Elizabethan Drama

ENGLISH MASTERPIECES · AN ANTHOLOGY OF
IMAGINATIVE LITERATURE FROM CHAUCER TO
T. S. ELIOT · UNDER THE GENERAL EDITOR-
SHIP OF MAYNARD MACK, YALE UNIVERSITY

Elizabethan Drama

edited by

LEONARD DEAN
Professor of English, University of Connecticut

Second Edition

PRENTICE-HALL, INC.
Englewood Cliffs, N. J.

TO THE READER

These volumes present a carefully proportioned collection of writings in English, from Chaucer to the present, which are primarily valuable as literary works of art. Writings in the less imaginative modes have been almost entirely excluded, and complete works have been preferred to excerpts. Where cutting or selection was necessary, an effort has been made to preserve what is crucial for an understanding of the artistic value of the whole piece. Since novels cannot be condensed or excerpted satisfactorily, they have been omitted. Separate reprints of prose fiction may be used to supplement the last two volumes of this set. The introductions try to focus the reader's attention on what is imaginatively interesting and valuable in the various selections. If they succeed, they will at the same time provide the justification for this anthology and distinguish it from the many other anthologies that are available.

77270

Contents

Elizabethan Drama

Background

The Renaissance, as everyone knows, was a period of fundamental change. In such a period the relations between imaginative writing and other cultural activities are unusually interesting. The Renaissance in England as elsewhere inherited from medieval and classical sources a picture or explanation of the universe. This picture was that of an ideally fixed community, arranged in descending order from God to inanimate things. Within this universal scheme, individuals and groups were assigned analogous organizations. Midway in the hierarchy stood man, part angel and part animal. He was a little universe, a microcosm, whose ideal order was one in which reason, the god-like faculty, ruled the passions and was in turn perfected by divine grace. The ideal political society, correspondingly, was a monarchy, governed by the Lord's lieutenant, and composed of a descending order of social classes or degrees in which each person fulfilled himself by performing the vocation or calling to which he had been born. The moral justification for this social hierarchy was the idea of equality of proportion. Equality existed in the otherwise unequal social structure, that is, because the character and ability of men were assumed to be proportionate to their positions. The king was entitled to his supreme position because he was theoretically supreme in reason and in the practice of Christian virtue.

When one turns from this ideal pattern to historical facts, however, the Renaissance is seen to be a period of violent change and disorder. The decentralized political system of feudalism was broken in England during the bloody Wars of the Roses and was remade by degrees into a strong national monarchy in which the middle classes held increasing power with the expansion of business. It was a dynamic situation, demanding and rewarding qualities of force or shrewdness which were condemned by the ideal pattern.

The typical Renaissance reactions to this conflict between practice and ideals will not be altogether unfamiliar to the modern reader. The group which had succeeded in eliminating rivals for political supremacy identified itself with the ideal and denounced rebellion as an attack against God's rule on earth. The spirit of one official Elizabethan homily or sermon "Against Disobedience and Wilfull Rebellion, appointed to be read in churches," is fairly expressed in this passage: "How horrible a sin against God and man rebellion is cannot possibly be expressed according to the greatness thereof. For he that nameth rebellion, nameth not a singular or one only sin, as is theft, robbery, murder, and such like, but he nameth the whole puddle and sink of all sins against God and man, against his prince, his country, his countrymen, his parents, his children, his kinsfolks, his friends, and against all men universally."

Another typical reaction was that of Sir Thomas More, who was well acquainted with practical politics under Henry VIII, but who believed in Christian and classical ideals and could not pretend that practice and belief were one. "Suppose I were with the French king," says Hythloday in More's *Utopia* (1515-16), "when he was discussing with his craftiest advisers how to enlarge his power and domain; and suppose that I, simple fool, should suggest that his real business was to rule France well; how do you think my advice would be received?" More is obliged to admit that such advice would not be well received, and he goes on to think of life as a stage play in which the real characters and motives of men are disguised. A person who steps in and calls things by their right names will break up the play. The best one can do is to work indirectly to reduce the hypocrisy in society, or to describe a utopian world which may serve as an attractive model for conduct.

A third reaction was Machiavelli's in *The Prince* (published 1532): "Many in their writings have feigned common-wealths and principalities that were never seen by others . . . ; and so great is the difference between the lives we do lead and the lives we should lead, that he which respects not what is done, but studies only to learn that which should be done, is likely by his knowledge to purchase his own subvertion." Machiavelli's proposal, in short, was that man should free himself from a paralyzing preoccupation with distant ideals and use any means to attain immediate social stability. The hero of *The Prince* is a consummate politician, infinitely cautious and adaptable, and completely unscrupulous. Having freed himself from old-fashioned ideas of right and wrong, he can use them to entangle simpler people in his program to master change and disorder. "Here is showed," wrote the anonymous Elizabethan translator of *The Prince,* "that we should not with a rude heat or natural instinct or by other example but artificially, as it were only for a further end, follow either virtue or vice, making no difference but by the profit we have occasion to use them." The chief hazard in the career of the prince as Machiavelli describes him is not the possible loss of his soul, but his bodily mortality and the unpredictable behavior of idealistic fools who may even give their lives to halt the prince's efficient dictatorship. A striking illustration is Machiavelli's admiring account of Caesar Borgia's suave and brutal rise to power. At the end occurs this sentence: "I remember he told me the same time that Julius the Second was chosen Pope that he had carefully forecast all inconveniences that might happen him by the death of his father, and had for every mischief provided a remedy, only this he dreamed not of, that when his father died, he himself should be in the like danger." The Elizabethan translator wrote opposite this passage: "Man proposeth, God disposeth." Machiavelli, however, continued with this: "When I therefore weigh and consider . . . the reasons of all the Duke's procedings, I cannot find anything wherein I may reprehend him."

It is clear that in Machiavelli's world, man rather than God is the center and measure of all things. Another spokesman for this shift toward modern secularism was Bacon. He heralds the change from metaphysics to physics, as Machiavelli does from the Christian prince to the politician. Bacon, having pigeon-holed theology and having dismissed the concept of the scientist as a Mephistopheles who sells his soul for learning, proceeds to describe the new Promethean hero who brings enlightenment to mankind by an objective study of man and nature. This new attitude invigorated Bacon, but it tortured the minds of many of his contemporaries. In a *Treatise of Humane Learning,* Fulke Greville (d. 1628) spoke for many when he said that "Knowledge is the forbidden tree, which man lusts after to be made his Maker." By striving to perfect himself without God's help and apart from divine ideals, man ironically perpetuates and even increases his fall from grace.

Poets, dramatists, and other writers reacted in varying ways to these inner tensions of changing Renaissance society. Many minor authors, then as now, were either complacently indifferent or horrified. Machiavelli, whose fictitious prince was uncomfortably like many real ones, was widely damned as a lying agent of the devil. History was combed for examples which could be dramatized as warnings against rebellion and change. The greater writers, however, caught up the basic issues of their time, and explored and resolved them imaginatively in the controlled fictions of art.

Some Conventions of the Elizabethan Drama and Theater

When we enter the plays reprinted in this volume, we in a sense enter new and separate worlds, and one of the conventions there is that most of the people speak poetry. True, we find that we can make inferences about character from the verse dialogue just as we do from the prose conversations of our own world; yet the crucial question remains: what is the justification for dialogue which is so remote from natural speech? One answer is suggested by the fact that in allowing the playwright to use poetic dialogue we in effect allow him to use a much richer language than he could if he confined himself to imitating actual conversation. An obvious gain from this wider use of the language is that characters, without giving the impression of being unnaturally self-conscious or communicative, can reveal themselves more fully and precisely than they ever would in real life. Sometimes, as will be pointed out in the introduction to *King Lear,* the use of poetic dialogue permits the growth and repetition of various language patterns, such as metaphors, that acquire an increasingly meaningful existence of their own, distinct from their revelation of character. When this happens, the themes of the play are carried on in the language as well as in the other elements. By using the language of poetry, then, the playwright may present and interpret his material more effectively than in a selection from real speech.

It is a little hard for us to accept a convention like poetic dialogue, even though we appreciate its advantages, because the usual relationship between audience and play in our theater differs from the Elizabethan. Audience and actors are separated by the physical construction of our theaters, by the sheer size of the auditorium, by the orchestra pit, the footlights, the recessed stage, and by the front curtain which is raised and lowered as if it were a movable wall. Under these conditions we assume rather easily that the actors are unaware of our presence in the theater, and that we are therefore spying on people who are behaving in a perfectly natural way. Obviously it would not be natural for them to talk in poetry.

The Elizabethan theater was relatively small, there was no front curtain, and of course no footlights, and the stage projected into the auditorium. This physical construction must have promoted a greater intimacy between audience and actors than we are accustomed to (except in certain experimental plays, in burlesque theaters with their runways, and in an occasional revue where the comedians deliberately involve the spectators in the action). Apparently the Elizabethan audience could pass back and forth more readily than we can from play world to real world. This accepted and practised flexibility made it possible for the playwright to violate rewardingly, as in the use of poetic dialogue, what seems to us the necessary illusion of life-likeness.

A clear sign of the intimacy between Elizabethan audience and actors is the so-called *aside,* in which an actor turns from the play and addresses the audience confidentially. An example, which has puzzled modern readers who are used to different conventions, is Prince Hal's comment on his tavern companions at the end of Act I, Scene ii, of *I Henry IV.* The speech appears to be a soliloquy in which Hal voices his private thoughts, but if we respond to it as we would to a comparable speech in our own theater, we can only conclude that Hal is a cold-blooded and hypocritical prig, and yet such a conclusion will not square with the author's general intention evidenced elsewhere to glorify Hal's character. An Elizabethan spectator would presumably not have this difficulty because he would understand, without conscious effort, that this soliloquy is to some extent an *aside.* Some fraction of the speech is meant to reveal character in a natural way, but another fraction of the speech is obviously "out of character," and must be understood as an expository comment on the action. It is as if Shakespeare used Hal the actor to interpret Hal the character. We are familiar with the two functions, but not in the same part at the same time. A radio play, for example, is normally composed of alternate narrations or explanations by the announcer and dramatizations by the players; in speeches like Hal's the two methods coalesce.

A related difficulty for readers who are conditioned to modern theatrical conventions is in knowing how to take Elizabethan characters that are varyingly symbolic and life-like. Consistently allegorical characters, like the Good and Evil Angels in *Doctor Faustus,* are not a serious problem because they are used only as personified abstractions and are so labeled. We may object that they are oversimplified analyses of value and experience, but we are not confused as to how to take them. A character like Edgar in *King Lear* is more puzzling. After he becomes a bedlam beggar in Act II, Scene iii, we find that it will not make sense if we respond to his actions as we had earlier when he was still openly Gloucester's son. It must now be arbitrarily assumed that his disguise is impenetrable, and it is no longer possible to make real-life inferences about his character from his speeches and actions. His function is symbolic. Still more puzzling in this respect is the character of Falstaff. He has, as a matter of fact, been interpreted all the way from a personified abstraction (a Shakespearian version of the medieval Vice) to a photographic study of an actual Elizabethan type. The difficulty seems to arise from the modern reader's lack of skill in attending to symbol and fact at the same time, and Falstaff is an extraordinarily subtle combination of the two.

The absence of a front curtain in the Elizabethan theater and the very small use of painted sets were limitations that the dramatist capitalized on with results that may also puzzle or disturb the modern reader. A play written for a relatively bare stage will of course have to supply its own setting in the actual dialogue. The descriptive passages in these plays may seem at first glance to be a rather poor substitute for our own elaborate painted sets, and certainly effects can now be achieved with electric lighting especially that Shakespeare, Marlowe, or Webster would have found useful. For a great writer, however, the necessity of remedying such defects through the use of descriptive language could be turned into a positive gain. A striking example is the series of storm scenes in *King Lear*. The emphasis in these scenes is not on the storm as it might be in a motion picture (The photography was wonderful!), nor is the symbolic meaning of the storm limited by a single painted set as it might be on the modern stage. In being described rather than photographed or staged, the storm in *King Lear* can be continuously varied and controlled to serve the author's purposes. He can use it, for example, to show the blindness of the coldly rational Cornwall, Regan, and Goneril; for them the storm is merely bad weather which they can escape by going indoors. He can use it more importantly to show the development of Lear's character. It serves to project, enlarge, and interpret Lear's inner turmoil, as we shall see later in more detail. Furthermore, a play that supplies its own setting can change the location of its action at will and at a word. This rapid alteration of locale makes possible a very full use of contrasting scenes, and through such contrast the action is interpreted, as in our frequent passage back and forth from tavern to court in *I Henry IV*. The technique is somewhat comparable to that of recent experimental movies where scenes dissolve into each other. A seeming limitation, therefore, may really be an opportunity for a capable writer to express his ideas with greater freedom and preciseness than he could otherwise. The structure of the modern play, with its pre-intermission climaxes and its few scenes, is determined in part by the physical theater. The mechanically crude Elizabethan playhouse made possible dramas with structures more responsive to their authors' artistic insights and desires. This in turn creates an unfamiliar responsibility and opportunity for the modern reader.

❧

Doctor Faustus

The story of Faust is potentially, like the story of Oedipus, a dramatic analysis of the power and limitation of human knowledge. It may show vividly what man can do, and it may contemplate man's predicament as a finite being. When the story is told by little minds, however, it tends to become a collection of magical tricks and a moralistic example, a Sunday sermon enlivened with tall stories, preaching the terrors of hell and the virtues of religious conformity. It was such a superficial version of the story that Marlowe worked with and revivified.

His source was an English translation of a German prose narrative, which had been published at Frankfort in 1587, and advertised as a warning to all Christians against pride and lust. The moral is emphasized by the English title: *The Historie of the damnable life, and deserued death of Doctor John Faustus*. The first five chapters give a rapid account of Faustus' sudden and perverse interest in necromancy and of his contract with the devil. The last three chapters are devoted to his fears of approaching death, his farewell speech of warning to his companions, and his horrible doom. The intervening fifty-four chapters, thus moralistically protected front and rear, describe the frivolous wonders and practical jokes which Faustus performed with his devilish powers.

An acquaintance with Marlowe's intellectual bent may sharpen a reader's perception of the ways in which he transformed his source. He was a violent free-thinker about religion. Many of his contemporaries were shocked by his doubts about the historical accuracy of the Old Testament, by his vulgarly expressed skepticism of the divinity of Christ, the virgin birth, and the morality of Mary, and by his tendency generally to talk about Christianity the way others talked about Mohammedanism. The comforts of a merely orthodox religious belief filled him with passionate disgust. Faith and reason were for him in tension because he thought about both of them profoundly rather than conventionally.

In *Tamburlaine,* which immediately preceded *Doctor Faustus,* Marlowe deliberately glorified purely human or secular achievement. Tamburlaine, the irresistible conqueror, asserts that

> Nature that framed us of four elements,
> Warring within our breasts for regiment,
> Doth teach us all to have aspiring minds:
> Our souls, whose faculties can comprehend
> The wondrous architecture of the world:
> And measure every wandering planet's course,
> Still climbing after knowledge infinite,
> And always moving as the restless spheres,
> Wills us to wear ourselves and never rest,
> Until we reach the ripest fruit of all,
> The perfect bliss and sole felicity,
> The sweet fruition of an earthly crown.   (II, vii, 18-29)

The conclusion that earthly success is "perfect bliss" and "sole felicity" is the argument of the whole play. Its shocking unorthodoxy is emphasized by being presented as a challenge to Christian phraseology and belief. *Tamburlaine* appears to be one of Marlowe's characteristically extreme attempts to gain a fresh hearing for the achievements of the world. The story, however, imposed certain limitations. Since the hero's victories are largely those of force rather than of intellect, they do not fairly symbolize the best of humanism and they do not dramatize the tension between religion and reason. The story of Faustus was a potentially better fiction for Marlowe because it remedied those defects.

Doctor Faustus is a better Everyman than Tamburlaine in the sense that he more fully represents man's intellectual aspirations, but he is carefully distinguished, as we should expect, from the merely average man. The latter is personified by the Scholars. In Scene II they hear that Faustus is learning magic, and they run in child-like horror to the Rector for help. They ask Faustus to show them Helen in Scene XIII, and although they are filled with admiration for the magician and for his creation, their wit, as they confess, is too simple to understand and praise her properly. In the last scene, when Faustus is convulsed with remorse and fear of hell, they first try to reduce the issue by suggesting that he is simply sick from being "over-solitary" or from over-eating. That failing, they urge him to think on heaven, which has always been easy enough for them to do; and then, after a moment of wavering courage, they leave to pray safely in another room while Faustus meets his terrible death alone. The Scholars, in short, are aware that there is an issue, but they cannot experience it fully. The contrast between them and Faustus suggests that only by observing a man who has gone beyond comfortable correctness can we find our true limitations and have an opportunity, thereby, to be truly religious.

Marlowe made other changes in his source for the purpose of distinguishing Faustus from the average man. For example, Faustus turns to magic in the play only after criticizing the arts and sciences which satisfy lesser minds. Logic leads merely to skill in disputation; medicine can cure disease but not mortality; law is "servile and illiberal" because it is subject to things, to "paltry legacies." All three, in Bacon's phrase, are "immersed in matter"; their mastery does not free man from his limitations, it emphasizes them. Faustus' criticism is unusually keen; his pride is exhilarating rather than conventionally petty. Marlowe makes us feel, as his source does not, that Faustus wants more than sensuous pleasure and power, that he is really moved by a fine scorn of what the world acclaims, that he wants to demonstrate that man may be greater than he is ordinarily content or even proud to be.

More striking than the elevation of Faustus' character is the change in the structure of the source so that in the play the end is not simply the conclusion of a formula, half of which had been given at the beginning and then forgotten, but rather the implied consequence of every preceding act and word. This change dramatizes the tension between faith and reason, between man's powers and limitations.

We have noticed that Faustus, for example, is an able critic of the widely acclaimed arts of logic, medicine, and law; but it is also made clear that his rationalism is undercut by rationalizing. His analysis is shrewd but partial. He thinks that he is objective, yet he unconsciously selects and distorts the evidence. We sense, for instance, his hidden real reasons in rejecting divinity. It is "hard," he complains, and goes on to denounce a system which predestines man to failure and death. This is invigorating, just as is Edmund's denunciation in *King Lear* of a social system which predestines bastards to a second place regardless of their ability. But both plays are designed to show that the two speakers, though refreshingly unorthodox, have actually only a limited truth because they argue from selected evidence and unexamined motives. Faustus, like Edmund, is convinced that the system is not a necessity but is really a monstrous trick used by an unscrupulous opposition to maintain its supremacy. An enlightened person will not be taken in, and if he is a man he will fight back. The world thus becomes a jungle in which the only virtue is selfish power, and the only possible relation between man and man or between man and God is a battle to the death. Both Faustus and Edmund perceive acutely that religious and social systems may repress rather than release valuable human abilities. Finding this "hard," they generalize that truth and virtue can never have any real existence, but are only fictitious and self-imposed fetters. In

liberating themselves, however, Edmund and Faustus reject the
ideals by which actions are evaluated. Brute force is thus enthroned,
and man in claiming recognition for his human abilities becomes,
perversely, subhuman.

That paradox is dramatized throughout the middle of the play.
As Faustus becomes more "manly," he becomes less acute and logical.
The most striking evidence fails to impress him. When Mephistophilis, the devil's very agent, laments his own fall from grace, and
exclaims: ". . . leave these frivolous demands, / Which strike a
terror to my fainting soul," Faustus answers blindly and patronizingly: "Learn thou of Faustus manly fortitude." His "liberated" powers, furthermore, have now no aim but indiscriminate self-expression.
One trick is as good as another, and all is farce.

The farcical scenes, which were probably composed and inserted by
another writer, may be justified as demonstrations of the necessary
frivolity of power detached from ideals, of the "expense of spirit"
which follows Faustus' "liberation," but they are usually felt to be
relatively "undramatic." An important reason for this is their single-
ness of aim and effect, their lack of real conflict. Faustus himself is
never wholly satisfied with sensations, or benumbed by them. The
continuing conflict in him, and in the universe, is shown in various
ways, but most successfully in those scenes, as we should expect, where
both human powers and limitations are justly and simultaneously
exhibited.

An example is the scene (XIII) containing the famous passage
about Helen. Faustus requests her as a moral opiate, as one "Whose
sweet embracings may extinguish clean / These thoughts [of heaven]
that do dissuade me from my vow . . . to Lucifer." The sight of her
fills him with scarce-believing wonder: "Was this the face that
launched a thousand ships, / And burnt the topless towers of Ilium?"
Her kind of beauty and the achievement it inspired are undeniably
real. She is "fairer than the evening air / Clad in the beauty of a
thousand stars," and brighter than flaming Jupiter. To possess her
or to strive for her is to be supremely heroic and chivalrous. It is
also to be burnt as were Ilium and Semele. She is the dual symbol
of man surpassing himself and destroying himself.

It is that predicament, the tension of man caught "in strange odds
between the earth and sky," that informs and strengthens the end
of the play. Marlowe's source had tried to be emphatic by picturing
Faustus' physical destruction. When the Scholars looked for Faustus
in the morning, they found "all the hall . . . besprinckled with
blood, his braines cleauing to the wall; for the Diuel had beaten him
from one wall against another, in one corner lay his eyes, in another

his teeth, a pitifull and fearfull sight to beholde. . . . lastly they came into the yarde where they found his bodie lying on the horse dung, most monstrously torne. . . . for his head and all his ioynts were dashed to pieces." In the play the emphasis is on the agony of Faustus, and of all thinking men, in reaching true self-knowledge. The idea of time, which at the beginning Faustus had considered to be merely an item in a legal contract, now becomes symbolic of man's mortality. It is only in the context of time that one can love Helen and achieve worldly greatness, but the passage of time is a sign of finiteness. In the midst of his ecstasy, any lover who is more than animal must cry out, *"O lente, lente currite, noctis equi!"* In the beginning Faustus had thought to surpass his human limitations by insisting that power is the sole virtue and by implicitly denying any difference between man and beast. Now, to escape from facing his true character and the consequences of his misunderstanding of it, he cries for the safety of extinction into brute nature. He would burn his books, the sign of man's superiority to the beast, and become a part of anonymous matter.

The last chorus, with its quiet regular rhythm, does not revel in the grisly details of Faustus' death as a warning against unorthodox behavior, nor does it suggest, as might some modern commentator, that Faustus failed because his science was old-fashioned or because he was not "well-adjusted" like the Scholars; it emphasizes, rather, the tragic sadness in an example, that is always "modern," of so much good perverted by lack of self-knowledge.

❧

King Lear

The legendary story of King Lear was well known to Elizabethans through the chroniclers, including Holinshed, and through an earlier play by an unidentified dramatist. Shakespeare accepted the traditional opening action in which the aged Lear disinherits Cordelia and divides the kingdom between Goneril and Regan according to their response to his test of their love for him. To work out the deductions from this beginning Shakespeare found it necessary to add to the basic Cinderella plot of his sources the story of Gloucester and his sons, Lear's madness, the Fool, Oswald, and the storm. He found it necessary, also, to draw a conclusion that was unlike the "happy ending" of the traditional versions in which Lear returns from France with

Cordelia, destroys the wicked sisters and their husbands, and rules in peace for two more years. These and other changes were more than the tinkering of a practical writer for the stage; they are factors in the transformation of a rather crude story of "poetic justice" into tragedy.

The first scene contains the premises for the action which follows: it sets up the basic groupings and conflicts. Lear enters, playing the role of the weary elder statesman, and arranges a test of his daughters' affection. He asserts that its purpose is to show him how to divide his kingdom on the grounds of merit; but the real reason for the test is apparent: he will be able to bask in the flattering protestations of love that he has now arranged to hear. Goneril and Regan answer with the expected extravagance. Their unction suggests selfish compliance, which they explicitly confirm at the end of the scene, and which is detected and underscored by Cordelia's asides. Lear, blinded by his vanity, turns to Cordelia with complacent anticipation: "Now, our joy, / Although our last and least, . . . what can you say to draw / A third more opulent than your sisters? Speak." He sits back smiling. The little scene, in which he is the loving, generous, and respected old father, is going well. This *is* a properly ordered world: children *are* dutiful, age *does* bring wisdom, words *are* cousin to the thought and deed. We are not surprised, therefore, at his astonished "Nothing?" to Cordelia's statement that she has nothing to say. Nor are we surprised at the anger in his voice as he warns her to mend her speech lest it mar her fortunes. We understand that Cordelia instinctively resents being cross-examined on a feeling like love that must be spontaneous to be valid and that cannot be forced or mechanically measured. Her refusal to comply enrages Lear, who becomes the embodiment of awful majesty grievously wronged. Kent urges him to "see better'"; but Lear, now rigidly arrogant, banishes both Kent and Cordelia and puts himself in the power of Goneril and Regan.

Lear's violent energy and lack of self-knowledge are necessary premises for tragedy. They predict that he will suffer great disillusionment, but that he may also learn greatly. The direction which his suffering and re-education will take is suggested by the opening scene. Lear has arrogantly assumed that his rights as father and king are absolute possessions, that they are his no matter what he does. He has not understood that the garments of authority are symbols, and that they are significant only as they are earned and re-earned. His wrong choice of daughters is an implicit denial that the values represented by Cordelia and Kent have any real existence. He must now learn what it is like to live in a world from which they have been banished. That experience may prepare him to see them finally at their true worth.

At the end of the first scene, Goneril and Regan draw their own conclusions from what has just happened. Their appraisal is thoroughly "scientific." If fathers and kings behave this way, if this is the true nature of the world, then clearly it does not pay to be a Cordelia or a Kent. Since the ideals of love and authority are apparently inoperative in practice, the coldly rational person will not let himself be handicapped by them, but will rather understand that they are mere verbalisms and will mouth them whenever it is expedient. Success will come to the practical psychologist who disciplines himself to take advantage of other people's emotionalism or idealism. Lear's behavior has brought this amoral attitude into power; the daughters are in a sense a projection of one part of his character. In their analysis of him, they demonstrate that they know that part very accurately.

Their deductions are emphasized at the beginning of the second scene by Edmund's reflections, which we have compared to Faustus'. Nature will be his goddess, for he has concluded that religion is merely a sanction used by respectable, legitimate people to maintain their unmerited supremacy. This conclusion has been forced upon him by the behavior of people like Lear and his own father. In the opening lines of the play, we have stood with him and heard his father, Gloucester, speak brazenly of the adultery that begot his illegitimate son. Gloucester's fault, his casual worldly cynicism, causes the same kind of amoral reaction in Edmund as Lear's fault had in Goneril and Regan. Gloucester errs through complacency and inattention. He, too, accepts his authority as a father and his "legitimate" social position as absolute possessions which do not have to be earned. Edmund very properly resents this, but in rebelling against the inequity of his lot, he repudiates the ideals of society along with its unjust conventional practices. The meaning of that repudiation is shown in the subsequent careers of Edmund, Goneril, and Regan.

The immediate consequence of the opening action is the practical success of the rationalists. Edmund easily dispossesses his brother Edgar. Gloucester is vaguely disturbed by the way things are going: ". . . brothers divide . . . And the noble and true-hearted Kent banished" (I, ii, 116-126); but he cannot see that he has erred. Perhaps the stars are unfavorable. Edmund smiles patronizingly: "An admirable evasion of whoremaster man, to lay his goatish disposition on the change of a star!" The implied analysis of human nature will not turn out to be as complete and accurate as Edmund thinks it is, but Gloucester deserves the criticism. His own moral relaxation under the protection of established relationships has brought them into disrepute and has made him vulnerable to precisely the kind of deception and inhuman treatment which he now begins to receive.

Lear also begins to learn what it means to have false values turned against oneself. The experience is dramatized in part through the elder daughters' measured reduction in his retinue. They argue coldly that he has no need for such a following now: "Idle old man, / That still would manage those authorities / That he hath given away" (I, iii, 16-18). Regan's conclusion is the logical one: "What need one?" (II, iv, 266). To which Lear cries in anguish: "O, reason not the need! . . . Allow not nature more than nature needs, / Man's life's as cheap as beast's." This kind of "reasoning" he begins to see is a denial of all feeling and affection. It is the counterpart of his own denial of such values in the opening scene.

To emphasize Lear's lesson Shakespeare introduces the Fool. His main function is to turn every word to the central fact of Lear's folly and its growing consequence. He is abnormally sensitive to human vanity, arrogance, and hypocrisy, and his position licenses him to be brutally frank in describing the harsh truth beneath conventional relationships. It is no news to him that daughters and sons may behave like Goneril, Regan, and Edmund. As Lear learns the Fool's gamin wisdom, we may feel that he is in effect starting to realize a heretofore stunted capacity for humility and self-knowledge. The Fool is as worldly-wise as Edmund or the elder sisters, but at the same time innocent. His speech is gnomic, suggestive—unlike the seemingly efficient directness of the rationalists; his loyalty to the dispossessed Lear is inexpedient. These qualities ally him with Cordelia and Kent; they imply a kind of devotion which cannot be coldly measured, and the existence in Lear of the potentiality for true authority, which the Fool, like Kent, "would fain call master."

The success of the rational opportunists and the concurrent disillusionment and suffering of Lear and Gloucester are carried to their logical extreme. Gloucester, betrayed by Edmund, his eyes gouged out by Cornwall and the elder sisters, concludes that there is no justice in the universe: "As flies to wanton boys, are we to the gods, / They kill us for their sport" (IV, i, 38-39). He tries to escape in a characteristically negative way through suicide. Lear, maddened by the growing conviction that all civilized relationships and institutions are essentially corrupt, would "Strike flat the thick rotundity o' the world! / Crack nature's moulds, all germens spill at once / That make ungrateful man" (III, ii, 7-9). Stripping off his clothes and the false sophistication which they seem to imply, he tries to lose himself in the violence of nature—in something elemental that is "real," that does not pretend like his false daughters to be other than it is. Hence, too, his desire for kinship with the primitive reality he takes Poor Tom to be.

But the play does not end in despair or cynicism; it follows the traditional pattern of tragedy from error, through disillusionment, to insight. The initial error of Lear and Gloucester was the easy belief that they and their world were already perfect, a confusion of appearance and reality. The deduction from that error was disillusionment; its severity made it impossible that they could ever again be sentimentally complacent or arrogant. Tragedy asserts, however, that it is unnecessary to stop at disillusionment. Cordelia, Kent, and Edgar may be driven into banishment and disguise for a while, but they are finally acknowledged at their true worth. Cordelia may die, but the ideal for which she stands continues to exist as a possibility. It has been said that every tragedy is a fairy story for the values which exist happily ever after, even if not for the carrier of the values. That is a different kind of fairy story from the one told by Shakespeare's sources.

An ending that is thoroughly critical yet affirmative spells disaster for the rationalists; it implies that they have misjudged the nature of man and the universe. That fact is dramatized in the relationship and self-destruction of Edmund, Goneril, Regan, and Cornwall. They come together inevitably. "Natures of such deep trust we shall much need" (II, i, 117-118), says Cornwall as he welcomes Edmund; but "deep trust" involves a quality of feeling that these hard-headed people have debunked out of existence. When it does appear they are surprised. Cornwall, for example, is mortally wounded by his own servant, who is revolted at the inhuman torture of Gloucester. The shrewd conspirator is caught off guard by the man of feeling. Goneril and Regan, in turn, are destroyed by their lust for Edmund. Having denied the reality of love by their actions at the beginning of the play, and having decided that the restraints and relationships of society are hypocritical fictions, the two have nothing to live for but selfish gratification. At the same time, in satisfying their lusts they necessarily relax the only kind of discipline which they have left, the code of the opportunist in a tooth-and-claw world, and as a result they become soft and vulnerable. Edmund's end is comparable, yet more complex, as might have been foreseen. He, too, becomes slack. His acceptance of Edgar's challenge to single combat is in him a sign of weakness, because it amounts to acceptance of the system of social obligations that he has rejected at the opening of the play. "By th' law of war thou wast not bound to answer / An unknown opposite," observes Goneril. "Thou are not vanquish'd, / But cozened and beguiled" (V, iii, 152-154). But his assertion "Some good I mean to

do, / Despite of mine own nature" (V, iii, 243-244) and his attempt
to halt the murder of Lear and Cordelia have led some readers to
believe that he finally sees his error and repents. The repentance is
so sudden, however, that it has seemed to other readers merely op-
portunistic. "The wheel has come full circle" (V, iii, 174), he admits
after he has been wounded and exposed by Edgar, and perhaps one
may feel that the reversal of fortune has brought back the strategically
subservient Edmund of the opening lines of the play.

The play makes its final affirmation not only negatively through the
self-destruction of the limited rationalists, but also positively through
the growing insight of Gloucester and Lear. The blinding of Gloucester symbolically opens his eyes to the true values of his situation: "I
stumbled when I saw" (IV, i, 21), and of Edgar: "Might I but live to
see thee in my touch / I'd say I had eyes again." His cynical statement that the gods "kill us for their sport" is soon qualified by an
access of self-knowledge: "Let the superfluous and lust-dieted man, /
That slaves your ordinance, that will not see / Because he does not
feel, feel your power quickly. . . ." (IV, i, 70-72). "I do remember
now. Henceforth I'll bear / Affliction till it do cry out itself /
'Enough, enough,' and die" (IV, vi, 76-77). At the conclusion, Edgar
reports that his father's "flaw'd heart, / Alack, too weak the conflict
to support! / 'Twixt two extremes of passion, joy and grief, / Burst
smilingly" (V, iii, 197-199).

Near the end of the play Lear is carried onto the stage asleep. The
attendants report that they have "put fresh garments on him"; and
we sense that these clothes will be truly expressive of the royal pre-
rogatives which he has finally earned and has come to understand
through suffering. Cordelia, noticing that he wakes, asks the doctor
to speak to him, but the doctor answers, "Madam, do you; 'tis fittest."
And we see that it is fittest not only because she is Lear's daughter,
but also because she represents the new aspect of nature to which he
is awakened. He thinks that he is in heaven, and that Cordelia is an
angel. He will try to understand, but this can scarcely be the actual
world that he has known. With a kind of childlike gravity he pricks
himself to see if he is alive. His new values are shown after he and
Cordelia have been captured by Edmund. She is ready to outface her
sisters, but Lear has no interest in practical action. "No, no, no, no!"
he exclaims impatiently. "Come, let's away to prison; / We two alone
will sing like birds i' the cage," and be entertained by the shifting,
inconsequential fortunes of the world. He is beyond practical good
and evil; he and Cordelia will view them under the aspect of eternity,
"As if they were God's spies." But Edmund, with his murdering
agent, is at hand to reassert the impossibility of being timeless in

time. When Lear reappears with the body of Cordelia in his arms he is maddened by her apparent death, and oblivious to everything but its meaning. He dies, not in despair, but affirming in the face of the facts that Cordelia still lives.

The play ends with a discussion of plans for carrying on the normal order of affairs. Cordelia will not live in all her perfect goodness; we cannot sing like birds in a cage and be innocent and irresponsible. But neither in the light of this experience can we be Edmund or the initial Lear. With Albany we will now for a while at least, "Speak what we feel, not what we ought to say."

A review, like the foregoing, of the play's theme as it grows out of the symbolic actions of the characters does not fairly account for the extraordinary power of certain scenes, especially the later ones, in which even single lines and phrases seem almost to "mean" the whole play. The depth or texture of the play, as distinct from its linear pattern, is a result of the way in which certain concepts—nature, justice, and so on—are explored and defined through repeated dramatizations, and of the way in which certain words are charged with increasing metaphoric significance. Scene vi of Act IV, for example, is powerful not only because it is the height of Lear's delirium and the climactic meeting between him and Gloucester, but also because the language by this time has built up a great potential of meaning. Gloucester asks, "Dost thou know me?" and Lear answers: "I remember thine eyes well enough. Dost thou squiny at me? No, do thy worst, blind Cupid, I'll not love." We are first shocked at what seems to be Lear's deliberate cruelty in calling attention to Gloucester's multilated eyes. Any normal person should be kind enough to gloss over the terrifying fact, to pretend, out of elementary consideration for the pathetic old man, that nothing is wrong. Then we realize at once that Lear's brutality is a further sign that he is beyond pathos, that his madness has been not a defense against the savage truth of the world but an abnormally sensitive realization of it. He was blind once, too, and now that he has been cruelly taught to see things as they are, he cannot afford to delude himself again. As he stares at the eyeless sockets they seem to squint at him coyly, like the side-long glance of a prostitute under the brothel sign of a blind Cupid. It is a look he remembers well enough. He mistook it once on the faces of Goneril and Regan for real affection, but now he believes that love does not exist, that love is always hypocritical, animal, commercial. He will not be fooled again: "No, do thy worst, blind Cupid, I'll not love." Subconsciously Lear knows that Gloucester is blind, but his actions show that he understands that physical blindness is inconsequential. "Read," he insistently orders Gloucester handing him an imaginary challenge. Without self-pity, Gloucester repeats the fact that he is eyeless. "Oh ho," exclaims Lear with delirious affability, "are you there with me?" are you in the same condition I am? "No eyes in your head, nor no money in your purse? . . . Yet you see how this world goes." "I see it feelingly," answers Gloucester. The several meanings come to us simultaneously: Without sight, I must know the world through other senses. I have been taught in a painful way to understand the world. I now have insight that gives me an imaginative comprehension of the world. Lear grasps all these meanings. "What, art mad?" Only mad persons like himself have this insight, and such insight drives one mad. Then, developing another meaning, "Look with thine ears," and you can see that the judge and the thief are equally corrupt. He elaborates his bitterly vivid knowledge of the world's hypocrisy in which "Robes and furred gowns hide all." "Reason in madness," comments Edgar. It is an accurate clinical observation; it also concentrates and expresses our feeling that the power of the scene comes from more than its theatrical effectiveness. Behind Edgar's comment are not only the observable surface facts, but all the play's dramatic statements about the insanity of cold rationality, the wisdom of folly, and the insight of madness. Behind the references to blindness-sight-insight and to clothes-appearances are all the earlier uses of those chains of metaphors. The power of the scene, in short, comes primarily from the interplay of concepts and images that have been growing in meaning since the beginning of the play. As a result the texture and the structure of the play reinforce each other.

❧

Volpone

The basic plot of *Volpone* (which Jonson derived from the Roman satirists) is the story of greedy men outwitting themselves. Legacy-hunters ply a rich, childless, and seemingly sick old man with gifts in order to be declared his heirs, but he is only feigning illness and age in order to increase his wealth at their expense. Finally, all are unmasked and punished. Jonson enriched this elementary situation in many ways.

First, the names which Jonson gave to the major characters suggest a beast fable in the background, but it is soon apparent that this is not a homely story of animals representing the virtues and vices of men. Volpone is not our sly childhood friend, Reynard; he is

Vulpes, the Machiavellian fox, whose seeming carrion attracts the vulture, the crow, and the raven. These are not animals illustrating humanity, but bestial men perversely using their human intelligence to be worse than animals. By the end of the play, the fox becomes wolf-like, and they all (like the Duchess of Malfi's brothers) feed on the weak and on each other. Mosca, the professional parasite, observes cynically that "All the wise world is little else in nature, / But parasites or sub-parasites." The final lines of the play remark that "Mischiefs feed / Like beasts, till they be fat, and then they bleed." The whole picture of bestial men feeding on men is a terrifying enlargement of the original theme of greed.

The basic plot calls, furthermore, for much of the action to take place in Volpone's bedroom, but again Jonson capitalizes on necessity. Mosca, ushering in the legacy-hunters, resembles a procurer. The figure on the bed, seductive yet disgusting, operates an endless tease, "Playing with their hopes . . . Letting the cherry knock against their lips, / And draw it by their mouths, and back again." What should be the place of rest and procreation becomes a scene of luxurious frustration, sterile, commercial, and demanding an exhausting alertness against fraud. The customers pay to watch a man die.

As a larger setting for his basic plot, Jonson chose Venice, thus reinforcing his play with the qualities of sophisticated vice and Machiavellian intrigue which Englishmen complacently and fearfully attributed to Italy. In addition to describing this urban Italian Renaissance setting directly, Jonson dramatizes the contrast between the North and the Mediterranean (and their human similarities) by adding to his cast two very British tourists, Sir Politic and Lady Would-Be. Sir Pol (parrot) is full of inaccurate inside information and Anglo-Saxon business know-how; Lady Would-Be is boringly vain of her attempted stylishness and superficial culture. They are accompanied by Peregrine (the pilgrim hawk), whose good sense is a norm which measures their affectation and who finally involves them in a farce which frees them from some of their self-delusion and comic predictability. The subterranean horror of Volpone's world is intensified by the obliviousness of these solid British types (or "humours," as Jonson would have called them). At the same time, Lady Would-Be, corseted by her loquaciousness and eccentric British insularity, is the only one who is safe in Volpone's bedroom. He shrinks in her presence, and perhaps even looks a little stagy.

In these days of the image-makers, the modern reader will not be surprised to find that Jonson further enlarged his subject by concentrating on the City's language itself. Most obvious is the voice

of the huckster. When Volpone must be disguised in order to catch
a glimpse of Celia, he is presented under her window as a mountebank or quack doctor, and we stand on the edge of the crowd with
the gullible Sir Pol and listen, guided by the ironic Peregrine, to
the familiar features of the patent-medicine hawker's spiel. "Excellent!" exclaims the admiring Pol. "Have you heard better language,
sir?" From beginning to end, from Volpone's initial glamorizing of
gold to the oratorical double-talk of the courtroom, Jonson creates
examples of the power and excitement of language and at the same
time exhibits its perversion. The cynical manipulation of language for
selfish purposes is the basic evil which we are asked to observe. It is
not safe, the play tells us, to respond directly and sincerely to language,
to the rhetoric of strong emotion, or to words of simple pathos.
This satiric view of language as an instrument closes off the primary
dramatic effects to which we respond directly and safely in Shakespeare's great plays—the heightened language of Lear in his agony
or the quiet heartbreak of Edgar's comment on his blinded father,
but Jonson's dialogue is nevertheless dramatic in a subtle and powerful way. A good example is the passage in which Mosca presents
Celia to Volpone when she has been dragged to the bedroom by her
husband Corvino (III, vii, 68-80):

> VOLP. [*Aside*] Thou art mine honor, Mosca, and my pride,
> My joy, my tickling, my delight! Go bring 'em.
> MOS. Please you draw near, sir.
> CORV.   Come on, what—
> You will not be rebellious? By that light—
> MOS. Sir, Signor Corvino, here, is come to see you.   5
> VOLP. Oh.
> MOS. And hearing of the consultation had,
> So lately, for your health, is come to offer,
> Or rather, sir, to prostitute—
> CORV.   Thanks, sweet Mosca.
> MOS. Freely, unasked, or unentreated—
> CORV.   Well.   10
> MOS. As the true fervent instance of his love,
> His own most fair and proper wife, the beauty
> Only of price in Venice—
> CORV.   'Tis well urged.
> MOS. To be your comfortress, and to preserve you.

We are moved here not only by the basic situation but also by the
play of language. In the center is the suavely assured Mosca, whose

speeches are dramatically adjusted to intensify the drama. The extended formal introduction of the helpless Celia tortures her and teasingly excites Volpone; it gives Mosca time to savor his own power and linguistic skill and to exhibit the husband's blind degradation. Corvino's comments direct our attention to this manipulation of language. He is openly thankful when Mosca replaces the mild "offer" with the hard sell of "prostitute," and he commends him ("'Tis well urged") for his high-pressure advertising of Celia's beauty.

It is Jonson's development of the character of Volpone, however, which adds the greatest dimension to the basic plot and theme. Volpone's opening speech to his gold tells us at once that he is no conventional miser. With Faustus-like daring he addresses his treasury as a "shrine" and his gold as a "saint." Separated (like Edmund in *King Lear*) from the restraints and ideals of Christian morality, he hears no more than Faustus did the old values in the religious terms which he uses to describe material wealth. Further distinguishing him from the mere man of property are his courtier-like grace and his contempt for security and productive labor. He is a creature of extraordinary daring and resourcefulness, delighting in the sheer exercise of unfettered intelligence. His flexibility as an impersonator and his conscious amorality set him above the rigid, hypocritical creatures who try to prey on him. He manipulates them with Iago-like skill. But his successes leave him unsatisfied. Mosca (devil-like) must constantly stimulate him with new challenges or with entertainment provided by his natural children (the dwarf, the eunuch, and the hermaphrodite), who also serve to externalize his own grotesqueness. The "heaven" toward which he moves is the golden flesh of Celia, offered up by her husband, Corvino, who invests her for profit. There is perhaps an air of melodrama about the attempted seduction of the heavenly Celia and her rescue by the good Bonario ("Forbear, foul ravisher!"), but the play's attention is on Corvino's degraded values and on Volpone. Assuming that Celia will prove to be "human" too, he offers her his riches and a life of endless sexual excitement; but her humanity includes a belief in the reality of honor, which he cannot understand and which makes his glowing appeal sound like the proposition of an international playboy. After this episode, the action leaves the bedroom, as the fox places himself in danger in order to gain new mastery and excitement, and moves logically toward an encounter between Volpone and Mosca, who (like an arrow or shooting star, as he says) is superior to the ordinary human parasite in the same way that his master surpasses the miser.

This movement out of the bedroom is also a movement toward a final dramatic study of social morality and civic justice. The play concludes with two trials. In the first, the innocent Celia and Bonario are declared guilty and justice miscarries; in the second, the guilty are unmasked and punished with poetic justice. The tone and meaning of these concluding actions have been variously interpreted. Many have felt them to be too somber or mechanically harsh to be appropriate for comedy and have suggested that *Volpone* leans toward tragedy or is at least a darkly comic imitation of tragedy. Certainly, Jonson's final image of society is far from the comic resolution symbolized by the natural freedom of the green world or by the festive release and harmony of a wedding party; yet his conclusion is social and secular, without the metaphysical overtones of tragedy. The first trial says that a court can be no better than the society which it represents. Appearance and language having become pervasively deceptive, guilt and innocence are inverted. The second trial says that such civic evil leads through excess to revulsion and harsh reform. This is the all-too-human City, as Jonson knew it and we know it, and the play about it is an uncompromisingly ironic comedy.

～～

The Duchess of Malfi

It is important to come to *The Duchess of Malfi* with the right expectations. If one looks for a straight-line plot or for realistic motivation, he will be disappointed. The play is built on different principles. The structure is that of analogous contrasting scenes which are essentially repetitive and symbolic rather than progressive and realistic.

The opening speeches picture contrasting values and governments. Antonio admiringly describes the court of a Christian prince, which is like a fountain from which flow silver drops to invigorate society. Opposed to this is the Machiavellian rule of the Duke and the Cardinal, who are like plum trees leaning crookedly over a stagnant pool and infested with parasites. The contrast is continued in the central action of the play, the attempt by the Duke and the Cardinal to prevent their sister, the Duchess, from remarrying. The realistic explanation provided for the attempt is their greedy desire to control her property, which might be endangered by the birth of an heir. This is not a very satisfactory explanation, however, because it ignores the fact that the Duchess already has a son by her first marriage. Here, as elsewhere, the more plausible and important significance is the symbolic one. The action of the brothers against the Duchess suggests that they and what they stand for are essentially sterile. Their relations with women, and with the world in general, are mercenary indulgences in self-gratification. In sharp contrast is the love between the Duchess and Antonio, which is spontaneous, unselfish and fruitful.

In seeing how other actions in the play are more than theatrical spectacles or horror for its own sake, it is important to observe the widespread use of imagery. The frequent comparisons involving animals, storm, fire, disease, drugs, decay, and other violent or pathological aspects of existence are generally functional rather than superficial. They help to define character and theme, and they provide a unifying atmosphere for the whole play. The metaphoric language is especially effective in revealing the subconscious disorder in abnormal characters like the Duke. On learning (II, v) that his sister has had a child, he imagines that he sees her laughing at him like a hyena, and then he urges the Cardinal to distract him with conversation so that he will not go on to visualize her in the very act of conception. This half-recognition that his mind is diseased fades as he indulges in a crescendo of denunciation. He would have the Duchess and her lover burned in a sealed coal pit or in the pitch-soaked sheets of their bed, and he would have the child boiled into a broth to renew the father's lust. It is not the Duchess who is being described in this outburst, of course, but rather the Duke himself. We measure his insanity by the quality of the images which possess his mind and by their distance from the truth. These images of animal violence serve also to unify the play. It is in terms of such images, for example, that the good characters inevitably define their own plight. When the Duchess woos Antonio (I, ii), she asserts that all discord outside of the circle of their love is only to be pitied and not feared, and that time will easily scatter the tempest. Just before her death (IV, ii), however, she realizes that the circle cannot hold, and she sends word to her animal-like brothers that they may soon "feed" on her in quiet. This metaphoric use of language is reinforced by symbolic stage spectacles. The Duchess surrounded by gibbering maniacs, Antonio answered by sardonic echoes, and the deaths by strangulation further suggest the claustrophobic world established by the forces of evil in the play.

The play ends like *Lear* or any true tragedy with the assertion that "noble use" can be made "of this great ruin" and that value will be more perfectly realized by those who have survived and understood the experience, but one may ask if much positive value has really been affirmed by the play as a whole or if perhaps Bosola is not nearer to

its central emphasis. Bosola is a character of divided mind and allegiance, of many disguises. Convenient in terms of plot because he
is intimate with all the characters, and can therefore learn and speak
their private thoughts, he is also the chief spokesman for the senten-
tious precepts and reflections that run through the play. They are frequently quotations or paraphrases from Sidney's *Arcadia,* Montaigne's
Essays and Donne's later poems. The play is enriched by association
for a spectator who knows the sources of these precepts, but the critical question is whether they form a firm scheme of values for the
whole play. It is generally felt that they do not, and perhaps this
feeling comes in part from the fact that so many of them are uttered
by the chameleon-like Bosola. It has also been suggested that the
play's over-all tone of disillusionment is a reflection of a growing
pessimism as the Elizabethan harmony of diverse beliefs began to
break and change. Certainly other writers of the seventeenth century
show the same philosophical melancholy. It is perhaps this mood and
the projection of states of feeling through imagery that have led
modern poets like Eliot to admire Webster and to use his studies of
disillusionment to reinforce their own.

A Note on the Texts

For *King Lear* the Globe text has been used, and for *Doctor Faustus*
the Quarto of 1604. The text of *Volpone* is that of the Folio of 1616, the
last edition corrected by Jonson. The text of *The Duchess of Malfi* is
based on the quarto of 1623 as reprinted by F. L. Lucas, *Complete Works,*
Vol. II, and by C. F. T. Brooke and N. B. Paradise, *English Drama: 1580-
1642,* New York, 1933. The spelling, punctuation, and capitalization have
been modernized in conformity with recent editorial practice.

The Tragical History
of Dr. Faustus

The Tragical History
of Dr. Faustus

DRAMATIS PERSONAE

THE POPE	OLD MAN
CARDINAL OF LORRAIN	SCHOLARS, FRIARS, *and* ATTENDANTS
EMPEROR OF GERMANY	DUCHESS OF VANHOLT
DUKE OF VANHOLT	LUCIFER
FAUSTUS	BELZEBUB
VALDES *and* CORNELIUS, *friends to Faustus*	MEPHISTOPHILIS
	GOOD ANGEL
WAGNER, *servant to Faustus*	EVIL ANGEL
CLOWN	THE SEVEN DEADLY SINS
ROBIN	DEVILS
RALPH	SPIRITS *in the shape of* ALEXANDER
VINTNER	THE GREAT, *of his* PARAMOUR,
HORSE-COURSER	*and of* HELEN OF TROY
KNIGHT	CHORUS

[*Enter* CHORUS.]

CHORUS. Not marching now in fields of Thrasimene,
Where Mars did mate the Carthaginians;
Nor sporting in the dalliance of love,
In courts of kings where state is overturned;
Nor in the pomp of proud audacious deeds, 5
Intends our Muse to vaunt his heavenly verse:

---

2. *mate:* side with (the Carthaginians who, led by Hannibal, defeated the Romans).

Only this, gentlemen,—we must perform
The form of Faustus' fortunes, good or bad.
To patient judgments we appeal our plaud,
And speak for Faustus in his infancy.   10
Now is he born, his parents base of stock,
In Germany, within a town called Rhodes;
Of riper years to Wittenberg he went,
Whereas his kinsmen chiefly brought him up.
So soon he profits in divinity,   15
The fruitful plot of scholarism graced,
That shortly he was graced with doctor's name,
Excelling all whose sweet delight disputes
In heavenly matters of theology;
Till swollen with cunning, of a self-conceit,   20
His waxen wings did mount above his reach,
And, melting, Heavens conspired his overthrow;
For, falling to a devilish exercise,
And glutted now with learning's golden gifts,
He surfeits upon cursed necromancy.   25
Nothing so sweet as magic is to him,
Which he prefers before his chiefest bliss.
And this the man that in his study sits!   [*Exit.*

I

[*Enter* FAUSTUS *in his Study.*]

FAUST. Settle thy studies, Faustus, and begin
To sound the depth of that thou wilt profess.   30
Having commenced, be a divine in show;
Yet level at the end of every art,
And live and die in Aristotle's works.
Sweet Analytics, 'tis thou hast ravished me,
Bene disserere est finis logices.   35
Is to dispute well logic's chiefest end?
Affords this art no greater miracle?
Then read no more, thou hast attained the end;
A greater subject fitteth Faustus' wit.
Bid ὄν καὶ μὴ ὄν farewell; Galen come,   40

---

9. *our plaud:* request for applause. 20. *cunning:* learning. 31. *commenced:* graduated. 32. *level:* aim. 34. *Analytics:* logic. 35. *Bene . . . logices:* The end of logic is to argue well. 40. *ὄν . . . ὄν:* being and non-being; *i.e.*, philosophy.

Seeing *Ubi desinit philosophus, ibi incipit medicus;*
Be a physician, Faustus, heap up gold,
And be eternised for some wondrous cure.
Summum bonum medicinae sanitas,
"The end of physic is our body's health."   45
Why, Faustus, hast thou not attained that end?
Is not thy common talk sound Aphorisms?
Are not thy bills hung up as monuments,
Whereby whole cities have escaped the plague,
And thousand desperate maladies been eased?   50
Yet art thou still but Faustus and a man.
Wouldst thou make men to live eternally,
Or, being dead, raise them to life again?
Then this profession were to be esteemed.
Physic, farewell.—Where is Justinian?   55
Si una eademque res legatur duobus, alter rem,
    alter valorem rei, &c.—
A pretty case of paltry legacies!
Exhaereditare filium non potest pater nisi, &c.—
Such is the subject of the Institute
And universal Body of the Law.   60
His study fits a mercenary drudge,
Who aims at nothing but external trash;
Too servile and illiberal for me.
When all is done, divinity is best;
Jerome's Bible, Faustus, view it well.   65
Stipendium peccati mors est. Ha! *Stipendium, &c.*
"The reward of sin is death." That's hard.
Si peccasse negamus, fallimur, et nulla est in nobis veritas.
"If we say that we have no sin we deceive ourselves and there's no
truth in us." Why then, belike we must sin and so conse-   [70
quently die.
Ay, we must die an everlasting death.
What doctrine call you this, *Che sera sera,*
"What will be shall be"? Divinity, adieu!

---

41. *Ubi . . . medicus:* Where the philosopher leaves off, the physician
begins. 45. *physic:* medicine. 47. *sound Aphorisms:* scientific medical
observations, like the Aphorisms of Hippocrates. 48. *bills:* prescriptions.
55. *Justinian:* Roman legal expert, author of the *Institutes* (l. 60). 56.
Si . . . &c.: if one and the same thing is willed to two persons, let one
take the thing and the other its value. 58. *Exhaereditare . . . &c.:* a father
cannot disinherit his son unless—. 61. *His:* its. 65. *Jerome's Bible:* the so-
called Vulgate, a Latin translation made by St. Jerome (c. 340-420).

These metaphysics of magicians   75
And necromantic books are heavenly;
Lines, circles, scenes, letters, and characters,
Ay, these are those that Faustus most desires.
O what a world of profit and delight,
Of power, of honour, of omnipotence   80
Is promised to the studious artisan!
All things that move between the quiet poles
Shall be at my command. Emperors and kings
Are but obeyed in their several provinces,
Nor can they raise the wind or rend the clouds;   85
But his dominion that exceeds in this
Stretcheth as far as doth the mind of man.
A sound magician is a mighty god:
Here, Faustus, try thy brains to gain a deity.
Wagner!

[Enter WAGNER.]

    Commend me to my dearest friends,   90
The German Valdes and Cornelius;
Request them earnestly to visit me.
  WAG. I will, sir.   *[Exit.*
  FAUST. Their conference will be a greater help to me
Than all my labours, plod I ne'er so fast.   95

[Enter GOOD ANGEL *and* EVIL ANGEL.]

  G. ANG. O Faustus! lay that damnèd book aside,
And gaze not upon it lest it tempt thy soul,
And heap God's heavy wrath upon thy head.
Read, read the Scriptures: that is blasphemy.
  E. ANG. Go forward, Faustus, in that famous art,   100
Wherein all nature's treasure is contained;
Be thou on earth as Jove is in the sky,
Lord and commander of these elements.   *[Exeunt* ANGELS.
  FAUST. How am I glutted with conceit of this!
Shall I make spirits fetch me what I please,   105
Resolve me of all ambiguities,
Perform what desperate enterprise I will?
I'll have them fly to India for gold,
Ransack the ocean for orient pearl,
And search all corners of the new-found world   110

---

81. *studious artisan:* scholarly practitioner. 99. *that:* the other. 104. *conceit:*
the thought.

For pleasant fruits and princely delicates;
I'll have them read me strange philosophy
And tell the secrets of all foreign kings;
I'll have them wall all Germany with brass,
And make swift Rhine circle fair Wittenberg;   115
I'll have them fill the public schools with silk,
Wherewith the students shall be bravely clad;
I'll levy soldiers with the coin they bring,
And chase the Prince of Parma from our land,
And reign sole king of all the provinces;   120
Yea, stranger engines for the brunt of war
Than was the fiery keel at Antwerp's bridge,
I'll make my servile spirits to invent.
Come, German Valdes and Cornelius,
And make me blest with your sage conference.   125

[*Enter* VALDES *and* CORNELIUS.]

Valdes, sweet Valdes, and Cornelius,
Know that your words have won me at the last
To practise magic and concealèd arts;
Yet not your words only, but mine own fantasy,
That will receive no object, for my head   130
But ruminates on necromantic skill.
Philosophy is odious and obscure;
Both law and physic are for petty wits;
Divinity is basest of the three,
Unpleasant, harsh, contemptible, and vile.   135
'Tis magic, magic, that hath ravished me.
Then, gentle friends, aid me in this attempt;
And I that have with concise syllogisms
Gravelled the pastors of the German church,
And made the flowering pride of Wittenberg   140
Swarm to my problems, as the infernal spirits
On sweet Musaeus, when he came to hell,
Will be as cunning as Agrippa was,
Whose shadows made all Europe honour him.
    VALD. Faustus, these books, thy wit, and our experience   145
Shall make all nations to canonise us.

---

111. *delicates:* delicacies. 117. *bravely:* splendidly. 122. *fiery keel:* fire ship.
130. *receive:* accept. 139. *Gravelled:* silenced. 141. *problems:* lectures. 143.
Agrippa: Cornelius Agrippa (1486-1535), a famous German student of
magic. 144. *shadows:* conjured spirits.

As Indian Moors obey their Spanish lords,
So shall the subjects of every element
Be always serviceable to us three;
Like lions shall they guard us when we please;   150
Like Almain rutters with their horsemen's staves,
Or Lapland giants, trotting by our sides;
Sometimes like women or unwedded maids,
Shadowing more beauty in their airy brows
Than have the white breasts of the queen of love.   155
From Venice shall they drag huge argosies,
And from America the golden fleece
That yearly stuffs old Philip's treasury;
If learnèd Faustus will be resolute.
   FAUST. Valdes, as resolute am I in this   160
As thou to live; therefore object it not.
   CORN. The miracles that magic will perform
Will make thee vow to study nothing else.
He that is grounded in astrology,
Enriched with tongues, well seen in minerals,   165
Hath all the principles magic doth require.
Then doubt not, Faustus, but to be renowned,
And more frequented for this mystery
Than heretofore the Delphian Oracle.
The spirits tell me they can dry the sea,   170
And fetch the treasure of all foreign wracks,
Ay, all the wealth that our forefathers hid
Within the massy entrails of the earth.
Then tell me, Faustus, what shall we three want?
   FAUST. Nothing, Cornelius! O this cheers my soul!   175
Come show me some demonstrations magical,
That I may conjure in some lusty grove,
And have these joys in full possession.
   VALD. Then haste thee to some solitary grove,
And bear wise Bacon's and Albanus's works,   180
The Hebrew Psalter and New Testament;
And whatsoever else is requisite
We will inform thee ere our conference cease.
   CORN. Valdes, first let him know the words of art;
And then, all other ceremonies learned,   185

---

151. *Almain rutters:* German riders. 154. *Shadowing:* showing. 165. *seen:*
instructed. 177. *lusty:* pleasant. 180. *Bacon's:* Roger Bacon; *Albanus's:*
perhaps Albertus Magnus, a contemporary of Bacon's.

Faustus may try his cunning by himself.

   VALD. First I'll instruct thee in the rudiments,
And then wilt thou be perfecter than I.

   FAUST. Then come and dine with me, and after meat,
We'll canvass every quiddity thereof;   190
For ere I sleep I'll try what I can do.
This night I'll conjure though I die therefore.   [*Exeunt.*

II

[*Enter two* SCHOLARS.]

   1 SCHOL. I wonder what's become of Faustus that was wont to make
our schools ring with *sic probo*?

   2 SCHOL. That shall we know, for see here comes his boy.   195

[*Enter* WAGNER.]

   1 SCHOL. How now, sirrah! Where's thy master?

   WAG. God in heaven knows!

   2 SCHOL. Why, dost not thou know?

   WAG. Yes, I know. But that follows not.   199

   1 SCHOL. Go to, sirrah! Leave your jesting, and tell us where he is.

   WAG. That follows not necessary by force of argument, that you,
being licentiate, should stand upon 't; therefore, acknowledge your
error and be attentive.

   2 SCHOL. Why, didst thou not say thou knew'st?

   WAG. Have you any witness on 't?   205

   1 SCHOL. Yes, sirrah, I heard you.

   WAG. Ask my fellow if I be a thief.

   2 SCHOL. Well, you will not tell us?

   WAG. Yes, sir, I will tell you; yet if you were not dunces, you would
never ask me such a question; for is not he *corpus naturale?*   [210
and is not that *mobile?* Then wherefore should you ask me such a
question? But that I am by nature phlegmatic, slow to wrath, and
prone to lechery (to love, I would say), it were not for you to come
within forty foot of the place of execution, although I do not doubt to
see you both hanged the next sessions. Thus having tri-   [215
umphed over you, I will set my countenance like a precisian, and begin
to speak thus:—Truly, my dear brethren, my master is within at
dinner, with Valdes and Cornelius, as this wine, if it could speak,
would inform your worships; and so the Lord bless you, pre-   [219

---

190. *quiddity:* element. 194. *sic probo:* thus I prove. 195. *boy:* pupil. 202.
licentiate: graduate student. 210. *corpus naturale:* natural body. 214. *place
of execution: i.e.,* the dining room. 216. *precisian:* Puritan.

serve you, and keep you, my dear brethren, my dear brethren. [*Exit.*

1 SCHOL. Nay, then, I fear he has fallen into that damned art, for which they two are infamous through the world.

2 SCHOL. Were he a stranger, and not allied to me, yet should I grieve for him. But come, let us go and inform the Rector, and see if he by his grave counsel can reclaim him.   225

1 SCHOL. O, I fear me nothing can reclaim him.

2 SCHOL. Yet let us try what we can do.   [*Exeunt.*

III

[*Enter* FAUSTUS *to conjure.*]

FAUST. Now that the gloomy shadow of the earth
Longing to view Orion's drizzling look,
Leaps from th' antarctic world unto the sky,   230
And dims the welkin with her pitchy breath,
Faustus, begin thine incantations,
And try if devils will obey thy hest,
Seeing thou has prayed and sacrificed to them.
Within this circle is Jehovah's name,   235
Forward and backward anagrammatised,
The 'breviated names of holy saints,
Figures of every adjunct to the heavens,
And characters of signs and erring stars,
By which the spirits are enforced to rise;   240
Then fear not, Faustus, but be resolute,
And try the uttermost magic can perform.

Sint mihi Dei Acherontis propitii! Valeat numen triplex Jehovae!
Ignei, aerii, aquatani spiritus, salvete! Orientis princeps Belzebub,
inferni ardentis monarcha, et Demogorgon, propitiamus   [245
vos, ut appareat et surgat Mephistophilis. Quid tu moraris? Per
Jehovam, Gehennam, et consecratam aquam quam nunc spargo,
signumque crucis quod nunc facio, et per vota nostra, ipse nunc
surgat nobis dicatus Mephistophilis!

---

224. *Rector:* head of the university. 231. *welkin:* sky. 233. *hest:* command.
238. *adjunct to:* planet in. 239. *characters of signs:* symbols of signs of the
zodiac; *erring:* wandering. 243-49. *Sint . . . Mephistophilis:* May the gods
of Acheron be favorable to me! Goodbye to the trinity of Jehovah. Hail,
spirits of fire, air, and water. Belzebub, prince of the East, monarch of
burning hell, and Demogorgon, we ask your favor that Mephistophilis may
rise and appear. Why do you delay? By Jehovah, hell, and the holy water
which I now sprinkle, and by the sign of the cross which I now make, and
by our vows, may Mephistophilis now arise to obey us.

[*Enter a* DEVIL.]

I charge thee to return and change thy shape;   250
Thou art too ugly to attend on me.
Go, and return an old Franciscan friar;
That holy shape becomes a devil best.   [*Exit* DEVIL.
I see there's virtue in my heavenly words;
Who would not be proficient in this art?   255
How pliant is this Mephistophilis,
Full of obedience and humility!
Such is the force of magic and my spells.
Now, Faustus, thou are conjuror laureate,
Thou canst command great Mephistophilis: 260
Quin redis Mephistophilis fratris imagine.

[*Re-enter* MEPHISTOPHILIS *like a Franciscan Friar.*]

MEPH. Now, Faustus, what would'st thou have me do?
FAUST. I charge thee wait upon me whilst I live,
To do whatever Faustus shall command,
Be it to make the moon drop from her sphere,   265
Or the ocean to overwhelm the world.
MEPH. I am a servant to great Lucifer,
And may not follow thee without his leave;
No more than he commands must we perform.
FAUST. Did he not charge thee to appear to me?   270
MEPH. No, I came hither of mine own accord.
FAUST. Did not my conjuring speeches raise thee? Speak.
MEPH. That was the cause, but yet *per accidens;*
For when we hear one rack the name of God,
Abjure the Scriptures and his Saviour Christ,   275
We fly in hope to get his glorious soul;
Nor will we come, unless he use such means
Whereby he is in danger to be damned;
Therefore the shortest cut for conjuring
Is stoutly o abjure the Trinity,   280
And pray devoutly to the prince of hell.
FAUST. So Faustus hath
Already done; and holds this principle,
There is no chief but only Belzebub,

---

254. *heavenly:* magical. 261. *Quin . . . imagine:* Why don't you return,
Mephistophilis, in the likeness of a friar? 273. *per accidens:* incidentally.
274. *rack:* torture and break (in anagrams).

To whom Faustus doth dedicate himself.   285
This word "damnation" terrifies not him,
For he confounds hell in Elysium;
His ghost be with the old philosophers!
But, leaving these vain trifles of men's souls,
Tell me what is that Lucifer thy lord?   290
   MEPH. Arch-regent and commander of all spirits.
   FAUST. Was not that Lucifer an angel once?
   MEPH. Yes, Faustus, and most dearly loved of God.
   FAUST. How comes it then that he is prince of devils?
   MEPH. O, by aspiring pride and insolence;   295
For which God threw him from the face of heaven.
   FAUST. And what are you that you live with Lucifer?
   MEPH. Unhappy spirits that fell with Lucifer,
Conspired against our God with Lucifer,
And are for ever damned with Lucifer.   300
   FAUST. Where are you damned?
   MEPH. In hell.
   FAUST. How comes it then that thou art out of hell?
   MEPH. Why this is hell, nor am I out of it.
Think'st thou that I who saw the face of God,   305
And tasted the eternal joys of heaven,
Am not tormented with ten thousand hells,
In being deprived of everlasting bliss?
O Faustus! leave these frivolous demands,
Which strike a terror to my fainting soul.   310
   FAUST. What, is great Mephistophilis so passionate
For being deprivèd of the joys of heaven?
Learn thou of Faustus manly fortitude,
And scorn those joys thou never shalt possess.
Go bear these tidings to great Lucifer: 315
Seeing Faustus hath incurred eternal death
By desperate thoughts against Jove's deity,
Say he surrenders up to him his soul,
So he will spare him four and twenty years,
Letting him live in all voluptuousness;   320
Having thee ever to attend on me;
To give me whatsoever I shall ask,
To tell me whatsoever I demand,
To slay mine enemies, and aid my friends,
And always be obedient to my will.   325

---

287. *confounds . . . Elysium:* does not believe in the distinction between
hell and heaven. 311. *passionate:* disturbed.

Go and return to mighty Lucifer,
And meet me in my study at midnight,
And then resolve me of thy master's mind.

MEPH. I will, Faustus.   [*Exit.*

FAUST. Had I as many souls as there be stars,   330
I'd give them all for Mephistophilis.
By him I'll be great emperor of the world,
And make a bridge through the moving air,
To pass the ocean with a band of men;
I'll join the hills that bind the Afric shore,   335
And make that country continent to Spain,
And both contributory to my crown.
The emperor shall not live but by my leave,
Nor any potentate of Germany.
Now that I have obtained what I desire,   340
I'll live in speculation of this art
Till Mephistophilis return again.   [*Exit.*

IV

[*Enter* WAGNER *and the* CLOWN.]

WAG. Sirrah, boy, come hither.

CLOWN. How, boy! Swowns, boy! I hope you have seen many boys
with such pickadevaunts as I have. Boy, quotha!   345

WAG. Tell me, sirrah, hast thou any comings in?

CLOWN. Ay, and goings out too. You may see else.

WAG. Alas, poor slave! See how poverty jesteth in his nakedness!
The villain is bare and out of service, and so hungry that I know he
would give his soul to the devil for a shoulder of mutton,   [350
though it were blood-raw.

CLOWN. How? My soul to the devil for a shoulder of mutton, though
'twere blood-raw! Not so, good friend. By 'r Lady, I had need have
it well roasted and good sauce to it, if I pay so dear.

WAG. Well, wilt thou serve me, and I'll make thee go like   [355
Qui mihi discipulus?

CLOWN. How, in verse?

WAG. No, sirrah; in beaten silk and stavesacre.

CLOWN. How, how, knave's acre! Ay, I thought that was all the land
his father left him. Do you hear? I would be sorry to   [36c
rob you of your living.

---

328. *resolve:* inform. 345. *pickadevaunts:* pointed beards. 346. *comings in*
income. 356. *Qui mihi discipulus:* my student. 358. *beaten silk:* ornamented
with beaten metal; *stavesacre:* lice powder.

WAG. Sirrah, I say in stavesacre.

CLOWN. Oho! Oho! Stavesacre! Why, then, belike if I were your man I should be full of vermin.

WAG. So thou shalt, whether thou beest with me or no. But,   [365 sirrah, leave your jesting, and bind yourself presently unto me for seven years, or I'll turn all the lice about thee into familiars, and they shall tear thee in pieces.

CLOWN. Do you hear, sir? You may save that labour; they are too familiar with me already. Swowns! they are as bold with my   [370 flesh as if they had paid for their meat and drink.

WAG. Well, do you hear, sirrah? Hold, take these guilders.

CLOWN. Gridirons! what be they?

WAG. Why, French crowns.

CLOWN. Mass, but for the name of French crowns, a man   [375 were as good have as many English counters. And what should I do with these?

WAG. Why, now, sirrah, thou art at an hour's warning, whensoever and wheresoever the devil shall fetch thee.

CLOWN. No, no. Here, take your gridirons again.   380

WAG. Truly I'll none of them.

CLOWN. Truly but you shall.

WAG. Bear witness I gave them him.

CLOWN. Bear witness I give them you again.

WAG. Well, I will cause two devils presently to fetch thee   [385 away—Baliol and Belcher.

CLOWN. Let your Baliol and your Belcher come here, and I'll knock them, they were never so knockt since they were devils. Say I should kill one of them, what would folks say? "Do you see yonder tall fellow in the round slop?—he has killed the devil." So I   [390 should be called kill-devil all the parish over.

[*Enter two* DEVILS; *the* CLOWN *runs up and down crying.*]

WAG. Baliol and Belcher! Spirits, away!   [*Exeunt* DEVILS.

CLOWN. What, are they gone? A vengeance on them, they have vile long nails! There was a he-devil, and a she-devil! I'll tell you how you shall know them: all he-devils has horns, and all she-   [395 devils has clifts and cloven feet.

WAG. Well, sirrah, follow me.

CLOWN. But, do you hear—if I should serve you, would you teach me to raise up Banios and Belcheos?

---

367. *familiars:* attendant spirits. 372. *guilders:* Dutch coins. 389. *tall:* strong; *round slop:* wide breeches.

WAG. I will teach thee to turn thyself to anything; to a dog,   [400
or a cat, or a mouse, or a rat, or anything.

CLOWN. How! a Christian fellow to a dog or a cat, a mouse or a
rat! No, no, sir. If you turn me into anything, let it be in the likeness
of a little pretty frisky flea, that I may be here and there and every-
where. Oh, I'll tickle the pretty wenches' plackets; I'll be   [405
amongst them, i' faith.

WAG. Well, sirrah, come.

CLOWN. But, do you hear, Wagner?

WAG. How!—Baliol and Belcher!

CLOWN. O Lord! I pray, sir, let Banio and Belcher go sleep.   410

WAG. Villain—call me Master Wagner, and let thy left eye be
diametarily fixt upon my right heel, with *quasi vestigias nostras insistere.*   [*Exit.*

CLOWN. God forgive him, he speaks Dutch fustian. Well,   [414
I'll follow him, I'll serve him, that's flat.   [*Exit.*

V

[*Enter* FAUSTUS *in his study.*]

FAUST. Now, Faustus, must
Thou needs be damned, and canst thou not be saved;
What boots it then to think of God or heaven?
Away with such vain fancies, and despair;
Despair in God, and trust in Belzebub.   420
Now go not backward: no, Faustus, be resolute.
Why waverest thou? O, something soundeth in mine ears,
"Abjure this magic, turn to God again!"
Ay, and Faustus will turn to God again.
To God?—He loves thee not—   425
The God thou serv'st is thine own appetite,
Wherein is fixed the love of Belzebub;
To him I'll build an altar and a church,
And offer lukewarm blood of new-born babes.

[*Enter* GOOD ANGEL *and* EVIL ANGEL.]

G. ANG. Sweet Faustus, leave that execrable art.   430
FAUST. Contrition, prayer, repentance! What of them?
G. ANG. O, they are means to bring thee unto heaven.

---

405. *plackets:* openings in petticoats. 412. *diametarily:* directly. 412-13.
quasi . . . insistere: as if to tread in our tracks (the Latin is ungrammati-
cal). 414. *fustian:* highfalutin' nonsense.

E. ANG. Rather illusions, fruits of lunacy,
That makes men foolish that do trust them most.
    G. ANG. Sweet Faustus, think of heaven, and heavenly things.   435
    E. ANG. No, Faustus, think of honour and of wealth.   [*Exeunt.*
    FAUST. Of wealth!
Why, the signiory of Emden shall be mine.
When Mephistophilis shall stand by me,
What God can hurt thee, Faustus? Thou art safe;   440
Cast no more doubts. Come, Mephistophilis,
And bring glad tidings from great Lucifer;—
Is 't not midnight? Come, Mephistophilis;
Veni, veni, Mephistophile!

[*Enter* MEPHISTOPHILIS.]

Now tell me, what says Lucifer thy lord?   445
    MEPH. That I shall wait on Faustus whilst he lives,
So he will buy my service with his soul.
    FAUST. Already Faustus hath hazarded that for thee.
    MEPH. But, Faustus, thou must bequeath it solemnly,
And write a deed of gift with thine own blood,   450
For that security craves great Lucifer.
If thou deny it, I will back to hell.
    FAUST. Stay, Mephistophilis! and tell me what good
Will my soul do thy lord.
    MEPH.   Enlarge his kingdom.
    FAUST. Is that the reason why he tempts us thus?   455
    MEPH. *Solamen miseris socios habuisse doloris.*
    FAUST. Why, have you any pain that torture others?
    MEPH. As great as have the human souls of men.
But tell me, Faustus, shall I have thy soul?
And I will be thy slave, and wait on thee,   460
And give thee more than thou hast wit to ask.
    FAUST. Ay, Mephistophilis, I give it thee.
    MEPH. Then, Faustus, stab thine arm courageously.
And bind thy soul that at some certain day
Great Lucifer may claim it as his own;   465
And then be thou as great as Lucifer.
    FAUST (*stabbing his arm*). Lo, Mephistophilis, for love of thee,
I cut mine arm, and with my proper blood
Assure my soul to be great Lucifer's,
Chief lord and regent of perpetual night!   470

---

438. *signiory:* domain. 456. *Solamen . . . doloris:* misery loves company
457. *that:* you who. 468. *proper:* own.

View here the blood that trickles from mine arm,
And let it be propitious for my wish.
   MEPH. But, Faustus, thou must
Write it in manner of a deed of gift.
   FAUST. Ay, so I will. But, Mephistophilis,   475
My blood congeals, and I can write no more.
   MEPH. I'll fetch thee fire to dissolve it straight.   [*Exit.*
   FAUST. What might the staying of my blood portend?
Is it unwilling I should write this bill?
Why streams it not that I may write afresh?   480
Faustus gives to thee his soul. Ah, there it stayed.
Why should'st thou not? Is not thy soul thine own?
Then write again, *Faustus gives to thee his soul.*

    [*Re-enter* MEPHISTOPHILIS *with a chafer of coals.*]

   MEPH. Here's fire. Come, Faustus, set it on.
   FAUST. So now the blood begins to clear again;   485
Now will I make an end immediately.
   MEPH. O what will not I do to obtain his soul.
   FAUST. *Consummatum est:* this bill is ended,
And Faustus hath bequeathed his soul to Lucifer—
But what is this inscription on mine arm?   490
Homo, fuge! Whither should I fly?
If unto God, he'll throw me down to hell.
My senses are deceived; here's nothing writ:—
I see it plain; here in this place is writ
Homo, fuge! Yet shall not Faustus fly.   495
   MEPH. I'll fetch him somewhat to delight his mind.   [*Exit.*

   [*Re-enter* MEPHISTOPHILIS *with* DEVILS, *giving crowns and rich
apparel to* FAUSTUS, *and they dance, and then depart.*]

   FAUST. Speak, Mephistophilis, what means this show?
   MEPH. Nothing, Faustus, but to delight thy mind withal,
And to show thee what magic can perform.
   FAUST. But may I raise up spirits when I please?   500
   MEPH. Ay, Faustus, and do greater things than these.
   FAUST. Then there's enough for a thousand souls.
Here, Mephistophilis, receive this scroll,
A deed of gift of body and of soul:

---

483. Stage direction: *chafer:* portable grate. 484. *it: i.e.,* saucer of blood.
488. *Consummatum est:* it is finished (a blasphemous use of Christ's words,
St. John xix, 30).

But yet conditionally that thou perform   505
All articles prescribed between us both.

MEPH. Faustus, I swear by hell and Lucifer
To effect all promises between us made.

FAUST. Then hear me read them: *On these conditions following.*
First, that Faustus may be a spirit in form and substance.   [510
Secondly, that Mephistophilis shall be his servant, and at his com-
mand. Thirdly, that Mephistophilis shall do for him and bring him
whatsoever he desires. Fourthly, that he shall be in his chamber or
house invisible. Lastly, that he shall appear to the said John Faustus,
at all times, in what form or shape soever he pleases. I, John   [515
Faustus, of Wittenberg, Doctor, by these presents do give both
body and soul to Lucifer, Prince of the East, and his minister, Mephis-
tophilis; and furthermore grant unto them, that twenty-four years
being expired, the articles above written inviolate, full power to
fetch or carry the said John Faustus, body and soul, flesh,   [520
blood, or goods, into their habitation wheresoever. By me, John
Faustus.

MEPH. Speak, Faustus, do you deliver this as your deed?

FAUST. Ay, take it, and the devil give thee good on't.

MEPH. Now, Faustus, ask what thou wilt.   525

FAUST. First will I question with thee about hell.
Tell me where is the place that men call hell?

MEPH. Under the heavens.

FAUST. Ay, but whereabout?

MEPH. Within the bowels of these elements,   530
Where we are tortured and remain for ever;
Hell hath no limits, nor is circumscribed
In one self place; for where we are is hell,
And where hell is there must we ever be.
And, to conclude, when all the world dissolves,   535
And every creature shall be purified,
All places shall be hell that is not heaven.

FAUST. Come, I think hell's a fable.

MEPH. Ay, think so still, till experience change thy mind.   539

FAUST. Why, think'st thou then that Faustus shall be damned?

MEPH. Ay, of necessity, for here's the scroll
Wherein thou hast given thy soul to Lucifer.

FAUST. Ay, and body too; but what of that?
Think'st thou that Faustus is so fond to imagine
That after this life, there is any pain?   545

---

544. *fond:* foolish.

Tush; these are trifles, and mere old wives' tales.

MEPH. But Faustus, I am an instance to prove the contrary,
For I am damnèd, and am now in hell.

FAUST. How! now in hell!
Nay, an this be hell, I'll willingly be damned here; 550
What? walking, disputing, &c.?
But, leaving off this, let me have a wife,
The fairest maid in Germany;
For I am wanton and lascivious,
And cannot live without a wife. 555

MEPH. How—a wife?
I prithee, Faustus, talk not of a wife.

FAUST. Nay, sweet Mephistophilis, fetch me one, for I will have
one.

MEPH. Well—thou wilt have one. Sit there till I come: 560
I'll fetch thee a wife in the devil's name. [Exit.

[Re-enter MEPHISTOPHILIS with a DEVIL dressed like
a woman, with fireworks.]

MEPH. Tell me, Faustus, how dost thou like thy wife?

FAUST. A plague on her for a hot whore!

MEPH. Tut, Faustus,
Marriage is but a ceremonial toy; 565
And if thou lovest me, think no more of it.
I'll cull thee out the fairest courtesans,
And bring them every morning to thy bed;
She whom thine eye shall like, thy heart shall have,
Be she as chaste as was Penelope, 570
As wise as Saba, or as beautiful
As was bright Lucifer before his fall.
Here, take this book, peruse it thoroughly.
The iterating of these lines brings gold;
The framing of this circle on the ground 575
Brings whirlwinds, tempests, thunder and lightning;
Pronounce this thrice devoutly to thyself,
And men in armour shall appear to thee,
Ready to execute what thou desir'st.

FAUST. Thanks, Mephistophilis; yet fain would I have a [580
book wherein I might behold all spells and incantations, that I
might raise up spirits when I please.

MEPH. Here they are, in this book. (Turns to them.)

_____

571. *Saba:* Sheba. 574. *iterating:* repeating.

FAUST. Now would I have a book where I might see all characters
and planets of the heavens, that I might know their motions   [585
and dispositions.

MEPH. Here they are too. (*Turns to them.*)

FAUST. Nay, let me have one book more,—and then I have done,—
wherein I might see all plants, herbs, and trees that grow upon the
earth.   590

MEPH. Here they be.

FAUST. O, thou art deceived.

MEPH. Tut, I warrant thee. (*Turns to them.*)   [*Exeunt.*

VI

[*Enter* FAUSTUS *and* MEPHISTOPHILIS.]

FAUST. When I behold the heavens, then I repent,
And curse thee, wicked Mephistophilis,   595
Because thou hast deprived me of those joys.

MEPH. Why, Faustus,
Thinkest thou heaven is such a glorious thing?
I tell thee 'tis not half so fair as thou,
Or any man that breathes on earth.   600

FAUST. How provest thou that?

MEPH. 'Twas made for man, therefore is man more excellent.

FAUST. If it were made for man, 'twas made for me;
I will renounce this magic and repent.

[*Enter* GOOD ANGEL *and* EVIL ANGEL.]

G. ANG. Faustus, repent; yet God will pity thee.   605

E. ANG. Thou art a spirit; God cannot pity thee.

FAUST. Who buzzeth in mine ears I am a spirit?
Be I a devil, yet God may pity me;
Ay, God will pity me if I repent.   609

E. ANG. Ay, but Faustus never shall repent.   [*Exeunt.*

FAUST. My heart's so hardened I cannot repent.
Scarce can I name salvation, faith, or heaven,
But fearful echoes thunder in mine ears
"Faustus, thou art damned!" Then swords and knives,
Poison, gun, halters, and envenomed steel   615
Are laid before me to despatch myself;
And long ere this I should have slain myself,
Had not sweet pleasure conquered deep despair.
Have I not made blind Homer sing to me

Of Alexander's love and Oenon's death?   620
And hath not he that built the walls of Thebes
With ravishing sound of his melodious harp,
Made music with my Mephistophilis?
Why should I die then, or basely despair?
I am resolved: Faustus shall ne'er repent.   625
Come, Mephistophilis, let us dispute again,
And argue of divine astrology.
Tell me, are there many heavens above the moon?
Are all celestial bodies but one globe,
As is the substance of this centric earth?   630
   MEPH. As are the elements, such are the spheres
Mutually folded in each other's orb,
And, Faustus,
All jointly move upon one axletree
Whose terminine is termed the world's wide pole;   635
Nor are the names of Saturn, Mars, or Jupiter
Feigned, but are erring stars.
   FAUST. But tell me, have they all one motion, both *situ et tempore?*
   MEPH. All jointly move from east to west in twenty-four hours
upon the poles of the world; but differ in their motion upon   [640
the poles of the zodiac.
   FAUST. Tush!
These slender trifles Wagner can decide;
Hath Mephistophilis no greater skill?
Who knows not the double motion of the planets?   645
The first is finished in a natural day;
The second thus: as Saturn in thirty years; Jupiter in twelve; Mars in
four; the Sun, Venus, and Mercury in a year; the moon in twenty-
eight days. Tush, these are freshmen's suppositions. But tell me,
hath every sphere a dominion or *intelligentia?*   650
   MEPH. Ay.
   FAUST. How many heavens, or spheres, are there?
   MEPH. Nine: the seven planets, the firmament, and the empyreal
heaven.
   FAUST. Well, resolve me in this question: Why have we not   [655
conjunctions, oppositions, aspects, eclipses, all at one time, but in
some years we have more, in some less?

---

620. *Alexander's:* Paris; *Oenon:* wife of Paris, whom he left for Helen and
who killed herself at his death. 621. *he:* Amphion. 638. *situ et tempore:*
in place and time. 650. *dominion or intelligentia:* ruling spirit.

MEPH. *Per inaequalem motum respectu totius.*
FAUST. Well, I am answered. Tell me who made the world.
MEPH. I will not.   660
FAUST. Sweet Mephistophilis, tell me.
MEPH. Move me not, for I will not tell thee.
FAUST. Villain, have I not bound thee to tell me anything?
MEPH. Ay, that is not against our kingdom; but this is.
Think thou on hell, Faustus, for thou are damned.   665
FAUST. Think, Faustus, upon God that made the world.
MEPH. Remember this.
FAUST. Ay, go, accursèd spirit, to ugly hell.
'Tis thou hast damned distressèd Faustus' soul.
Is't not too late?   670

[*Re-enter* GOOD ANGEL *and* EVIL ANGEL.]

E. ANG. Too late.
G. ANG. Never too late, if Faustus can repent.
E. ANG. If thou repent, devils shall tear thee in pieces.
G. ANG. Repent, and they shall never raze thy skin.   [*Exeunt.*
FAUST. Ah, Christ, my Saviour,   675
Seek to save distressèd Faustus' soul.

[*Enter* LUCIFER, BELZEBUB, *and* MEPHISTOPHILIS.]

LUC. Christ cannot save thy soul, for he is just;
There's none but I have interest in the same.
FAUST. O, who art thou that look'st so terrible?
LUC. I am Lucifer,   680
And this is my companion prince in hell.
FAUST. O Faustus! they are come to fetch away thy soul!
LUC. We come to tell thee thou dost injure us;
Thou talk'st of Christ contrary to thy promise;
Thou should'st not think of God: think of the devil,   685
And of his dam, too.
FAUST. Nor will I henceforth: pardon me in this,
And Faustus vows never to look to heaven,
Never to name God, or to pray to him;
To burn his Scriptures, slay his ministers,   690
And make my spirits pull his churches down.
LUC. Do so, and we will highly gratify thee. Faustus, we are
come from hell to show thee some pastime. Sit down, and thou shalt
see all the Seven Deadly Sins appear in their proper shapes.

---

658. *Per . . . totius:* because of their unequal motion relative to the whole.
674. *raze:* scratch.

FAUST. That sight will be pleasing unto me,   695
As Paradise was to Adam the first day
Of his creation.

LUC. Talk not of Paradise nor creation, but mark this show; talk
of the devil, and nothing else.—Come away!   699

[*Enter the* SEVEN DEADLY SINS.]

Now, Faustus, examine them of their several names and dispositions.

FAUST. What art thou—the first?

PRIDE. I am Pride. I disdain to have any parents. I am like
to Ovid's flea: I can creep into every corner of a wench; sometimes, like a periwig, I sit upon her brow; or like a fan of feathers,
I kiss her lips; indeed I do—what do I not? But, fie, what a   [705
scent is here! I'll not speak another word, except the ground were
perfumed, and covered with cloth of arras.

FAUST. What art thou—second?

COVET. I am Covetousness, begotten of an old churl in an old
leathern bag; and might I have my wish I would desire that   [710
this house and all the people in it were turned to gold, that I might
lock you up in my good chest. O, my sweet gold!

FAUST. What art thou—the third?

WRATH. I am Wrath. I had neither father nor mother: I leapt out
of a lion's mouth when I was scarce half an hour old; and   [715
ever since I have run up and down the world with this case of rapiers
wounding myself when I had nobody to fight withal. I was born in
hell; and look to it, for some of you shall be my father.

FAUST. What art thou—the fourth?

ENVY. I am Envy, begotten of a chimney sweeper and an   [720
oyster-wife. I cannot read, and therefore wish all books were burnt.
I am lean with seeing others eat. O that there would come a famine
through all the world, that all might die, and I live alone! then thou
should'st see how fat I would be. But must thou sit and I stand!
Come down with a vengeance!   725

FAUST. Away, envious rascal! What art thou—the fifth?

GLUT. Who, I, sir? I am Gluttony. My parents are all dead, and
the devil a penny they have left me, but a bare pension, and that is
thirty meals a day and ten bevers—a small trifle to suffice nature. O,
I come of a royal parentage! My grandfather was a Gam-   [730
mon of Bacon, my grandmother a Hogshead of Claret-wine; my
godfathers were these, Peter Pickleherring, and Martin Martlemas-
beef. O but my godmother, she was a jolly gentlewoman, and

729. bevers: snacks.

well beloved in every good town and city; her name was Mistress
Margery Marchbeer. Now, Faustus, thou hast heard all my   [735
progeny, wilt thou bid me to supper?

FAUST. No, I'll see thee hanged; thou wilt eat up all my victuals.

GLUT. Then the devil choke thee!

FAUST. Choke thyself, glutton! Who art thou—the sixth?

SLOTH. I am Sloth. I was begotten on a sunny bank, where   [740
I have lain ever since; and you have done me great injury to bring
me from thence. Let me be carried thither again by Gluttony and
Lechery. I'll not speak another word for a king's ransom.

FAUST. What are you, Mistress Minx, the seventh and last?

LECH. Who, I, sir? I am one that loves an inch of raw   [745
mutton better than an ell of fried stockfish; and the first letter of
my name begins with Lechery.

LUC. Away to hell, to hell! (*Exeunt the* SINS.) Now, Faustus,
how dost thou like this?

FAUST. O, this feeds my soul!   750

LUC. Tut, Faustus, in hell is all manner of delight.

FAUST. O might I see hell, and return again. How happy were I
then!

LUC. Thou shalt; I will send for thee at midnight.
In meantime take this book; peruse it thoroughly,   755
And thou shalt turn thyself into what shape thou wilt.

FAUST. Great thanks, mighty Lucifer!
This will I keep as chary as my life.

LUC. Farewell, Faustus, and think on the devil.

FAUST. Farewell, great Lucifer! Come, Mephistophilis.   760
                                                  [*Exeunt omnes.*

[*Enter* WAGNER.]

WAGNER. Learnèd Faustus,
To know the secrets of astronomy,
Graven in the book of Jove's high firmament,
Did mount himself to scale Olympus' top,
Being seated in a chariot burning bright,   765
Drawn by the strength of yoky dragons' necks.
He now is gone to prove cosmography,
And, as I guess, will first arrive at Rome,
To see the Pope and manner of his court,
And take some part of holy Peter's feast,   770
That to this day is highly solemnised.   [*Exit.*

---

746. *mutton:* prostitute.

VII

[*Enter* FAUSTUS *and* MEPHISTOPHILIS.]

FAUST. Having now, my good Mephistophilis,
Passed with delight the stately town of Trier,
Environed round with airy mountain-tops,
With walls of flint, and deep entrenchèd lakes,   775
Not to be won by any conquering prince;
From Paris next, coasting the realm of France,
We saw the river Maine fall into Rhine,
Whose banks are set with groves of fruitful vines;
Then up to Naples, rich Campania,   780
Whose buildings fair and gorgeous to the eye,
The streets straight forth, and paved with finest brick,
Quarter the town in four equivalents.
There saw we learnèd Maro's golden tomb,
The way he cut, an English mile in length,   785
Thorough a rock of stone in one night's space;
From thence to Venice, Padua, and the rest,
In one of which a sumptuous temple stands,
That threats the stars with her aspiring top;
Thus hitherto has Faustus spent his time.   790
But tell me, now, what resting-place is this?
Hast thou, as erst I did command,
Conducted me within the walls of Rome?
  MEPH. Faustus, I have; and because we will not be unprovided, I
have taken up his Holiness' privy-chamber for our use.   795
  FAUST. I hope his Holiness will bid us welcome.
  MEPH. Tut, 'tis no matter, man, we'll be bold with his good cheer.
And now, my Faustus, that thou may'st perceive
What Rome containeth to delight thee with,
Know that this city stands upon seven hills   800
That underprop the groundwork of the same.
Just through the midst runs flowing Tiber's stream,
With winding banks that cut it in two parts,
Over the which four stately bridges lean,
That make safe passage to each part of Rome.   805
Upon the bridge called Ponto Angelo
Erected is a castle passing strong,
Within whose walls such store of ordnance are,

---

784. *Maro's:* Virgil, once believed to be a magician.

And double cannons, framed of carvèd brass,
As match the days within one complete year;   810
Besides the gates and high pyramids,
Which Julius Caesar brought from Africa.

    FAUST. Now by the kingdoms of infernal rule,
Of Styx, of Acheron, and the fiery lake
Of ever-burning Phlegethon, I swear   815
That I do long to see the monuments
And situation of bright-splendent Rome:
Come therefore, let's away.

    MEPH. Nay, Faustus, stay; I know you'd fain see the Pope,
And take some part of holy Peter's feast,   820
Where thou shalt see a troop of bald-pate friars,
Whose *summum bonum* is in belly-cheer.

    FAUST. Well, I'm content to compass then some sport,
And by their folly make us merriment.
Then charm me, Mephistophilis, that I   825
May be invisible, to do what I please
Unseen of any whilst I stay in Rome.

        [MEPHISTOPHILIS *charms him.*]

    MEPH. So, Faustus, now
Do what thou wilt, thou shalt not be discerned.

    [*Sound a sennet. Enter the* POPE *and the* CARDINAL OF LORRAIN
        to the banquet, with FRIARS *attending.*]

    POPE. My Lord of Lorrain, wilt please you draw near?   830
    FAUST. Fall to, and the devil choke you an you spare!
    POPE. How now! Who's that which spake?—Friars, look about.
    I FRIAR. Here's nobody, if it like your Holiness.
    POPE. My lord, here is a dainty dish was sent me from the Bishop
of Milan.   835
    FAUST. I thank you, sir. (*Snatches it.*)
    POPE. How now! Who's that which snatched the meat from me?
Will no man look? My lord, this dish was sent me from the Cardinal
of Florence.
    FAUST. You say true; I'll ha 't. (*Snatches it.*)   840
    POPE. What, again! My lord, I'll drink to your Grace.
    FAUST. I'll pledge your Grace. (*Snatches the cup.*)
    C. OF LOR. My lord, it may be some ghost newly crept out of Purga-

---

829. Stage direction: *sennet:* trumpet notes.

tory, come to beg a pardon of your Holiness.

POPE. It may be so. Friars, prepare a dirge to lay the fury　　[845
of this ghost. Once again, my lord, fall to. (*The* POPE *crosseth himself.*)

FAUST. What, are you crossing of yourself?
Well, use that trick no more I would advise you.

[*The* POPE *crosses himself again.*]

Well, there's the second time. Aware the third, I give you　　[850
fair warning.

[*The* POPE *crosses himself again, and* FAUSTUS *hits him
a box of the ear; and they all run away.*]

Come on, Mephistophilis, what shall we do?

MEPH. Nay, I know not. We shall be cursed with bell, book, and
candle.

FAUST. How! bell, book, and candle,—candle, book, and bell,
Forward and backward to curse Faustus to hell!　　　　　856
Anon you shall hear a hog grunt, a calf bleat, and an ass bray,
Because it is Saint Peter's holiday.

[*Re-enter all the* FRIARS *to sing the Dirge.*]

I FRIAR. Come, brethren, let's about our business with good devotion.　　　　　　　　　　　　　　　　　　　　　860

[*They sing:*]

Cursed be he that stole away his Holiness' meat from the table!
　　Maledicat Dominus!
Cursed be he that struck his Holiness a blow on the face! *Maledicat
　　Dominus!*
Cursed be he that took friar Sandelo a blow on the pate! *Maledicat
　　Dominus!*
Cursed be he that disturbeth our holy dirge! *Maledicat Dominus!*
Cursed be he that took away his Holiness' wine! *Maledicat Dominus!*
　　Et omnes sancti! Amen!　　　　　　　　　　　　865

[MEPHISTOPHILIS *and* FAUSTUS *beat the* FRIARS, *and fling
fireworks among them: and so exeunt.*]

[*Enter* CHORUS.]

CHORUS. When Faustus had with pleasure ta'en the view

853-54. *bell, book, and candle:* formally excommunicated. 861. *Maledicat
Dominus:* may the Lord curse him. 865. *Et omnes sancti:* and all the saints.

Of rarest things, and royal courts of kings,
He stayed his course, and so returnèd home;
Where such as bear his absence but with grief,
I mean his friends, and near'st companions,   870
Did gratulate his safety with kind words,
And in their conference of what befell,
Touching his journey through the world and air,
They put forth questions of astrology,
Which Faustus answered with such learnèd skill,   875
As they admired and wondered at his wit.
Now is his fame spread forth in every land;
Amongst the rest the Emperor is one,
Carolus the Fifth, at whose palace now
Faustus is feasted 'mongst his noblemen.   880
What there he did in trial of his art,
I leave untold—your eyes shall see performed.   [*Exit.*

VIII

[Enter ROBIN *the Ostler with a book in his hand.]*

ROBIN. O, this is admirable! here I ha' stolen one of Dr. Faustus'
conjuring books, and i' faith I mean to search some circles for my
own use. Now will I make all the maidens in our parish   [885
dance at my pleasure, stark naked before me; and so by that means
I shall see more than e'er I felt or saw yet.

[Enter RALPH *calling* ROBIN.]*

RALPH. Robin, prithee come away; there's a gentleman tarries to
have his horse, and he would have his things rubbed and made clean.
He keeps such a chafing with my mistress about it; and   [890
she has sent me to look thee out. Prithee come away.

ROBIN. Keep out, keep out, or else you are blown up; you are dis-
membered, Ralph, keep out, for I am about a roaring piece of work.

RALPH. Come, what dost thou with that same book? Thou canst
not read.   895

ROBIN. Yes, my master and mistress shall find that I can read, he
for his forehead, she for her private study; she's born to bear with
me, or else my art fails.

RALPH. Why, Robin, what book is that?

ROBIN. What book! Why, the most intolerable book for   [900
conjuring that e'er was invented by any brimstone devil.

RALPH. Canst thou conjure with it?

ROBIN. I can do all these things easily with it: first, I can make thee

drunk with ippocras at any tavern in Europe for nothing; that's one
of my conjuring works.   905

RALPH. Our Master Parson says that's nothing.

ROBIN. True, Ralph; and more, Ralph, if thou hast any mind to
Nan Spit, our kitchenmaid, then turn her and wind her to thy own
use as often as thou wilt, and at midnight.

RALPH. O brave Robin, shall I have Nan Spit, and to mine   [910
own use? On that condition I'll feed thy devil with horse-bread as
long as he lives, of free cost.

ROBIN. No more, sweet Ralph; let's go and make clean our boots,
which lie foul upon our hands, and then to our conjuring   [914
in the devil's name.   [Exeunt.

IX

[Enter ROBIN and RALPH with a silver goblet.]

ROBIN. Come, Ralph, did not I tell thee we were for ever made by
this Doctor Faustus' book? *Ecce signum,* here's a simple purchase
for horse-keepers; our horses shall eat no hay as long as this lasts.

[Enter the VINTNER.]

RALPH. But, Robin, here comes the vintner.

ROBIN. Hush! I'll gull him supernaturally. Drawer, I hope   [920
all is paid: God be with you.—Come, Ralph.

VINT. Soft, sir; a word with you. I must yet have a goblet paid
from you, ere you go.

ROBIN. I, a goblet, Ralph; I, a goblet! I scorn you, and you are but
a &c. I, a goblet! search me.   925

VINT. I mean so, sir, with your favour.

ROBIN. How say you now?

VINT. I must say somewhat to your fellow. You, sir!

RALPH. Me, sir! me, sir! search your fill. Now, sir, you may be
ashamed to burden honest men with a matter of truth.   930

VINT. Well, t' one of you hath this goblet about you.

ROBIN. You lie, drawer, 'tis afore me.—Sirrah you, I'll teach ye to
impeach honest men; stand by;—I'll scour you for a goblet!—stand
aside you had best, I charge you in the name of Belzebub. Look to
the goblet, Ralph.   935

VINT. What mean you, sirrah?

---

904. *ippocras:* spiced wine. 917. *Ecce . . . purchase:* behold the evidence,
here's a free bargain. 920. *gull him supernaturally:* trick him with magic;
Drawer: bartender. 930. *matter of truth:* question about their honesty.

ROBIN. I'll tell you what I mean. *Sanctobulorum, Periphrasticon—*
Nay, I'll tickle you, vintner. Look to the goblet, Ralph. *Polypragmos*
Belseborams framanto pacostiphos tostu, Mephistophilis, &c.

[*Enter* MEPHISTOPHILIS, *sets squibs at their backs,*
and then exits. They run about.]

VINT. *O nomine Domini!* what meanest thou, Robin?   [940
Thou hast no goblet.

RALPH. *Peccatum peccatorum!* Here's thy goblet, good vintner.

ROBIN. *Misericordia pro nobis!* What shall I do? Good devil, forgive me now, and I'll never rob thy library more.

[*Re-enter to them* MEPHISTOPHILIS.]

MEPH. Monarch of hell, under whose black survey   945
Great potentates do kneel with awful fear,
Upon whose altars thousand souls do lie,
How am I vexèd with these villains' charms?
From Constantinople am I hither come
Only for pleasure of these damnèd slaves.   950

ROBIN. How from Constantinople? You have had a great journey.
Will you take sixpence in your purse to pay for your supper, and
begone?

MEPH. Well, villains, for your presumption, I transform thee into
an ape, and thee into a dog; and so begone.   955

ROBIN. How, into an ape? That's brave! I'll have fine sport with
the boys. I'll get nuts and apples enow.

RALPH. And I must be a dog.

ROBIN. I' faith thy head will never be out of the pottage pot.
[*Exeunt.*

X

[*Enter* EMPEROR, FAUSTUS, *and a* KNIGHT *with attendants.*]

EMP. Master Doctor Faustus, I have heard strange report   [960
of thy knowledge in the black art, how that none in my empire
nor in the whole world can compare with thee for the rare effects of
magic; they say thou hast a familiar spirit, by whom thou canst
accomplish what thou list. This, therefore, is my request, that thou
let me see some proof of thy skill, that mine eyes may be   [965

937-39. Burlesque Latin. 939. Stage directions: *squibs:* firecrackers. 942.
Peccatum peccatorum: sin of sins. 943. *Misericordia pro nobis:* mercy on us.

witnesses to confirm what mine ears have heard reported; and here I
swear to thee by the honour of mine imperial crown, that, whatever
thou doest, thou shalt be no ways prejudiced or endamaged.

KNIGHT (*aside*). I' faith he looks much like a conjuror.

FAUST. My gracious Sovereign, though I must confess my-   [970
self far inferior to the report men have published, and nothing
answerable to the honour of your imperial Majesty, yet for that love
and duty binds me thereunto, I am content to do whatsoever your
Majesty shall command me.

EMP. Then, Doctor Faustus, mark what I shall say.   975
As I was sometime solitary set
Within my closet, sundry thoughts arose
About the honour of mine ancestors,
How they had won by prowess such exploits,
Got such riches, subdued so many kingdoms,   980
As we that do succeed, or they that shall
Hereafter possess our throne, shall
(I fear me) ne'er attain to that degree
Of high renown and great authority;
Amongst which kings is Alexander the Great,   985
Chief spectacle of the world's pre-eminence,
The bright shining of whose glorious acts
Lightens the world with his reflecting beams,
As, when I heard but motion made of him,
It grieves my soul I never saw the man.   990
If, therefore, thou by cunning of thine art
Canst raise this man from hollow vaults below,
Where lies entombed this famous conqueror,
And bring with him his beauteous paramour,
Both in their right shapes, gesture, and attire   995
They used to wear during their time of life,
Thou shalt both satisfy my just desire,
And give me cause to praise thee whilst I live.

FAUST. My gracious lord, I am ready to accomplish your request so
far forth as by art, and power of my spirit, I am able to   [1000
perform.

KNIGHT (*aside*). I' faith that's just nothing at all.

FAUST. But, if it like your Grace, it is not in my ability to present
before your eyes the true substantial bodies of those two deceased
princes, which long since are consumed to dust.   1005

KNIGHT (*aside*). Ay, marry, Master Doctor, now there's a sign
of grace in you, when you will confess the truth.

FAUST. But such spirits as can lively resemble Alexander and his paramour shall appear before your Grace in that manner that they best lived in, in their most flourishing estate; which I doubt   [1010 not shall sufficiently content your imperial Majesty.

EMP. Go to, Master Doctor, let me see them presently.

KNIGHT. Do you hear, Master Doctor? You bring Alexander and his paramour before the Emperor!

FAUST. How then, sir?   1015

KNIGHT. I' faith that's as true as Diana turned me to a stag!

FAUST. No, sir, but when Actaeon died, he left the horns for you. Mephistophilis, begone.   [*Exit* MEPHISTOPHILIS.

KNIGHT. Nay, an you go to conjuring, I'll begone.   [*Exit.*

FAUST. I'll meet with you anon for interrupting me so.   [1020 Here they are, my gracious lord.

[*Re-enter* MEPHISTOPHILIS *with* ALEXANDER *and his* PARAMOUR.]

EMP. Master Doctor, I heard this lady while she lived had a wart or mole in her neck: how shall I know whether it be so or no?

FAUST. Your Highness may boldly go and see.   [*Exeunt,* SPIRITS.

EMP. Sure these are no spirits, but the true substantial   [1025 bodies of those two deceased princes.

FAUST. Will 't please your Highness now to send for the knight that was so pleasant with me here of late?

EMP. One of you call him forth.   [*Exit* ATTENDANT.

[*Re-enter the* KNIGHT *with a pair of horns on his head.*]

How now, sir knight! why I had thought thou had'st been   [1030 a bachelor, but now I see thou hast a wife, that not only gives thee horns, but makes thee wear them. Feel on thy head.

KNIGHT. Thou damned wretch and execrable dog,
Bred in the concave of some monstrous rock,
How darest thou thus abuse a gentleman?   1035
Villain, I say, undo what thou hast done!

FAUST. O, not so fast, sir; there's no haste; but, good, are you re-membered how you crossed me in my conference with the Emperor? I think I have met with you for it.

EMP. Good Master Doctor, at my entreaty release him;   [1040 he hath done penance sufficient.

FAUST. My gracious lord, not so much for the injury he offered

---

1017. *Actaeon:* While hunting, he saw chaste Diana bathing, whereupon she changed him into a stag and he was torn to pieces by his own dogs. A husband was said to have *horns* when his wife was unfaithful.

me here in your presence, as to delight you with some mirth, hath
Faustus worthily requited this injurious knight; which, being all I
desire, I am content to release him of his horns; and, sir   [1045
knight, hereafter speak well of scholars. Mephistophilis, transform
him straight. Now, my good lord, having done my duty I humbly
take my leave.

EMP. Farewell, Master Doctor; yet, ere you go,   1049
Expect from me a bounteous reward.   [*Exeunt.*

XI

[*Enter* FAUSTUS *and* MEPHISTOPHILIS.]

FAUST. Now, Mephistophilis, the restless course
That time doth run with calm and silent foot,
Shortening my days and thread of vital life,
Calls for the payment of my latest years;
Therefore, sweet Mephistophilis, let us   1055
Make haste to Wittenberg.

MEPH. What, will you go on horseback or on foot?

FAUST. Nay, till I'm past this fair and pleasant green,
I'll walk on foot.

[*Enter a* HORSE-COURSER.]

HORSE-C. I have been all this day seeking one Master   [1060
Fustian: mass, see where he is! God save you, Master Doctor!

FAUST. What, horse-courser! You are well met.

HORSE-C. Do you hear, sir? I have brought you forty dollars for
your horse.   1064

FAUST. I cannot sell him so; if thou likest him for fifty, take him.

HORSE-C. Alas, sir, I have no more.—I pray you speak for me.

MEPH. I pray you let him have him; he is an honest fellow, and
he has a great charge, neither wife nor child.

FAUST. Well, come, give me your money. My boy will deliver him
to you. But I must tell you one thing before you have him;   [1070
ride him not into the water at any hand.

HORSE-C. Why, sir, will he not drink of all waters?

FAUST. O yes, he will drink of all waters, but ride him not into
the water; ride him over hedge or ditch, or where you wilt, but not
into the water.   1075

HORSE-C. Well, sir.—Now I am made man for ever. I'll not leave
my horse for forty. If he had but the quality of hey-ding-ding, hey-

---

1068. *charge:* burden. 1071. *at any hand:* in any case. 1077. *hey-ding-ding:*
could dance.

ding-ding, I'd make a brave living on him: he has a buttock as slick
as an eel. Well, God b' wi' ye, sir, your boy will deliver him me; but
hark ye, sir, if my horse be sick or ill at ease, if I bring   [1080
his water to you, you'll tell me what it is?

FAUST. Away, you villain; what, dost think I am a horse-doctor?
                                                    [*Exit* HORSE-COURSER.
What art thou, Faustus, but a man condemned to die?
Thy fatal time doth draw to final end;
Despair doth drive distrust unto my thoughts—   1085
Confound these passions with a quiet sleep:
Tush, Christ did call the thief upon the cross;
Then rest thee, Faustus, quiet in conceit. (*Sleeps in his chair.*)

             [*Re-enter* HORSE-COURSER, *all wet, crying.*]

HORSE-C. Alas, alas! Doctor Fustian, quotha? Mass, Doctor Lopus
was never such a doctor. Has given me a purgation has   [1090
purged me of forty dollars; I shall never see them more. But yet,
like an ass as I was, I would not be ruled by him, for he bade me I
should ride him into no water. Now I, thinking my horse had had
some rare quality that he would not have had me known of, I, like
a venturous youth, rid him into the deep pond at the   [1095
town's end. I was no sooner in the middle of the pond, but my
horse vanished away, and I sat upon a bottle of hay, never so near
drowning in my life. But I'll seek out my Doctor, and have my
forty dollars again, or I'll make it the dearest horse!—O, yonder is
his snipper-snapper.—Do you hear? You hey-pass, where's   [1100
your master?

MEPH. Why, sir, what would you? You cannot speak with him.

HORSE-C. But I will speak with him.

MEPH. Why, he's fast asleep. Come some other time.

HORSE-C. I'll speak with him now, or I'll break his glass   [1105
windows about his ears.

MEPH. I tell thee he has not slept this eight nights.

HORSE-C. An he have not slept this eight weeks, I'll speak with him.

MEPH. See where he is, fast asleep.

HORSE-C. Ay, this is he. God save you, Master Doctor!   [1110
Master Doctor, Master Doctor Fustian!—Forty dollars, forty dollars
for a bottle of hay!

MEPH. Why, thou seest he hears thee not.

HORSE-C. So ho, ho!—so ho, ho! (*Hollas in his ear.*) No, will you

---

1086. *Confound these passions:* overcome these worries. 1088. *conceit:* mind.
1097. *bottle:* bundle. 1100. *hey-pass:* magician's assistant.

not wake? I'll make you wake ere I go. (*Pulls* FAUSTUS *by* [1115
the leg, and pulls it away.) Alas, I am undone! What shall I do?

FAUST. O my leg, my leg! Help, Mephistophilis! call the officers.
My leg, my leg!

MEPH. Come, villain, to the constable.

HORSE-C. O lord, sir, let me go, and I'll give you forty [1120
dollars more.

MEPH. Where be they?

HORSE-C. I have none about me. Come to my ostry and I'll give
them you.

MEPH. Begone quickly. [HORSE-COURSER *runs away.*

FAUST. What, is he gone? Farewell he! Faustus has his [1126
leg again, and the horse-courser, I take it, a bottle of hay for his
labour. Well, this trick shall cost him forty dollars more.

[*Enter* WAGNER.]

How now, Wagner, what's the news with thee?

WAG. Sir, the Duke of Vanholt doth earnestly entreat your [1130
company.

FAUST. The Duke of Vanholt! an honourable gentleman, to whom
I must be no niggard of my cunning. Come, Mephistophilis, let's
away to him. [*Exeunt.*

XII

[*Enter the* DUKE, *the* DUCHESS, FAUSTUS, *and* MEPHISTOPHILIS.]

DUKE. Believe me, Master Doctor, this merriment hath [1135
much pleased me.

FAUST. My gracious lord, I am glad it contents you so well.—But
it may be, madam, you take no delight in this. I have heard that
great-bellied-women do long for some dainties or other. What is
it, madam? Tell me, and you shall have it. 1140

DUCHESS. Thanks, good Master Doctor; and for I see your courteous intent to pleasure me, I will not hide from you the thing my
heart desires; and were it now summer, as it is January and the
dead time of the winter, I would desire no better meat than a dish of
ripe grapes. 1145

FAUST. Alas, madam, that's nothing! Mephistophilis, begone.

[*Exit* MEPHISTOPHILIS.

Were it a greater thing than this, so it would content you, you should
have it.

1123. *ostry:* inn.

[*Re-enter* MEPHISTOPHILIS *with the grapes.*]

Here they be, madam; wilt please you taste on them?

DUKE. Believe me, Master Doctor, this makes me wonder   [1150
above the rest, that being in the dead time of winter, and in the
month of January, how you should come by these grapes.

FAUST. If it like your Grace, the year is divided into two circles
over the whole world, that, when it is here winter with us, in the
contrary circle it is summer with them, as in India, Saba,   [1155
and farther countries in the East; and by means of a swift spirit that
I have, I had them brought hither, as ye see.—How do you like them,
madam; be they good?

DUCHESS. Believe me, Master Doctor, they be the best grapes that
I e'er tasted in my life before.   1160

FAUST. I am glad they content you so, madam.

DUKE. Come, madam, let us in, where you must well reward this
learned man for the great kindness he hath showed to you.

DUCHESS. And so I will, my lord; and whilst I live, rest beholding
for this courtesy.   1165

FAUST. I humbly thank your Grace.

DUKE. Come, Master Doctor, follow us and receive your reward.
[*Exeunt.*

XIII

[*Enter* WAGNER, *solus.*]

WAG. I think my master means to die shortly,
For he hath given to me all his goods;
And yet, methinks, if that death were near,   1170
He would not banquet and carouse and swill
Amongst the students, as even now he doth,
Who are at supper with such belly-cheer
As Wagner ne'er beheld in all his life.
See where they come! Belike the feast is ended.   1175

[*Enter* FAUSTUS, *with two or three* SCHOLARS *and* MEPHISTOPHILIS]

1 SCHOL. Master Doctor Faustus, since our conference about fair
ladies, which was the beautifullest in all the world, we have determined with ourselves that Helen of Greece was the admirablest lady
that ever lived; therefore, Master Doctor, if you will do us that favour,
as to let us see that peerless dame of Greece, whom all   [1180
the world admires for majesty, we should think ourselves much beholding unto you.

FAUST. Gentlemen.
For that I know your friendship is unfeigned,

And Faustus' custom is not to deny   1185
The just requests of those that wish him well,
You shall behold that peerless dame of Greece,
No otherways for pomp and majesty
Than when Sir Paris crossed the seas with her,
And brought the spoils to rich Dardania.   1190
Be silent, then, for danger is in words.

　　　[*Music sounds, and* HELEN *passeth over the stage.*]

　　2 SCHOL. Too simple is my wit to tell her praise,
Whom all the world admires for majesty.
　　3 SCHOL. No marvel though the angry Greeks pursued
With ten years' war the rape of such a queen,   1195
Whose heavenly beauty passeth all compare.
　　1 SCHOL. Since we have seen the pride of nature's works,
And only paragon of excellence,

　　　　　　　　[*Enter an* OLD MAN.]

Let us depart; and for this glorious deed
Happy and blest be Faustus evermore.   1200
　　FAUSTUS. Gentlemen, farewell—the same I wish to you.
　　　　　　　　　　[*Exeunt* SCHOLARS *and* WAGNER.
　　OLD MAN. Ah, Doctor Faustus, that I might prevail
To guide thy steps unto the way of life,
By which sweet path thou may'st attain the goal
That shall conduct thee to celestial rest!   1205
Break heart, drop blood, and mingle it with tears,
Tears falling from repentant heaviness
Of thy most vile and loathsome filthiness,
The stench whereof corrupts the inward soul
With such flagitious crimes of heinous sins   1210
As no commiseration may expel,
But mercy, Faustus, of thy Saviour sweet,
Whose blood alone must wash away thy guilt.
　　FAUST. Where art thou, Faustus? Wretch, what hast thou done?
Damned art thou, Faustus, damned; despair and die!   1215
Hell calls for right, and with a roaring voice
Says "Faustus! come! thine hour is almost come!"
And Faustus now will come to do thee right.

　　　[MEPHISTOPHILIS *gives him a dagger.*]

　　OLD MAN. Ah stay, good Faustus, stay thy desperate steps!
I see an angel hovers o'er thy head,   1220

And, with a vial full of precious grace,
Offers to pour the same into thy soul.
Then call for mercy, and avoid despair.
    FAUST. Ah, my sweet friend, I feel
Thy words do comfort my distressèd soul.   1225
Leave me a while to ponder on my sins.
    OLD MAN. I go, sweet Faustus, but with heavy cheer,
Fearing the ruin of thy hopeless soul.   [*Exit.*
    FAUST. Accursèd Faustus, where is mercy now?
I do repent; and yet I do despair;   1230
Hell strives with grace for conquest in my breast.
What shall I do to shun the snares of death?
    MEPH. Thou traitor, Faustus, I arrest thy soul
For disobedience to my sovereign lord;
Revolt, or I'll in piecemeal tear thy flesh.   1235
    FAUST. Sweet Mephistophilis, entreat thy lord
To pardon my unjust presumption,
And with my blood again I will confirm
My former vow I made to Lucifer.
    MEPH. Do it now then quickly, with unfeigned heart,   1240
Lest danger do attend thy drift.
    FAUST. Torment, sweet friend, that base and crooked age,
That durst dissuade me from my Lucifer,
With greatest torments that our hell affords.
    MEPH. His faith is great, I cannot touch his soul;   1245
But what I may afflict his body with
I will attempt, which is but little worth.
    FAUST. One thing, good servant, let me crave of thee,
To glut the longing of my heart's desire,—
That I might have unto my paramour   1250
That heavenly Helen, which I saw of late,
Whose sweet embracings may extinguish clean
These thoughts that do dissuade me from my vow,
And keep mine oath I made to Lucifer.
    MEPH. Faustus, this or what else thou shalt desire   1255
Shall be performed in twinkling of an eye.

             [*Re-enter* HELEN.]

    FAUST. Was this the face that launched a thousand ships,
And burnt the topless towers of Ilium?
Sweet Helen, make me immortal with a kiss.

1235. *Revolt:* turn back from repentance. 1242. *age:* old man.

Her lips suck forth my soul; see where it flies!—   1260
Come, Helen, come, give me my soul again.
Here will I dwell, for heaven be in these lips,
And all is dross that is not Helena.

[*Enter* OLD MAN.]

I will be Paris, and for love of thee,
Instead of Troy, shall Wittenberg be sacked;   1265
And I will combat with weak Menelaus,
And wear thy colours on my plumèd crest;
Yea, I will wound Achilles in the heel,
And then return to Helen for a kiss.
Oh, thou art fairer than the evening air   1270
Clad in the beauty of a thousand stars;
Brighter art thou than flaming Jupiter
When he appeared to hapless Semele;
More lovely than the monarch of the sky
In wanton Arethusa's azured arms;   1275
And none but thou shalt be my paramour.   [*Exeunt.*
  OLD MAN. Accursèd Faustus, miserable man,
That from thy soul exclud'st the grace of heaven,
And fly'st the throne of his tribunal seat!

[*Enter* DEVILS.]

Satan begins to sift me with his pride;   1280
As in this furnace God shall try my faith,
My faith, vile hell, shall triumph over thee.
Ambitious fiends! see how the heavens smiles
At your repulse, and laughs your state to scorn!   1284
Hence, hell! for hence I fly unto my God.   [*Exeunt.*

XIV

[*Enter* FAUSTUS *with the* SCHOLARS.]

FAUST. Ah, gentlemen!
  I SCHOL. What ails Faustus?
FAUST. Ah, my sweet chamber-fellow, had I lived with thee, then
had I lived still! but now I die eternally. Look, comes he not, comes
he not?   1290

———

1273. *hapless:* unfortunate, because she was burned by the vision. 1280.
sift me: Luke xxii, 31: "Satan hath desired to have you, that he may sift you
as wheat"; *pride:* power.

2 SCHOL. What means Faustus?

3 SCHOL. Belike he is grown into some sickness by being over solitary.

1 SCHOL. If it be so, we'll have physicians to cure him. 'Tis but
a surfeit. Never fear, man.   1295

FAUST. A surfeit of deadly sin that hath damned both body and soul.

2 SCHOL. Yet, Faustus, look up to heaven; remember God's mercies
are infinite.

FAUST. But Faustus' offences can never be pardoned; the serpent
that tempted Eve may be saved but not Faustus. Ah, gentle-   [1300
men, hear me with patience, and tremble not at my speeches! Though
my heart pants and quivers to remember that I have been a student
here these thirty years, oh, would I had never seen Wittenberg, never
read book! And what wonders I have done, all Germany can witness,
yea, the world; for which Faustus hath lost both Germany   [1305
and the world, yea heaven itself, heaven, the seat of God, the throne
of the blessed, the kingdom of joy; and must remain in hell for ever,
hell, ah, hell, for ever! Sweet friends! what shall become of Faustus
being in hell for ever?

3 SCHOL. Yet, Faustus, call on God.   1310

FAUST. On God, whom Faustus hath abjured! on God, whom Faustus
hath blasphemed! Ah, my God, I would weep, but the devil draws in
my tears. Gush forth blood instead of tears! Yea, life and soul! Oh,
he stays my tongue! I would lift up my hands, but see, they hold
them, they hold them!   1315

ALL. Who, Faustus?

FAUST. Lucifer and Mephistophilis. Ah, gentlemen, I gave them
my soul for my cunning!

ALL. God forbid!

FAUST. God forbade it indeed; but Faustus hath done it.   [1320
For vain pleasure of twenty-four years hath Faustus lost eternal joy
and felicity. I writ them a bill with mine own blood: the date is
expired; the time will come, and he will fetch me.

1 SCHOL. Why did not Faustus tell us of this before, that divines
might have prayed for thee?   1325

FAUST. Oft have I thought to have done so; but the devil threatened
to tear me in pieces if I named God; to fetch both body and soul if I
once gave ear to divinity, and now 'tis too late. Gentlemen, away!
lest you perish with me.

2 SCHOL. Oh, what shall we do to save Faustus?   1330

FAUST. Talk not of me, but save yourselves, and depart.

3 SCHOL. God will strengthen me. I will stay with Faustus.

1 SCHOL. Tempt not God, sweet friend; but let us into the next
room, and there pray for him.

1295. *surfeit:* over-eating.

FAUST. Ay, pray for me, pray for me! and what noise so-   [1335
ever ye hear, come not unto me, for nothing can rescue me.

2 SCHOL. Pray thou, and we will pray that God may have mercy
upon thee.

FAUST. Gentlemen, farewell! If I live till morning I'll visit you: if
not—Faustus is gone to hell.   1340

ALL. Faustus, farewell!

[*Exeunt* SCHOLARS. *The clock strikes eleven.*

FAUST. Ah, Faustus,
Now hast thou but one bare hour to live,
And then thou must be damned perpetually!
Stand still, you ever-moving spheres of heaven,   1345
That time may cease, and midnight never come;
Fair nature's eye, rise, rise again and make
Perpetual day; or let this hour be but
A year, a month, a week, a natural day,
That Faustus may repent and save his soul!   1350
O lente, lente, currite noctis equi!
The stars move still, time runs, the clock will strike,
The devil will come, and Faustus must be damned.
O, I'll leap up to my God! Who pulls me down?
See, see where Christ's blood streams in the firmament!   1355
One drop would save my soul—half a drop: ah, my Christ!
Ah, rend not my heart for naming of my Christ!
Yet will I call on him: O spare me, Lucifer!—
Where is it now? 'Tis gone; and see where God
Stretcheth out his arm, and bends his ireful brows!   1360
Mountain and hills come, come and fall on me,
And hide me from the heavy wrath of God!
No! no!
Then will I headlong run into the earth;
Earth gape! O no, it will not harbour me!   1365
You stars that reigned at my nativity,
Whose influence hath allotted death and hell,
Now draw up Faustus like a foggy mist
Into the entrails of yon labouring clouds,
That when they vomit forth into the air,   1370
My limbs may issue from their smoky mouths,
So that my soul may but ascend to heaven.

[*The watch strikes.*]

Ah, half the hour is past! 'Twill all be past anon!
O God!

1351. *O . . . equi:* run slowly, slowly, horses of the night (from Ovid's
Amores, I, 13).

If thou wilt not have mercy on my soul,   1375
Yet for Christ's sake whose blood hath ransomed me,
Impose some end to my incessant pain;
Let Faustus live in hell a thousand years—
A hundred thousand, and at last be saved!
O, no end is limited to damned souls!   1380
Why wert thou not a creature wanting soul?
Or why is this immortal that thou hast?
Ah, Pythagoras' metempsychosis! were that true,
This soul should fly from me, and I be changed
Unto some brutish beast! All beasts are happy,   1385
For, when they die,
Their souls are soon dissolved in elements;
But mine must live, still to be plagued in hell.
Curst be the parents that engendred me!
No, Faustus; curse thyself; curse Lucifer   1390
That hath deprived thee of the joys of heaven.

[*The clock striketh twelve.*]

O, it strikes, it strikes! Now, body, turn to air,
Or Lucifer will bear thee quick to hell.

[*Thunder and lightning.*]

O soul, be changed into little water-drops,
And fall into the ocean—ne'er be found.   1395
My God! my God! look not so fierce on me!

[*Enter* DEVILS.]

Adders and serpents, let me breathe awhile!
Ugly hell, gape not! come not, Lucifer!
I'll burn my books!—Ah Mephistophilis!
                          [*Exeunt* DEVILS *with* FAUSTUS.

[*Enter* CHORUS]

    CHO. Cut is the branch that might have grown full straight,   1400
And burnèd is Apollo's laurel bough,
That sometimes grew within this learned man.
Faustus is gone; regard his hellish fall,
Whose fiendful fortune may exhort the wise
Only to wonder at unlawful things,   1405
Whose deepness doth entice such forward wits
To practise more than heavenly power permits.   [*Exit.*

1401. *Apollo's laurel bough:* symbol of knowledge.

King Lear

King Lear

DRAMATIS PERSONAE

LEAR, *King of Britain*
KING OF FRANCE
DUKE OF BURGUNDY
DUKE OF CORNWALL
DUKE OF ALBANY
EARL OF KENT
EARL OF GLOUCESTER
EDGAR, *son to Gloucester*
EDMUND, *bastard son to Gloucester*
CURAN, *a courtier*
OLD MAN, *tenant to Gloucester*
DOCTOR
FOOL

OSWALD, *steward to Goneril*
A CAPTAIN *employed by Edmund*
GENTLEMAN *attendant on Cordelia*
HERALD
SERVANTS *to Cornwall*
GONERIL
REGAN } *daughters to Lear*
CORDELIA
KNIGHTS *of Lear's train*, CAPTAINS, MESSENGERS, SOLDIERS, *and* ATTENDANTS
SCENE—*Britain.*

Act I

SCENE I. KING LEAR'S *palace.*

[*Enter* KENT, GLOUCESTER, *and* EDMUND.]

KENT. I thought the King had more affected the Duke of Albany than Cornwall.

GLO. It did always seem so to us. But now, in the division of the kingdom, it appears not which of the Dukes he values most, for

---

ACT I, SC. I: I. *affected:* favored.

equalities are so weighed that curiosity in neither can make   [5
choice of either's moiety.

KENT. Is not this your son, my lord?

GLO. His breeding, sir, hath been at my charge. I have so often
blushed to acknowledge him that now I am brazed to it.

KENT. I cannot conceive you.   10

GLO. Sir, this young fellow's mother could. Whereupon she grew
round-wombed, and had indeed, sir, a son for her cradle ere she had
a husband for her bed. Do you smell a fault?

KENT. I cannot wish the fault undone, the issue of it being so proper.

GLO. But I have, sir, a son by order of law, some year elder   [15
than this, who yet is no dearer in my account. Though this knave
came something saucily into the world before he was sent for, yet was
his mother fair, there was good sport at his making, and the whoreson
must be acknowledged. Do you know this noble gentleman, Edmund?

EDM. No, my lord.   20

GLO. My Lord of Kent. Remember him hereafter as my honorable
friend.

EDM. My services to your lordship.

KENT. I must love you, and sue to know you better.

EDM. Sir, I shall study deserving.   25

GLO. He hath been out nine years, and away he shall again. The
King is coming.

[*Sennet. Enter one bearing a coronet,* KING LEAR, CORNWALL, ALBANY,
GONERIL, REGAN, CORDELIA, *and* ATTENDANTS.]

LEAR. Attend the lords of France and Burgundy, Gloucester.

GLO. I shall, my liege.   [*Exeunt* GLOUCESTER *and* EDMUND.

LEAR. Meantime we shall express our darker purpose.   30
Give me the map there. Know that we have divided
In three our kingdom. And 'tis our fast intent
To shake all cares and business from our age,
Conferring them on younger strengths while we
Unburdened crawl toward death. Our son of Cornwall,   35
And you, our no less loving son of Albany,
We have this hour a constant will to publish
Our daughters' several dowers, that future strife

5-6. *equalities . . . moiety:* shares are so balanced that examination (*curiosity*) cannot choose between shares (*moiety*). 9. *brazed:* hardened. 14. *proper:*
handsome. 25. *study deserving:* try to deserve your acquaintance. 26. *out:*
abroad. Stage direction. *Sennet:* trumpet sounds; *coronet:* small crown.
35. *son: i.e.,* son-in-law. 37. *publish:* announce. 38. *several:* individual.

May be prevented now. The princes, France and Burgundy,
Great rivals in our youngest daughter's love,   40
Long in our court have made their amorous sojourn,
And here are to be answered. Tell me, my daughters,
Since now we will divest us both of rule,
Interest of territory, cares of state,
Which of you shall we say doth love us most?   45
That we our largest bounty may extend
Where nature doth with merit challenge. Goneril,
Our eldest-born, speak first.
    GON. Sir, I love you more than words can wield the matter,
Dearer than eyesight, space, and liberty,   50
Beyond what can be valued, rich or rare,
No less than life, with grace, health, beauty, honor,
As much as child e'er loved or father found;
A love that makes breath poor and speech unable;
Beyond all manner of so much I love you.   55
    COR. [*Aside*] What shall Cordelia do? Love, and be silent.
    LEAR. Of all these bounds, even from this line to this,
With shadowy forests and with champaigns riched,
With plenteous rivers and wide-skirted meads,
We make thee lady. To thine and Albany's issue   60
Be this perpetual. What says our second daughter,
Our dearest Regan, wife to Cornwall? Speak.
    REG. I am made of that self metal as my sister,
And prize me at her worth. In my true heart
I find she names my very deed of love,   65
Only she comes too short; that I profess
Myself an enemy to all other joys
Which the most precious square of sense possesses,
And find I am alone felicitate
In your dear Highness' love.
    COR.   [*Aside*] Then poor Cordelia!   70
And yet not so, since I am sure my love's
More ponderous than my tongue.
    LEAR. To thee and thine hereditary ever
Remain this ample third of our fair kingdom,
No less in space, validity and pleasure   75

---

39. *prevented:* forestalled. 47. *nature . . . challenge:* instinct and merit
claim reward. 50. *space:* freedom. 58. *champaigns riched:* enriched with
fertile fields. 63. *self:* same. 66. *that:* in that. 68. *precious square of sense:*
delicate sensibility. 69. *felicitate:* made happy. 75. *validity:* value.

Than that conferred on Goneril. Now, our joy,
Although the last, not least, to whose young love
The vines of France and milk of Burgundy
Strive to be interested, what can you say to draw
A third more opulent than your sisters? Speak.   80
    COR. Nothing, my lord.
    LEAR. Nothing!
    COR. Nothing.
    LEAR. Nothing will come of nothing. Speak again.
    COR. Unhappy that I am, I cannot heave   85
My heart into my mouth. I love your Majesty
According to my bond, no more nor less.
    LEAR. How, how, Cordelia! Mend your speech a little,
Lest it may mar your fortunes.
    COR.   Good my lord,
You have begot me, bred me, loved me. I   90
Return those duties back as are right fit,
Obey you, love you, and most honor you.
Why have my sisters husbands if they say
They love you all? Haply, when I shall wed,
That lord whose hand must take my plight shall carry   95
Half my love with him, half my care and duty.
Sure, I shall never marry like my sisters,
To love my father all.
    LEAR. But goes thy heart with this?
    COR.   Aye, good my lord.
    LEAR. So young, and so untender?   100
    COR. So young, my lord, and true.
    LEAR. Let it be so. Thy truth then be thy dower.
For, by the sacred radiance of the sun,
The mysteries of Hecate, and the night,
By all the operation of the orbs   105
From whom we do exist and cease to be,
Here I disclaim all my paternal care,
Propinquity, and property of blood,
And as a stranger to my heart and me
Hold thee from this forever. The barbarous Scythian,   110

---

79. *interested:* have a share in. 87. *bond: i.e.,* as a daughter should. 104. *mysteries of Hecate:* secret rites of the goddess of witchcraft and the underworld. 105. *operation of the orbs:* influence of the stars. 108. *Propinquity:* relationship; *property:* identity. 110. *Scythian:* believed since classical times to represent extreme savagery.

Or he that makes his generation messes
To gorge his appetite shall to my bosom
Be as well neighbored, pitied, and relieved
As thou my sometime daughter.
    KENT.   Good my liege——
    LEAR. Peace, Kent!   115
Come not between the dragon and his wrath.
I loved her most, and thought to set my rest
On her kind nursery. Hence, and avoid my sight!
So be my grave my peace, as here I give
Her father's heart from her! Call France. Who stirs?   120
Call Burgundy. Cornwall and Albany,
With my two daughters' dowers digest this third.
Let pride, which she calls plainness, marry her.
I do invest you jointly with my power,
Pre-eminence, and all the large effects   125
That troop with majesty. Ourself, by monthly course,
With reservation of a hundred knights
By you to be sustained, shall our abode
Make with you by due turns. Only we still retain
The name and all the additions to a king.   130
The sway, revenue, execution of the rest,
Belovèd sons, be yours, which to confirm,
This coronet part betwixt you.
    KENT.   Royal Lear,
Whom I have ever honored as my King,
Loved as my father, as my master followed,   135
As my great patron thought on in my prayers——
    LEAR. The bow is bent and drawn, make from the shaft.
    KENT. Let it fall rather, though the fork invade
The region of my heart. Be Kent unmannerly
When Lear is mad. What would'st thou do, old man?   140
Think'st thou that duty shall have dread to speak
When power to flattery bows? To plainness honor's bound
When majesty stoops to folly. Reverse thy doom,
And in thy best consideration check
This hideous rashness. Answer my life my judgment,   145

---

111. *generation messes:* children food. 116. *dragon:* British royal symbol
or crest; *wrath: i.e.,* object of his wrath. 117. *set my rest:* rely without
reservation, and find peace in. 118. *avoid:* leave. 123. *plainness:* honesty.
126. *course:* turn. 130. *additions:* ceremony. 137. *make:* stand away. 138.
fall: fly; *fork:* pronged head. 143. *doom:* judgment. 145. *Answer . . .
judgment:* I'll stake my life on my judgment.

Thy youngest daughter does not love thee least,
Nor are those empty-hearted whose low sound
Reverbs no hollowness.

LEAR.   Kent, on thy life, no more.

KENT. My life I never held but as a pawn
To wage against thy enemies, nor fear to lose it,   150
Thy safety being the motive.

LEAR.   Out of my sight!

KENT. See better, Lear, and let me still remain
The true blank of thine eye.

LEAR. Now, by Apollo——

KENT.   Now, by Apollo, King,
Thou swear'st thy gods in vain.

LEAR.   O vassal! Miscreant!   155
                          [*Laying his hand on his sword.*

ALB. & CORN. Dear sir, forbear.

KENT. Do.
Kill thy physician, and the fee bestow
Upon the foul disease. Revoke thy doom,
Or whilst I can vent clamor from my throat   160
I'll tell thee thou dost evil.

LEAR.   Hear me, recreant!
On thy allegiance, hear me!
Since thou hast sought to make us break our vow,
Which we durst never yet, and with strained pride
To come between our sentence and our power;   165
Which nor our nature nor our place can bear,
Our potency made good—take thy reward.
Five days we do allot thee, for provision
To shield thee from diseases of the world,
And on the sixth to turn thy hated back   170
Upon our kingdom. If on the tenth day following
Thy banished trunk be found in our dominions,
The moment is thy death. Away! By Jupiter,
This shall not be revoked.

    KENT. Fare thee well, King. Sith thus thou wilt appear,   175
Freedom lives hence, and banishment is here.
[*To* CORDELIA] The gods to their dear shelter take thee, maid,

---

148. *Reverbs:* reverberates with. 150. *wage:* wager. 153. *blank:* bullseye.
155. *Miscreant:* heathen. 161. *recreant:* traitor. 164. *strained:* extreme. 165.
power: execution; explained by *Our potency made good* (l. 167): our authority put into effect. 172. *trunk:* body. 175. *Sith:* since.

That justly think'st and hast most rightly said!
[*To* REGAN *and* GONERIL] And your large speeches may your deeds
　　approve,
That good effects may spring from words of love.　　　　　180
Thus Kent, O princes, bids you all adieu.
He'll shape his old course in a country new.　　　　　[*Exit.*

[*Flourish. Re-enter* GLOUCESTER, *with* FRANCE, BURGUNDY,
　　　　　and ATTENDANTS.]

GLO. Here's France and Burgundy, my loble lord.
　　LEAR. My lord of Burgundy,
We first address toward you, who with this King　　　　　185
Hath rivaled for our daughter. What, in the least,
Will you require in present dower with her,
Or cease your quest of love?
　　BUR.　　　　　Most royal Majesty,
I crave no more than what your Highness offered,
Nor will you tender less.
　　LEAR.　　　　　Right noble Burgundy,　　　　　190
When she was dear to us, we did hold her so,
But now her price is fall'n. Sir, there she stands.
If aught within that little seeming substance,
Or all of it, with our displeasure pieced
And nothing more, may fitly like your Grace,　　　　　195
She's there, and she is yours.
　　BUR.　　　　　I know no answer.
　　LEAR. Will you, with those infirmities she owes,
Unfriended, new-adopted to our hate,
Dowered with our curse and strangered with our oath,
Take her, or leave her?
　　BUR.　　　　　Pardon me, royal sir,　　　　　200
Election makes not up on such conditions.
　　LEAR. Then leave her, sir. For, by the power that made me,
I tell you all her wealth. [*To* FRANCE] For you, great King,
I would not from your love make such a stray,
To match you where I hate. Therefore beseech you　　　　　205
To avert your liking a more worthier way
Than on a wretch whom nature is ashamed
Almost to acknowledge hers.
　　FRANCE.　　　　　This is most strange,

179. *approve:* substantiate. 182. Stage direction. *Flourish:* trumpet fanfare.
194. *pieced:* added. 195. *like:* please. 197. *owes:* has. 201. *Election makes
not up:* One's choice is not affirmative. 206. *avert:* turn.

That she that even but now was your best object,
The argument of your praise, balm of your age,   210
Most best, most dearest, should in this trice of time
Commit a thing so monstrous, to dismantle
So many folds of favor. Sure, her offense
Must be of such unnatural degree
That monsters it, or your forevouched affection   215
Fall'n into taint. Which to believe of her
Must be a faith that reason without miracle
Could never plant in me.
    COR.   I yet beseech your Majesty—
If for I want that glib and oily art,
To speak and purpose not, since what I well intend   220
I'll do 't before I speak—that you make known
It is no vicious blot, murder, or foulness,
No unchaste action or dishonored step,
That hath deprived me of your grace and favor,
But even for want of that for which I am richer,   225
A still-soliciting eye, and such a tongue
As I am glad I have not, though not to have it
Hath lost me in your liking.
    LEAR.   Better thou
Hadst not been born than not to have pleased me better.
    FRANCE. Is it but this? A tardiness in nature   230
Which often leaves the history unspoke
That it intends to do? My Lord of Burgundy,
What say you to the lady? Love's not love
When it is mingled with regards that stand
Aloof from the entire point. Will you have her?   235
She is herself a dowry.
    BUR.   Royal Lear,
Give but that portion which yourself proposed,
And here I take Cordelia by the hand,
Duchess of Burgundy.
    LEAR. Nothing. I have sworn, I am firm.   240
    BUR. I am sorry then you have so lost a father
That you must lose a husband.
    COR.   Peace be with Burgundy!
Since that respects of fortune are his love,
I shall not be his wife.

---

210. *argument:* subject. 230. *tardiness in nature:* natural reticence. 235.
entire: main. 243. *respects of fortune:* concern about money.

FRANCE. Fairest Cordelia, that art most rich being poor, 245
Most choice forsaken, and most loved despised,
Thee and thy virtues here I seize upon;
Be it lawful I take up what's cast away.
Gods, gods! 'Tis strange that from their cold'st neglect
My love should kindle to inflamed respect. 250
Thy dowerless daughter, King, thrown to my chance,
Is queen of us, of ours, and our fair France.
Not all the dukes of waterish Burgundy
Can buy this unprized precious maid of me.
Bid them farewell, Cordelia, though unkind. 255
Thou losest here, a better where to find.
　　LEAR. Thou hast her, France. Let her be thine, for we
Have no such daughter, nor shall ever see
That face of hers again. Therefore be gone
Without our grace, our love, our benison. 260
Come, noble Burgundy. [*Flourish. Exeunt all but* FRANCE, GONERIL,
　　　　　　　　　　　　　　　　REGAN, *and* CORDELIA.

　　FRANCE. Bid farewell to your sisters.
　　COR. The jewels of our father, with washed eyes
Cordelia leaves you. I know you what you are,
And, like a sister, am most loath to call 265
Your faults as they are named. Use well our father.
To your professèd bosoms I commit him.
But yet, alas, stood I within his grace,
I would prefer him to a better place.
So farewell to you both. 270
　　REG. Prescribe not us our duties.
　　GON.　　　　　　　　　　　Let your study
Be to content your lord, who hath received you
At fortune's alms. You have obedience scanted,
And well are worth the want that you have wanted.
　　COR. Time shall unfold what plaited cunning hides. 275
Who cover faults, at last shame them derides.
Well may you prosper!
　　FRANCE.　　　　　　　Come, my fair Cordelia.
　　　　　　　　　　　　[*Exeunt* FRANCE *and* CORDELIA.

---

253. *waterish:* many-rivered, and also unmanly. 260. *benison:* blessing.
263. *washed:* wet, and clear. 267. *professèd:* insincere. 269. *prefer:* recommend. 273. *fortune's alms:* petty charity; *scanted:* neglected. 274. *well
. . . wanted:* are entitled to as little love as you have shown. 275. *plaited:*
deviously enfolded.

GON. Sister, it is not a little I have to say of what most nearly appertains to us both. I think our father will hence tonight.   [279

REG. That's most certain, and with you; next month with us.

GON. You see how full of changes his age is; the observation we have made of it hath not been little. He always loved our sister most, and with what poor judgment he hath now cast her off appears too grossly.

REG. 'Tis the infirmity of his age. Yet he hath ever but   [285 slenderly known himself.

GON. The best and soundest of his time hath been but rash. Then must we look to receive from his age not alone the imperfections of long-ingrafted condition, but therewithal the unruly waywardness that infirm and choleric years bring with them.   290

REG. Such unconstant starts are we like to have from him as this of Kent's banishment.

GON. There is further compliment of leave-taking between France and him. Pray you, let's hit together. If our father carry authority with such dispositions as he bears, this last surrender of   [295 his will but offend us.

REG. We shall further think on 't.

GON. We must do something, and i' the heat.   [*Exeunt.*

SCENE II. *The* EARL OF GLOUCESTER'S *castle.*

[*Enter* EDMUND, *with a letter.*]

EDM. Thou, Nature, art my goddess; to thy law
My services are bound. Wherefore should I
Stand in the plague of custom, and permit
The curiosity of nations to deprive me,
For that I am some twelve or fourteen moonshines   5
Lag of a brother? Why bastard? Wherefore base?
When my dimensions are as well compact,
My mind as generous and my shape as true,
As honest madam's issue? Why brand they us
With base? With baseness? Bastardy? Base, base?   10
Who in the lusty stealth of nature take
More composition and fierce quality
Than doth, within a dull, stale, tired bed,

---

291. *unconstant starts:* unpredictable outbursts. 293. *compliment:* ceremony. 294. *hit:* agree. 296. *but offend:* only harm.

sc. II: 3. *stand . . . custom:* be harmed by accepted conventions. 4. *curiosity:* over-fine legal distinctions. 7. *compact:* composed. 8. *generous:* noble.

Go to the creating a whole tribe of fops
Got 'tween asleep and wake? Well then,   15
Legitimate Edgar, I must have your land.
Our father's love is to the bastard Edmund
As to the legitimate—fine word, "legitimate"!
Well, my legitimate, if this letter speed
And my invention thrive, Edmund the base   20
Shall top the legitimate. I grow, I prosper.
Now, gods, stand up for bastards!

[*Enter* GLOUCESTER.]

GLO. Kent banished thus! And France in choler parted!
And the King gone tonight! Subscribed his power!
Confined to exhibition! All this done   25
Upon the gad! Edmund, how now! What news?
  EDM. So please your lordship, none.   [*Putting up the letter.*
  GLO. Why so earnestly seek you to put up that letter?
  EDM. I know no news, my lord.
  GLO. What paper were you reading?   30
  EDM. Nothing, my lord.
  GLO. No? What needed then that terrible dispatch of it into your
pocket? The quality of nothing hath not such need to hide itself.
Let's see. Come, if it be nothing, I shall not need spectacles.
  EDM. I beseech you, sir, pardon me. It is a letter from my   [35
brother that I have not all o'erread, and for so much as I have perused,
I find it not fit for your o'erlooking.
  GLO. Give me the letter, sir.
  EDM. I shall offend, either to detain or give it. The contents, as
in part I understand them, are to blame.   40
  GLO. Let's see, let's see.
  EDM. I hope, for my brother's justification, he wrote this but as an
essay or taste of my virtue.
  GLO. [*Reads.*] "This policy and reverence of age makes the world
bitter to the best of our times, keeps our fortunes from us   [45
till our oldness cannot relish them. I begin to find an idle and fond
bondage in the oppression of aged tyranny, who sways not as it
hath power, but as it is suffered. Come to me, that of this I may
speak more. If our father would sleep till I waked him, you should

---

15. *Got:* begotten. 20. *invention:* plot. 24. *Subscribed:* signed away. 25.
exhibition: living allowance. 26. *gad:* good, spur of the moment. 43. *essay:*
test. 44. *policy . . . age:* convention of revering age. 45. *best of our times:*
i.e., when we are young. 46. *fond:* foolish. 48. *suffered:* submitted to.

enjoy half his revenue forever, and live the beloved of your   [50
brother,   EDGAR."
Hum! Conspiracy!—"Sleep till I waked him, you should enjoy half
his revenue!"—My son Edgar! Had he a hand to write this? A heart
and brain to breed it in? When came this to you? Who brought it?

EDM. It was not brought me, my lord, there's the cunning   [55
of it. I found it thrown in at the casement of my closet.

GLO. You know the character to be your brother's?

EDM. If the matter were good, my lord, I durst swear it were his,
but in respect of that, I would fain think it were not.

GLO. It is his.   60

EDM. It is his hand, my lord, but I hope his heart is not in the
contents.

GLO. Hath he never heretofore sounded you in this business?

EDM. Never, my lord. But I have heard him oft maintain it to be
fit that, sons at perfect age and fathers declining, the father   [65
should be as ward to the son, and the son manage his revenue.

GLO. Oh, villain, villain! His very opinion in the letter! Abhorred
villain! Unnatural, detested, brutish villain! Worse than brutish!
Go, sirrah, seek him; I'll apprehend him. Abominable villain!
Where is he?   70

EDM. I do not well know, my lord. If it shall please you to suspend
your indignation against my brother till you can derive from him
better testimony of his intent, you should run a certain course.
Where, if you violently proceed against him, mistaking his purpose,
it would make a great gap in your own honor and shake in   [75
pieces the heart of his obedience. I dare pawn down my life for him
that he hath wrote this to feel my affection to your honor and to no
further pretense of danger.

GLO. Think you so?

EDM. If your honor judge it meet, I will place you where   [80
you shall hear us confer of this, and by an auricular assurance have
your satisfaction, and that without any further delay than this very
evening.

GLO. He cannot be such a monster—

EDM. Nor is not, sure.   85

GLO. —to his father, that so tenderly and entirely loves him.
Heaven and earth! Edmund, seek him out, wind me into him, I

---

56. *closet:* room. 57. *character:* handwriting. 69. *apprehend:* arrest. 77.
feel: test. 78. *pretense of danger:* dangerous purpose. 87. *wind me into him:*
worm your way into his confidence.

pray you. Frame the business after your own wisdom. I would
unstate myself, to be in a due resolution.

EDM. I will seek him, sir, presently, convey the business as   [90
I shall find means, and acquaint you withal.

GLO. These late eclipses in the sun and moon portend no good to
us. Though the wisdom of nature can reason it thus and thus, yet
nature finds itself scourged by the sequent effects. Love cools, friendship falls off, brothers divide. In cities, mutinies; in coun-   [95
tries, discord; in palaces, treason; and the bond cracked 'twixt son
and father. This villain of mine comes under the prediction, there's
son against father. The King falls from bias of nature, there's father
against child. We have seen the best of our time. Machinations, hollowness, treachery, and all ruinous disorders follow us dis-   [100
quietly to our graves. Find out this villain, Edmund, it shall lose thee
nothing. Do it carefully. And the noble and true-hearted Kent
banished! His offense, honesty! 'Tis strange.   [Exit.

EDM. This is the excellent foppery of the world, that when we are
sick in fortune—often the surfeit of our own behavior—we   [105
make guilty of our disasters the sun, the moon, and the stars, as if
we were villains by necessity, fools by heavenly compulsion; knaves,
thieves, and treachers by spherical predominance; drunkards, liars,
and adulterers by an enforced obedience of planetary influence; and
all that we are evil in, by a divine thrusting on—an admira-   [110
ble evasion of whoremaster man, to lay his goatish disposition to the
charge of a star! My father compounded with my mother under the
dragon's tail, and my nativity was under Ursa Major, so that it follows I am rough and lecherous. Fut, I should have been that I am
had the maidenliest star in the firmament twinkled on my   [115
bastardizing. Edgar—— [Enter EDGAR.] And pat he comes like the
catastrophe of the old comedy. My cue is villainous melancholy, with
a sigh like Tom o' Bedlam. Oh, these eclipses do portend these divisions! Fa, sol, la, mi.

EDG. How now, brother Edmund! What serious contem-   [120
plation are you in?

EDM. I am thinking, brother, of a prediction I read this other day,
what should follow these eclipses.

---

89. *unstate:* give up my rank and estate; *due resolution:* complete certainty.
90. *presently:* immediately; *convey:* manage. 93. *wisdom of nature:* science
of astronomy. 94. *sequent:* resulting. 98. *bias:* path. 104. *excellent foppery:*
remarkable folly. 108. *treachers:* traitors; *spherical predominance:* forced by
a planet. 111. *goatish:* lecherous. 113. *Ursa Major:* the Great Bear. 118.
Tom o' Bedlam: name given to inmates of Bethlehem (Bedlam) hospital
for the insane who were sent out to beg.

EDG. Do you busy yourself about that?

EDM. I promise you the effects he writes of succeed unhap-   [125
pily, as of unnaturalness between the child and the parent; death,
dearth, dissolutions of ancient amities; divisions in state, menaces and
maledictions against king and nobles; needless diffidences, banishment
of friends, dissipation of cohorts, nuptial breaches, and I know not
what.   130

EDG. How long have you been a sectary astronomical?

EDM. Come, come, when saw you my father last?

EDG. Why, the night gone by.

EDM. Spake you with him?

EDG. Aye, two hours together.   135

EDM. Parted you in good terms? Found you no displeasure in him
by word or countenance?

EDG. None at all.

EDM. Bethink yourself wherein you may have offended him. And
at my entreaty forbear his presence till some little time hath   [140
qualified the heat of his displeasure, which at this instant so rageth in
him that with the mischief of your person it would scarcely allay.

EDG. Some villain hath done me wrong.

EDM. That's my fear. I pray you have a continent forbearance till
the speed of his rage goes slower, and, as I say, retire with   [145
me to my lodging, from whence I will fitly bring you to hear my lord
speak. Pray ye, go, there's my key. If you do stir abroad, go armed.

EDG. Armed, brother!

EDM. Brother, I advise you to the best—go armed. I am no honest
man if there be any good meaning toward you. I have told   [150
you what I have seen and heard, but faintly, nothing like the image
and horror of it. Pray you, away.

EDG. Shall I hear from you anon?

EDM. I do serve you in this business.   [*Exit* EDGAR.
A credulous father, and a brother noble,   155
Whose nature is so far from doing harms
That he suspects none, on whose foolish honesty
My practices ride easy. I see the business.
Let me, if not by birth, have lands by wit.   159
All with me's meet that I can fashion fit.   [*Exit.*

---

125. *succeed:* follow. 128. *needless diffidences:* unfounded suspicions. 129.
dissipation: scattering. 131. *sectary astronomical:* believer in astrology.
141. *qualified:* lessened. 142. *mischief . . . allay:* hardly be satisfied even
with attacking you bodily. 144. *continent:* self-controlled. 160. *meet . . .
fit:* proper that I can opportunistically manipulate.

SCENE III. *The* DUKE OF ALBANY'S *palace.*

[*Enter* GONERIL *and* OSWALD, *her steward.*]

GON. Did my father strike my gentleman for chiding of his fool?
OSW. Yes, madam.
GON. By day and night he wrongs me. Every hour
He flashes into one gross crime or other
That sets us all at odds. I'll not endure it.   5
His knights grow riotous, and himself upbraids us
On every trifle. When he returns from hunting,
I will not speak with him. Say I am sick.
If you come slack of former services,
You shall do well; the fault of it I'll answer.   10
  OSW. He's coming, madam, I hear him.   [*Horns within.*
  GON. Put on what weary negligence you please,
You and your fellows; I'd have it come to question.
If he distaste it, let him to our sister,
Whose mind and mine, I know, in that are one,   15
Not to be overruled. Idle old man,
That still would manage those authorities
That he hath given away! Now, by my life,
Old fools are babes again, and must be used
With checks as flatteries when they are seen abused.   20
Remember what I tell you.
  OSW.   Very well, madam.
  GON. And let his knights have colder looks among you.
What grows of it, no matter; advise your fellows so.
I would breed from hence occasions, and I shall,
That I may speak. I'll write straight to my sister   25
To hold my very course. Prepare for dinner.   [*Exeunt.*

SCENE IV. *A hall in the same.*

[*Enter* KENT, *disguised.*]

KENT. If but as well I other accents borrow
That can my speech defuse, my good intent
May carry through itself to that full issue
For which I razed my likeness. Now, banished Kent,

SC. III: 9. *come . . . services:* serve less efficiently than before. 13. *question:* a showdown. 20. *as:* in face of; *seen abused:* seen to be misguided. 24. *occasions:* opportunities for action.
  SC. IV: 2. *defuse:* disguise. 4. *razed:* erased.

If thou canst serve where thou dost stand condemned,   5
So may it come, thy master whom thou lovest
Shall find thee full of labors.

[*Horns within. Enter* LEAR, KNIGHTS, *and* ATTENDANTS.]

LEAR. Let me not stay a jot for dinner. Go get it ready. [*Exit an*
ATTENDANT.] How now! What art thou?
KENT. A man, sir.   10
LEAR. What dost thou profess? What wouldst thou with us?
KENT. I do profess to be no less than I seem—to serve him truly that
will put me in trust, to love him that is honest, to converse with him
that is wise and says little, to fear judgment, to fight when I cannot
choose, and to eat no fish.   15
LEAR. What art thou?
KENT. A very honest-hearted fellow, and as poor as the King.
LEAR. If thou be as poor for a subject as he is for a king, thou art
poor enough. What wouldst thou?
KENT. Service.   20
LEAR. Who wouldst thou serve?
KENT. You.
LEAR. Dost thou know me, fellow?
KENT. No, sir, but you have that in your countenance which I
would fain call master.   25
LEAR. What's that?
KENT. Authority.
LEAR. What services canst thou do?
KENT. I can keep honest counsel, ride, run, mar a curious tale in
telling it, and deliver a plain message bluntly. That which   [30
ordinary men are fit for, I am qualified in, and the best of me is
diligence.
LEAR. How old art thou?
KENT. Not so young, sir, to love a woman for singing, nor so old to
dote on her for anything. I have years on my back forty-eight.   [35
LEAR. Follow me; thou shalt serve me. If I like thee no worse after
dinner, I will not part from thee yet. Dinner, ho, dinner! Where's
my knave? My fool? Go you, and call my fool hither. [*Exit an* AT-
TENDANT. *Enter* OSWALD.] You, you, sirrah, where's my daughter?
OSW. So please you——   40
[*Exit.*

---

5. *serve:* be a servant. 12. *profess:* do for a trade. 14. *judgment:* Day of
Judgment. 15. *eat no fish:* hence a Protestant and loyal. 29. *mar a curious
tale:* condense an affectedly wordy story.

LEAR. What says the fellow there? Call the clotpoll back. [*Exit a*
KNIGHT.] Where's my fool, ho? I think the world's asleep. [*Re-enter*
KNIGHT.] How now! Where's that mongrel?

KNIGHT. He says, my lord, your daughter is not well.   44

LEAR. Why came not the slave back to me when I called him?

KNIGHT. Sir, he answered me, in the roundest manner, he would not.

LEAR. He would not!

KNIGHT. My lord, I know not what the matter is, but, to my judgment, your Highness is not entertained with that ceremonious affection as you were wont. There's a great abatement of kindness   [50
appears as well in the general dependents as in the Duke himself also
and your daughter.

LEAR. Ha! Sayest thou so?

KNIGHT. I beseech you pardon me, my lord, if I be mistaken, for
my duty cannot be silent when I think your Highness wronged.

LEAR. Thou but rememberest me of mine own conception.   [56
I have perceived a most faint neglect of late, which I have rather
blamed as mine own jealous curiosity than as a very pretense and
purpose of unkindness. I will look further into 't. But where's my
fool? I have not seen him this two days.   60

KNIGHT. Since my young lady's going into France, sir, the fool hath
much pined away.

LEAR. No more of that, I have noted it well. Go you, and tell my
daughter I would speak with her. [*Exit an* ATTENDANT.] Go you,
call hither my fool. [*Exit an* ATTENDANT. *Re-enter* OSWALD.]   [65
Oh, you sir, you, come you hither, sir. Who am I, sir?

OSW. My lady's father.

LEAR. My lady's father! My lord's knave. You whoreson dog! You
slave! You cur!

OSW. I am none of these, my lord, I beseech your pardon.   70

LEAR. Do you bandy looks with me, you rascal?   [*Striking him.*

OSW. I'll not be struck, my lord.

KENT. Nor tripped neither, you base football player.

[*Tripping up his heels.*

LEAR. I thank thee, fellow. Thou servest me, and I'll love thee.

KENT. Come, sir, arise, away! I'll teach you differences.   [75
Away, away! If you will measure your lubber's length again, tarry.
But away! Go to, have you wisdom? So.   [*Pushes* OSWALD *out.*

---

41. *clotpoll:* blockhead. 46. *roundest:* flattest. 49. *entertained:* treated. 51.
dependents: servants. 58. *jealous curiosity:* undue sensitiveness; *very pretense:* actual intention. 75. *differences:* proper distinctions in rank.

LEAR. Now, my friendly knave, I thank thee. There's earnest of thy
service.   [*Giving* KENT *money.*

[*Enter* FOOL.]

FOOL. Let me hire him too. Here's my coxcomb.   80
                                        [*Offering* KENT *his cap.*
LEAR. How now, my pretty knave! How dost thou?
FOOL. Sirrah, you were best take my coxcomb.
KENT. Why, fool?
FOOL. Why, for taking one's part that's out of favor. Nay, an thou
canst not smile as the wind sits, thou'lt catch cold shortly.   [85
There, take my coxcomb. Why, this fellow hath banished two on's
daughters, and done the third a blessing against his will. If thou
follow him, thou must needs wear my coxcomb. How now, nuncle!
Would I had two coxcombs and two daughters!
LEAR. Why, my boy?   90
FOOL. If I gave them all my living, I'd keep my coxcombs myself.
There's mine; beg another of thy daughters.
LEAR. Take heed, sirrah, the whip.
FOOL. Truth's a dog must to kennel. He must be whipped out,
when Lady the brach may stand by the fire and stink.   95
LEAR. A pestilent gall to me!
FOOL. Sirrah, I'll teach thee a speech.
LEAR. Do.
FOOL. Mark it, nuncle:
                "Have more than thou showest,   100
                Speak less than thou knowest,
                Lend less than thou owest,
                Ride more than thou goest,
                Learn more than thou trowest,
                Set less than thou throwest.   105
                Leave thy drink and thy whore,
                And keep in-a-door,
                And thou shalt have more
                Than two tens to a score."
KENT. This is nothing, fool.   110
FOOL. Then 'tis like the breath of an unfee'd lawyer. You gave me
nothing for 't. Can you make no use of nothing, nuncle?
LEAR. Why, no, boy, nothing can be made out of nothing.

---

78. *earnest:* down payment. 88. *nuncle:* contraction of mine uncle. 95.
brach: bitch (flattery). 102. *owest:* own. 103. *goest:* walk. 104. *trowest:*
know. 105. *Set:* bet; *throwest:* win.

FOOL. [*To* KENT] Prithee tell him so much the rent of his land
comes to. He will not believe a fool.   115

LEAR. A bitter fool!

FOOL. Dost thou know the difference, my boy, between a bitter fool
and a sweet fool?

LEAR. No, lad, teach me.

FOOL.   "That lord that counseled thee   120
                          To give away thy land,
                       Come place him here by me,
                          Do thou for him stand.
                       The sweet and bitter fool
                          Will presently appear—   125
                       The one in motley here,
                          The other found out there."

LEAR. Dost thou call me fool, boy?

FOOL. All thy other titles thou hast given away. That thou wast
born with.   130

KENT. This is not altogether fool, my lord.

FOOL. No, faith, lords and great men will not let me. If I had a
monopoly out, they would have part on 't. And ladies too, they will
not let me have all the fool to myself; they'll be snatching. Give me
an egg, nuncle, and I'll give thee two crowns.   135

LEAR. What two crowns shall they be?

FOOL. Why, after I have cut the egg in the middle and eat up the
meat, the two crowns of the egg. When thou clovest thy crown i' the
middle and gavest away both parts, thou borest thine ass on thy back
o'er the dirt. Thou hadst little wit in thy bald crown when   [140
thou gavest thy golden one away. If I speak like myself in this, let
him be whipped that first finds it so. [*Singing*]
                  "Fools had ne'er less wit in a year,
                     For wise men are grown foppish,
                   And know not how their wits to wear,   145
                     Their manners are so apish."

LEAR. When were you wont to be so full of songs, sirrah?

FOOL. I have used it, nuncle, ever since thou madest thy daughters
thy mother. For when thou gavest them the rod and puttest down
thine own breeches, [*Singing*]   150
                  "Then they for sudden joy did weep,
                     And I for sorrow sung,
                   That such a king should play bopeep,
                     And go the fools among."

_____

133. *out:* granted me.

Prithee, nuncle, keep a schoolmaster that can teach thy fool to   [155
lie. I would fain learn to lie.

LEAR. An you lie, sirrah, we'll have you whipped.

FOOL. I marvel what kin thou and thy daughters are. They'll have
me whipped for speaking true, thou'lt have me whipped for lying,
and sometimes I am whipped for holding my peace. I had   [160
rather be any kind o' thing than a fool. And yet I would not be thee,
nuncle. Thou hast pared thy wit o' both sides and left nothing i' the
middle. Here comes one o' the parings.

[Enter GONERIL.]

LEAR. How now, daughter! What makes that frontlet on? Methinks you are too much of late i' the frown.   165

FOOL. Thou wast a pretty fellow when thou hadst no need to care
for her frowning. Now thou art an O without a figure. I am better
than thou art now. I am a fool, thou art nothing. [*To* GONERIL] Yes,
forsooth, I will hold my tongue; so your face bids me, though you
say nothing.   170

      "Mum, mum.
      He that keeps nor crust nor crumb,
      Weary of all, shall want some."

[*Pointing to* LEAR] That's a shealed peascod.

GON. Not only, sir, this your all-licensed fool,   175
But other of your insolent retinue
Do hourly carp and quarrel, breaking forth
In rank and not-to-be-endurèd riots. Sir,
I had thought, by making this well known unto you,
To have found a safe redress, but now grow fearful   180
By what yourself too late have spoke and done
That you protect this course and put it on
By your allowance. Which if you should, the fault
Would not 'scape censure, nor the redresses sleep,
Which, in the tender of a wholesome weal,   185
Might in their working do you that offense
Which else were shame, that then necessity
Will call discreet proceeding.

FOOL. For, you know, nuncle,
"The hedge sparrow fed the cuckoo so long   190

---

164. *frontlet:* frown. 174. *shealed peascod:* shelled peapod. 175. *all-licensed:*
allowed to take all liberties. 177. *carp:* complain. 182. *put it on:* inspire it.
187. *that then necessity:* but which force of circumstances.

That it had it head bit off by it young."
So out went the candle, and we were left darkling.
　　LEAR. Are you our daughter?
　　GON. Come, sir.
I would you would make use of that good wisdom　　　　195
Whereof I know you are fraught, and put away
These dispositions that of late transform you
From what you rightly are.
　　FOOL. May not an ass know when the cart draws the horse? Whoop,
Jug! I love thee.　　　　200
　　LEAR. Doth any here know me? This is not Lear.
Doth Lear walk thus? Speak thus? Where are his eyes?
Either his notion weakens, his discernings
Are lethargied—— Ha! Waking? 'Tis not so.
Who is it that can tell me who I am?　　　　205
　　FOOL. Lear's shadow.
　　LEAR. I would learn that; for, by the marks of sovereignty, knowl-
edge, and reason, I should be false persuaded I had daughters.
　　FOOL. Which they will make an obedient father.
　　LEAR. Your name, fair gentlewoman?　　　　210
　　GON. This admiration, sir, is much o' the savor
Of other your new pranks. I do beseech you
To understand my purposes aright.
As you are old and reverend, you should be wise.
Here do you keep a hundred knights and squires,　　　　215
Men so disordered, so deboshed and bold,
That this our court, infected with their manners,
Shows like a riotous inn. Epicurism and lust
Make it more like a tavern or a brothel
Than a graced palace. The same itself doth speak　　　　220
For instant remedy. Be then desired
By her, that else will take the thing she begs,
A little to disquantity your train,
And the remainder that shall still depend,
To be such men as may besort your age,　　　　225
Which know themselves and you.
　　LEAR.　　　　　　　　　Darkness and devils!
Saddle my horses, call my train together.

_____

196. _fraught:_ stored. 203. _notion:_ understanding. 209. _which:_ whom. 211.
admiration: pretended puzzlement. 216. _deboshed:_ debauched. 220. _graced:_
honorable. 223. _train:_ attendants. 224. _depend:_ serve. 225. _besort:_ befit.

Degenerate bastard! I'll not trouble thee.
Yet have I left a daughter.

   GON. You strike my people, and your disordered rabble   230
Make servants of their betters.

[*Enter* ALBANY.]

   LEAR. Woe, that too late repents.—[*To* ALBANY] Oh, sir, are you
     come?
Is it your will? Speak, sir. Prepare my horses.
Ingratitude, thou marble-hearted fiend,
More hideous when thou show'st thee in a child   235
Than the sea monster!
   ALB.   Pray, sir, be patient.
   LEAR. [*To* GONERIL] Detested kite! Thou liest.
My train are men of choice and rarest parts,
That all particulars of duty know,
And in the most exact regard support   240
The worships of their name. O most small fault,
How ugly didst thou in Cordelia show!
That, like an engine, wrenched my frame of nature
From the fixed place, drew from my heart all love
And added to the gall. O Lear, Lear, Lear!   245
Beat at this gate, that let thy folly in   [*Striking his head*
And thy dear judgment out! Go, go, my people.
   ALB. My lord, I am guiltless, as I am ignorant
Of what hath moved you.
   LEAR.   It may be so, my lord.
Hear, Nature, hear; dear goddess, hear!   250
Suspend thy purpose if thou didst intend
To make this creature fruitful.
Into her womb convey sterility.
Dry up in her the organs of increase,
And from her derogate body never spring   255
A babe to honor her! If she must teem,
Create her child of spleen, that it may live
And be a thwart disnatured torment to her.
Let it stamp wrinkles in her brow of youth,
With cadent tears fret channels in her cheeks,   260
Turn all her mother's pains and benefits

---

237. *kite:* bird of prey. 238. *parts:* abilities. 240-1. *support . . . name:* earn
respect. 255. *derogate:* blighted. 256. *teem:* be fruitful. 258. *thwart disnatured:* obstinate and unnatural. 260. *cadent:* falling.

To laughter and contempt, that she may feel
How sharper than a serpent's tooth it is
To have a thankless child! Away, away!   [*Exit.*
   ALB. Now, gods that we adore, whereof comes this?   265
   GON. Never afflict yourself to know the cause,
But let his disposition have that scope
That dotage gives it.

[Re-enter LEAR.]

   LEAR. What, fifty of my followers at a clap!
Within a fortnight!
   ALB.   What's the matter, sir?   270
   LEAR. I'll tell thee. [*To* GONERIL] Life and death! I am ashamed
That thou hast power to shake my manhood thus,
That these hot tears, which break from me perforce,
Should make thee worth them. Blasts and fogs upon thee!
The untented woundings of a father's curse   275
Pierce every sense about thee! Old fond eyes,
Beweep this cause again, I'll pluck ye out
And cast you with the waters that you lose
To temper clay. Yea, is it come to this?
Let it be so. Yet have I left a daughter   280
Who I am sure is kind and comfortable.
When she shall hear this of thee, with her nails
She'll flay thy wolvish visage. Thou shalt find
That I'll resume the shape which thou dost think
I have cast off forever. Thou shalt, I warrant thee.   285
[Exeunt LEAR, KENT, and ATTENDANTS.
   GON. Do you mark that, my lord?
   ALB. I cannot be so partial, Goneril,
To the great love I bear you——
   GON. Pray you, content. What, Oswald, ho!   289
[*To the* FOOL] You, sir, more knave than fool, after your master.
   FOOL. Nuncle Lear, nuncle Lear, tarry, take the fool with thee.
"A fox, when one has caught her,
And such a daughter,
Should sure to the slaughter,
If my cap would buy a halter.   295
So the fool follows after."   [*Exit.*
   GON. This man hath had good counsel. A hundred knights!
'Tis politic and safe to let him keep

---

275. *untented:* not swabbed; hence raw. 276. *fond:* foolish.

At point a hundred knights. Yes, that on every dream,
Each buzz, each fancy, each complaint, dislike,   300
He may enguard his dotage with their powers
And hold our lives in mercy. Oswald, I say!
   ALB. Well, you may fear too far.
   GON.   Safer than trust too far.
Let me still take away the harms I fear,
Not fear still to be taken. I know his heart.   305
What he hath uttered I have writ my sister.
If she sustain him and his hundred knights
When I have showed the unfitness——
                [*Re-enter* OSWALD.] How now, Oswald!
What, have you writ that letter to my sister?
   OSW. Yes, madam.   310
   GON. Take you some company, and away to horse.
Inform her full of my particular fear,
And thereto add such reasons of your own
As may compact it more. Get you gone,
And hasten your return. [*Exit* OSWALD.] No, no, my lord,   315
This milky gentleness and course of yours
Though I condemn not, yet, under pardon,
You are much more attasked for want of wisdom
Than praised for harmful mildness.
   ALB. How far your eyes may pierce I cannot tell.   320
Striving to better, oft we mar what's well.
   GON. Nay, then——
   ALB. Well, well, the event.   [*Exeunt.*

SCENE V. *Court before the same.*

[*Enter* LEAR, KENT, *and* FOOL.]

   LEAR. Go you before to Gloucester with these letters. Acquaint my
daughter no further with anything you know than comes from her
demand out of the letter. If your diligence be not speedy, I shall be
there afore you.
   KENT. I will not sleep, my lord, till I have delivered your   [5
letter.   [*Exit.*
   FOOL. If a man's brains were in 's heels, were 't not in danger of
kibes?

---

299. *At point:* fully equipped. 314. *compact:* strengthen and tighten. 318.
attasked: blamed. 323. *event:* outcome (will decide).
   sc. v: 8. *kibes:* chilblains.

LEAR. Aye, boy.

FOOL. Then I prithee be merry. Thy wit shall ne'er go slipshod. 10

LEAR. Ha, ha, ha!

FOOL. Shalt see thy other daughter will use thee kindly, for though she's as like this as a crab's like an apple, yet I can tell what I can tell.

LEAR. Why, what canst thou tell, my boy?

FOOL. She will taste as like this as a crab does to a crab. [15 Thou canst tell why one's nose stands i' the middle on 's face?

LEAR. No.

FOOL. Why, to keep one's eyes of either side 's nose, that what a man cannot smell out he may spy into.

LEAR. I did her wrong—— 20

FOOL. Canst tell how an oyster makes his shell?

LEAR. No.

FOOL. Nor I neither, but I can tell why a snail has a house.

LEAR. Why?

FOOL. Why, to put 's head in; not to give it away to his [25 daughters and leave his horns without a case.

LEAR. I will forget my nature.—So kind a father!—Be my horses ready?

FOOL. Thy asses are gone about 'em. The reason why the seven stars are no more than seven is a pretty reason. 30

LEAR. Because they are not eight?

FOOL. Yes, indeed. Thou wouldst make a good fool.

LEAR. To take 't again perforce! Monster ingratitude!

FOOL. If thou wert my fool, nuncle, I'd have thee beaten for being old before thy time. 35

LEAR. How's that?

FOOL. Thou shouldst not have been old till thou hadst been wise.

LEAR. Oh, let me not be mad, not mad, sweet heaven! Keep me in temper. I would not be mad!

[*Enter* GENTLEMAN.] How now! Are the horses ready? 40

GENT. Ready, my lord.

LEAR. Come, boy.

FOOL. She that's a maid now and laughs at my departure Shall not be a maid long, unless things be cut shorter.   [*Exeunt.*

---

10. *slipshod:* in slippers (worn when one has chilblains). 12. *kindly:* according to her nature. 13. *crab's:* crab-apple. 33. *To . . . perforce:* to recover it (my kingdom) by force. 39. *in temper:* within bounds of my normal temperament; sane.

Act II

SCENE I. *The* EARL OF GLOUCESTER's *castle.*

[*Enter* EDMUND *and* CURAN, *meeting.*]

EDM. Save thee, Curan.

CUR. And you, sir. I have been with your father, and given him notice that the Duke of Cornwall and Regan his duchess will be here with him this night.

EDM. How comes that?   5

CUR. Nay, I know not. You have heard of the news abroad—I mean the whispered ones, for they are yet but ear-kissing arguments?

EDM. Not I. Pray you what are they?

CUR. Have you heard of no likely wars toward 'twixt the dukes of Cornwall and Albany?   10

EDM. Not a word.

CUR. You may do, then, in time. Fare you well, sir.   [*Exit.*

EDM. The Duke be here tonight? The better! Best!
This weaves itself perforce into my business.
My father hath set guard to take my brother,   15
And I have one thing, of a queasy question,
Which I must act. Briefness and fortune, work!
Brother, a word, descend. Brother, I say!
[*Enter* EDGAR.] My father watches. O sir, fly this place.
Intelligence is given where you are hid.   20
You have now the good advantage of the night.
Have you not spoken 'gainst the Duke of Cornwall?
He's coming hither, now, i' the night, i' the haste,
And Regan with him. Have you nothing said
Upon his party 'gainst the Duke of Albany?   25
Advise yourself.

EDG.   I am sure on 't, not a word.

EDM. I hear my father coming. Pardon me;
In cunning I must draw my sword upon you.
Draw. Seem to defend yourself. Now quit you well.
Yield. Come before my father. Light, ho, here!   30

ACT II, SC. I: 16. *queasy question:* delicate nature. 18. *descend:* from his hiding place (in the balcony). 20. *intelligence:* information. 25. *party:* behalf. 28. *cunning:* pretense. 29. *quit:* acquit.

Fly, brother. Torches, torches! So farewell.   [*Exit* EDGAR.
Some blood drawn on me would beget opinion   [*Wounds his arm.*
Of my more fierce endeavor. I have seen drunkards
Do more than this in sport. Father, father!
Stop, stop! No help?   35

      [*Enter* GLOUCESTER *and* SERVANTS *with torches.*]

GLO. Now, Edmund, where's the villain?
EDM. Here stood he in the dark, his sharp sword out,
Mumbling of wicked charms, conjuring the moon
To stand 's auspicious mistress.
  GLO.   But where is he?
EDM. Look, sir, I bleed.
  GLO.   Where is the villain, Edmund?   40
EDM. Fled this way, sir. When by no means he could——
GLO. Pursue him, ho!—Go after.   [*Exeunt some* SERVANTS.
                    "By no means" what?
EDM. Persuade me to the murder of your lordship,
But that I told him the revenging gods
'Gainst parricides did all their thunders bend,   45
Spoke with how manifold and strong a bond
The child was bound to the father. Sir, in fine,
Seeing how loathly opposite I stood
To his unnatural purpose, in fell motion
With his preparèd sword he charges home   50
My unprovided body, lanced mine arm.
But when he saw my best alarumed spirits
Bold in the quarrel's right, roused to the encounter,
Or whether gasted by the noise I made,
Full suddenly he fled.
  GLO.   Let him fly far.   55
Not in this land shall he remain uncaught;
And found—dispatch. The noble Duke my master,
My worthy arch and patron, comes tonight.
By his authority I will proclaim it,
That he which finds him shall deserve our thanks,   60
Bringing the murderous caitiff to the stake.
He that conceals him, death.

---

32. *beget opinion:* give the impression. 44. *that:* when. 47. *fine:* short.
49. *fell:* deadly. 50. *preparèd:* drawn. 51. *unprovided:* unprotected. 54.
gasted: frightened. 57. *dispatch:* kill him. 58. *arch:* chief. 61. *caitiff:* rascal.

EDM. When I dissuaded him from his intent
And found him pight to do it, with curst speech
I threatened to discover him. He replied,   65
"Thou unpossessing bastard! Dost thou think,
If I would stand against thee, could the reposal
Of any trust, virtue, or worth in thee
Make thy words faithed? No. What I should deny—
As this I would, aye, though thou didst produce   70
My very character—I'd turn it all
To thy suggestion, plot, and damnèd practice.
And thou must make a dullard of the world
If they not thought the profits of my death
Were very pregnant and potential spurs   75
To make thee seek it."
    GLO.   Strong and fastened villain!
Would he deny his letter? I never got him.   [*Tucket within*
Hark, the Duke's trumpets! I know not why he comes.
All ports I'll bar; the villain shall not 'scape,
The Duke must grant me that. Besides, his picture   80
I will send far and near, that all the kingdom
May have due note of him; and of my land,
Loyal and natural boy, I'll work the means
To make thee capable.

[*Enter* CORNWALL, REGAN, *and* ATTENDANTS.]

    CORN. How now, my noble friend! Since I came hither,   85
Which I can call but now, I have heard strange news.
    REG. If it be true, all vengeance comes too short
Which can pursue the offender. How dost, my lord?
    GLO. Oh, madam, my old heart is cracked, is cracked!
    REG. What, did my father's godson seek your life?   90
He whom my father named? Your Edgar?
    GLO. Oh, lady, lady, shame would have it hid!
    REG. Was he not companion with the riotous knights
That tend upon my father?
    GLO. I know not, madam. 'Tis too bad, too bad.   95
    EDM. Yes, madam, he was of that consort.

---

64. *pight:* determined; *curst:* violent. 66. *unpossessing:* without rights of
inheritance. 71. *character:* handwriting; *turn it:* make it appear to be. 72.
practice: scheming. 75. *pregnant and potential spurs:* full and strong in-
centives. 76. *fastened:* confirmed. 77. *got:* begot; Stage direction. *tucket:*
trumpet notes. 83. *natural:* proper and normal. 84. *capable: i.e.,* of in-
heriting.

REG. No marvel then, though he were ill affected.
'Tis they have put him on the old man's death,
To have the waste and spoil of his revènues.
I have this present evening from my sister　　　100
Been well informed of them, and with such cautions
That if they come to sojourn at my house,
I'll not be there.
　　CORN.　　　　　Nor I, assure thee, Regan.
Edmund, I hear that you have shown your father
A childlike office.
　　EDM.　　　　　'Twas my duty, sir.　　　105
　　GLO. He did bewray his practice, and received
This hurt you see, striving to apprehend him.
　　CORN. Is he pursued?
　　GLO.　　　　　Aye, my good lord.
　　CORN. If he be taken, he shall never more
Be feared of doing harm. Make your own purpose,　　110
How in my strength you please. For you, Edmund,
Whose virtue and obedience doth this instant
So much commend itself, you shall be ours.
Natures of such deep trust we shall much need.
You we first seize on.
　　EDM.　　　　　I shall serve you, sir,　　115
Truly, however else.
　　GLO.　　　　　For him I thank your Grace.
　　CORN. You know not why we came to visit you——
　　REG. Thus out of season, threading dark-eyed night.
Occasions, noble Gloucester, of some poise,
Wherein we must have use of your advice.　　120
Our father he hath writ, so hath our sister,
Of differences, which I least thought it fit
To answer from our home. The several messengers
From hence attend dispatch. Our good old friend,
Lay comforts to your bosom, and bestow　　125
Your needful counsel to our business,
Which craves the instant use.
　　GLO.　　　　　I serve you, madam.
Your Graces are right welcome.　　　[*Flourish. Exeunt.*

---

97. *though . . . affected:* if he was hostile. 105. *childlike office:* true son's
service. 106. *bewray his practice:* disclose his plot. 110-11. *Make . . . please:*
use my authority to do as you wish. 119. *poise:* weight. 123. *from:* when
away from. 124. *attend dispatch:* wait to be sent.

SCENE II. *Before* GLOUCESTER'S *castle.*

[*Enter* KENT *and* OSWALD, *severally.*]

OSW. Good dawning to thee, friend. Art of this house?
KENT. Aye.
OSW. Where may we set our horses?
KENT. I' the mire.
OSW. Prithee, if thou lovest me, tell me.   5
KENT. I love thee not.
OSW. Why, then I care not for thee.
KENT. If I had thee in Lipsbury pinfold, I would make thee care
for me.
OSW. Why dost thou use me thus? I know thee not.   10
KENT. Fellow, I know thee.
OSW. What dost thou know me for?
KENT. A knave, a rascal, an eater of broken meats; a base, proud,
shallow, beggarly, three-suited, hundred-pound, filthy, worsted-
stocking knave; a lily-livered, action-taking knave; a whore-   [15
son, glass-gazing, superserviceable, finical rogue; one-trunk-inherit-
ing slave; one that wouldst be a bawd in way of good service, and
art nothing but the composition of a knave, beggar, coward, pander,
and the son and heir of a mongrel bitch—one whom I will beat into
clamorous whining if thou deniest the least syllable of thy   [20
addition.
OSW. Why, what a monstrous fellow art thou, thus to rail on one
that is neither known of thee nor knows thee!
KENT. What a brazen-faced varlet art thou, to deny thou knowest
me! Is it two days ago since I tripped up thy heels and beat   [25
thee before the King? Draw, you rogue. For though it be night,
yet the moon shines. I'll make a sop o' the moonshine of you. Draw,
you whoreson cullionly barber-monger, draw. [*Drawing his sword.*
OSW. Away! I have nothing to do with thee.
KENT. Draw, you rascal. You come with letters against the   [30
King, and take vanity the puppet's part against the royalty of her
father. Draw, you rogue, or I'll so carbonado your shanks. Draw,
you rascal, come your ways.

SC. II: 8. *Lipsbury pinfold:* pound for stray animals. 15. *action-taking:*
one who takes legal action rather than contending openly. 16. *superserviceable:* obsequious and dishonorable. 27. *sop . . . you:* a sponge out of you
that will soak up moonshine. 28. *cullionly barber-monger:* low beauty-
parlor habitué. 31. *vanity . . . part:* the side of Lady Vanity (an evil pup-
pet-show character). 32. *carbonado:* cross-cut, as for broiling.

osw. Help, ho! Murder! Help!

KENT. Strike, you slave. Stand, rogue, stand, you neat slave,   [35
strike.   [*Beating him.*

osw. Help, ho! Murder! Murder!

> [*Enter* EDMUND, *with his rapier drawn,* CORNWALL,
> REGAN, GLOUCESTER, *and* SERVANTS.]

EDM. How now! What's the matter?   [*Parting them.*

KENT. With you, goodman boy, an you please.
Come, I'll flesh you, come on, young master.   40

GLO. Weapons! Arms! What's the matter here?

CORN. Keep peace, upon your lives.
He dies that strikes again. What is the matter?

REG. The messengers from our sister and the King.

CORN. What is your difference? Speak.   45

osw. I am scarce in breath, my lord.

KENT. No marvel, you have so bestirred your valor. You cowardly
rascal; nature disclaims in thee. A tailor made thee.

CORN. Thou art a strange fellow—a tailor make a man?

KENT. Aye, a tailor, sir. A stonecutter or a painter could   [50
not have made him so ill, though he had been but two hours at
the trade.

CORN. Speak yet, how grew your quarrel?

osw. This ancient ruffian, sir, whose life I have spared at suit of
his gray beard——   55

KENT. Thou whoreson zed! Thou unnecessary letter! My lord, if
you will give me leave, I will tread this unbolted villain into mortar,
and daub the walls of a jakes with him. Spare my gray beard, you
wagtail?

CORN. Peace, sirrah!   60
You beastly knave, know you no reverence?

KENT. Yes, sir, but anger hath a privilege.

CORN. Why art thou angry?

KENT. That such a slave as this should wear a sword,
Who wears no honesty. Such smiling rogues as these,   65
Like rats, oft bite the holy cords a-twain
Which are too intrinse to unloose; smooth every passion

---

35. *neat:* dandyish. 48. *nature disclaims in thee:* nature denies having
made you. 56. *zed:* the letter "z," which is unnecessary because "s" can
take its place. 57. *unbolted:* unsifted, low-grade. 58. *jakes:* privy. 59. *wagtail:* a comically active little bird (with reference to Oswald's bowing and
scraping before rank). 66. *holy cords:* bonds of marriage and family. 67.
too intrinse to unloose: too firmly tied to come apart otherwise; *smooth:*
cater to.

That in the natures of their lords rebel;
Bring oil to fire, snow to their colder moods;
Renege, affirm, and turn their halcyon beaks   70
With every gale and vary of their masters,
Knowing naught, like dogs, but following.
A plague upon your epileptic visage!
Smile you my speeches, as I were a fool?
Goose, if I had you upon Sarum plain,   75
I'd drive ye cackling home to Camelot.
    CORN. What, art thou mad, old fellow?
    GLO. How fell you out? Say that.
    KENT. No contraries hold more antipathy
Than I and such a knave.   80
    CORN. Why dost thou call him knave? What is his fault?
    KENT. His countenance likes me not.
    CORN. No more perchance does mine, nor his, nor hers.
    KENT. Sir, 'tis my occupation to be plain.
I have seen better faces in my time   85
Than stands on any shoulder that I see
Before me at this instant.
    CORN.   This is some fellow
Who, having been praised for bluntness, doth affect
A saucy roughness, and constrains the garb
Quite from his nature. He cannot flatter, he—   90
An honest mind and plain—he must speak truth!
An they will take it, so. If not, he's plain.
These kind of knaves I know, which in this plainness
Harbor more craft and more corrupter ends
Than twenty silly ducking observants   95
That stretch their duties nicely.
    KENT. Sir, in good faith, in sincere verity,
Under the allowance of your great aspéct,
Whose influence, like the wreath of radiant fire
On flickering Phoebus' front——
    CORN.   What mean'st by this?   100
    KENT. To go out of my dialect, which you discommend so much.
I know, sir, I am no flatterer. He that beguiled you in a plain accent
was a plain knave, which, for my part, I will not be, though I should
win your displeasure to entreat me to 't.

---

70. *Renege:* deny; *halcyon:* the kingfisher when hung by the neck was
believed to turn his beak into the wind. 89-90. *constrains . . . nature:* puts
on a forced appearance which is the opposite of his real nature. 96. *stretch:*
earnestly perform; *nicely:* punctiliously.

CORN. What was the offense you gave him?   105
OSW. I never gave him any.
It pleased the King his master very late
To strike at me, upon his misconstruction,
When he, conjunct, and flattering his displeasure,
Tripped me behind; being down, insulted, railed,   110
And put upon him such a deal of man
That worthied him, got praises of the King
For him attempting who was self-subdued,
And in the fleshment of this dread exploit
Drew on me here again.
          KENT.   None of these rogues and cowards   115
But Ajax is their fool.
          CORN.   Fetch forth the stocks!
You stubborn ancient knave, you reverend braggart,
We'll teach you——
          KENT.   Sir, I am too old to learn.
Call not your stocks for me. I serve the King,
On whose employment I was sent to you.   120
You shall do small respect, show too bold malice
Against the grace and person of my master,
Stocking his messenger.
          CORN. Fetch forth the stocks! As I have life and honor,
There shall he sit till noon.   125
          REG. Till noon! Till night, my lord, and all night too.
          KENT. Why, madam, if I were your father's dog,
You should not use me so.
          REG.   Sir, being his knave, I will.
          CORN. This is a fellow of the selfsame color
Our sister speaks of. Come, bring away the stocks!   130
                              [Stocks brought out
          GLO. Let me beseech your Grace not to do so.
His fault is much, and the good King his master
Will check him for 't. Your purposed low correction
Is such as basest and contemned'st wretches
For pilferings and most common trespasses   135
Are punished with. The King must take it ill
That he, so slightly valued in his messenger,

---

108. *misconstruction:* lies about me. 109. *conjunct:* siding with the King.
111-12. *put . . . him:* acted like such a he-man that he got credit. 113.
attempting . . . self-subdued: attacking him who chose not to fight. 114.
fleshment: heroic heat. 116. *Ajax:* type of the loud-mouthed coward. 117.
reverend: old. 134. *contemned'st:* most despised.

Should have him thus restrained.
 CORN.   I'll answer that.
 REG. My sister may receive it much more worse
To have her gentleman abused, assaulted,   140
For following her affairs. Put in his legs [KENT *is put in the stocks.*
Come, my good lord, away. [*Exeunt all but* GLOUCESTER *and* KENT.
 GLO. I am sorry for thee, friend. 'Tis the Duke's pleasure,
Whose disposition all the world well knows
Will not be rubbed nor stopped. I'll entreat for thee. 145
 KENT. Pray do not, sir. I have watched and traveled hard;
Some time I shall sleep out, the rest I'll whistle.
A good man's fortune may grow out at heels.
Give you good morrow!   149
 GLO. The Duke's to blame in this; 'twill be ill-taken. [*Exit.*
 KENT. Good King, that must approve the common saw,
Thou out of heaven's benediction comest
To the warm sun!
Approach, thou beacon to this underglobe,
That by thy comfortable beams I may   155
Peruse this letter! Nothing almost sees miracles
But misery. I know 'tis from Cordelia,
Who hath most fortunately been informed
Of my obscurèd course, and shall find time
From this enormous state, seeking to give   160
Losses their remedies. All weary and o'erwatched,
Take vantage, heavy eyes, not to behold
This shameful lodging.
Fortune, good night. Smile once more; turn thy wheel! [*Sleeps.*

SCENE III. *A wood.*

[*Enter* EDGAR.]

 EDG. I heard myself proclaimed,
And by the happy hollow of a tree
Escaped the hunt. No port is free, no place,
That guard and most unusual vigilance
Does not attend my taking. Whiles I may 'scape   5
I will preserve myself, and am bethought

---

151. *that . . . saw:* who must be an illustration of the proverb. 152. *bene-diction:* blessing (of shade). 159. *obscurèd course:* actions while disguised. 160. *enormous state:* evil times.
 SC. III: 5. *attend my taking:* attempt my arrest.

To take the basest and most poorest shape
That ever penury in contempt of man
Brought near to beast. My face I'll grime with filth,
Blanket my loins, elf all my hair in knots,   10
And with presented nakedness outface
The winds and persecutions of the sky.
The country gives me proof and precedent
Of Bedlam beggars, who with roaring voices
Strike in their numbed and mortified bare arms   15
Pins, wooden pricks, nails, sprigs of rosemary,
And with this horrible object, from low farms,
Poor pelting villages, sheepcotes and mills,
Sometime with lunatic bans, sometime with prayers,
Enforce their charity. Poor Turlygod! Poor Tom!   20
That's something yet. Edgar I nothing am.   [*Exit.*

SCENE IV. *Before* GLOUCESTER's *castle.* KENT *in
the stocks.*

[*Enter* LEAR, FOOL, *and* GENTLEMAN.]

LEAR. 'Tis strange that they should so depart from home
And not send back my messenger.
GENT.   As I learned,
The night before there was no purpose in them
Of this remove.
KENT.   Hail to thee, noble master!
LEAR. Ha!   5
Makest thou this shame thy pastime?
KENT.   No, my lord.
FOOL. Ha, ha! He wears cruel garters. Horses are tied by the heads,
dogs and bears by the neck, monkeys by the loins, and men by the
legs. When a man's overlusty at legs, then he wears wooden nether-
stocks.   10
LEAR. What's he that hath so much thy place mistook
To set thee here?
KENT.   It is both he and she,
Your son and daughter.
LEAR. No.

---

10. *elf:* tangle, as by mischievous elves. 17. *object:* appearance; *low:* poor.
18. *pelting:* of no account. 19. *bans:* curses.
  sc. IV: 7. *cruel:* with a pun on "crewel" (worsted). 9-10. *netherstocks:*
stockings.

KENT. Yes.   15
LEAR. No, I say.
KENT. I say yea.
LEAR. No, no, they would not.
KENT. Yes, they have.
LEAR. By Jupiter, I swear no.   20
KENT. By Juno, I swear aye.
LEAR.   They durst not do 't,
They could not, would not do 't. 'Tis worse than murder
To do upon respect such violent outrage.
Resolve me with all modest haste which way
Thou mightest deserve, or they impose, this usage,   25
Coming from us.
    KENT.   My lord, when at their home
I did commend your Highness' letters to them,
Ere I was risen from the place that showed
My duty kneeling, came there a reeking post,
Stewed in his haste, half-breathless, panting forth   30
From Goneril his mistress salutations;
Delivered letters, spite of intermission,
Which presently they read. On whose contents
They summoned up their meiny, straight took horse,
Commanded me to follow and attend   35
The leisure of their answer, gave me cold looks.
And meeting here the other messenger,
Whose welcome, I perceived, had poisoned mine—
Being the very fellow that of late
Displayed so saucily against your Highness—   40
Having more man than wit about me, drew.
He raised the house with loud and coward cries.
Your son and daughter found this trespass worth
The shame which here it suffers.
    FOOL. Winter's not gone yet if the wild geese fly that way.   [45
                "Fathers that wear rags
                    Do make their children blind,
                But fathers that bear bags
                    Shall see their children kind.
                Fortune, that arrant whore,   50
                    Ne'er turns the key to the poor."

24. *resolve:* tell. 29. *reeking post:* sweating messenger. 32. *intermission:* interruption (by the arrival of the messenger). 33. *presently:* at that time; *On:* as a result of. 34. *meiny:* servants. 48. *bear bags:* are rich.

But for all this, thou shalt have as many dolors for thy daughters as
thou canst tell in a year.

    LEAR. Oh, how this mother swells up toward my heart!
Hysterica passio, down, thou climbing sorrow,   55
Thy element's below! Where is this daughter?

    KENT. With the earl, sir, here within.

    LEAR. Follow me not; stay here.   [*Exit.*

    GENT. Made you no more offense but what you speak of?

    KENT. None.   60
How chance the King comes with so small a train?

    FOOL. An thou hadst been set i' the stocks for that question, thou
hadst well deserved it.

    KENT. Why, fool?

    FOOL. We'll set thee to school to an ant, to teach thee there's   [65
no laboring i' the winter. All that follow their noses are led by their
eyes but blind men, and there's not a nose among twenty but can
smell him that's stinking. Let go thy hold when a great wheel runs
down a hill, lest it break thy neck with following it, but the great one
that goes up the hill, let him draw thee after. When a wise   [70
man gives thee better counsel, give me mine again. I would have
none but knaves follow it, since a fool gives it.

> "That sir which serves and seeks for gain,
>   And follows but for form,
> Will pack when it begins to rain,   75
>   And leave thee in the storm.
>
> "But I will tarry, the fool will stay,
>   And let the wise man fly.
> The knave turns fool that runs away,
>   The fool no knave, perdy."   80

    KENT. Where learned you this, fool?

    FOOL. Not i' the stocks, fool.

        [*Re-enter* LEAR, *with* GLOUCESTER.]

    LEAR. Deny to speak with me? They are sick? They are weary?
They have traveled all the night? Mere fetches,
The images of revolt and flying off.   85
Fetch me a better answer.

    GLO.   My dear lord,
You know the fiery quality of the Duke,

---

52. *dolors:* griefs, with a pun on "dollars." 53. *tell:* count. 54. *mother:*
hysteria. 56. *element's:* proper place. 84. *fetches:* excuses. 85. *images:* clear
signs.

How unremovable and fixed he is
In his own course.

LEAR. Vengeance! Plague! Death! Confusion!   [90
Fiery? What quality? Why, Gloucester, Gloucester,
I'd speak with the Duke of Cornwall and his wife.

GLO. Well, my good lord, I have informed them so.

LEAR. Informed them! Dost thou understand me, man?

GLO. Aye, my good lord.   95

LEAR. The King would speak with Cornwall; the dear father
Would with his daughter speak, commands her service.
Are they informed of this? My breath and blood!
"Fiery"? "The fiery Duke"? Tell the hot Duke that——
No, but not yet. Maybe he is not well.   100
Infirmity doth still neglect all office
Whereto our health is bound. We are not ourselves
When nature being oppressed commands the mind
To suffer with the body. I'll forbear,
And am fall'n out with my more headier will,   105
To take the indisposed and sickly fit
For the sound man. [*Looking on* KENT] Death on my state! Where-
        fore
Should he sit here? This act persuades me
That this remotion of the Duke and her
Is practice only. Give me my servant forth.   110
Go tell the Duke and's wife I'd speak with them,
Now, presently. Bid them come forth and hear me,
Or at their chamber door I'll beat the drum
Till it cry sleep to death.   114

GLO. I would have all well betwixt you.   [*Exit.*

LEAR. Oh, me, my heart, my rising heart! But down!

FOOL. Cry to it, nuncle, as the cockney did to the eels when she
put 'em i' the paste alive. She knapped 'em o' the coxcombs with a
stick, and cried "Down, wantons, down!" 'Twas her brother that, in
pure kindness to his horse, buttered his hay.   120

[*Re-enter* GLOUCESTER, *with* CORNWALL, REGAN, *and* SERVANTS.]

LEAR. Good morrow to you both.

CORN. Hail to your Grace!   [KENT *is set at liberty.*

REG. I am glad to see your Highness.

101-02. *Infirmity . . . bound:* sickness always causes a man to neglect duties
which he would do if well. 109. *remotion:* keeping themselves away from
me. 110. *practice:* scheming. 118. *knapped:* rapped.

LEAR. Regan, I think you are; I know what reason
I have to think so. If thou shouldst not be glad,   125
I would divorce me from thy mother's tomb,
Sepúlchring an adultress. [*To* KENT] Oh, are you free?
Some other time for that. Belovèd Regan,
Thy sister's naught. O Regan, she hath tied
Sharp-toothed unkindness, like a vulture, here.   130
                                        [*Points to his heart.*
I can scarce speak to thee; thou'lt not believe
With how depraved a quality—— O Regan!
    REG. I pray you, sir, take patience. I have hope
You less know how to value her desert
Than she to scant her duty.
    LEAR.   Say, how is that?   135
    REG. I cannot think my sister in the least
Would fail her obligation. If, sir, perchance
She have restrained the riots of your followers,
'Tis on such ground and to such wholesome end
As clears her from all blame.   140
    LEAR. My curses on her!
    REG.   Oh, sir, you are old;
Nature in you stands on the very verge
Of her confine. You should be ruled and led
By some discretion that discerns your state
Better than you yourself. Therefore I pray you   145
That to our sister you do make return.
Say you have wronged her, sir.
    LEAR.   Ask her forgiveness?
Do you but mark how this becomes the house.—
[*Kneeling*] "Dear daughter, I confess that I am old;
Age is unnecessary. On my knees I beg   150
That you'll vouchsafe me raiment, bed, and food."
    REG. Good sir, no more; these are unsightly tricks.
Return you to my sister.
    LEAR.   [*Rising*] Never, Regan.
She hath abated me of half my train,
Looked black upon me, struck me with her tongue,   155
Most serpentlike, upon the very heart.
All the stored vengeances of heaven fall
On her ingrateful top! Strike her young bones,
You taking airs, with lameness.

---

129. *naught:* wicked. 148. *becomes the house:* is becoming of family relationship. 159. *taking:* infectious.

CORN.   Fie, sir, fie!

LEAR. You nimble lightnings, dart your blinding flames   160
Into her scornful eyes. Infect her beauty,
You fen-sucked fogs, drawn by the powerful sun
To fall and blast her pride.

REG. Oh, the blest gods! So will you wish on me
When the rash mood is on.   165

LEAR. No, Regan, thou shalt never have my curse.
Thy tender-hefted nature shall not give
Thee o'er to harshness. Her eyes are fierce, but thine
Do comfort and not burn. 'Tis not in thee
To grudge my pleasures, to cut off my train,   170
To bandy hasty words, to scant my sizes,
And in conclusion to oppose the bolt
Against my coming in. Thou better know'st
The offices of nature, bond of childhood,
Effects of courtesy, dues of gratitude.   175
Thy half o' the kingdom hast thou not forgot,
Wherein I thee endowed.

REG.   Good sir, to the purpose.

LEAR. Who put my man i' the stocks?   [Tucket within.

CORN.   What trumpet's that?

REG. I know 't, my sister's. This approves her letter,
That she would soon be here.

[Enter OSWALD.]   Is your lady come?   180

LEAR. This is a slave whose easy-borrowed pride
Dwells in the fickle grace of her he follows.
Out, varlet, from my sight!

CORN.   What means your Grace?

LEAR. Who stocked my servant? Regan, I have good hope
Thou didst not know on 't. Who comes here?

[Enter GONERIL.]   O heavens,   185
If you do love old men, if your sweet sway
Allow obedience, if yourselves are old,
Make it your cause. Send down, and take my part!

[To GONERIL] Art not ashamed to look upon this beard?
O Regan, wilt thou take her by the hand?   190

GON. Why not by the hand, sir? How have I offended?
All's not offense that indiscretion finds
And dotage terms so.

---

163. *fall:* fall upon. 167. *hefted:* framed. 171. *sizes:* allowances. 179. *approves:* confirms. 187. *allow:* approve.

LEAR.　　　　　　　　O sides, you are too tough,
Will you yet hold? How came my man i' the stocks?
　　CORN. I set him there, sir. But his own disorders　　　　195
Deserved much less advancement.
　　LEAR.　　　　　　　　　　You! Did you?
　　REG. I pray you, father, being weak, seem so.
If till the expiration of your month
You will return and sojourn with my sister,
Dismissing half your train, come then to me.　　　　　　200
I am now from home and out of that provision
Which shall be needful for your entertainment.
　　LEAR. Return to her, and fifty men dismissed?
No, rather I abjure all roofs, and choose
To wage against the enmity o' the air,　　　　　　　　205
To be a comrade with the wolf and owl—
Necessity's sharp pinch! Return with her?
Why, the hot-blooded France, that dowerless took
Our youngest-born—I could as well be brought
To knee his throne and, squirelike, pension beg　　　　210
To keep base life afoot. Return with her?
Persuade me rather to be slave and sumpter
To this detested groom.　　　　　　　[*Pointing at* OSWALD.
　　GON.　　　　　　　At your choice, sir.
　　LEAR. I prithee, daughter, do not make me mad.
I will not trouble thee, my child. Farewell.　　　　　215
We'll no more meet, no more see one another.
But yet thou art my flesh, my blood, my daughter,
Or rather a disease that's in my flesh
Which I must needs call mine. Thou art a boil,
A plague sore, an embossed carbuncle,　　　　　　　220
In my corrupted blood. But I'll not chide thee.
Let shame come when it will, I do not call it.
I do not bid the thunderbearer shoot,
Nor tell tales of thee to high-judging Jove.
Mend when thou canst, be better at thy leisure.　　　　225
I can be patient, I can stay with Regan,
I and my hundred knights.
　　REG.　　　　　　　　Not altogether so.
I looked not for you yet, nor am provided
For your fit welcome. Give ear, sir, to my sister;
For those that mingle reason with your passion　　　　230

---

196. *advancement:* honor. 212. *sumpter:* beast of burden. 220. *embossed:*
swollen. 230. *mingle . . . passion:* analyze your emotional behavior.

Must be content to think you old, and so——
But she knows what she does.
    LEAR.   Is this well spoken?
    REG. I dare avouch it, sir. What, fifty followers?
Is it not well? What should you need of more?
Yea, or so many, sith that both charge and danger   235
Speak 'gainst so great a number? How in one house
Should many people under two commands
Hold amity? 'Tis hard, almost impossible.
    GON. Why might not you, my lord, receive attendance
From those that she calls servants or from mine?   240
    REG. Why not, my lord? If then they chanced to slack you,
We could control them. If you will come to me,
For now I spy a danger, I entreat you
To bring but five and twenty. To no more
Will I give place or notice.   245
    LEAR. I gave you all——
    REG.   And in good time you gave it.
    LEAR. Made you my guardians, my depositaries,
But kept a reservation to be followed
With such a number. What, must I come to you
With five and twenty, Regan? Said you so?   250
    REG. And speak 't again, my lord, no more with me.
    LEAR. Those wicked creatures yet do look well-favored,
When others are more wicked. Not being the worst
Stands in some rank of praise. [*To* GONERIL] I'll go with thee.
Thy fifty yet doth double five and twenty,   255
And thou art twice her love.
    GON.   Hear me, my lord.
What need you five and twenty, ten, or five,
To follow in a house where twice so many
Have a command to tend you?
    REG.   What need one?
    LEAR. Oh, reason not the need. Our basest beggars   260
Are in the poorest thing superfluous.
Allow not nature more than nature needs,
Man's life's as cheap as beast's. Thou art a lady.
If only to go warm were gorgeous,
Why, nature needs not what thou gorgeous wear'st,   265
Which scarcely keeps thee warm. But for true need——
You heavens, give me that patience, patience I need!

---

241. *slack:* neglect. 261. *superfluous:* more than they absolutely need.

You see me here, you gods, a poor old man,
As full of grief as age, wretched in both.
If it be you that stirs these daughters' hearts   270
Against their father, fool me not so much
To bear it tamely. Touch me with noble anger,
And let not women's weapons, water drops,
Stain my man's cheeks! No, you unnatural hags,
I will have such revenges on you both   275
That all the world shall—— I will do such things——
What they are, yet I know not, but they shall be
The terrors of the earth. You think I'll weep.
No, I'll not weep.
I have full cause of weeping, but this heart   280
Shall break into a hundred thousand flaws
Or ere I'll weep. O fool, I shall go mad!

                          [Exeunt LEAR, GLOUCESTER, KENT, *and* FOOL.
  CORN. Let us withdraw, 'twill be a storm.   *[Storm and tempest.*
  REG. This house is little. The old man and his people
Cannot be well bestowed.   285
  GON. 'Tis his own blame. Hath put himself from rest,
And must needs taste his folly.
  REG. For his particular, I'll receive him gladly,
But not one follower.
  GON.   So am I purposed.
Where is my Lord of Gloucester?   290
  CORN. Followed the old man forth. He is returned.

               [Re-enter GLOUCESTER.]

  GLO. The King is in high rage.
  CORN.   Whither is he going?
  GLO. He calls to horse, but will I know not whither.
  CORN. 'Tis best to give him way, he leads himself.
  GON. My lord, entreat him by no means to stay.   290, 295
  GLO. Alack, the night comes on, and the bleak winds
Do sorely ruffle. For many miles about
There's scarce a bush.
  REG.   Oh, sir, to willful men
The injuries that they themselves procure
Must be their schoolmasters. Shut up your doors.   300
He is attended with a desperate train,
And what they may incense him to, being apt

---

288. *his particular:* him alone. 302. *apt to have his ear abused:* predisposed to accept bad advice.

To have his ear abused, wisdom bids fear.

corn. Shut up your doors, my lord, 'tis a wild night.   304
My Regan counsels well. Come out o' the storm.   [*Exeunt.*

Act III

scene i. *A heath.*

[*Storm still. Enter* kent *and a* gentleman, *meeting.*]

kent. Who's there, besides foul weather?
gent. One minded like the weather, most unquietly.
kent. I know you. Where's the King?
gent. Contending with the fretful elements.
Bids the wind blow the earth into the sea,   5
Or swell the curlèd waters 'bove the main,
That things might change or cease; tears his white hair,
Which the impetuous blasts, with eyeless rage,
Catch in their fury, and make nothing of;
Strives in his little world of man to outscorn   10
The to-and-fro-conflicting wind and rain.
This night, wherein the cub-drawn bear would couch,
The lion and the belly-pinchèd wolf
Keep their fur dry, unbonneted he runs,
And bids what will take all.
kent.   But who is with him?   15
gent. None but the fool, who labors to outjest
His heart-struck injuries.
kent.   Sir, I do know you,
And dare, upon the warrant of my note,
Commend a dear thing to you. There is division,
Although as yet the face of it be covered   20
With mutual cunning, 'twixt Albany and Cornwall,
Who have—as who have not that their great stars
Throned and set high?—servants, who seem no less,
Which are to France the spies and speculations
Intelligent of our state; what hath been seen,   25
Either in snuffs and packings of the dukes,

---

act iii, sc. i: 6. *main:* land. 12. *cub-drawn:* nursed dry, and therefore hungry. 18. *warrant of my note:* assurance of what I have seen of you. 24-5. *speculations . . . state:* informers who give information about our affairs. 26. *snuffs and packings:* irritations and deceptions.

Or the hard rein which both of them have borne
Against the old kind King, or something deeper,
Whereof perchance these are but furnishings;
But true it is, from France there comes a power　　　30
Into this scattered kingdom, who already,
Wise in our negligence, have secret feet
In some of our best ports and are at point
To show their open banner. Now to you.
If on my credit you dare build so far　　　35
To make your speed to Dover, you shall find
Some that will thank you, making just report
Of how unnatural and bemadding sorrow
The King hath cause to plain.
I am a gentleman of blood and breeding,　　　40
And from some knowledge and assurance offer
This office to you.
　　GENT. I will talk further with you.
　　KENT.　　　　　　　　　　　　No, do not.
For confirmation that I am much more
Than my outwall, open this purse and take　　　45
What it contains. If you shall see Cordelia—
As fear not but you shall—show her this ring,
And she will tell you who your fellow is
That yet you do not know. Fie on this storm!
I will go seek the King.
　　GENT.　　　　　　　Give me your hand.　　　50
Have you no more to say?
　　KENT. Few words, but, to effect, more than all yet—
That when we have found the King—in which your pain
That way, I'll this—he that first lights on him　　　54
Holloa the other.　　　　　　　　　　　[*Exeunt severally.*

SCENE II. *Another part of the heath. Storm still.*

[*Enter* LEAR *and* FOOL.]

　　LEAR. Blow, winds, and crack your cheeks! Rage! Blow!
You cataracts and hurricanoes, spout
Till you have drenched our steeples, drowned the cocks!
You sulphurous and thought-executing fires,

---

29. *furnishings:* good rather than real reasons. 35. *credit:* word. 39. *plain:* complain. 42. *office:* assignment. 45. *outwall:* appearance. 48. *fellow:* present companion. 53. *pain:* task (lies).

SC. II: 2. *hurricanoes:* water-spouts. 3. *cocks:* weathercocks. 4. *thought-executing:* acting with the speed of thought.

Vaunt-couriers to oak-cleaving thunderbolts,   5
Singe my white head! And thou, all-shaking thunder,
Smite flat the thick rotundity o' the world!
Crack nature's molds, all germens spill at once
That make ingrateful man!

FOOL. O nuncle, court holy water in a dry house is better   [10
than this rain water out o' door. Good nuncle, in, and ask thy daughters' blessing. Here's a night pities neither wise man nor fool.

LEAR. Rumble thy bellyful! Spit, fire! Spout, rain!
Nor rain, wind, thunder, fire, are my daughters.
I tax not you, you elements, with unkindness.   15
I never gave you kingdom, called you children,
You owe me no subscription. Then let fall
Your horrible pleasure. Here I stand, your slave,
A poor, infirm, weak, and despised old man.
But yet I call you servile ministers   20
That have with two pernicious daughters joined
Your high-engendered battles 'gainst a head
So old and white as this. Oh, oh! 'Tis foul!

FOOL. He that has a house to put 's head in has a good headpiece.

      "The codpiece that will house   25
        Before the head has any,
      The head and he shall louse
        So beggars marry many.
      The man that makes his toe
        What he his heart should make   30
      Shall of a corn cry woe,
        And turn his sleep to wake."

For there was never yet fair woman but she made mouths in a glass.

LEAR. No, I will be the pattern of all patience,
I will say nothing.   35

               [Enter KENT.]

KENT. Who's there?

FOOL. Marry, here's grace and a codpiece—that's a wise man and
a fool.

KENT. Alas, sir, are you here? Things that love night
Love not such nights as these. The wrathful skies   40
Gallow the very wanderers of the dark
And make them keep their caves. Since I was man,

---

5. *Vaunt-couriers:* forerunners. 8. *germens:* seeds. 10. *court holy water:*
flattery. 17. *subscription:* obedience. 20. *ministers:* agents. 25. *codpiece:*
male sexual organ. 41. *Gallow:* terrify.

Such sheets of fire, such bursts of horrid thunder,
Such groans of roaring wind and rain, I never
Remember to have heard. Man's nature cannot carry   45
The affliction nor the fear.
    LEAR.   Let the great gods,
That keep this dreadful pother o'er our heads,
Find out their enemies now. Tremble, thou wretch,
That hast within thee undivulgèd crimes
Unwhipped of justice. Hide thee, thou bloody hand,   50
Thou perjured, and thou simular man of virtue
That art incestuous. Caitiff, to pieces shake,
That under covert and convenient seeming
Hast practiced on man's life. Close pent-up guilts,
Rive your concealing continents and cry   55
These dreadful summoners grace. I am a man
More sinned against than sinning.
    KENT.   Alack, bareheaded!
Gracious my lord, hard by here is a hovel;
Some friendship will it lend you 'gainst the tempest.
Repose you there while I to this hard house—   60
More harder than the stones whereof 'tis raised,
Which even but now, demanding after you,
Denied me to come in—return, and force
Their scanted courtesy.
    LEAR.   My wits begin to turn.
Come on, my boy. How dost, my boy? Art cold?   65
I am cold myself. Where is this straw, my fellow?
The art of our necessities is strange,
That can make vile things precious. Come, your hovel.
Poor fool and knave, I have one part in my heart
That's sorry yet for thee.   70
    FOOL. [*Singing*]
        "He that has and a little tiny wit—
           With hey, ho, the wind and the rain—
           Must make content with his fortunes fit,
           For the rain it raineth every day."
    LEAR. True, my good boy. Come, bring us to this hovel.   75
                     [*Exeunt* LEAR *and* KENT.
    FOOL. This is a brave night to cool a courtesan.
I'll speak a prophecy ere I go:

---

47. *pother:* turmoil. 51. *simular:* hypocritical. 55. *Rive:* rip open; *continents:* coverings. 73. *content:* contentment.

"When priests are more in word than matter,
When brewers mar their malt with water,
When nobles are their tailors' tutors,   80
No heretics burned, but wenches' suitors,
When every case in law is right,
No squire in debt, nor no poor knight,
When slanders do not live in tongues,
Nor cutpurses come not to throngs,   85
When usurers tell their gold i' the field,
And bawds and whores do churches build—
Then shall the realm of Albion
Come to great confusion.
Then comes the time, who lives to see 't,   90
That going shall be used with feet."
This prophecy Merlin shall make, for I live before his time.   [*Exit.*

SCENE III. GLOUCESTER'S *castle.*

[*Enter* GLOUCESTER *and* EDMUND.]

GLO. Alack, alack, Edmund, I like not this unnatural dealing. When I desired their leave that I might pity him, they took from me the use of mine own house, charged me, on pain of their perpetual displeasure, neither to speak of him, entreat for him, nor any way sustain him.   5

EDM. Most savage and unnatural!

GLO. Go to, say you nothing. There's a division betwixt the Dukes, and a worse matter than that. I have received a letter this night, 'tis dangerous to be spoken.—I have locked the letter in my closet. These injuries the King now bears will be revenged home. There   [10 is part of a power already footed. We must incline to the King. I will seek him and privily relieve him. Go you, and maintain talk with the Duke, that my charity be not of him perceived. If he ask for me, I am ill and gone to bed. Though I die for it, as no less is threatened me, the King my old master must be relieved. There is some   [15 strange thing toward, Edmund. Pray you be careful.   [*Exit.*

EDM. This courtesy, forbid thee, shall the Duke
Instantly know, and of that letter too.
This seems a fair deserving, and must draw me

---

88. *Albion:* Britain. 91. *going . . . feet:* men shall walk on their own two feet.

sc. III: 5. *sustain:* relieve. 11. *footed:* landed; *incline to:* side with. 17. *forbid:* forbidden to. 19. *fair deserving:* a good opportunity to do something that will deserve reward.

That which my father loses, no less than all.   20
The younger rises when the old doth fall.   [*Exit.*

SCENE IV. *The heath. Before a hovel.*

[*Enter* LEAR, KENT, *and* FOOL.]

KENT. Here is the place, my lord. Good my lord, enter.
The tyranny of the open night's too rough
For nature to endure.   [*Storm still.*
     LEAR.   Let me alone.
KENT. Good my lord, enter here.
     LEAR.   Wilt break my heart?
KENT. I had rather break mine own. Good my lord, enter.   5
     LEAR. Thou think'st 'tis much that this contentious storm
Invades us to the skin. So 'tis to thee,
But where the greater malady is fixed
The lesser is scarce felt. Thou'dst shun a bear,
But if thy flight lay toward the raging sea   10
Thou'dst meet the bear i' the mouth. When the mind's free
The body's delicate. The tempest in my mind
Doth from my senses take all feeling else
Save what beats there. Filial ingratitude!
Is it not as this mouth should tear this hand   15
For lifting food to 't? But I will punish home.
No, I will weep no more. In such a night
To shut me out! Pour on, I will endure.
In such a night as this! O Regan, Goneril!
Your old kind father, whose frank heart gave all——   20
Oh, that way madness lies; let me shun that;
No more of that.
     KENT.   Good my lord, enter here.
     LEAR. Prithee, go in thyself; seek thine own ease.
This tempest will not give me leave to ponder
On things would hurt me more. But I'll go in.   25
[*To the* FOOL] In, boy, go first. You houseless poverty——
Nay, get thee in. I'll pray, and then I'll sleep.   [FOOL *goes in.*
Poor naked wretches, wheresoe'er you are,
That bide the pelting of this pitiless storm,
How shall your houseless heads and unfed sides,   30
Your looped and windowed raggedness, defend you
From seasons such as these? Oh, I have ta'en

sc. IV: 15. *as:* as if. 29. *bide:* endure.

Too little care of this! Take physic, pomp.
Expose thyself to feel what wretches feel,
That thou mayst shake the superflux to them   35
And show the heavens more just.

EDG. [Within] Fathom and half, fathom and half!
Poor Tom!   [*The* FOOL *runs out from the hovel.*

FOOL. Come not in here, nuncle, here's a spirit.
Help me, help me!   40

KENT. Give me thy hand. Who's there?

FOOL. A spirit, a spirit. He says his name's Poor Tom.

KENT. What art thou that dost grumble there i' the straw?
Come forth.

[*Enter* EDGAR *disguised as a madman.*]

EDG. Away! The foul fiend follows me!   45
"Through the sharp hawthorn blows the cold wind."
Hum! Go to thy cold bed and warm thee.

LEAR. Hast thou given all to thy two daughters?
And art thou come to this?

EDG. Who gives anything to Poor Tom? Whom the foul   [50
fiend hath led through fire and through flame, through ford and
whirlpool, o'er bog and quagmire, that hath laid knives under his
pillow and halters in his pew, set ratsbane by his porridge, made
him proud of heart to ride on a bay trotting horse over four-inched
bridges, to course his own shadow for a traitor. Bless thy   [55
five wits! Tom's a-cold. Oh, do de, do de, do de. Bless thee from
whirlwinds, star-blasting, and taking! Do Poor Tom some charity,
whom the foul fiend vexes. There could I have him now, and there,
and there again, and there.   [*Storm still.*

LEAR. What, have his daughters brought him to this pass?   60
Couldst thou save nothing? Didst thou give them all?

FOOL. Nay, he reserved a blanket, else we had been all shamed.

LEAR. Now, all the plagues that in the pendulous air
Hang fated o'er men's faults light on thy daughters!

KENT. He hath no daughters, sir.   65

LEAR. Death, traitor! Nothing could have subdued nature
To such a lowness but his unkind daughters.
Is it the fashion that discarded fathers
Should have thus little mercy on their flesh?

---

35. *Shake the superflux:* cast down what you do not really need. 52-3.
knives . . . ratsbane: instruments of suicide by stabbing, hanging, and
poisoning. 55. *course:* hunt. 57. *taking:* infection. 63. *pendulous:* low-
hanging.

Judicious punishment! 'Twas this flesh begot   70
Those pelican daughters.

   EDG. "Pillicock sat on Pillicock Hill.
      Halloo, halloo, loo, loo!"

   FOOL. This cold night will turn us all to fools and madmen.

   EDG. Take heed o' the foul fiend. Obey thy parents; keep   [75
thy word justly; swear not; commit not with man's sworn spouse;
set not thy sweet heart on proud array. Tom's a-cold.

   LEAR. What hast thou been?

   EDG. A servingman, proud in heart and mind, that curled my hair,
wore gloves in my cap, served the lust of my mistress's heart   [80
and did the act of darkness with her, swore as many oaths as I spake
words and broke them in the sweet face of heaven. One that slept
in the contriving of lust and waked to do it. Wine loved I deeply,
dice dearly, and in woman outparamoured the Turk. False of heart,
light of ear, bloody of hand, hog in sloth, fox in stealth,   [85
wolf in greediness, dog in madness, lion in prey. Let not the creak-
ing of shoes nor the rustling of silks betray thy poor heart to woman.
Keep thy foot out of brothels, thy hand out of plackets, thy pen from
lenders' books, and defy the foul fiend.
      "Still through the hawthorn blows the cold wind.   90
      Says suum, mun, ha, no, nonny.
      Dolphin my boy, my boy, sessa! Let him trot by."
                                     [*Storm still.*

   LEAR. Why, thou wert better in thy grave than to answer with thy
uncovered body this extremity of the skies. Is man no more than
this? Consider him well. Thou owest the worm no silk, the   [95
beast no hide, the sheep no wool, the cat no perfume. Ha! Here's
three on 's are sophisticated. Thou art the thing itself. Unaccom-
modated man is no more but such a poor, bare, forked animal as
thou art. Off, off, you lendings! Come, unbutton here.
                           [*Tearing off his clothes.*

   FOOL. Prithee, nuncle, be contented; 'tis a naughty night   [100
to swim in. Now a little fire in a wild field were like an old lecher's
heart; a small spark, all the rest on 's body cold. Look, here comes
a walking fire.

      [*Enter* GLOUCESTER, *with a torch.*]

   EDG. This is the foul fiend Flibbertigibbet. He begins at curfew
and walks till the first cock, he gives the web and the pin,   [105

---

71. *pelican:* young pelicans were thought to live by their mother's blood.
88. *plackets:* slits in petticoats. 96. *cat:* civet cat. 105. *web and the pin:*
cataract of the eye.

squints the eye and makes the harelip, mildews the white wheat
and hurts the poor creature of earth.

> "Saint Withhold footed thrice the 'old;
> He met the nightmare and her ninefold.
> Bid her alight,   110
> And her troth plight,
> And aroint thee, witch, aroint thee!"

KENT. How fares your Grace?

LEAR. What's he?

KENT. Who's there? What is 't you seek?   115

GLO. What are you there? Your names?

EDG. Poor Tom, that eats the swimming frog, the toad, the tadpole,
the wall newt, and the water; that in the fury of his heart, when the
foul fiend rages, eats cow dung for sallets; swallows the old rat and
the ditch dog; drinks the green mantle of the standing pool;   [120
who is whipped from tithing to tithing, and stock-punished, and
imprisoned; who hath had three suits to his back, six shirts to his
body, horse to ride, and weapon to wear.

> "But mice and rats and such small deer
> Have been Tom's food for seven long year."   125

Beware my follower. Peace, Smulkin, peace, thou fiend!

GLO. What, hath your Grace no better company?

EDG. The Prince of Darkness is a gentleman.
Modo he's called, and mahu.

GLO. Our flesh and blood is grown so vile, my lord,   130
That it doth hate what gets it.

EDG. Poor Tom's a-cold.

GLO. Go in with me. My duty cannot suffer
To obey in all your daughters' hard commands.
Though their injunction be to bar my doors   135
And let this tyrannous night take hold upon you,
Yet have I ventured to come seek you out
And bring you where both fire and food is ready.

LEAR. First let me talk with this philosopher.
What is the cause of thunder?   140

KENT. Good my lord, take his offer, go into the house.

LEAR. I'll talk a word with this same learnèd Theban.
What is your study?

EDG. How to prevent the fiend and to kill vermin.

---

108. *'old:* wold or pasture. 109. *ninefold:* offspring. 112. *aroint:* begone.
118. *wall . . . water:* newts (lizards) living in the wall and in the water.
119. *sallets:* salads. 120. *ditch:* dead; *mantle:* scum. 121. *tithing:* parish.
124. *deer:* animals. 131. *gets:* begets. 133. *suffer:* permit me. 142. *Theban:*
i.e., Greek philosopher.

LEAR. Let me ask you one word in private.   145
  KENT. Impórtune him once more to go, my lord.
His wits begin to unsettle.
  GLO. Canst thou blame him?   [*Storm still.*
His daughters seek his death. Ah, that good Kent!
He said it would be thus, poor banished man!   150
Thou say'st the King grows mad. I'll tell thee, friend,
I am almost mad myself. I had a son,
Now outlawed from my blood. He sought my life
But lately, very late. I loved him, friend,
No father his son dearer. Truth to tell thee,   155
The grief hath crazed my wits. What a night's this!
I do beseech your Grace——
  LEAR.   Oh, cry you mercy, sir.
Noble philosopher, your company.
  EDG. Tom's a-cold.
  GLO. In, fellow, there, into the hovel. Keep thee warm.   160
  LEAR. Come, let's in all.
  KENT.   This way, my lord.
  LEAR.   With him,
I will keep still with my philosopher.
  KENT. Good my lord, soothe him; let him take the fellow.
  GLO. Take him you on.
  KENT. Sirrah, come on; go along with us.   165
  LEAR. Come, good Athenian.
  GLO. No words, no words. Hush.
  EDG. "Child Rowland to the dark tower came.
          His word was still 'Fie, foh, and fum,   169
          I smell the blood of a British man.'"   [*Exeunt.*

SCENE V. GLOUCESTER's *castle.*

[*Enter* CORNWALL *and* EDMUND.]

  CORN. I will have my revenge ere I depart his house.
  EDM. How, my lord, I may be censured, that nature thus gives way
to loyalty, something fears me to think of.
  CORN. I now perceive it was not altogether your brother's evil disposition made him seek his death, but a provoking merit, set   [5
a-work by a reprovable badness in himself.
  EDM. How malicious is my fortune, that I must repent to be just!

_____

168. *Child:* candidate for knighthood.
  SC. V: 2. *nature:* natural affection for my father. 5-6. *but . . . himself:*
righteous indignation aroused by actual badness in Gloucester.

This is the letter he spoke of, which approves him an intelligent party to the advantages of France. Oh heavens, that this treason were not, or not I the detector!   10

CORN. Go with me to the Duchess.

EDM. If the matter of this paper be certain, you have mighty business in hand.

CORN. True or false, it hath made thee Earl of Gloucester. Seek out where thy father is, that he may be ready for our apprehension.

EDM. [*Aside*] If I find him comforting the King, it will   [16 stuff his suspicion more fully.—I will persevere in my course of loyalty, though the conflict be sore between that and my blood.

CORN. I will lay trust upon thee, and thou shalt find a dearer   [19 father in my love.   [*Exeunt.*

SCENE VI. *A chamber in a farmhouse adjoining the castle.*

[*Enter* GLOUCESTER, LEAR, KENT, FOOL, *and* EDGAR.]

GLO. Here is better than the open air; take it thankfully. I will piece out the comfort with what addition I can. I will not be long from you.

KENT. All the power of his wits has given way to his impatience. The gods reward your kindness!   [*Exit* GLOUCESTER.

EDG. Fraretetto calls me, and tells me Nero is an angler in   [6 the lake of darkness. Pray, innocent, and beware the foul fiend.

FOOL. Prithee, nuncle, tell me whether a madman be a gentleman or a yeoman.

LEAR. A king, a king!   10

FOOL. No, he's a yeoman that has a gentleman to his son, for he's a mad yeoman that sees his son a gentleman before him.

LEAR. To have a thousand with red burning spits
Come hissing in upon 'em——

EDG. The foul fiend bites my back.   15

FOOL. He's mad that trusts in the tameness of a wolf, a horse's health, a boy's love, or a whore's oath.

LEAR. It shall be done; I will arraign them straight.
[*To* EDGAR] Come, sit thou here, most learned justicer.
[*To the* FOOL] Thou, sapient sir, sit here. Now, you she-foxes!

---

8. *approves:* proves; *intelligent party:* spy. 15. *apprehension:* arrest. 18. *blood:* ties of blood.

SC. VI: 19. *justicer:* judge. 20. *sapient:* wise.

EDG. Look where he stands and glares! Wantest thou eyes   [21
at trial, madam?

> "Come o'er the bourn, Bessy, to me."

FOOL.   "Her boat hath a leak,
                   And she must not speak   25
               Why she dares not come over to thee."

EDG. The foul fiend haunts poor Tom in the voice of a nightingale.
Hopdance cries in Tom's belly for two white herring. Croak not,
black angel, I have no food for thee.

KENT. How do you, sir? Stand you not so amazed.   30
Will you lie down and rest upon the cushions?

LEAR. I'll see their trial first. Bring in the evidence.
[*To* EDGAR] Thou robèd man of justice, take thy place.
[*To the* FOOL] And thou, his yokefellow of equity,
Bench by his side. [*To* KENT] You are o' the commission,   35
Sit you too.

EDG. Let us deal justly.

> "Sleepest or wakest thou, jolly shepherd?
>   Thy sheep be in the corn,
>   And for one blast of thy minikin mouth,   40
>   Thy sheep shall take no harm."

Purr! The cat is gray.

LEAR. Arraign her first. 'Tis Goneril. I here take my oath befoie
this honorable assembly, she kicked the poor King her father.

FOOL. Come hither, mistress. Is your name Goneril?   45

LEAR. She cannot deny it.

FOOL. Cry you mercy, I took you for a joint stool.

LEAR. And here's another, whose warped looks proclaim
What store her heart is made on. Stop her there!
Arms, arms, sword, fire! Corruption in the place!   50
False justicer, why hast thou let her 'scape?

EDG. Bless thy five wits!

KENT. Oh, pity! Sir, where is the patience now,
That you so oft have boasted to retain?

EDG. [*Aside*] My tears begin to take his part so much   55
They'll mar my counterfeiting.

LEAR. The little dogs and all,
Tray, Blanch, and Sweetheart, see, they bark at me.

---

21. *he: i.e.,* the imaginary fiend. 21-2. *Wantest . . . madam:* Did you desire spectators at your trial, madam (Goneril or Regan)? 23. *bourn:* brook.
35. *Bench:* mount the judge's bench. 40. *for:* during; *minikin:* pretty littll.
49. *store:* stuff; *on:* of. 50. *place:* high place, court.

EDG. Tom will throw his head at them. Avaunt, you curs!
   Be thy mouth or black or white,   60
   Tooth that poisons if it bite,
   Mastiff, greyhound, mongrel grim,
   Hound or spaniel, brach or lym,
   Or bobtail tike or trundletail,
   Tom will make them weep and wail.   65
   For, with throwing thus my head,
   Dogs leap the hatch, and all are fled.
Do de, de, de. Sessa! Come, march to wakes and fairs and market
towns. Poor Tom, thy horn is dry.
  LEAR. Then let them anatomize Regan; see what breeds [70
about her heart. Is there any cause in nature that makes these hard
hearts? [*To* EDGAR] You, sir, I entertain for one of my hundred;
only I do not like the fashion of your garments. You will say they
are Persian attire, but let them be changed.
  KENT. Now, good my lord, lie here and rest awhile.   75
  LEAR. Make no noise, make no noise. Draw the curtains.
So, so, so. We'll go to supper i' the morning. So, so, so.
  FOOL. And I'll go to bed at noon.

     [*Re-enter* GLOUCESTER.]

  GLO. Come hither, friend. Where is the King my master?
  KENT. Here, sir, but trouble him not. His wits are gone. 80
  GLO. Good friend, I prithee take him in thy arms.
I have o'erheard a plot of death upon him.
There is a litter ready; lay him in 't,
And drive toward Dover, friend, where thou shalt meet
Both welcome and protection. Take up thy master.   85
If thou shouldst dally half an hour, his life,
With thine and all that offer to defend him,
Stand in assurèd loss. Take up, take up,
And follow me, that will to some provision
Give thee quick conduct.
  KENT.   Oppressèd nature sleeps.   90
This rest might yet have balmed thy broken sinews,
Which, if convenience will not allow,
Stand in hard cure. [*To the* FOOL] Come, help to bear thy master.
Thou must not stay behind.

---

63. *brach:* bitch; *lym:* bloodhound. 64. *trundletail:* long hang-tail. 69. *horn:*
bottle. 72. *entertain:* employ. 74. *Persian:* magnificent. 89. *provision:* protection. 91. *balmed:* soothed; *sinews:* nerves. 93. *Stand . . . cure:* will be
very difficult to cure.

GLO.   Come, come, away.
                                    [*Exeunt all but* EDGAR.
EDG. When we our betters see bearing our woes,   95
We scarcely think our miseries our foes.
Who alone suffers suffers most i' the mind,
Leaving free things and happy shows behind.
But then the mind much sufferance doth o'erskip
When grief hath mates, and bearing fellowship.   100
How light and portable my pain seems now
When that which makes me bend makes the King bow,
He childed as I fathered! Tom, away!
Mark the high noises, and thyself bewray
When false opinion, whose wrong thought defiles thee,   105
In thy just proof repeals and reconciles thee.
What will hap more tonight, safe 'scape the King!
Lurk, lurk.   [*Exit.

SCENE VII. GLOUCESTER'S *castle.*

[*Enter* CORNWALL, REGAN, GONERIL, EDMUND, *and* SERVANTS.]

CORN. Post speedily to my lord your husband. Show him this letter.
The army of France is landed. Seek out the traitor Gloucester.
                              [*Exeunt some of the* SERVANTS.
REG. Hang him instantly.
GON. Pluck out his eyes.
CORN. Leave him to my displeasure. Edmund, keep you   [5
our sister company. The revenges we are bound to take upon your
traitorous father are not fit for your beholding. Advise the Duke,
where you are going, to a most festinate preparation. We are bound
to the like. Our posts shall be swift and intelligent betwixt us. Fare-
well, dear sister. Farewell, my Lord of Gloucester.   10
[*Enter* OSWALD.] How now! Where's the King?
OSW. My Lord of Gloucester hath conveyed him hence.
Some five or six and thirty of his knights,
Hot questrists after him, met him at gate,
Who, with some other of the lords dependents,   15

---

98. *free:* carefree; *happy shows:* signs of happiness. 100. *bearing fellowship:*
in bearing miseries. 103. *He . . . fathered:* he suffers from children, I
from a father. 104. *high noises:* dangerous signs; *bewray:* reveal. 106. *In
. . . repeals:* recalls you from hiding when your innocence is justly proved.
108. *Lurk:* lie low.

SC. VII: 8. *to . . . festinate:* to make immediate. 10. *Lord of Gloucester:*
Edmund. 14. *questrists:* searchers. 15. *dependents:* of his party.

Are gone with him toward Dover, where they boast
To have well-armèd friends.
    CORN.   Get horses for your mistress.
    GON. Farewell, sweet lord, and sister.
    CORN. Edmund, farewell. [*Exeunt* GONERIL, EDMUND, *and* OSWALD.
                    Go seek the traitor Gloucester.
Pinion him like a thief; bring him before us.   20
                        [*Exeunt other* SERVANTS.
Though well we may not pass upon his life
Without the form of justice, yet our power
Shall do a courtesy to our wrath, which men
May blame but not control. Who's there? The traitor?

      [*Enter* GLOUCESTER, *brought in by two or three.*]

    REG. Ungrateful fox! 'Tis he.   25
    CORN. Bind fast his corky arms.
    GLO. What mean your Graces? Good my friends, consider
You are my guests. Do me no foul play, friends.
    CORN. Bind him, I say.   [SERVANTS *bind him.*
    REG.   Hard, hard. O filthy traitor!
    GLO. Unmerciful lady as you are, I'm none.   30
    CORN. To this chair bind him. Villain, thou shalt find——-
                    [REGAN *plucks his beard.*
    GLO. By the kind gods, 'tis most ignobly done
To pluck me by the beard.
    REG. So white, and such a traitor!
    GLO.   Naughty lady,
These hairs which thou dost ravish from my chin   35
Will quicken and accuse thee. I am your host.
With robbers' hands my hospitable favors
You should not ruffle thus. What will you do?
    CORN. Come, sir, what letters had you late from France?
    REG. Be simple answerer, for we know the truth.   40
    CORN. And what confederacy have you with the traitors
Late footed in the kingdom?
    REG. To whose hands have you sent the lunatic King?
Speak.
    GLO. I have a letter guessingly set down,   45
Which came from one that's of a neutral heart,
And not from one opposed.

---

21. *pass:* final judgment. 26. *corky:* old and withered. 34. *Naughty:* evil.
36. *quicken:* come to life. 37. *favors:* face. 40. *Be simple:* talk straight.

CORN.   Cunning.
REG.   And false.
CORN. Where hast thou sent the King?
GLO.   To Dover.
REG. Wherefore to Dover? Wast thou not charged at peril——
CORN. Wherefore to Dover? Let him first answer that.   50
GLO. I am tied to the stake, and I must stand the course.
REG. Wherefore to Dover, sir?
GLO. Because I would not see thy cruel nails
Pluck out his poor old eyes, nor thy fierce sister
In his anointed flesh stick boarish fangs.   55
The sea, with such a storm as his bare head
In hell-black night endured, would have buoyed up,
And quenched the stellèd fires.
Yet, poor old heart, he holp the heavens to rain.
If wolves had at thy gate howled that stern time,   60
Thou shouldst have said, "Good porter, turn the key,"
All cruels else subscribed. But I shall see
The wingèd vengeance overtake such children.
    CORN. See 't shalt thou never. Fellows, hold the chair.
Upon these eyes of thine I'll set my foot.   65
    GLO. He that will think to live till he be old,
Give me some help! Oh, cruel! Oh, you gods!
                        [GLOUCESTER's *eye is put out.*
    REG. One side will mock another; the other too.
    CORN. If you see vengeance——
    1. SERV.   Hold your hand, my lord.
I have served you ever since I was a child,   70
But better service have I never done you
Than now to bid you hold.
    REG.   How now, you dog!
    1. SERV. If you did wear a beard upon your chin,
I'd shake it on this quarrel. What do you mean?
    CORN. My villain!
                                                             75
        [*They draw and fight.* CORNWALL *is wounded.*
    1. SERV. Nay, then, come on, and take the chance of anger.
    REG. Give me thy sword. A peasant stand up thus!
        [*Takes a sword and runs at him behind.*

—————————

51. *I . . . course:* I am tied like a bear and I must endure being baited by
the dogs. 55. *anointed:* royal. 57. *buoyed:* surged. 58. *stellèd fires:* stars.
59. *holp:* helped. 60. *howled:* i.e., for shelter. 62. *All . . . subscribed:* All
cruel creatures except you recognized the need for compassion.

1. SERV. Oh, I am slain! My lord, you have one eye left
To see some mischief on him. Oh!   [*Dies.*
  CORN. Lest it see more, prevent it. Out, vile jelly!   80
Where is thy luster now?   [*Puts out* GLOUCESTER'S *other eye.*
  GLO. All dark and comfortless. Where's my son Edmund?
Edmund, enkindle all the sparks of nature,
To quit this horrid act.
  REG.   Out, treacherous villain!
Thou call'st on him that hates thee. It was he   85
That made the overture of thy treasons to us,
Who is too good to pity thee.
  GLO. Oh, my follies! Then Edgar was abused.
Kind gods, forgive me that, and prosper him!
  REG. Go thrust him out at gates, and let him smell   90
His way to Dover.   [*Exit one with* GLOUCESTER.
          How is 't, my lord? How look you?
  CORN. I have received a hurt. Follow me, lady.
Turn out that eyeless villain. Throw this slave
Upon the dunghill. Regan, I bleed apace.
Untimely comes this hurt. Give me your arm.   95
           [*Exit* CORNWALL, *led by* REGAN.
  2. SERV. I'll never care what wickedness I do
If this man come to good.
  3. SERV.   If she live long,
And in the end meet the old course of death,
Women will all turn monsters.
  2. SERV. Let's follow the old Earl, and get the bedlam   100
To lead him where he would. His roguish madness
Allows itself to anything.
  3. SERV. Go thou. I'll fetch some flax and whites of eggs
To apply to his bleeding face. Now, heaven help him!
                  [*Exeunt severally.*

---

83. *nature:* natural affection. 84. *quit:* revenge. 86. *overture:* revelation.
98. *meet . . . death:* die naturally. 101-02. *His . . . anything:* The fact
that he (Edgar) is a rogue (vagabond) and insane gives him license to do
anything.

Act IV

SCENE I. *The heath.*

[*Enter* EDGAR.]

EDG. Yet better thus, and known to be contemned,
Than still contemned and flattered. To be worst,
The lowest and most dejected thing of fortune,
Stands still in esperance, lives not in fear.
The lamentable change is from the best;   5
The worst returns to laughter. Welcome then,
Thou unsubstantial air that I embrace!
The wretch that thou hast blown unto the worst
Owes nothing to thy blasts.—But who comes here?

[*Enter* GLOUCESTER, *led by an* OLD MAN.]

My father, poorly led? World, world, O world!   10
But that thy strange mutations make us hate thee,
Life would not yield to age.
    OLD MAN. Oh, my good lord, I have been your tenant, and your
father's tenant, these fourscore years.
    GLO. Away, get thee away. Good friend, be gone.   15
Thy comforts can do me no good at all;
Thee they may hurt.
    OLD MAN. Alack, sir, you cannot see your way.
    GLO. I have no way and therefore want no eyes.
I stumbled when I saw. Full oft 'tis seen,   20
Our means secure us, and our mere defects
Prove our commodities. Ah, dear son Edgar,
The food of thy abusèd father's wrath,
Might I but live to see thee in my touch,
I'd say I had eyes again!
    OLD MAN.   How now! Who's there?   25
    EDG. [*Aside*] Oh gods! Who is 't can say "I am at the worst"?
I am worse than e'er I was.
    OLD MAN.   'Tis poor mad Tom.

ACT IV, SC. I: 1. *contemned:* despised. 4. *esperance:* hope. 21-2. *means
. . . commodities:* prosperity makes us careless, and our greatest privations
prove to be our blessings. 23. *food:* object.

EDG. [*Aside*] And worse I may be yet. The worst is not
So long as we can say "This is the worst."
  OLD MAN. Fellow, where goest?
  GLO.   Is it a beggarman?   30
  OLD MAN. Madman and beggar too.
  GLO. He has some reason, else he could not beg.
I' the last night's storm I such a fellow saw,
Which made me think a man a worm. My son
Came then into my mind, and yet my mind   35
Was then scarce friends with him. I have heard more since.
As flies to wanton boys are we to the gods,
They kill us for their sport.
  EDG.   [*Aside*] How should this be?
Bad is the trade that must play fool to sorrow,
Angering itself and others. Bless thee, master!   40
  GLO. Is that the naked fellow?
  OLD MAN.   Aye, my lord.
  GLO. Then, prithee get thee gone. If for my sake
Thou wilt o'ertake us hence a mile or twain
I' the way toward Dover, do it for ancient love,
And bring some covering for this naked soul,   45
Who I'll entreat to lead me.
  OLD MAN.   Alack, sir, he is mad.
  GLO. 'Tis the times' plague when madmen lead the blind.
Do as I bid thee, or rather do thy pleasure.
Above the rest, be gone.
  OLD MAN. I'll bring him the best 'parel that I have,   50
Come on 't what will.   [*Exit.*
  GLO. Sirrah, naked fellow——
  EDG. Poor Tom's a-cold. [*Aside*] I cannot daub it further.
  GLO. Come hither, fellow.   54
  EDG. [*Aside*] And yet I must.—Bless thy sweet eyes, they bleed.
  GLO. Know'st thou the way to Dover?
  EDG. Both stile and gate, horseway and footpath. Poor Tom hath
been scared out of his good wits. Bless thee, good man's son, from
the foul fiend! Five fiends have been in Poor Tom at once—of lust,
as Obidicut; Hobbididence, prince of dumbness; Mahu, of   [60
stealing; Modo, of murder; Flibbertigibbet, of mopping and mowing,
who since possesses chambermaids and waiting-women. So, bless
thee, master!

---

40. *Angering:* paining. 53. *daub:* cover up. 61. *mopping and mowing:*
making faces.

GLO. Here, take this purse, thou whom the heavens' plagues
Have humbled to all strokes. That I am wretched　　　　65
Makes thee the happier. Heavens, deal so still!
Let the superfluous and lust-dieted man,
That slaves your ordinance, that will not see
Because he doth not feel, feel your power quickly.
So distribution should undo excess　　　　70
And each man have enough. Dost thou know Dover?
　EDG. Aye, master.
　GLO. There is a cliff whose high and bending head
Looks fearfully in the confinèd deep.
Bring me but to the very brim of it,　　　　75
And I'll repair the misery thou dost bear
With something rich about me. From that place
I shall no leading need.
　EDG.　　　　　Give me thy arm.
Poor Tom shall lead thee.　　　　　[Exeunt.

SCENE II. Before the DUKE OF ALBANY's palace.

[Enter GONERIL and EDMUND.]

GON. Welcome, my lord. I marvel our mild husband
Not met us on the way.
　　　[Enter OSWALD.] Now, where's your master?
　OSW. Madam, within, but never man so changed.
I told him of the army that was landed.
He smiled at it. I told him you were coming.　　　　5
His answer was "The worse." Of Gloucester's treachery
And of the loyal service of his son
When I informed him, then he called me sot
And told me I had turned the wrong side out.
What most he should dislike seems pleasant to him,　　　　10
What like, offensive.
　GON. [To EDMUND] Then shall you go no further.
It is the cowish terror of his spirit,
That dares not undertake. He'll not feel wrongs
Which tie him to an answer. Our wishes on the way
May prove effects. Back, Edmund, to my brother.　　　　15

67. superfluous and lust-dieted man: the man who has more than he needs
and who feeds all his lusts or desires. 68. slaves your ordinance: makes a
slave of heaven's plan. 73. bending: overhanging.
　SC. II: 13. undertake: act. 14. tie: force. 15. prove effects: come true.

Hasten his musters and conduct his powers.
I must change arms at home and give the distaff
Into my husband's hands. This trusty servant
Shall pass between us. Ere long you are like to hear,
If you dare venture in your own behalf,   20
A mistress's command. Wear this. Spare speech.   [*Giving a favor.*
Decline your head. This kiss, if it durst speak,
Would stretch thy spirits up into the air.
Conceive, and fare thee well.

    EDM. Yours in the ranks of death.   25
    GON. My most dear Gloucester!   [*Exit* EDMUND.
Oh, the difference of man and man!
To thee a woman's services are due,
My fool ursurps my body.

    OSW.   Madam, here comes my lord.   [*Exit.*

[*Enter* ALBANY.]

    GON. I have been worth the whistle.
    ALB.   O Goneril!   30
You are not worth the dust which the rude wind
Blows in your face. I fear your disposition.
That nature which contemns it origin
Cannot be bordered certain in itself.
She that herself will sliver and disbranch   35
From her material sap, perforce must wither
And come to deadly use.

    GON. No more; the text is foolish.
    ALB. Wisdom and goodness to the vile seem vile.
Filths savor but themselves. What have you done?   40
Tigers, not daughters, what have you performed?
A father, and a gracious agèd man
Whose reverence even the head-lugged bear would lick,
Most barbarous, most degenerate, have you madded!
Could my good brother suffer you to do it?   45
A man, a prince, by him so benefited!
If that the heavens do not their visible spirits
Send quickly down to tame these vile offenses,
It will come,

---

17. *change arms:* exchange roles. 28. *fool:* husband. 33. *it origin:* its father.
34. *Cannot . . . itself:* has no inner discipline. 36. *material sap:* basic nour-
ishment. 38. *text: i.e.,* of the sermon. 45. *brother suffer:* Cornwall permit.

Humanity must perforce prey on itself,   50
Like monsters of the deep.
   GON.   Milk-livered man!
That bear'st a cheek for blows, a head for wrongs,
Who hast not in thy brows an eye discerning
Thine honor from thy suffering; that not know'st
Fools do those villains pity who are punished   55
Ere they have done their mischief. Where's thy drum?
France spreads his banners in our noiseless land,
With plumèd helm thy state begins to threat,
Whiles thou, a moral fool, sit'st still and criest
"Alack, why does he so?"
   ALB.   See thyself, devil!   60
Proper deformity seems not in the fiend
So horrid as in woman.
   GON.   O vain fool!
   ALB. Thou changèd and self-covered thing, for shame,
Bemonster not thy feature. Were 't my fitness
To let these hands obey my blood,   65
They are apt enough to dislocate and tear
Thy flesh and bones. Howe'er thou art a fiend,
A woman's shape doth shield thee.
   GON. Marry, your manhood! Mew!

[Enter a MESSENGER.]

   ALB. What news?   70
   MESS. O my good lord, the Duke of Cornwall's dead,
Slain by his servant, going to put out
The other eye of Gloucester.
   ALB.   Gloucester's eyes!
   MESS. A servant that he bred, thrilled with remorse,
Opposed against the act, bending his sword   75
To his great master, who thereat enraged
Flew on him and amongst them felled him dead,
But not without that harmful stroke which since
Hath plucked him after.
   ALB.   This shows you are above,

53-4. *Who . . . suffering:* Who cannot distinguish necessary suffering from insults that dishonor you. 55-6. *Fools . . . mischief:* only fools object to preventive punishment. 59. *moral:* weakly moralizing. 61. *Proper:* characteristically diabolical. 63. *self-covered:* true self hidden. 64. *my fitness:* proper for me. 65. *blood:* angry impulse. 74. *thrilled with remorse:* moved with pity.

You justicers, that these our nether crimes   80
So speedily can venge. But, oh, poor Gloucester!
Lost he his other eye?
   MESS.   Both, both, my lord.
This letter, madam, craves a speedy answer.
'Tis from your sister.
   GON.   [*Aside*] One way I like this well;
But being widow, and my Gloucester with her,   85
May all the building in my fancy pluck
Upon my hateful life. Another way,
The news is not so tart.—I'll read, and answer.   [*Exit.*
   ALB. Where was his son when they did take his eyes?
   MESS. Come with my lady hither.
   ALB.   He is not here.   90
   MESS. No, my good lord, I met him back again.
   ALB. Knows he the wickedness?
   MESS. Aye, my good lord, 'twas he informed against him,
And quit the house on purpose, that their punishment
Might have the freer course.
   ALB.   Gloucester, I live   95
To thank thee for the love thou show'dst the King,
And to revenge thine eyes. Come hither, friend.
Tell me what more thou know'st.   [*Exeunt.*

SCENE III. *The French camp near Dover.*

[*Enter* KENT *and a* GENTLEMAN.]

   KENT. Why the King of France is so suddenly gone back know you
the reason?
   GENT. Something he left imperfect in the state which since his com-
ing-forth is thought of, which imports to the kingdom so much fear
and danger that his personal return was most required and necessary.
   KENT. Who hath he left behind him general?   6
   GENT. The Marshal of France, Monsieur La Far.
   KENT. Did your letters pierce the Queen to any demonstration of
grief?
   GENT. Aye, sir. She took them, read them in my presence,   10
And now and then an ample tear trilled down
Her delicate cheek. It seemed she was a queen

---

80. *nether:* lower, earthly. 86. *building . . . pluck:* dreams about Edmund
pull down.

Over her passion, who most rebel-like
Sought to be king o'er her.

KENT.	Oh, then it moved her.

GENT. Not to a rage. Patience and sorrow strove	15
Who should express her goodliest. You have seen
Sunshine and rain at once. Her smiles and tears
Were like a better way. Those happy smilets
That played on her ripe lip seemed not to know
What guests were in her eyes, which parted thence	20
As pearls from diamonds dropped. In brief,
Sorrow would be a rarity most beloved
If all could so become it.

KENT.	Made she no verbal question?

GENT. Faith, once or twice she heaved the name of "father"
Pantingly forth, as if it pressed her heart;	25
Cried "Sisters! Sisters! Shame of ladies! Sisters!
Kent! Father! Sisters! What, i' the storm? i' the night?
Let pity not be believed!" There she shook
The holy water from her heavenly eyes,
And clamor moistened. Then away she started	30
To deal with grief alone.

KENT.	It is the stars,
The stars above us, govern our conditions;
Else one self mate and mate could not beget
Such different issues. You spoke not with her since?

GENT. No.	35

KENT. Was this before the King returned?

GENT.	No, since.

KENT. Well, sir, the poor distressèd Lear's i' the town,
Who sometime in his better tune remembers
What we are come about, and by no means
Will yield to see his daughter.

GENT.	Why, good sir?	40

KENT. A sovereign shame so elbows him. His own unkindness
That stripped her from his benediction, turned her
To foreign casualties, gave her dear rights
To his doghearted daughters. These things sting
His mind so venomously that burning shame	45
Detains him from Cordelia.

GENT.	Alack, poor gentleman!

KENT. Of Albany's and Cornwall's powers you heard not?

SC. III: 13. *passion:* emotion. 18. *a better way:* only more beautiful. 32. *conditions:* characters. 33. *self:* same. 34. *issues:* children. 41. *sovereign:* overwhelming; *elbows:* attends. 43. *casualties:* hazards.

GENT. 'Tis so, they are afoot.

KENT. Well, sir, I'll bring you to our master Lear,
And leave you to attend him. Some dear cause   50
Will in concealment wrap me up awhile.
When I am known aright, you shall not grieve
Lending me this acquaintance. I pray you, go
Along with me.   [*Exeunt.*

SCENE IV. *The same. A tent.*

[*Enter, with drum and colors,* CORDELIA, DOCTOR, *and* SOLDIERS.]

COR. Alack, 'tis he. Why, he was met even now
As mad as the vexed sea, singing aloud,
Crowned with rank fumiter and furrow weeds,
With burdocks, hemlock, nettles, cuckoo flowers,
Darnel, and all the idle weeds that grow   5
In our sustaining corn. A century send forth.
Search every acre in the high-grown field,
And bring him to our eye. [*Exit an* OFFICER.] What can man's
      wisdom
In the restoring his bereavèd sense?
He that helps him take all my outward worth.   10

DOCT. There is means, madam.
Our foster nurse of nature is repose,
The which he lacks. That to provoke in him
Are many simples operative, whose power
Will close the eye of anguish.

COR.   All blest secrets,   15
All you unpublished virtues of the earth,
Spring with my tears! Be aidant and remediate
In the good man's distress! Seek, seek for him,
Lest his ungoverned rage dissolve the life
That wants the means to lead it.

[*Enter a* MESSENGER.]

MESS.   News, madam.   20
The British powers are marching hitherward.

COR. 'Tis known before; our preparation stands
In expectation of them. O dear father,

---

sc. IV: 6. *sustaining corn:* food-giving grain; *century:* a hundred soldiers.
10. *outward worth:* material wealth. 13. *provoke:* induce. 14. *simples
operative:* effective herbs. 17. *aidant and remediate:* helpful and remedial.

It is thy business that I go about;
Therefore great France　　　　　　　　　　　　25
My mourning and important tears hath pitied.
No blown ambition doth our arms incite,
But love, dear love, and our aged father's right.
Soon may I hear and see him!　　　　　　　　[*Exeunt.*

SCENE V. GLOUCESTER'S *castle.*

[*Enter* REGAN *and* OSWALD.]

REG. But are my brother's powers set forth?
OSW.　　　　　　　　　　　　　　Aye, madam.
REG. Himself in person there?
OSW.　　　　　　　　　Madam, with much ado.
Your sister is the better soldier.
　REG. Lord Edmund spake not with your lord at home?
OSW. No, madam.　　　　　　　　　　　　　5
REG. What might import my sister's letter to him?
OSW. I know not, lady.
　REG. Faith, he is posted hence on serious matter.
It was great ignorance, Gloucester's eyes being out,
To let him live. Where he arrives he moves　　　10
All hearts against us. Edmund, I think, is gone,
In pity of his misery, to dispatch
His nighted life; moreover to descry
The strength o' the enemy.
　OSW. I must needs after him, madam, with my letter.　15
　REG. Our troops set forth tomorrow. Stay with us;
The ways are dangerous.
　OSW.　　　　　　　I may not, madam.
My lady charged my duty in this business.
　REG. Why should she write to Edmund? Might not you
Transport her purposes by word? Belike,　　　20
Something—I know not what—— I'll love thee much;
Let me unseal the letter.
　OSW.　　　　　　Madam, I had rather——
　REG. I know your lady does not love her husband;
I am sure of that. And at her late being here
She gave strange œillades and most speaking looks　25
To noble Edmund. I know you are of her bosom.

---

26. *important:* importunate. 27. *blown:* inflated.
　SC. V: 9. *ignorance:* lack of foresight. 18. *my duty:* me to be dutiful. 25.
œillades: come-hither glances. 26. *of her bosom:* in her confidence.

osw. I, madam?

reg. I speak in understanding. You are, I know 't.
Therefore I do advise you, take this note.
My lord is dead; Edmund and I have talked,   30
And more convenient is he for my hand
Than for your lady's. You may gather more.
If you do find him, pray you give him this,
And when your mistress hears thus much from you,
I pray desire her call her wisdom to her.   35
So, fare you well.
If you do chance to hear of that blind traitor,
Preferment falls on him that cuts him off.

osw. Would I could meet him, madam! I should show   39
What party I do follow.

reg.   Fare thee well.   [Exeunt.

SCENE VI. *Fields near Dover.*

[*Enter* GLOUCESTER, *and* EDGAR *dressed like a peasant.*]

glo. When shall we come to the top of that same hill?
edg. You do climb up it now. Look how we labor.
glo. Methinks the ground is even.
edg.   Horrible steep.
Hark, do you hear the sea?
glo.   No, truly.
edg. Why then your other senses grow imperfect   5
By your eyes' anguish.
glo.   So may it be, indeed.
Methinks thy voice is altered, and thou speak'st
In better phrase and matter than thou didst.
edg. You're much deceived. In nothing am I changed
But in my garments.
glo.   Methinks you're better-spoken.   10
edg. Come on, sir, here's the place. Stand still. How fearful
And dizzy 'tis to cast one's eyes so low!
The crows and choughs that wing the midway air
Show scarce so gross as beetles. Halfway down
Hangs one that gathers samphire, dreadful trade!   15
Methinks he seems no bigger than his head.
The fishermen that walk upon the beach

---

29. *take this note:* mark this. 38. *Preferment:* advancement.
  sc. vi: 14. *gross:* large. 15. *samphire:* aromatic herb.

Appear like mice, and yond tall anchoring bark
Diminished to her cock—her cock, a buoy
Almost too small for sight. The murmuring surge   20
That on the unnumbered idle pebbles chafes
Cannot be heard so high. I'll look no more,
Lest my brain turn and the deficient sight
Topple down headlong.
    GLO.   Set me where you stand.
    EDG. Give me your hand. You are now within a foot   25
Of the extreme verge. For all beneath the moon
Would I not leap upright.
    GLO.   Let go my hand.
Here, friend, 's another purse; in it a jewel
Well worth a poor man's taking. Fairies and gods
Prosper it with thee! Go thou further off.   30
Bid me farewell, and let me hear thee going.
    EDG. Now fare you well, good sir.
    GLO.   With all my heart.
    EDG. Why I do trifle thus with his despair
Is done to cure it.
    GLO. [*Kneeling*] O you mighty gods!
This world I do renounce, and in your sights   35
Shake patiently my great affliction off.
If I could bear it longer and not fall
To quarrel with your great opposeless wills,
My snuff and loathèd part of nature should
Burn itself out. If Edgar live, oh, bless him!   40
Now, fellow, fare thee well.   [*He falls forward.*
    EDG.   Gone, sir. Farewell.
And yet I know not how conceit may rob
The treasury of life when life itself
Yields to the theft. Had he been where he thought,
By this had thought been past. Alive or dead?   45
Ho, you sir! Friend! Hear you, sir! Speak!
Thus might he pass indeed. Yet he revives.
What are you, sir?
    GLO.   Away, and let me die.
    EDG. Hadst thou been aught but gossamer, feathers, air,
So many fathom down precipitating,   50
Thou'dst shivered like an egg. But thou dost breathe,
Hast heavy substance, bleed'st not, speak'st, art sound.

18-9. *bark . . . cock:* ship reduced to the size of her small-boat. 39. *snuff:*
candle stub. 42. *conceit:* imagination. 47. *pass:* die.

Ten masts at each make not the altitude
Which thou hast perpendicularly fell.
Thy life's a miracle. Speak yet again.   55
  GLO. But have I fall'n, or no?
  EDG. From the dread summit of this chalky bourn.
Look up a-height; the shrill-gorged lark so far
Cannot be seen or heard. Do but look up.
  GLO. Alack, I have no eyes.   60
Is wretchedness deprived that benefit,
To end itself by death? 'Twas yet some comfort
When misery could beguile the tyrant's rage
And frustrate his proud will.
  EDG.   Give me your arm.
Up, so. How is 't? Feel you your legs? You stand.   65
  GLO. Too well, too well.
  EDG.   This is above all strangeness.
Upon the crown o' the cliff, what thing was that
Which parted from you?
  GLO.   A poor unfortunate beggar.
  EDG. As I stood here below, methought his eyes
Were two full moons, he had a thousand noses,   70
Horns whelked and waved like the enridgèd sea.
It was some fiend; therefore, thou happy father,
Think that the clearest gods, who make them honors
Of men's impossibilities, have preserved thee.
  GLO. I do remember now. Henceforth I'll bear   75
Affliction till it do cry out itself
"Enough, enough," and die. That thing you speak of,
I took it for a man. Often 'twould say
"The fiend, the fiend." He led me to that place.
  EDG. Bear free and patient thoughts. But who comes here?   80

    [*Enter* LEAR, *fantastically dressed with wild flowers.*]

The safer sense will n'er accommodate
His master thus.
  LEAR. No; they cannot touch me for coining; I am the King himself.
  EDG. O thou side-piercing sight!   84

---

53. *at each:* end to end. 57. *bourn:* boundary cliff. 58. *shrill-gorged:* shrill-
throated. 63. *beguile:* cheat (by suicide) 71. *whelked:* protuberant. 73.
clearest: divinest. 74. *men's impossibilities:* miracles. 80. *free:* cheerful.
81-2. *The . . . thus:* a sane man would never dress in this way. 83. *touch:*
convict; *coining:* making coins.

LEAR. Nature's above art in that respect. There's your press money. That fellow handles his bow like a crowkeeper; draw me a clothier's yard. Look, look, a mouse! Peace, peace, this piece of toasted cheese will do 't. There's my gauntlet; I'll prove it on a giant. Bring up the brown bills. Oh, well-flown bird! I' the clout, i' the clout. Hewgh! Give the word.   90

EDG. Sweet marjoram.

LEAR. Pass.

GLO. I know that voice.

LEAR. Ha! Goneril, with a white beard! They flattered me like a dog, and told me I had white hairs in my beard ere the black   [95 ones were there. To say "aye" and "no" to everything that I said! "Aye" and "no" too was no good divinity. When the rain came to wet me once and the wind to make me chatter, when the thunder would not peace at my bidding, there I found 'em, there I smelt 'em out. Go to, they are not men o' their words. They told me I was everything. 'Tis a lie, I am not ague-proof.   101

GLO. The trick of that voice I do well remember.
Is 't not the King?

LEAR.   Aye, every inch a king.
When I do stare, see how the subject quakes.
I pardon that man's life. What was thy cause?   105
Adultery?
Thou shalt not die. Die for adultery! No.
The wren goes to 't, and the small gilded fly
Does lecher in my sight.
Let copulation thrive, for Gloucester's bastard son   110
Was kinder to his father than my daughters
Got 'tween the lawful sheets.
To 't, luxury, pell-mell! For I lack soldiers.
Behold yond simpering dame,
Whose face between her forks presages snow,   115
That minces virtue and does shake the head
To hear of pleasure's name.
The fitchew, nor the soilèd horse, goes to 't
With a more riotous appetite.

---

85. *Nature's above art:* a king's natural rights are beyond the law; *press money:* money for being drafted or impressed as a soldier. 86. *crowkeeper:* one who keeps (scares) away the crows. 87. *clothier's yard:* yard-long arrow. 88. *gauntlet:* token of challenge; *prove:* make it good. 89. *brown bills:* weapons painted brown and used by infantry; *bird:* arrow. 90. *clout:* bullseye. 113. *luxury:* lust. 115. *forks:* legs; *snow:* chastity. 118. *fitchew:* skunk; *soilèd:* well fed on grass in the spring.

Down from the waist they are Centaurs,   120
Though women all above.
But to the girdle do the gods inherit,
Beneath is all the fiends'.
There's hell, there's darkness, there's the sulphurous pit,
Burning, scalding, stench, consumption, fie, fie, fie!   125
Pah, pah! Give me an ounce of civet, good apothecary, to sweeten my
imagination. There's money for thee.
   GLO. Oh, let me kiss that hand!
   LEAR. Let me wipe it first; it smells of mortality.
   GLO. O ruined piece of nature! This great world   130
Shall so wear out to naught. Dost thou know me?
   LEAR. I remember thine eyes well enough. Dost thou squiny at me?
No, do thy worst, blind Cupid; I'll not love. Read thou this challenge,
mark but the penning on 't.
   GLO. Were all the letters suns, I could not see one.   135
   EDG. I would not take this from report. It is,
And my heart breaks at it.
   LEAR. Read.
   GLO. What, with the case of eyes?   139
   LEAR. Oh ho, are you there with me? No eyes in your head, nor
no money in your purse? Your eyes are in a heavy case, your purse
in a light. Yet you see how this world goes.
   GLO. I see it feelingly.
   LEAR. What, art mad? A man may see how this world goes with no
eyes. Look with thine ears. See how yond Justice rails upon   [145
yond simple thief. Hark, in thine ear. Change places and, handy-
dandy, which is the Justice, which is the thief? Thou hast seen a
farmer's dog bark at a beggar?
   GLO. Aye, sir.   149
   LEAR. And the creature run from the cur? There thou mightst
behold the great image of authority.
A dog's obeyed in office.
Thou rascal beadle, hold thy bloody hand!
Why dost thou lash that whore? Strip thine own back.
Thou hotly lust'st to use her in that kind   155
For which thou whip'st her. The usurer hangs the cozener.
Through tattered clothes small vices do appear;

---

120. *Centaurs:* lustful creatures, half man and half horse. 126. *civet:* perfume. 132. *squiny:* look sideways. 133. *blind Cupid:* prostitute; the sign
over a brothel. 141. *case:* sockets. 153. *beadle:* officer. 156. *cozener:* crook.

Robes and furred gowns hide all. Plate sin with gold
And the strong lance of justice hurtless breaks.
Arm it in rags, a pigmy's straw does pierce it.   160
None does offend, none, I say, none, I'll able 'em.
Take that of me, my friend, who have the power
To seal the accuser's lips. Get thee glass eyes
And, like a scurvy politician, seem
To see the things thou dost not.   165
Now, now, now, now. Pull off my boots. Harder, harder. So.
    EDG. Oh, matter and impertinency mixed!
Reason in madness!
    LEAR. If thou wilt weep my fortunes, take my eyes.
I know thee well enough. Thy name is Gloucester.   170
Thou must be patient; we came crying hither.
Thou know'st the first time that we smell the air,
We wawl and cry. I will preach to thee. Mark.
    GLO. Alack, alack the day!
    LEAR. When we are born, we cry that we are come   175
To this great stage of fools. This 's a good block.
It were a delicate stratagem to shoe
A troop of horse with felt. I'll put 't in proof,
And when I have stol'n upon these sons-in-law,
Then, kill, kill, kill, kill, kill, kill!   180

        [*Enter a* GENTLEMAN, *with* ATTENDANTS.]

    GENT. Oh, here he is. Lay hand upon him. Sir,
Your most dear daughter——
    LEAR. No rescue? What, a prisoner? I am even
The natural fool of fortune. Use me well;
You shall have ransom. Let me have a surgeon;   185
I am cut to the brains.
    GENT.   You shall have anything.
    LEAR. No seconds? All myself?
Why, this would make a man a man of salt,
To use his eyes for garden waterpots,
Aye, and laying autumn's dust.   190
    GENT. Good sir——
    LEAR. I will die bravely, like a smug bridegroom. What!

---

161. *able:* give free authority to. 163. *glass eyes:* spectacles. 167. *matter and impertinency:* sense and nonsense. 176. *block:* hat, or mold over which felt is formed. 178. *in proof:* to the test. 184. *natural:* born. 188. *salt:* tears. 192. *die:* a pun (sexual intercourse); *bravely:* in style; *smug:* smooth.

I will be jovial. Come, come, I am a king,
My masters, know you that.
   GENT. You are a royal one, and we obey you.   195
   LEAR. Then there's life in 't. Nay, an you get it, you shall get it by
running. Sa, sa, sa, sa.   [*Exit running.* ATTENDANTS *follow.*
   GENT. A sight most pitiful in the meanest wretch,
Past speaking of in a king! Thou hast one daughter
Who redeems nature from the general curse   200
Which twain have brought her to.
   EDG. Hail, gentle sir.
   GENT.   Sir, speed you. What's your will?
   EDG. Do you hear aught, sir, of a battle toward?
   GENT. Most sure and vulgar. Everyone hears that
Which can distinguish sound.
   EDG.   But, by your favor,   205
How near's the other army?
   GENT. Near and on speedy foot; the main descry
Stands on the hourly thought.
   EDG.   I thank you, sir. That's all.
   GENT. Though that the Queen on special cause is here,   209
Her army is moved on.
   EDG.   I thank you, sir.   [*Exit* GENTLEMAN
   GLO. You ever-gentle gods, take my breath from me.
Let not my worser spirit tempt me again
To die before you please!
   EDG.   Well pray you, father.
   GLO. Now, good sir, what are you?
   EDG. A most poor man, made tame to fortune's blows,   **215**
Who, by the art of known and feeling sorrows,
Am pregnant to good pity. Give me your hand.
I'll lead you to some biding.
   GLO.   Hearty thanks.
The bounty and the benison of heaven
To boot, and boot!

[*Enter* OSWALD.]

   OSW.   A proclaimed prize! Most happy!   **220**
That eyeless head of thine was first framed flesh
To raise my fortunes. Thou old unhappy traitor,

---

203. *toward:* at hand. 204. *vulgar:* commonly known. 207-08. *main . . .
thought:* main body of troops will be in sight soon. 217. *pregnant to:* able
to conceive. 218. *biding:* resting. 219. *benison:* blessing.

Briefly thyself remember. The sword is out
That must destroy thee.
    GLO.   Now let thy friendly hand
Put strength enough to 't.   [EDGAR *interposes*.
    OSW.   Wherefore, bold peasant,   225
Darest thou support a published traitor? Hence,
Lest that the infection of his fortune take
Like hold on thee! Let go his arm.
    EDG. Chill not let go, zir, without vurther 'casion.
    OSW. Let go, slave, or thou diest!   230
    EDG. Good gentleman, go your gait, and let poor volk pass. An
chud ha' been zwaggered out of my life, 'twould not ha' been zo long
as 'tis by a vortnight. Nay, come not near th' old man; keep out, che
vor ye, or I'se try whether your costard or my ballow be the harder.
Chill be plain with you.   235
    OSW. Out, dunghill!   [*They fight*.
    EDG. Chill pick your teeth, zir. Come, no matter vor your foins.
                                  [OSWALD *falls*.
    OSW. Slave, thou hast slain me. Villain, take my purse.
If ever thou wilt thrive, bury my body,
And give the letters which thou find'st about me   240
To Edmund Earl of Gloucester. Seek him out
Upon the British party. Oh, untimely death!
Death!   [*Dies*.
    EDG. I know thee well—a serviceable villain,
As duteous to the vices of thy mistress   245
As badness would desire.
    GLO.   What, is he dead?
    EDG. Sit you down, father, rest you.
Let's see these pockets. The letters that he speaks of
May be my friends. He's dead. I am only sorry
He had no other deathsman. Let us see.   250
Leave, gentle wax, and, manners, blame us not.
To know our enemies' minds, we'd rip their hearts;
Their papers is more lawful.   [*Reads*.
    "Let our reciprocal vows be remembered. You have many oppor-
tunities to cut him off. If your will want not, time and place   [255
will be fruitfully offered. There is nothing done if he return the con-
queror. Then am I the prisoner, and his bed my jail; from the loathed

---

223. *thyself remember*: examine yourself in preparation for death. 229.
Chill: I'll. 233-4. *che vor ye*: I warn you. 234. *costard*: apple (head); *ballow*: staff. 237. *foins*: sword thrusts. 251. *Leave*: permit me.

warmth whereof deliver me, and supply the place for your labor.
  "Your—wife, so I would say—affectionate servant,   GONERIL."
Oh, undistinguished space of woman's will!   260
A plot upon her virtuous husband's life,
And the exchange my brother! Here, in the sands,
Thee I'll rake up, the post unsanctified
Of murderous lechers, and in the mature time
With this ungracious paper strike the sight   265
Of the death-practiced Duke. For him 'tis well
That of thy death and business I can tell.
  GLO. The King is mad. How stiff is my vile sense,
That I stand up, and have ingenious feeling
Of my huge sorrows! Better I were distract.   270
So should my thoughts be severed from my griefs,
And woes by wrong imaginations lose
The knowledge of themselves.   [*Drum afar off.*
    EDG.   Give me your hand.
Far off methinks I hear the beaten drum.   274
Come, father, I'll bestow you with a friend.   [*Exeunt.*

SCENE VII. *A tent in the French camp.* LEAR *on a bed asleep,
    soft music playing,* GENTLEMAN, *and others attending.*

        [*Enter* CORDELIA, KENT, *and* DOCTOR.]
  COR. O thou good Kent, how shall I live and work,
To match thy goodness? My life will be too short,
And every measure fail me.
  KENT. To be acknowledged, madam, is o'erpaid.
All my reports go with the modest truth,   5
Nor more nor clipped, but so.
    COR.   Be better suited.
These weeds are memories of those worser hours.
I prithee put them off.
    KENT.   Pardon me, dear madam;
Yet to be known shortens my made intent.
My boon I make it that you know me not   10
Till time and I think meet.

---

260. *undistinguished space:* boundless extent; *will:* desires. 263. *rake up:*
bury. 266. *death-practiced:* whose death is plotted. 268. *stiff:* stubbornly
strong; *sense:* reason. 269. *ingenious feeling:* consciousness. 270. *distract:*
insane.
  SC. VII: 7. *weeds:* clothes. 9. *Yet . . . intent:* to be recognized now makes
me fall short of my goal. 10. *boon:* favor.

COR. Then be 't so, my good lord. [*To the* DOCTOR] How does the
    King?
DOCT. Madam, sleeps still.
COR. O you kind gods,
Cure this great breach in his abusèd nature!   15
The untuned and jarring senses, oh, wind up
Of this child-changèd father!
DOCT.   So please your Majesty
That we may wake the King. He hath slept long.
COR. Be governed by your knowledge, and proceed
I' the sway of your own will. Is he arrayed?   20
GENT. Aye, madam. In the heaviness of his sleep
We put fresh garments on him.
DOCT. Be by, good madam, when we do awake him.
I doubt not of his temperance.
COR.   Very well.
DOCT. Please you, draw near. Louder the music there!   25
COR. O my dear father! Restoration hang
Thy medicine on my lips, and let this kiss
Repair those violent harms that my two sisters
Have in thy reverence made!
KENT.   Kind and dear Princess!
COR. Had you not been their father, these white flakes   30
Had challenged pity of them. Was this a face
To be opposed against the warring winds?
To stand against the deep dread-bolted thunder?
In the most terrible and nimble stroke
Of quick, cross lightning? To watch—poor perdu!—   35
With this thin helm? Mine enemy's dog,
Though he had bit me, should have stood that night
Against my fire; and wast thou fain, poor father,
To hovel thee with swine and rogues forlorn
In short and musty straw? Alack, alack!   40
'Tis wonder that thy life and wits at once
Had not concluded all. He wakes. Speak to him.
DOCT. Madam, do you, 'tis fittest.
COR. How does my royal lord? How fares your Majesty?
LEAR. You do me wrong to take me out o' the grave.   45
Thou art a soul in bliss, but I am bound
Upon a wheel of fire that mine own tears
Do scald like molten lead.

---

24. *temperance:* sanity. 35. *cross:* forked; *perdu:* exposed sentinel. 46. *bliss:*
heaven. 47. *that:* so that.

COR.   Sir, do you know me?
LEAR. You are a spirit, I know. When did you die?
COR. Still, still far wide!   50
DOCT. He's scarce awake. Let him alone awhile.
LEAR. Where have I been? Where am I? Fair daylight?
I am mightily abused. I should e'en die with pity
To see another thus. I know not what to say.
I will not swear these are my hands. Let's see,   55
I feel this pin prick. Would I were assured
Of my condition!
COR.   Oh, look upon me, sir,
And hold your hands in benediction o'er me.
No, sir, you must not kneel.
LEAR.   Pray do not mock me.
I am a very foolish fond old man,   60
Fourscore and upward, not an hour more nor less,
And, to deal plainly,
I fear I am not in my perfect mind.
Methinks I should know you and know this man,
Yet I am doubtful, for I am mainly ignorant   65
What place this is; and all the skill I have
Remembers not these garments, nor I know not
Where I did lodge last night. Do not laugh at me,
For, as I am a man, I think this lady
To be my child Cordelia.
COR.   And so I am, I am.   70
LEAR. Be your tears wet? Yes, faith. I pray weep not.
If you have poison for me, I will drink it.
I know you do not love me, for your sisters
Have, as I do remember, done me wrong.
You have some cause, they have not.
COR.   No cause, no cause.   75
LEAR. Am I in France?
KENT.   In your own kingdom, sir.
LEAR. Do not abuse me.
DOCT. Be comforted, good madam. The great rage,
You see, is killed in him. And yet it is danger
To make him even o'er the time he has lost.   80
Desire him to go in; trouble him no more
Till further settling.
COR. Will 't please your Highness walk?

---

80. *even o'er:* piece together.

LEAR.   You must bear with me.
Pray you now, forget and forgive. I am old and foolish.

      [Exeunt all but KENT *and* GENTLEMAN.

GENT. Holds it true, sir, that the Duke of Cornwall was so slain?
KENT. Most certain, sir.   86
GENT. Who is conductor of his people?
KENT. As 'tis said, the bastard son of Gloucester.
GENT. They say Edgar, his banished son, is with the Earl of Kent
in Germany.   90
KENT. Report is changeable. 'Tis time to look about. The powers
of the kingdom approach apace.
GENT. The arbitrament is like to be bloody. Fare you well, sir.

                 [Exit.

KENT. My point and period will be throughly wrought,   94
Or well or ill, as this day's battle's fought.   *[Exit.*

Act V

SCENE I. *The British camp near Dover.*

[Enter, with drum and colors, EDMUND, REGAN,
GENTLEMEN, *and* SOLDIERS.]

EDM. Know of the Duke if his last purpose hold,
Or whether since he is advised by aught
To change the course. He's full of alteration
And self-reproving. Bring his constant pleasure.

      [To a GENTLEMAN, *who goes out.*

REG. Our sister's man is certainly miscarried.   5
EDM. 'Tis to be doubted, madam.
REG.   Now, sweet lord,
You know the goodness I intend upon you.
Tell me, but truly, but then speak the truth,
Do you not love my sister?
EDM.   In honored love.
REG. But have you never found my brother's way   10
To the forfended place?
EDM.   That thought abuses you.

---

91. *Report is changeable:* rumors vary; *powers:* soldiers. 93. *arbitrament:*
decisive battle. 94. *My . . . wrought:* my fate will be conclusively decided.
 ACT V, SC. I: 1. *Know:* learn. 4. *constant pleasure:* final desire. 6. *doubted:*
feared. 11. *forfended:* forbidden; *abuses:* deceives.

REG. I am doubtful that you have been conjunct
And bosomed with her, as far as we call hers.
   EDM. No, by mine honor, madam.
   REG. I never shall endure her. Dear my lord,   15
Be not familiar with her.
   EDM.   Fear me not.—
She and the Duke her husband!

   [*Enter, with drum and colors,* ALBANY, GONERIL, *and* SOLDIERS.]

   GON. [*Aside*] I had rather lose the battle than that sister
Should loosen him and me.
   ALB. Our very loving sister, well bemet.   20
Sir, this I hear: The King is come to his daughter,
With others whom the rigor of our state
Forced to cry out. Where I could not be honest,
I never yet was valiant. For this business,
It toucheth us, as France invades our land,   25
Not bolds the King, with others, whom I fear
Most just and heavy causes make oppose.
   EDM. Sir, you speak nobly.
   REG.   Why is this reasoned?
   GON. Combine together 'gainst the enemy,
For these domestic and particular broils   30
Are not the question here.
   ALB.   Let's then determine
With the ancient of war on our proceedings.
   EDM. I shall attend you presently at your tent.
   REG. Sister, you'll go with us?
   GON. No.   35
   REG. 'Tis most convenient. Pray you go with us.
   GON. [*Aside*] Oh ho, I know the riddle.—I will go.
             [*As they are going out, enter* EDGAR *disguised.*
   EDG. If e'er your Grace had speech with man so poor,
Hear me one word.
   ALB.   I'll overtake you. Speak.
            [*Exeunt all but* ALBANY *and* EDGAR.
   EDG. Before you fight the battle, ope this letter.   40
If you have victory, let the trumpet sound

---

12. *doubtful:* suspicious. 13. *as . . . hers:* all the way. 22. *state:* rule. 23.
cry out: protest. 26. *bolds:* encourages. 27. *make oppose:* make them opposed to us. 28. *Why . . . reasoned:* Why discuss the reasons. 30. *domestic
and particular broils:* family and personal quarrels. 32. *ancient of war:*
veteran officers.

For him that brought it. Wretched though I seem,
I can produce a champion that will prove
What is avouchèd there. If you miscarry,
Your business of the world hath so an end,   45
And machination ceases. Fortune love you!
    ALB. Stay till I have read the letter.
    EDG.   I was forbid it.
When time shall serve, let but the herald cry
And I'll appear again.   49
    ALB. Why, fare thee well. I will o'erlook thy paper.   [*Exit* EDGAR.

[Re-enter EDMUND.]

    EDM. The enemy's in view. Draw up your powers.
Here is the guess of their true strength and forces
By diligent discovery, but your haste
Is now urged on you.
    ALB.   We will greet the time.   [*Exit.*
    EDM. To both these sisters have I sworn my love,   55
Each jealous of the other, as the stung
Are of the adder. Which of them shall I take?
Both? One? Or neither? Neither can be enjoyed
If both remain alive. To take the widow
Exasperates, makes mad her sister Goneril,   60
And hardly shall I carry out my side,
Her husband being alive. Now then we'll use
His countenance for the battle, which being done,
Let her who would be rid of him devise
His speedy taking-off. As for the mercy   65
Which he intends to Lear and to Cordelia,
The battle done, and they within our power,
Shall never see his pardon, for my state
Stands on me to defend, not to debate.   [*Exit.*

SCENE II. *A field between the two camps.*

[Alarum within. Enter, with drum and colors, LEAR, CORDELIA,
and SOLDIERS, *over the stage; and exeunt. Enter* EDGAR
and GLOUCESTER.]

    EDG. Here, father, take the shadow of this tree
For your good host. Pray that the right may thrive.
If ever I return to you again,

---

56. *jealous:* wary. 63. *countenance:* help.

I'll bring you comfort.

GLO.   Grace go with you, sir!   [*Exit* EDGAR.

[*Alarum and retreat within. Re-enter* EDGAR.]

EDG. Away, old man. Give me thy hand, away!   5
King Lear hath lost, he and his daughter ta'en.
Give me thy hand, come on.

GLO. No farther, sir. A man may rot even here.

EDG. What, in ill thoughts again? Men must endure
Their going hence, even as their coming hither.   10
Ripeness is all. Come on.

GLO.   And that's true too.   [*Exeunt.*

SCENE III. *The British camp near Dover.*

[*Enter, in conquest, with drum and colors,* EDMUND; LEAR *and*
CORDELIA, *as prisoners;* CAPTAIN, SOLDIERS, *etc.*]

EDM. Some officers take them away. Good guard,
Until their greater pleasures first be known
That are to censure them.

COR.   We are not the first
Who with best meaning have incurred the worst.
For thee, oppressèd King, am I cast down.   5
Myself could else outfrown false fortune's frown.
Shall we not see these daughters and these sisters?

LEAR. No, no, no, no! Come, let's away to prison.
We two alone will sing like birds i' the cage.
When thou dost ask me blessing, I'll kneel down   10
And ask of thee forgiveness. So we'll live,
And pray, and sing, and tell old tales, and laugh
At gilded butterflies, and hear poor rogues
Talk of court news. And we'll talk with them too,
Who loses and who wins, who's in, who's out,   15
And take upon 's the mystery of things
As if we were God's spies. And we'll wear out,
In a walled prison, packs and sects of great ones
That ebb and flow by the moon.

EDM.   Take them away.

LEAR. Upon such sacrifices, my Cordelia,   20
The gods themselves throw incense. Have I caught thee?

SC. III: 2. *greater pleasures:* desires of my superiors. 3. *censure:* judge.
13. *gilded butterflies:* people at court.

He that parts us shall bring a brand from Heaven,
And fire us hence like foxes. Wipe thine eyes.
The goodyears shall devour them, flesh and fell,
Ere they shall make us weep. We'll see 'em starve first.   25
Come.   [*Exeunt* LEAR *and* CORDELIA, *guarded.*
     EDM. Come hither, captain, hark.
Take thou this note. Go follow them to prison.
One step I have advanced thee. If thou dost
As this instructs thee, thou dost make thy way
To noble fortunes. Know thou this, that men   30
Are as the time is. To be tender-minded
Does not become a sword. Thy great employment
Will not bear question. Either say thou'lt do 't,
Or thrive by other means.
     CAPT.   I'll do 't, my lord.
     EDM. About it, and write happy when thou hast done.   35
Mark, I say, instantly, and carry it so
As I have set it down.
     CAPT. I cannot draw a cart, nor eat dried oats.
If it be man's work, I'll do 't.   [*Exit.*

          [*Flourish. Enter* ALBANY, GONERIL, REGAN, *another*
                    CAPTAIN, *and* SOLDIERS.]

     ALB. Sir, you have shown today your valiant strain,   40
And fortune led you well. You have the captives
That were the opposites of this day's strife.
We do require them of you, so to use them
As we shall find their merits and our safety
May equally determine.
     EDM.   Sir, I thought it fit   45
To send the old and miserable King
To some retention and appointed guard;
Whose age has charms in it, whose title more,
To pluck the common bosom on his side
And turn our impressed lances in our eyes   50
Which do command them. With him I sent the Queen,
My reason all the same, and they are ready
Tomorrow or at further space to appear
Where you shall hold your session. At this time

---

24. *goodyears*: devil; *fell*: skin. 40. *strain*: character. 42. *opposites*: oppo-
nents. 49. *pluck the common bosom*: gain the hearts of the rank and file.
50. *impressed lances*: drafted soldiers. 51. *Which*: who.

We sweat and bleed. The friend hath lost his friend,   55
And the best quarrels, in the heat, are cursed
By those that feel their sharpness.
The question of Cordelia and her father
Requires a fitter place.
   ALB.   Sir, by your patience,
I hold you but a subject of this war,   60
Not as a brother.
   REG.   That's as we list to grace him.
Methinks our pleasure might have been demanded
Ere you had spoke so far. He led our powers,
Bore the commission of my place and person;
The which immediacy may well stand up   65
And call itself your brother.
   GON.   Not so hot.
In his own grace he doth exalt himself
More than in your addition.
   REG.   In my rights,
By me invested, he compeers the best.
   GON. That were the most, if he should husband you.   70
   REG. Jesters do oft prove prophets.
   GON.   Holloa, holloa!
That eye that told you so looked but a-squint.
   REG. Lady, I am not well; else I should answer
From a full-flowing stomach. General,
Take thou my soldiers, prisoners, patrimony;   75
Dispose of them, of me; the walls are thine.
Witness the world that I create thee here
My lord and master.
   GON.   Mean you to enjoy him?
   ALB. The let-alone lies not in your goodwill.
   EDM. Nor in thine, lord.
   ALB.   Half-blooded fellow, yes.   80
   REG. [To EDMUND] Let the drum strike, and prove my title thine.
   ALB. Stay yet; hear reason. Edmund, I arrest thee
On capital treason, and in thine attaint
This gilded serpent. [Pointing to GONERIL] For your claim, fair sister,
I bar it in the interest of my wife.   85

---

60. *subject:* subordinate. 61. *list to grace him:* please to honor him. 65.
immediacy: closeness to my authority. 66. *brother:* equal. 69. *compeers:*
equals. 74. *stomach:* anger. 76. *the walls are thine:* you have broken
through my defenses. 79. *let-alone:* permission. 80. *Half-blooded:* bastard.
83. *in thine attaint:* as an accomplice in your treason I impeach.

'Tis she is subcontracted to this lord,
And I, her husband, contradict your bans.
If you will marry, make your loves to me;
My lady is bespoke.
GON.   An interlude!
ALB. Thou art armed, Gloucester. Let the trumpet sound.   90
If none appear to prove upon thy person
Thy heinous, manifest, and many treasons,
There is my pledge. [*Throwing down a glove*] I'll prove it on thy
    heart
Ere I taste bread, thou art in nothing less
Than I have here proclaimed thee.
REG.   Sick, oh, sick!   95
GON. [*Aside*] If not, I'll ne'er trust medicine.
EDM. [*Throwing down a glove*] There's my exchange. What in
    the world he is
That names me traitor, villainlike he lies.
Call by thy trumpet. He that dares approach,
On him, on you—who not?—I will maintain   100
My truth and honor firmly.
ALB. A herald, ho!
EDM.   A herald, ho, a herald!
ALB. Trust to thy single virtue, for thy soldiers,
All levied in my name, have in my name
Took their discharge.
REG.   My sickness grows upon me.   105
ALB. She is not well. Convey her to my tent.   [*Exit* REGAN, *led.*
[*Enter a* HERALD.] Come hither, herald.—Let the trumpet sound.—
And read out this.
CAPT. Sound, trumpet!   [*A trumpet sounds.*
HER. [*Reads.*] "If any man of quality or degree within the   [110
lists of the army will maintain upon Edmund, supposed Earl of
Gloucester, that he is a manifold traitor, let him appear by the third
sound of the trumpet. He is bold in his defense."   113
EDM. Sound!   [*First trumpet.*
HER. Again!   [*Second trumpet.*
Again!   [*Third trumpet.*
                                  [*Trumpet answers within.*

[*Enter* EDGAR *at the third sound, armed, with a trumpet before him.*]

----

89. *interlude:* cheap wit. 96. *medicine:* poison. 110. *degree:* aristocratic
position.

ALB. Ask him his purposes, why he appears
Upon this call o' the trumpet.
  HER.   What are you?
Your name, your quality? And why you answer
This present summons?
  EDG.   Know my name is lost, 120
By treason's tooth bare-gnawn and canker-bit.
Yet am I noble as the adversary
I come to cope.
  ALB.   Which is that adversary?
  EDG. What's he that speaks for Edmund, Earl of Gloucester?
  EDM. Himself. What say'st thou to him?
  EDG.   Draw thy sword, 125
That if my speech offend a noble heart,
Thy arm may do thee justice. Here is mine.
Behold, it is the privilege of mine honors,
My oath, and my profession. I protest,
Maugre thy strength, youth, place, and eminence, 130
Despite thy victor sword and fire-new fortune,
Thy valor and thy heart, thou art a traitor,
False to thy gods, thy brother, and thy father,
Conspirant 'gainst this high illustrious prince,
And from the extremest upward of thy head 135
To the descent and dust below thy foot
A most toad-spotted traitor. Say thou "No,"
This sword, this arm, and my best spirits are bent
To prove upon thy heart, whereto I speak,
Thou liest.
  EDM. In wisdom I should ask thy name, 140
But since thy outside looks so fair and warlike
And that thy tongue some say of breeding breathes,
What safe and nicely I might well delay
By rule of knighthood, I disdain and spurn.
Back do I toss these treasons to thy head; 145
With the hell-hated lie o'erwhelm thy heart,
Which for they yet glance by and scarcely bruise,
This sword of mine shall give them instant way
Where they shall rest forever. Trumpets, speak!
      [*Alarums. They fight.* EDMUND *falls.*

---

129. *oath, profession:* as a knight. 130. *Maugre:* in spite of. 131. *fire-new:* newly minted. 137. *toad-spotted:* poisonous. 142. *say:* accent. 143. *nicely:* according to the letter of the law.

ALB. Save him, save him!

GON.　　　　　　　　　This is practice, Gloucester.　　150
By the law of arms thou wast not bound to answer
An unknown opposite. Thou art not vanquished,
But cozened and beguiled.

ALB.　　　　　　　　Shut your mouth, dame,
Or with this paper shall I stop it. Hold, sir;
Thou worse than any name, read thine own evil.　　155
No tearing, lady. I perceive you know it.

GON. Say if I do, the laws are mine, not thine.
Who can arraign me for 't?

ALB.　　　　　　　　Most monstrous!
Know'st thou this paper?

GON.　　　　　　　　Ask me not what I know. 　[*Exit.*
ALB. Go after her. She's desperate; govern her.　　160
EDM. What you have charged me with, that have I done,
And more, much more. The time will bring it out.
'Tis past, and so am I. But what art thou
That hast this fortune on me? If thou 'rt noble,
I do forgive thee.

EDG.　　　　　　　Let's exchange charity.　　165
I am no less in blood than thou art, Edmund.
If more, the more thou hast wronged me.
My name is Edgar, and thy father's son.
The gods are just, and of our pleasant vices
Make instruments to plague us.　　170
The dark and vicious place where thee he got
Cost him his eyes.

EDM.　　　　　　　Thou hast spoken right, 'tis true.
The wheel is come full circle; I am here.

ALB. Methought thy very gait did prophesy
A royal nobleness. I must embrace thee.　　175
Let sorrow split my heart if ever I
Did hate thee or thy father!

EDG.　　　　　　　Worthy prince, I know't.
ALB. Where have you hid yourself?
How have you known the miseries of your father?

EDG. By nursing them, my lord. List a brief tale,　　180
And when 'tis told, oh, that my heart would burst!
The bloody proclamation to escape

---

150. *practice:* a trick. 153. *cozened and beguiled:* cheated and imposed upon.
160. *govern:* hold. 171. *got:* begot. 173. *wheel:* of fortune. 182. *The . . .
escape:* in order to escape the proclamation for my arrest.

That followed me so near— Oh, our lives' sweetness!
That we the pain of death would hourly die
Rather than die at once!—taught me to shift   185
Into a madman's rags, to assume a semblance
That very dogs disdained. And in this habit
Met I my father with his bleeding rings,
Their precious stones new-lost; became his guide,
Led him, begged for him, saved him from despair;   190
Never—oh, fault!—revealed myself unto him
Until some half-hour past, when I was armed.
Not sure, though hoping, of this good success,
I asked his blessing, and from first to last
Told him my pilgrimage. But his flawed heart—   195
Alack, too weak the conflict to support!—
'Twixt two extremes of passion, joy and grief,
Burst smilingly.
    EDM.   This speech of yours hath moved me,
And shall perchance do good. But speak you on.
You look as you had something more to say.   200
    ALB. If there be more, more woeful, hold it in,
For I am almost ready to dissolve,
Hearing of this.
    EDG.   This would have seemed a period
To such as love not sorrow, but another,
To amplify too much, would make much more,   205
And top extremity.
Whilst I was big in clamor, came there in a man
Who, having seen me in my worst estate,
Shunned my abhorred society. But then, finding
Who 'twas that so endured, with his strong arms   210
He fastened on my neck, and bellowed out
As he'd burst heaven, threw him on my father,
Told the most piteous tale of Lear and him
That ever ear received. Which in recounting
His grief grew puissant, and the strings of life   215
Began to crack. Twice then the trumpets sounded,
And there I left him tranced.
    ALB.   But who was this?
    EDG. Kent, sir, the banished Kent, who in disguise
Followed his enemy King, and did him service
Improper for a slave.   220

---

203. *period:* end. 207. *big in clamor:* loud in lament. 215. *puissant:* intense;
strings of life: heartstrings. 217. *tranced:* unconscious.

[*Enter a* GENTLEMAN, *with a bloody knife.*]

GENT. Help, help, oh, help!

EDG.   What kind of help?

ALB.   Speak, man.

EDG. What means this bloody knife?

GENT.   'Tis hot, it smokes.
It came even from the heart of—oh, she's dead!

ALB. Who dead? Speak, man.

GENT. Your lady, sir, your lady. And her sister   225
By her is poisoned. She hath confessed it.

EDM. I was contracted to them both. All three
Now marry in an instant.

EDG.   Here comes Kent.

ALB. Produce the bodies, be they alive or dead.

                                        [*Exit* GENTLEMAN.
This judgment of the heavens, that makes us tremble,   230
Touches us not with pity.
              [*Enter* KENT.] Oh, is this he?
The time will not allow the compliment
Which very manners urges.

KENT.   I am come
To bid my King and master aye good night.
Is he not here?

ALB.   Great thing of us forgot!   235
Speak, Edmund, where's the King? And where's Cordelia?
See's thou this object, Kent?

                    [*The bodies of* GONERIL *and* REGAN *are brought in.*
KENT. Alack, why thus?

EDM.   Yet Edmund was beloved.
The one the other poisoned for my sake,
And after slew herself.   240

ALB. Even so. Cover their faces.

EDM. I pant for life. Some good I mean to do,
Despite of mine own nature. Quickly send—
Be brief in it—to the castle, for my writ
Is on the life of Lear and on Cordelia.   245
Nay, send in time.

ALB.   Run, run, oh, run!

EDG. To who, my lord? Who hath the office? Send
Thy token of reprieve.

EDM. Well thought on. Take my sword.   249
Give it the captain.

---

234. *aye:* forever. 244. *writ:* order of execution.

ALB.   Haste thee, for thy life.   [*Exit* EDGAR.

EDM. He hath commission from thy wife and me
To hang Cordelia in the prison and
To lay the blame upon her own despair,
That she fordid herself.

ALB. The gods defend her! Bear him hence awhile.   255

[EDMUND *is borne off.*

[*Re-enter* LEAR, *with* CORDELIA *dead in his arms,* EDGAR, CAPTAIN,
and others following.]

LEAR. Howl, howl, howl, howl! Oh, you are men of stones.
Had I your tongues and eyes, I'd use them so
That heaven's vault should crack. She's gone forever!
I know when one is dead and when one lives.
She's dead as earth. Lend me a looking-glass.   260
If that her breath will mist or stain the stone,
Why, then she lives.

KENT.   Is this the promised end?

EDG. Or image of that horror?

ALB.   Fall and cease.

LEAR. This feather stirs; she lives. If it be so,
It is a chance which does redeem all sorrows   265
That ever I have felt.

KENT.   [*Kneeling*] Oh, my good master!

LEAR. Prithee, away.

EDG.   'Tis noble Kent, your friend.

LEAR. A plague upon you, murderers, traitors all!
I might have saved her. Now she's gone forever!
Cordelia, Cordelia! Stay a little. Ha!   270
What is 't thou say'st? Her voice was ever soft,
Gentle and low, an excellent thing in woman.
I killed the slave that was a-hanging thee.

CAPT. 'Tis true, my lords, he did.

LEAR.   Did I not, fellow?
I have seen the day with my good biting falchion   275
I would have made them skip. I am old now,
And these same crosses spoil me. Who are you?
Mine eyes are not o' the best, I'll tell you straight.

---

254. *fordid:* killed. 261. *stone:* glass. 262. *promised end:* prophesied end of
the world. 263. *Fall and cease:* let the doom fall and all things cease. 275.
falchion: sword. 277. *crosses:* hardships.

KENT. If fortune brag of two she loved and hated,
One of them we behold.   280
    LEAR. This is a dull sight. Are you not Kent?
    KENT.   The same,
Your servant Kent. Where is your servant Caius?
    LEAR. He's a good fellow, I can tell you that.
He'll strike, and quickly too. He's dead and rotten.
    KENT. No, my good lord, I am the very man——   285
    LEAR. I'll see that straight.
    KENT. That from your first of difference and decay
Have followed your sad steps.
    LEAR.   You are welcome hither.
    KENT. Nor no man else. All's cheerless, dark, and deadly.
Your eldest daughters have fordone themselves,   290
And desperately are dead.
    LEAR.   Aye, so I think.
    ALB. He knows not what he says, and vain is it
That we present us to him.
    EDG.   Very bootless.

[Enter a CAPTAIN.]

    CAPT. Edmund is dead, my lord.
    ALB.   That's but a trifle here.
You lords and noble friends, know our intent.   295
What comfort to this great decay may come
Shall be applied. For us, we will resign,
During the life of this old Majesty,
To him our absolute power.
        [*To* EDGAR *and* KENT] You, to your rights,
With boot, and such addition as your honors   300
Have more than merited. All friends shall taste
The wages of their virtue, and all foes
The cup of their deservings. Oh, see, see!
    LEAR. And my poor fool is hanged! No, no, no life!
Why should a dog, a horse, a rat, have life   305
And thou no breath at all? Thou'lt come no more,
Never, never, never, never, never!
Pray you, undo this button. Thank you, sir.

---

280. *If . . . behold:* Lear must be one of the two men who have suffered
greatest changes in fortune. 287. *Your first of difference:* beginning of your
change. 290. *foredone:* killed. 291. *desperately:* in despair. 293. *bootless:*
useless. 296. *great decay:* wreck of a great man (Lear). 300. *boot:* interest.
304. *fool:* darling (Cordelia).

Do you see this? Look on her, look, her lips,
Look there, look there!   [*Dies.*

    EDG.   He faints. My lord, my lord!   310
    KENT. Break, heart, I prithee break!
    EDG.   Look up, my lord.
    KENT. Vex not his ghost. Oh, let him pass! He hates him
That would upon the rack of this tough world
Stretch him out longer.
    EDG.   He is gone indeed.
    KENT. The wonder is he hath endured so long.   315
He but usurped his life.
    ALB. Bear them from hence. Our present business
Is general woe. [*To* KENT *and* EDGAR] Friends of my soul, you twain
Rule in this realm and the gored state sustain.
    KENT. I have a journey, sir, shortly to go.   320
My master calls me, I must not say no.
    ALB. The weight of this sad time we must obey,
Speak what we feel, not what we ought to say.
The oldest hath borne most. We that are young
Shall never see so much, nor live so long.   325
                 [*Exeunt, with a dead march.*

---

312. *ghost:* departing spirit.

Volpone, or The Fox

Volpone, or The Fox

A Comedy

TO THE MOST NOBLE AND MOST EQUAL SISTERS, THE TWO FAMOUS UNI-
VERSITIES, FOR THEIR LOVE AND ACCEPTANCE SHOWN TO HIS POEM IN
THE PRESENTATION, BEN JONSON, THE GRATEFUL ACKNOWLEDGER, DEDI-
CATES BOTH IT AND HIMSELF.

DRAMATIS PERSONAE

VOLPONE, *a magnifico*
MOSCA, *his parasite*
VOLTORE, *an advocate*
CORBACCIO, *an old gentleman*
CORVINO, *a merchant*
BONARIO, *a young gentleman*
POLITIC WOULD-BE, *a knight*
PEREGRINE, *a gentleman travel-
ler*
NANO, *a dwarf*
CASTRONE, *an eunuch*
ANDROGYNO, *a hermaphrodite*

GREGE, *mob*
COMMANDADORI, *officers*
MERCATORI, *three merchants*
AVOCATORI, *four magistrates*
NOTARIO, *the register*
SERVITORE, *a servant*

MADAM WOULD-BE, *the knight's
wife*
CELIA, *Corvino's wife*
WOMEN

SCENE—*Venice.*

THE ARGUMENT

V OLPONE, childless, rich, feigns sick, despairs,
O ffers his state to hopes of several heirs,
L ies languishing; his parasite receives
P resents of all, assures, deludes; then weaves
O ther cross plots, which ope themselves, are told.
N ew tricks for safety are sought; they thrive: when, bold,
E ach tempts th' other again, and all are sold.

CHARACTERS. *Mosca:* a fly; *Voltore:* vulture; *Corbaccio:* raven; *Corvino:*
crow; *Bonario:* good; *Celia:* heavenly. ARGUMENT. *sold:* defrauded.

Prologue

Now, luck yet send us, and a little wit
  Will serve to make our play hit;
According to the palates of the season,
  Here is rhyme, not empty of reason.
This we were bid to credit from our poet,   5
  Whose true scope, if you would know it,
In all his poems still hath been this measure,
  To mix profit with your pleasure;
And not as some, whose throats their envy failing,
  Cry hoarsely, "All he writes is railing,"   10
And when his plays come forth, think they can flout them,
  With saying he was a year about them.
To this there needs no lie, but this his creature,
  Which was two months since no feature;
And, though he dares give them five lives to mend it,   15
  'Tis known, five weeks fully penned it,
From his own hand, without a coadjutor,
  Novice, journeyman, or tutor.
Yet thus much I can give you as a token
  Of his play's worth: no eggs are broken,   20
Nor quaking custards with fierce teeth affrighted,
  Wherewith your rout are so delighted;
Nor hales he in a gull, old ends reciting,
  To stop gaps in his loose writing;
With such a deal of monstrous and forced action,   25
  As might make Beth'lem a faction,
Nor made he his play for jests stol'n from each table,
  But makes jests to fit his fable;
And so presents quick comedy refined,
  As best critics have designed;   30
The laws of time, place, persons he observeth,
  From no needful rule he swerveth.
All gall and copperas from his ink he draineth;
  Only, a little salt remaineth;
Wherewith he'll rub your cheeks, till, red with laughter,   35
  They shall look fresh a week after.

PROLOGUE: 21. *quaking custard:* allusion to stage burlesques of the huge
custard set on the Lord Mayor's table for fools to jump in. 23. *gull:* a
fool. *old ends:* old scraps of poetry. 26. *Beth'lem a faction:* Bethlehem
(Bedlam, insane asylum) more disorderly. 33. *copperas:* vitriol.

Act I

SCENE I. *A room in Volpone's house.*

[*Enter* VOLPONE *and* MOSCA.]

VOLP. Good morning to the day; and next, my gold.
Open the shrine, that I may see my saint.
Hail the world's soul, and mine. More glad than is
The teeming earth to see the longed-for sun
Peep through the horns of the celestial Ram,   5
Am I, to view thy splendor darkening his;
That, lying here, amongst my other hoards,
Showest like a flame by night, or like the day
Struck out of chaos, when all darkness fled
Unto the center. O thou son of Sol,   10
But brighter than thy father, let me kiss,
With adoration, thee, and every relic
Of sacred treasure in this blessèd room.
Well did wise poets, by thy glorious name,
Title that age which they would have the best;   15
Thou being the best of things, and far transcending
All style of joy, in children, parents, friends,
Or any other waking dream on earth.
Thy looks when they to Venus did ascribe,
They should have given her twenty thousand Cupids;   20
Such are thy beauties and our loves! Dear saint,
Riches, the dumb god, that giv'st all men tongues,
That canst do nought, and yet makest men do all things;
The price of souls; even hell, with thee to boot,
Is made worth heaven. Thou art virtue, fame,   25
Honor, and all things else! Who can get thee,
He shall be noble, valiant, honest, wise—
    MOS. And what he will, sir. Riches are in fortune
A greater good than wisdom is in nature.
    VOLP. True, my beloved Mosca. Yet I glory   30
More in the cunning purchase of my wealth
Than in the glad possession, since I gain
No common way; I use no trade, no venture;
I wound no earth with ploughshares, fat no beasts

ACT I, sc. I: 5, *Ram:* zodiacal sign which the sun enters in late March.
8. *day:* first day of Creation. 10. *son of Sol:* i.e., gold, reputedly ripened
in the earth by the sun. 15. *that age:* the Golden Age. I: 22. *dumb
god:* silence is golden. 31. *purchase:* acquisition. 33. *venture:* investments.

To feed the shambles; have no mills for iron,   35
Oil, corn, or men, to grind 'em into powder;
I blow no subtle glass, expose no ships
To threat'nings of the furrow-faced sea;
I turn no monies in the public bank,
No usure private—
   MOS.   No, sir, nor devour   40
Soft prodigals. You shall ha' some will swallow
A melting heir as glibly as your Dutch
Will pills of butter, and ne'er purge for 't;
Tear forth the fathers of poor families
Out of their beds, and coffin them alive   45
In some kind clasping prison, where their bones
May be forthcoming, when the flesh is rotten.
But your sweet nature doth abhor these courses;
You loathe the widow's or the orphan's tears
Should wash your pavements, or their piteous cries   50
Ring in your roofs, and beat the air for vengeance.
   VOLP. Right, Mosca; I do loathe it.—
   MOS.   And, besides, sir,
You are not like the thresher that doth stand
With a huge flail, watching a heap of corn,
And, hungry, dares not taste the smallest grain,   55
But feeds on mallows, and such bitter herbs;
Nor like the merchant, who hath filled his vaults
With Romagnía, rich and Candian wines,
Yet drinks the lees of Lombard's vinegar.
You will not lie in straw, whilst moths and worms   60
Feed on your sumptuous hangings and soft beds.
You know the use of riches, and dare give now
From that bright heap, to me, your poor observer,
Or to your dwarf, or your hermaphrodite,
Your eunuch, or what other household trifle   65
Your pleasure allows maintenance.—
   VOLP.   Hold thee, Mosca;
Take of my hand; thou strikest on truth in all,
And they are envious term thee parasite.
Call forth my dwarf, my eunuch, and my fool,
And let 'em make me sport.   [*Exit* MOSCA.
                What should I do,   70

---

37. *subtle:* fine Venetian. 40. *usure:* usury, loans at exorbitant rates. 58.
Romagnía: Greek wine; *Candian:* Cretan. 63. *observer:* servant.

But cocker up my genius, and live free
To all delights my fortune calls me to?
I have no wife, no parent, child, ally,
To give my substance to; but whom I make
Must be my heir; and this makes men observe me.   75
This draws new clients daily to my house,
Women and men of every sex and age,
That bring me presents, send me plate, coin, jewels,
With hope that when I die (which they expect
Each greedy minute) it shall then return   80
Tenfold upon them; whilst some, covetous
Above the rest, seek to engross me whole,
And counter work the one unto the other,
Contend in gifts, as they would seem in love;
All which I suffer, playing with their hopes,   85
And am content to coin 'em into profit,
And look upon their kindness, and take more,
And look on that; still bearing them in hand,
Letting the cherry knock against their lips,
And draw it by their mouths, and back again.—   90
How now!

SCENE II

[*Enter* MOSCA *with* NANO, ANDROGYNO, *and* CASTRONE.]

NAN. Now, room for fresh gamesters, who do will you to know
They do bring you neither play nor university show,
And therefore do entreat you that whatsoever they rehearse
May not fare a whit the worse for the false pace of the verse.
If you wonder at this, you will wonder more ere we pass; 5
For know, here is enclosed the soul of Pythagoras,
That juggler divine, as hereafter shall follow,
Which soul, fast and loose, sir, came first from Apollo,
And was breathed into Aethalides, Mercurius his son,
Where it had the gift to remember all that ever was done. 10
From thence it fled forth, and made quick transmigration
To goldy-locked Euphorbus, who was killed, in good fashion,
At the siege of old Troy, by the cuckold of Sparta.

---

71. *cocker . . . genius:* cater to my inclination. 82. *engross:* monopolize.
88. *bearing . . . hand:* leading them on. 89. *cherry:* as in the game of
bob-cherry.

   SC. II: 6. *here:* i.e., in Androgyno. 8. *fast and loose:* an early version of
the shell game. 9. *Aethalides:* son of Mercury and herald of the Argonauts.
13. *cuckold of Sparta:* Menelaus.

Hermotimus was next (I find it in my charta);
To whom it did pass, where no sooner it was missing,   15
But with one Pyrrhus of Delos it learned to go a-fishing;
And thence did it enter the sophist of Greece.
From Pythagore, she went into a beautiful piece,
Hight Aspasia, the meretrix; and the next toss of her
Was again of a whore—she became a philosopher,   20
Crates the cynic, as itself doth relate it.
Since, kings, knights, and beggars, knaves, lords, and fools
   gat it,
Besides ox and ass, camel, mule, goat, and brock,
In all which it hath spoke, as in the cobbler's cock.
But I come not here to discourse of that matter,   25
Or his one, two, or three, or his great oath, "By QUATER!"
His musics, his trigon, his golden thigh,
Or his telling how elements shift; but I
Would ask, how of late thou hast suffered translation,
And shifted thy coat in these days of reformation.   30
   AND. Like one of the reformed, a fool, as you see,
Counting all old doctrine heresy.
   NAN. But not on thine own forbid meats hast thou ventured?
   AND. On fish, when first a Carthusian I entered.
   NAN. Why, then thy dogmatical silence hath left thee?   35
   AND. Of that an obstreperous lawyer bereft me.
   NAN. O wonderful change! When sir lawyer forsook thee,
For Pythagore's sake, what body then took thee?
   AND. A good dull mule.
   NAN.   And how! by that means
Thou wert brought to allow of the eating of beans?   40
   AND. Yes.
   NAN.   But from the mule into whom didst thou pass?
   AND. Into a very strange beast, by some writers called an ass;
By others a precise, pure, illuminate brother

---

14. *Hermotimus:* Greek philosopher (perhaps legendary) of the 6th century B.C., whose soul is reported by Plutarch to have had the habit of leaving his body. 19. *Hight:* named. *meretrix:* prostitute. 23. *brock:* badger.
24. *cobbler's cock:* This section on the transmigration of souls is based on
Lucian's dialogue of the cobbler and the cock. 26. *By QUATER:* By four.
This and subsequent allusions to trigon (mystical triangle), fish, and dogmatical silence reflect the Pythagorean philosophy based on the first four
numbers and the rules and legends developed by the Pythagorean sect—all
a running satire on greed for gold or religious extremism. 31. *reformed:*
i.e., "Protestants," Puritans. 34. *Carthusian:* Roman Catholic religious order. 35. *lawyer:* notorious talkers. 43. *precise:* puritanical; *illuminate:* i.e.,
having "inner light."

Of those devour flesh—and sometimes one another;
And will drop you forth a libel, or a sanctified lie,   45
Betwixt every spoonful of a nativity-pie.
     NAN. Now quit thee, fore Heaven, of that profane nation;
And gently report thy next transmigration.
     AND. To the same that I am.
     NAN.   A creature of delight,
And, what is more than a fool, an hermaphrodite!   50
Now, pray thee, sweet soul, in all thy variation,
Which body wouldst thou choose to take up thy station?
     AND. Troth, this I am in; even here would I tarry.
     NAN. 'Cause here the delight of each sex thou canst vary?
     AND. Alas, those pleasures be stale and forsaken;   55
No, 'tis your fool wherewith I am so taken,
The only one creature that I can call blessed;
For all other forms I have proved most distressed.
     NAN. Spoke true, as thou wert in Pythagoras still.
This learned opinion we celebrate will,   60
Fellow eunuch, as behoves us, with all our wit and art,
To dignify that whereof ourselves are so great and special a part.
     VOLP. Now, very, very pretty. Mosca, this
Was thy invention?
     MOS.   If it please my patron,
Not else.
     VOLP. It doth, good Mosca.   65
     MOS.   Then it was, sir.   [Sings.

          Fools they are the only nation
          Worth men's envy or admiration;
          Free from care or sorrow taking,
          Selves and others merry making:
          All they speak or do is sterling.   70
          Your fool he is your great man's dearling,
          And your ladies' sport and pleasure;
          Tongue and bauble are his treasure.
          E'en his face begetteth laughter,
          And he speaks truth free from slaughter;   75
          He's the grace of every feast,
          And sometimes the chiefest guest;
          Hath his trencher and his stool,
          When wit waits upon the fool.

44. *those:* those who. 46. *nativity-pie:* Christmas pie; strict Puritans avoided the Popish word "Christ mass." 75. *slaughter:* punishment.

O, who would not be   80
He, he, he?

        [One knocks without.

VOLP. Who's that? Away! Look, Mosca.
MOS.   Fool, begone!

    [Exeunt NANO, CASTRONE, *and* ANDROGYNO.

'Tis Signior Voltore, the advocate;
I know him by his knock.
  VOLP.   Fetch me my gown,
My furs, and nightcaps; say my couch is changing,   85
And let him entertain himself awhile
Without, i' th' gallery. *[Exit* MOSCA.] Now, now my clients
Begin their visitation! Vulture, kite,
Raven, and gorcrow, all my birds of prey,
That think me turning carcass, now they come;   90
I am not for 'em yet.

    [Re-enter MOSCA, *with the gown, etc.]*
     How now! the news?
  MOS. A piece of plate, sir.
  VOLP.   Of what bigness?
  MOS.   Huge,
Massy, and antique, with your name inscribed,
And arms engraven.
  VOLP.   Good! and not a fox
Stretched on the earth, with fine delusive sleights,   95
Mocking a gaping crow? ha, Mosca?
  MOS.   Sharp, sir.
  VOLP. Give me my furs.—Why dost thou laugh so, man?
  MOS. I cannot choose, sir, when I apprehend
What thoughts he has without now, as he walks:
That this might be the last gift he should give,   100
That this would fetch you; if you died today,
And gave him all, what he should be tomorrow;
What large return would come of all his ventures;
How he should worshipped be, and reverenced;
Ride with his furs and footcloths, waited on   105
By herds of fools and clients; have clear way
Made for his mule, as lettered as himself;
Be called the great and learned advocate!

---

89. *gorcrow:* scavenger crow. 92. *plate:* dish of gold. 96. *Mocking . . . crow:* as in Aesop's fable, where the fox flatters the crow into singing and thus dropping a cheese.

And then concludes there's nought impossible.

VOLP. Yes, to be learned, Mosca.

MOS.   O, no! rich   110
Implies it. Hood an ass with reverend purple,
So you can hide his two ambitious ears,
And he shall pass for a cathedral doctor.

VOLP. My caps, my caps, good Mosca. Fetch him in.

MOS. Stay, sir; your ointment for your eyes.

VOLP.   That's true;   115
Dispatch, dispatch; I long to have possession
Of my new present.

MOS.   That, and thousands more,
I hope to see you lord of.

VOLP.   Thanks, kind Mosca.

MOS. And that, when I am lost in blended dust,
And hundred such as I am, in succession—   120

VOLP. Nay, that were too much, Mosca.

MOS.   You shall live
Still to delude these harpies.

VOLP.   Loving Mosca!
'Tis well; my pillow now, and let him enter.   [*Exit* MOSCA.
Now, my feigned cough, my phthisic, and my gout,
My apoplexy, palsy, and catarrhs,   125
Help, with your forced functions this my posture,
Wherein, this three year, I have milked their hopes .
He comes; I hear him— Uh, uh, uh, uh!—Oh!

SCENE III

[*Enter* MOSCA *with* VOLTORE.]

MOS. You still are what you were, sir. Only you,
Of all the rest, are he commands his love,
And you do wisely to preserve it thus,
With early visitation and kind notes
Of your good meaning to him, which, I know,   5
Cannot but come most grateful. Patron! sir!
Here's Signior Voltore is come—

VOLP.   What say you?

109. *learned:* i.e., one thing that would be impossible for him.
115. *ointment:* to make his eyes appear old and mattering (cf. Act I, sc.
IV, 48). 124. *phthisic:* consumption. 126. *posture:* deception.
sc. III: 2. *he:* the one who.

MOS. Sir, Signior Voltore is come this morning
To visit you.
    VOLP.   I thank him.
    MOS.   And hath brought
A piece of antique plate, bought of St. Mark,   10
With which he here presents you.
    VOLP.   He is welcome.
Pray him to come more often.
    MOS.   Yes.
    VOLT.   What says he?
MOS. He thanks you, and desires you see him often.
VOLP. Mosca.
    MOS.   My patron!
    VOLP.   Bring him near. Where is he?
I long to feel his hand.
    MOS.   The plate is here, sir.   15
VOLT. How fare you, sir?
    VOLP.   I thank you, Signior Voltore.
Where is the plate? mine eyes are bad.
    VOLT.   I'm sorry
To see you still thus weak.
    MOS. [*Aside*]   That he is not weaker.
VOLP. You are too munificent.
    VOLT.   No, sir; would to heaven
I could as well give health to you, as that plate.   20
    VOLP. You give, sir, what you can. I thank you. Your love
Hath taste in this, and shall not be unanswered.
I pray you see me often.
    VOLT.   Yes, I shall, sir.
VOLP. Be not far from me.
    MOS.   Do you observe that, sir?
VOLT. Hearken unto me still; it will concern you.   25
MOS. You are a happy man; sir; know your good.
VOLP. I cannot now last long—
    MOS. [*Aside*]   You are his heir, sir.
VOLT. [*Aside*] Am I?
    VOLP. I feel me going—uh, uh, uh, uh!—
I'm sailing to my port—uh, uh, uh, uh!—
And I am glad I am so near my haven.   30
    MOS. Alas, kind gentleman; well, we must all go—
VOLT. But, Mosca—

---

10. *St. Mark:* goldsmith in St. Mark's Square.

MOS.   Age will conquer.
VOLT.   'Pray thee, hear me.
Am I inscribed his heir, for certain?
MOS.   Are you!
I do beseech you, sir, you will vouchsafe
To write me in your family. All my hopes   35
Depend upon your worship. I am lost
Except the rising sun do shine on me.
  VOLT. It shall both shine, and warm thee, Mosca.
MOS.   Sir,
I am a man that hath not done your love
All the worst offices: here I wear your keys,   40
See all your coffers and your caskets locked,
Keep the poor inventory of your jewels,
Your plate, and monies; am your steward, sir,
Husband your goods here.
  VOLT.   But am I sole heir?
  MOS. Without a partner, sir; confirmed this morning;   45
The wax is warm yet, and the ink scarce dry
Upon the parchment.
  VOLT.   Happy, happy me!
By what good chance, sweet Mosca?
  MOS.   Your desert, sir;
I know no second cause.
  VOLT.   Thy modesty
Is loth to know it; well, we shall requite it.   50
  MOS. He ever liked your course, sir; that first took him.
I oft have heard him say how he admired
Men of your large profession, that could speak
To every cause, and things mere contraries,
Till they were hoarse again, yet all be law;   55
That, with most quick agility, could turn,
And return; make knots, and undo them;
Give forkèd counsel; take provoking gold
On either hand, and put it up; these men,
He knew, would thrive with their humility.   60
And, for his part, he thought he should be blest
To have his heir of such a suffering spirit,

---

35. *write . . . family*: enroll me among your servants. 51. *course*: behavior (ordinarily used to describe a reprehensible action). 54. *To . . . contraries*: i.e., on both sides of a question. 58. *forkèd*: i.e., that looks two ways (with suggestion of a serpent's forked tongue). 59. *put it up*: pocket it.

So wise, so grave, of so perplexed a tongue,
And loud withal, that would not wag, nor scarce
Lie still, without a fee; when every word   65
Your worship but lets fall, is a *cecchine!*

                                          [Another knocks.

Who's that? One knocks; I would not have you seen, sir.
And yet—pretend you came and went in haste;
I'll fashion an excuse. And, gentle sir,
When you do come to swim in golden lard,   70
Up to the arms in honey, that your chin
Is borne up stiff with fatness of the flood,
Think on your vassal; but remember me:
I ha' not been your worst of clients.
    VOLT.   Mosca—
    MOS. When will you have your inventory brought, sir?   75
Or see a copy of the will?—Anon.—
I'll bring 'em to you, sir. Away, begone,
Put business i' your face.   *[Exit* VOLTORE.
    VOLP.   Excellent Mosca!
Come hither, let me kiss thee.
    MOS.   Keep you still, sir.
Here is Corbaccio.
    VOLP.   Set the plate away.   86
The vulture's gone, and the old raven's come.

SCENE. IV

[MOSCA, CORBACCIO, *and* VOLPONE.]

    MOS. Betake you to your silence, and your sleep.—
[To the plate] Stand there and multiply.—*[Aside]* Now shall we see
A wretch who is indeed more impotent
Than this can feign to be; yet hopes to hop
Over his grave.— Signior Corbaccio!   5
You're very welcome, sir.
    CORB.   How does your patron?
    MOS. Troth, as he did, sir; no amends.
    CORB.   What? mends he?
    MOS. No, sir: he is rather worse.

---

63. *perplexed:* intricate. 66. *cecchine:* a Venetian gold coin.
sc. iv: 4. *this:* i.e., Volpone. 7. Corbaccio is deaf.

CORB.   That's well. Where is he?
MOS. Upon his couch, sir, newly fall'n asleep.
CORB. Does he sleep well?
MOS.   No wink, sir, all this night,   10
Nor yesterday; but slumbers.
CORB.   Good! he should take
Some counsel of physicians. I have brought him
An opiate here, from mine own doctor—
MOS. He will not hear of drugs.
CORB.   Why? I myself
Stood by while 'twas made, saw all th' ingredients,   15
And know it cannot but most gently work.
My life for his, 'tis but to make him sleep.
  VOLP. [*Aside*] Ay, his last sleep, if he would take it.
MOS.   Sir,
He has no faith in physic.
CORB.   Say you? say you?
  MOS. He has no faith in physic; he does think   20
Most of your doctors are the greater danger,
And worse disease, t' escape. I often have
Heard him protest that your physician
Should never be his heir.
CORB.   Not I his heir?
MOS. Not your physician, sir.
CORB.   O, no, no, no;   25
I do not mean it.
  MOS.   No, sir, nor their fees
He cannot brook; he says they flay a man
Before they kill him.
CORB.   Right, I do conceive you.
  MOS. And then they do it by experiment;
For which the law not only doth absolve 'em,   30
But gives them great reward; and he is loth
To hire his death so.
CORB.   It is true, they kill
With as much licence as a judge.
MOS.   Nay, more;
For he but kills, sir, where the law condemns,
And these can kill him too.
CORB.   Ay, or me,   35

---

11. *slumbers:* dozes. 21. *your:* colloquial usage meaning simply "a."

Or any man. How does his apoplex?
Is that strong on him still?
    MOS.   Most violent.
His speech is broken, and his eyes are set,
His face drawn longer than 'twas wont—
    CORB.   How? how?
Stronger than he was wont?
    MOS.   No, sir; his face   40
Drawn longer than 'twas wont.
    CORB.   O, good.
    MOS.   His mouth
Is ever gaping, and his eyelids hang.
    CORB.   Good.
    MOS. A freezing numbness stiffens all his joints,
And makes the color of his flesh like lead.
    CORB.   'Tis good.
    MOS. His pulse beats slow, and dull.
    CORB.   Good symptoms still.   45
    MOS. And from his brain—
    CORB.   Ha? How? Not from his brain?
    MOS. Yes, sir, and from his brain—
    CORB.   I conceive you; good.
    MOS. Flows a cold sweat, with a continual rheum,
Forth the resolved corners of his eyes.
    CORB. Is 't possible? Yet I am better, ha!   50
How does he with the swimming of his head?
    MOS. O, sir, 'tis past the scotomy; he now
Hath lost his feeling, and hath left to snort;
You hardly can perceive him, that he breathes.
    CORB. Excellent, excellent; sure I shall outlast him;   55
This makes me young again, a score of years.
    MOS. I was a-coming for you, sir.
    CORB.   Has he made his will?
What has he giv'n me?
    MOS.   No, sir.
    CORB.   Nothing? ha?
    MOS. He has not made his will, sir.
    CORB.   Oh, oh, oh.
What then did Voltore, the lawyer, here?   60
    MOS. He smelt a carcass, sir, when he but heard

---

49. *resolved:* rotting. 52. *scotomy:* dizziness. 53. *left to snort:* stopped
snoring.

My master was about his testament;
As I did urge him to it for your good—
   CORB. He came unto him, did he? I thought so.
   MOS. Yes, and presented him this piece of plate.   65
   CORB. To be his heir?
   MOS.   I do not know, sir.
   CORB.   True;
I know it too.
   MOS.[*Aside*] By your own scale, sir.
   CORB.   Well,
I shall prevent him yet. See, Mosca, look,
Here I have brought a bag of bright *cecchines,*
Will quite weigh down his plate.
   MOS.   Yea, marry, sir.   70
This is true physic, this your sacred medicine;
No talk of opiates to this great elixir!
   CORB. 'Tis *aurum palpabile,* if not *potabile.*
   MOS. It shall be ministered to him in his bowl!
   CORB. Ay, do, do, do.
   MOS.   Most blessed cordial!   75
This will recover him.
   CORB.   Yes, do, do, do.
   MOS. I think it were not best, sir.
   CORB.   What?
   MOS.   To recover him.
   CORB. O, no, no, no; by no means.
   MOS.   Why, sir, this
Will work some strange effect, if he but feel it.
   CORB. 'Tis true; therefore forbear. I'll take my venture;   80
Give me 't again.
   MOS.   At no hand; pardon me,
You shall not do yourself that wrong, sir. I
Will so advise you, you shall have it all.
   CORB. How?
   MOS.   All, sir; 'tis your right, your own; no man
Can claim a part; 'tis yours without a rival,   85
Decreed by destiny.
   CORB.   How, how, good Mosca?

---

68. *prevent:* get ahead of. 73. *aurum . . . potabile:* gold that can be
touched if not drunk; the latter elixir was known as the sovereign remedy
75. *cordial:* heart medicine. 81. *At no hand:* by no means.

MOS. I'll tell you, sir. This fit he shall recover—
CORB. I do conceive you.
MOS.   And, on first advantage
Of his gained sense, will I re-importune him
Unto the making of his testament,   90
And show him this.   [*Points to the money.*
    CORB.   Good, good.
    MOS.   'Tis better yet,
If you will hear, sir.
    CORB.   Yes, with all my heart.
    MOS. Now would I counsel you, make home with speed;
There, frame a will; whereto you shall inscribe
My master your sole heir.
    CORB.   And disinherit   95
My son?
    MOS.   O, sir, the better; for that color
Shall make it much more taking.
    CORB.   O, but color?
    MOS. This will, sir, you shall send it unto me.
Now, when I come to enforce, as I will do,
Your cares, your watchings, and your many prayers,   100
Your more than many gifts, your this day's present,
And last, produce your will; where (without thought
Or least regard unto your proper issue,
A son so brave, and highly meriting)
The stream of your diverted love hath thrown you   105
Upon my master, and made him your heir;
He cannot be so stupid or stone-dead,
But, out of conscience and mere gratitude—
    CORB. He must pronounce me his?
    MOS.   'Tis true.
    CORB.   This plot
Did I think on before.
    MOS.   I do believe it.   110
    CORB. Do you not believe it?
    MOS.   Yes, sir.
    CORB.   Mine own project.
    MOS. Which, when he hath done, sir—
    CORB.   Published me his heir?
    MOS. And you so certain to survive him—

---

96. *color:* pretense. **99.** *enforce:* emphasize. **103.** *proper issue:* own child.

CORB.   Ay.
MOS. Being so lusty a man—
CORB.   'Tis true.
MOS.   Yes, sir—
CORB. I thought on that too. See, how he should be   115
The very organ to express my thoughts!
MOS. You have not only done yourself a good—
CORB. But multiplied it on my son!
MOS.   'Tis right, sir.
CORB. Still, my invention.
MOS.   'Las, sir! Heaven knows,
It hath been all my study, all my care,   120
(I e'en grow gray withal) how to work things—
CORB. I do conceive, sweet Mosca.
MOS.   You are he
For whom I labor here.
CORB.   You are he
I'll straight about it.
MOS. [Aside]   Rook go with you, raven.
CORB. I know thee honest.
MOS.   You do lie, sir—
CORB.   And—   125
MOS. Your knowledge is no better than your ears, sir.
CORB. I do not doubt to be a father to thee.
MOS. Nor I to gull my brother of his blessing.
CORB. I may ha' my youth restored to me, why not?
MOS. Your worship is a precious ass—
CORB.   What say'st thou?   130
MOS. I do desire your worship to make haste, sir.
CORB. 'Tis done, 'tis done; I go.   [Exit.
VOLP. [Leaping from his couch] Oh, I shall burst!
Let out my sides, let out my sides—
MOS.   Contain
Your flux of laughter, sir; you know this hope
Is such a bait, it covers any hook.   135
VOLP. O, but thy working, and thy placing it!
I cannot hold; good rascal, let me kiss thee;
I never knew thee in so rare a humor.

---

124. _Rook . . . you:_ may you be rooked (with a pun on rook:raven); this
and the next four speeches by Mosca are not quite caught by Corbaccio.
134. _flux:_ flow.

MOS. Alas, sir, I but do as I am taught;
Follow your grave instruction, give 'em words,   140
Pour oil into their ears, and send them hence.
   VOLP. 'Tis true, 'tis true. What a rare punishment
Is avarice to itself!
   MOS.   Ay, with our help, sir.
   VOLP. So many cares, so many maladies,
So many fears attending on old age.   145
Yea, death so often called on, as no wish
Can be more frequent with 'em, their limbs faint,
Their senses dull, their seeing, hearing, going,
All dead before them; yea, their very teeth,
Their instruments of eating, failing them.   150
Yet this is reckoned life! Nay, here was one,
Is now gone home, that wishes to live longer!
Feels not his gout, nor palsy; feigns himself
Younger by scores of years, flatters his age
With confident belying it, hopes he may   155
With charms like Aeson have his youth restored;
And with these thoughts so battens, as if fate
Would be as easily cheated on as he;
And all turns air! Who's that there, now? a third?
                            [*Another knocks.*
   MOS. Close; to your couch again; I hear his voice.   160
It is Corvino, our spruce merchant.
   VOLP. [*Lying down*]   Dead.
   MOS. Another bout, sir, with your eyes. [*Anointing them*]—Who's
there?

SCENE V

[*Enter* CORVINO.]

Signior Corvino! come most wish'd for! Oh,
How happy were you, if you knew it, now!
   CORV. Why? what? wherein?
   MOS.   The tardy hour is come, sir.
   CORV. He is not dead?
   MOS.   Not dead, sir, but as good;
He knows no man.

---

148. *going:* motion. 156. *Aeson:* Jason's father rejuvenated by Medea's
magic. 157. *battens:* feeds and fattens.

CORV.   How shall I do then?
MOS.   Why, sir?   5
CORV. I have brought him here a pearl.
MOS.   Perhaps he has
So much remembrance left as to know you, sir.
He still calls on you; nothing but your name
Is in his mouth. Is your pearl orient, sir?
  CORV. Venice was never owner of the like.   10
  VOLP. Signior Corvino!
MOS.   Hark!
VOLP.   Signior Corvino.
  MOS. He calls you; step and give it him.—He's here, sir.
And he has brought you a rich pearl.
  CORV.   How do you, sir?—
Tell him it doubles the twelfth carat.
MOS.   Sir,
He cannot understand: his hearing's gone;   15
And yet it comforts him to see you—
  CORV.   Say
I have a diamond for him, too.
MOS.   Best show 't sir;
Put it into his hand; 'tis only there
He apprehends; he has his feeling yet.
See, how he grasps it!
  CORV.   'Las, good gentleman!   2(
How pitiful the sight is!
MOS.   Tut, forget, sir.
The weeping of an heir should still be laughter
Under a visor.
  CORV.   Why, am I his heir?
  MOS. Sir, I am sworn, I may not show the will
Till he be dead. But here has been Corbaccio,   25
Here has been Voltore, here were others too—
I cannot number 'em, they were so many—
All gaping here for legacies; but I,
Taking the vantage of his naming you,
"Signior Corvino, Signior Corvino," took   30
Paper, and pen, and ink, and there I asked him
Whom he would have his heir! "Corvino." Who
Should be executor? "Corvino." And

_____

sc. v: 9. *orient:* of high quality. 14. *doubles . . . carat:* perfect, the equal of 24-carat or pure gold. 23. *visor:* mask.

To any question he was silent to,
I still interpreted the nods he made,   35
Through weakness, for consent; and sent home th' others,
Nothing bequeathed them, but to cry and curse.
   CORV. Oh, my dear Mosca. [*They embrace.*] Does he not perceive us?
   MOS. No more than a blind harper. He knows no man,
No face of friend, nor name of any servant,   40
Who 'twas that fed him last, or gave him drink;
Not those he hath begotten, or brought up,
Can he remember.
   CORV.   Has he children?
   MOS.   Bastards,
Some dozen, or more, that he begot on beggars,
Gypsies, and Jews, and black-moors, when he was drunk.   45
Knew you not that, sir? 'Tis the common fable.
The dwarf, the fool, the eunuch, are all his;
He's the true father of his family,
In all save me. But he has given 'em nothing.
   CORV. That's well, that's well. Art sure he does not hear us?   50
   MOS. Sure, sir! Why, look you, credit your own sense. [*Shouts in* VOLPONE'S *ear.*]
The pox approach, and add to your diseases,
If it would send you hence the sooner, sir;
For your incontinence it hath deserved it
Throughly and throughly, and the plague to boot!—   55
You may come near, sir.—Would you would once close
Those filthy eyes of yours, that flow with slime
Like two frog-pits; and those same hanging cheeks,
Cover'd with hide instead of skin—Nay, help, sir—
That look like frozen dishclouts set on end.   60
   CORV. Or like an old smoked wall, on which the rain
Ran down in streaks.
   MOS.   Excellent, sir! speak out;
You may be louder yet; a culverin
Discharged in his ear would hardly bore it.
   CORV. His nose is like a common sewer, still running.   65
   MOS. 'Tis good! And what his mouth?
   CORV.   A very draught.

---

46. *fable:* gossip. 52. *pox:* venereal disease. 58. *frog-pits:* i.e., beslimed with frogs' eggs. 59. *help:* i.e., to abuse Volpone. 63. *culverin:* cannon. 66. *draught:* cesspool.

MOS. O, stop it up—
CORV.   By no means.
MOS.   Pray you, let me;
Faith, I could stifle him rarely with a pillow
As well as any woman that should keep him.
  CORV. Do as you will; but I'll be gone.
  MOS.   Be so;   70
It is your presence makes him last so long.
  CORV. I pray you use no violence.
  MOS.   No, sir? why?
Why should you be thus scrupulous, 'pray you, sir?
  CORV. Nay, at your discretion.
  MOS.   Well, good sir, begone.
  CORV. I will not trouble him now to take my pearl?   75
  MOS. Pooh, nor your diamond. What a needless care
Is this afflicts you? Is not all here yours?
Am not I here, whom you have made, your creature,
That owe my being to you?
  CORV.   Grateful Mosca!
Thou art my friend, my fellow, my companion,   80
My partner, and shalt share in all my fortunes,
  MOS. Excepting one.
  CORV.   What's that?
  MOS.   Your gallant wife, sir.
                              [*Exit* CORVINO.
Now is he gone; we had no other means
To shoot him hence but this.
  VOLP.   My divine Mosca!
Thou hast today outgone thyself. Who's there?   85
                              [*Another knocks.*
I will be troubled with no more. Prepare
Me music, dances, banquets, all delights;
The Turk is not more sensual in his pleasures
Than will Volpone. [*Exit* MOSCA.] Let me see; a pearl!
A diamond! plate! *cecchines!* Good morning's purchase.   90
Why, this is better than rob churches, yet;
Or fat, by eating, once a month, a man—

                    [*Re-enter* MOSCA.]

Who is 't?

_____

68. *rarely:* quickly. 90. *purchase:* loot.

MOS.   The beauteous Lady Would-be, sir,
Wife to the English knight, Sir Politic Would-be—
This is the style, sir, is directed me—   95
Hath sent to know how you have slept tonight,
And if you would be visited.
    VOLP.   Not now.
Some three hours hence—
    MOS.   I told the squire so much.
    VOLP. When I am high with mirth and wine; then, then.
'Fore heaven, I wonder at the desperate valor   100
Of the bold English, that they dare let loose
Their wives to all encounters!
    MOS.   Sir, this knight
Had not his name for nothing: he is politic,
And knows, howe'er his wife affect strange airs,
She hath not yet the face to be dishonest.   105
But had she Signior Corvino's wife's face—
    VOLP. Hath she so rare a face?
    MOS.   O, sir, the wonder,
The blazing star of Italy! a wench
Of the first year! a beauty ripe as harvest!
Whose skin is whiter than a swan, all over!   110
Than silver, snow, or lilies! a soft lip,
Would tempt you to eternity of kissing!
And flesh that melteth in the touch to blood!
Bright as your gold! and lovely as your gold!
    VOLP. Why had not I known this before?
    MOS.   Alas, sir,   115
Myself but yesterday discovered it.
    VOLP. How might I see her?
    MOS.   Oh, not possible;
She's kept as warily as is your gold;
Never does come abroad, never takes air
But at a window. All her looks are sweet,   120
As the first grapes or cherries, and are watched
As near as they are.
    VOLP.   I must see her—
    MOS.   Sir,
There is a guard of ten spies thick upon her,

---

95. *style:* Mosca parodies the affected grand manner of Lady Would-be. 98.
squire: servant. 105. *dishonest:* unfaithful; *face:* (1) boldness (2) beauty.
113. *blood:* passion.

All his whole household; each of which is set
Upon his fellow, and have all their charge,   125
When he goes out, when he comes in, examined.
 VOLP. I will go see her, though but at her window.
 MOS. In some disguise then.
 VOLP.   That is true; I must
Maintain mine own shape still the same; we'll think.

              [Exeunt.

Act II

SCENE I. *Before Corvino's house in St. Mark's Square.*

[*Enter* SIR POLITIC WOULD-BE, *and* PEREGRINE.]

 POL. Sir, to a wise man, all the world's his soil:
It is not Italy, nor France, nor Europe,
That must bound me, if my fates call me forth.
Yet I protest, it is no salt desire
Of seeing countries, shifting a religion,   5
Nor any disaffection to the state
Where I was bred, and unto which I owe
My dearest plots, hath brought me out; much less
That idle, antic, stale, grey-headed project
Of knowing men's minds and manners, with Ulysses!   10
But a peculiar humor of my wife's
Laid for this height of Venice, to observe,
To quote, to learn the language, and so forth—
I hope you travel, sir, with license?
 PER.   Yes.
 POL. I dare the safelier converse.—How long, sir,   15
Since you left England?
 PER.   Seven weeks.
 POL.   So lately!
You ha' not been with my Lord Ambassador?
 PER.   Not yet, sir.
 POL. Pray you, what news, sir, vents our climate?

---

125. *charge:* parcels.

 ACT II, sc. 1: 4. *salt:* intense. 8. *dearest plots:* the dreams and accomplishments which made me what I am today. 12. *Laid . . . Venice:* directed toward Venice. 13. *quote:* note. 14. *license:* government permission
—required of nobility. 18. *vents our climate:* comes from England.

I heard last night a most strange thing reported
By some of my Lord's followers, and I long   20
To hear how 'twill be seconded!
   PER.   What was't, sir?
   POL. Marry, sir, of a raven that should build
In a ship royal of the king's.
   PER. [*Aside*]   This fellow,
Does he gull me, trow? or is gulled—Your name, sir?
   POL. My name is Politic Would-be.
   PER. [*Aside*]   O, that speaks him.—   25
A knight, sir?
   POL.   A poor knight, sir.
   PER.   Your lady
Lies here in Venice, for intelligence
Of tires and fashions and behavior,
Among the courtesans? The fine Lady Would-be?
   POL. Yes, sir; the spider and the bee ofttimes   30
Suck from one flower.
   PER.   Good Sir Politic!
I cry you mercy; I have heard much of you.
'Tis true, sir, of your raven.
   POL.   On your knowledge?
   PER. Yes, and your lion's whelping in the Tower.
   POL. Another whelp!
   PER.   Another, sir.
   POL.   Now heaven!   35
What prodigies be these? The fires at Berwick!
And the new star! These things concurring, strange!
And full of omen! Saw you those meteors?
   PER. I did, sir.
   POL.   Fearful! Pray you, sir, confirm me,
Were there three porpoises seen, above the Bridge,   40
As they give out?
   PER.   Six, and a sturgeon, sir.
   POL. I am astonished!
   PER.   Nay, sir, be not so;
I'll tell you a greater prodigy then these—
   POL. What should these things portend?

---

21. *how . . . seconded:* what will come of it. 22. *raven:* perhaps a dark
hint of a traitor in the royal household. 24. *trow:* I wonder. 28. *tires:*
styles. 34. *Tower:* of London, where a lion was born August 5, 1604, and
another on February 26, 1606. 36. *fires:* meteors.

PER.   The very day,
Let me be sure, that I put forth from London,   45
There was a whale discovered in the river,
As high as Woolwich, that had waited there,
Few know how many months, for the subversion
Of the Stode fleet.
       POL.   Is't possible? Believe it,
'Twas either sent from Spain, or the Archduke's!   50
Spinola's whale, upon my life, my credit!
Will they not leave these projects? Worthy sir,
Some other news.
       PER.   Faith, Stone, the fool, is dead,
And they do lack a tavern fool extremely.
       POL. Is Mas' Stone dead?
       PER.   He's dead, sir; why, I hope   55
You thought him not immortal?—[*Aside*] Oh, this knight,
Were he well known, would be a precious thing
To fit our English stage. He that should write
But such a fellow, should be thought to feign
Extremely, if not maliciously.
       POL.   Stone dead!   60
       PER. Dead.—Lord! how deeply, sir, you apprehend it!
He was no kinsman to you?
       POL.   That I know of.
Well! that same fellow was an unknown fool.
       PER. And yet you knew him, it seems?
       POL.   I did so. Sir,
I knew him one of the most dangerous heads   65
Living within the state, and so I held him.
       PER. Indeed, sir?
       POL.   While he lived, in action,
He has received weekly intelligence,
Upon my knowledge, out of the Low Countries,
For all parts of the world, in cabbages;   70
And those dispensed again to ambassadors,
In oranges, muskmelons, apricots,
Lemons, pome-citrons, and such like; sometimes

48-9. *subversion . . . fleet:* to destroy the fleet from Stode, near Hamburg.
50. *Archduke's:* i.e., the Netherlands, at this time under Archduke Albert
of Austria and Spain and his wife, the Spanish Infanta Isabella. 51. *Spinola:*
Spanish general who captured Ostend in 1604 and used novel weapons. 53.
fool: court fool to James I. 62. *That:* not that. 63. *unknown:* pretended.
64-5. *knew:* (1) saw through. (2) were acquainted with.

In Colchester oysters, and your Selsey cockles.
  PER. You make me wonder!
  POL.   Sir, upon my knowledge.   75
Nay, I have observed him, at your public ordinary,
Take his advertisement from a traveller
(A concealed statesman) in a trencher of meat;
And instantly, before the meal was done,
Convey an answer in a toothpick.
  PER.   Strange!   80
How could this be, sir?
  POL.   Why, the meat was cut
So like his character, and so laid as he
Must easily read the cipher.
  PER.   I have heard
He could not read, sir.
  POL.   So 'twas given out,
In polity, by those that did employ him;   85
But he could read, and had your languages,
And to 't, as sound a noddle—
  PER.   I have heard, sir,
That your baboons were spies, and that they were
A kind of subtle nation near to China.
  POL. Ay, ay, your Mamaluchi. Faith, they had   90
Their hand in a French plot or two; but they
Were so extremely given to women, as
They made discovery of all: yet I
Had my advices here, on Wednesday last,
From one of their own coat, they were returned,   95
Made their relations, as the fashion is,
And now stand fair for fresh employment.
  PER. [Aside]   Heart!
This Sir Pol will be ignorant of nothing.—
It seems, sir, you know all.
  POL.   Not all, sir. But
I have some general notions. I do love   100
To note and to observe. Though I live out,

---

74. *Selsey:* on the Sussex coast. 76. *ordinary:* tavern. 77. *advertisement:*
information. 82. *character:* writing. 85. *In polity:* cunningly. 87. *And to' t:*
in addition. 90. *Mamaluchi:* actually Mamelukes, or white slaves converted
to Islamism and powerful in Egypt from the 13th century. 92. *as:* that. 95.
coat: party. 96. *relations:* reports.

Free from the active torrent, yet I'd mark
The currents and the passages of things
For mine own private use; and know the ebbs
And flows of state.
PER.   Believe it, sir, I hold   105
Myself in no small tie unto my fortunes,
For casting me thus luckily upon you,
Whose knowledge, if your bounty equal it,
May do me great assistance, in instruction
For my behavior, and my bearing, which   110
Is yet so rude and raw—
POL.   Why? came you forth
Empty of rules for travel?
PER.   Faith, I had
Some common ones, from out that vulgar grammar,
Which he that cried Italian to me, taught me.
POL. Why, this it is that spoils all our brave bloods,
Trusting our hopeful gentry unto pedants,
Fellows of outside, and mere bark. You seem
To be a gentleman of ingenuous race.—
I not profess it, but my fate hath been
To be where I have been consulted with,   120
In this high kind, touching some great men's sons,
Persons of blood and honor.—
PER.   Who be these, sir?

SCENE II

[*Enter* MOSCA *and* NANO *disguised, with workmen who erect a stage.*]

MOS. Under that window, there 't must be. The same.
POL. Fellows to mount a bank! Did your instructor
In the dear tongues never discourse to you
Of the Italian mountebanks?
PER.   Yes, sir.
POL.   Why,
Here shall you see one.
PER.   They are quacksalvers,   5
Fellows that live by venting oils and drugs!

---

106. *tie:* obligation. 114. *cried:* taught. 118. *ingenuous race:* honorable birth.
sc. II: 2. *bank:* platform (with pun on *mountebank*). 6. *venting:* selling.

POL. Was that the character he gave you of them?
PER. As I remember.
POL.   Pity his ignorance.
They are the only knowing men of Europe!
Great general scholars, excellent physicians,   10
Most admired statesmen, professed favorites
And cabinet counsellors to the greatest princes!
The only languaged men of all the world!
PER. And, I have heard, they are most lewd impostors;
Made all of terms and shreds; no less beliers   15
Of great men's favors, than their own vile med'cines;
Which they will utter upon monstrous oaths;
Selling that drug for twopence, ere they part,
Which they have valued at twelve crowns before.
POL. Sir, calumnies are answered best with silence.   20
Yourself shall judge.—Who is it mounts, my friends?
MOS. Scoto of Mantua, sir.
POL.   Is 't he? Nay, then
I'll proudly promise, sir, you shall behold
Another man than has been phant'sied to you.
I wonder yet, that he should mount his bank   25
Here in this nook, that has been wont t' appear
In face of the Piazza! Here he comes.

[*Enter* VOLPONE, *disguised as a mountebank doctor, and followed
by a crowd of people.*]

VOLP. [*To* NANO] Mount, zany.
GRE.   Follow, follow, follow, follow, follow.
POL. See how the people follow him! he's a man
May write ten thousand crowns in bank here. Note,   30
Mark but his gesture—I do use to observe
The state he keeps in getting up!
PER.   'Tis worth it, sir.
VOLP. Most noble gentlemen, and my worthy patrons, it may seem
strange that I, your Scoto Mantuano, who was ever wont to fix
my bank in the face of the public Piazza, near the shelter   [35
of the portico to the Procuratia, should now, after eight months'
absence from this illustrious city of Venice, humbly retire myself
into an obscure nook of the Piazza.

---

14. *lewd:* ignorant. 15. *terms and shreds:* parroted scraps of learning. 17.
utter: sell; *oaths:* testimonials. 22. *Scoto of Mantua:* an Italian juggler, then
in England. 24. *phant'sied:* imaginatively described. 28. *GRE:* i.e., Gregis,
Latin for "crowd."

POL. Did not I now object the same?

PER.   Peace, sir.

VOLP. Let me tell you: I am not, as your Lombard proverb   [40
saith, cold on my feet; or content to part with my commodities at a
cheaper rate than I accustomed—look not for it. Nor that the
calumnious reports of that impudent detractor, and shame to our
profession (Alessandro Buttone, I mean), who gave out, in public,
I was condemn'd *a' sforzato* to the galleys, for poisoning the   [45
Cardinal Bembo's—cook, hath at all attached, much less dejected me.
No, no, worthy gentlemen; to tell you true, I cannot endure to see the
rabble of these ground *ciarlitani* that spread their cloaks on the pave-
ment, as if they meant to do feats of activity, and then come in lamely,
with their mouldy tales out of Boccaccio, like stale Tabarin,   [50
the fabulist; some of them discoursing their travels, and of their
tedious captivity in the Turk's galleys, when, indeed, were the truth
known, they were the Christian's galleys, where very temperately they
ate bread, and drunk water, as a wholesome penance, enjoined them
by their confessors, for base pilferies.   55

POL. Note but his bearing, and contempt of these.

VOLP. These turdy-facy-nasty-paty-lousy-fartical rogues, with one
poor groat's-worth of unprepared antimony, finely wrapped up
in several *scartoccios,* are able, very well, to kill their twenty a
week, and play; yet these meagre, starved spirits, who have   [60
half stopped the organs of their minds with earthy oppilations, want
not their favorers among your shrivelled salad-eating artisans, who
are overjoyed that they may have their half-pe'rth of physic; though
it purge 'em into another world, 't makes no matter.

POL. Excellent! ha' you heard better language, sir?   65

VOLP. Well, let 'em go. And, gentlemen, honorable gentlemen,
know that for this time our bank, being thus removed from the
clamours of the *canaglia,* shall be the scene of pleasure and delight;
for I have nothing to sell, little or nothing to sell.

POL. I told you, sir, his end.

PER.   You did so, sir.   70

VOLP. I protest I and my six servants are not able to make of this
precious liquor so fast as it is fetched away from my lodging by
gentlemen of your city, strangers of the terra-firma, worshipful

45. *a' sforzato:* at forced labor. 46. *Bembo:* secretary to Pope Leo X; the
pause indicated by the dash after Bembo suggests that Volpone was about
to say something like "mistress" rather than "cook." 48. *ciarlitani:* small-
time charlatans. 51. *fabulist:* storyteller. 59. *scartoccios:* papers, also a
charge of gunpowder. 61. *oppilations:* obstructions of the vital spirits. 63.
half-pe'rth: half-pennyworth. 68. *canaglia:* canaille, rabble. 73. *terra-
firma:* mainland.

merchants, ay, and senators, too, who, ever since my arrival, have
detained me to their uses, by their splendidous liberalities.   [75
And worthily. For what avails your rich man to have his magazines
stuffed with *moscadelli,* or of the purest grape, when his physicians
prescribe him, on pain of death, to drink nothing but water cocted
with aniseeds? O health! health! the blessing of the rich! the riches
of the poor! who can buy thee at too dear a rate, since there   [80
is no enjoying this world without thee? Be not then so sparing of
your purses, honorable gentlemen, as to abridge the natural course
of life—

PER. You see his end.

POL.   Ay, is 't not good?

VOLP. For, when a humid flux, or catarrh, by the mutability   [85
of air, falls from your head into an arm or shoulder, or any other
part, take you a ducat, or your *cecchine* of gold, and apply to the place
affected; see what good effect it can work. No, no; 'tis this blessed
unguento, this rare extraction, that hath only power to disperse all
malignant humors that proceed either of hot, cold, moist, or   [90
windy causes—

PER. I would he had put in dry too.

POL.   'Pray you, observe.

VOLP. To fortify the most indigest and crude stomach, ay, were it
of one that, through extreme weakness, vomited blood, applying
only a warm napkin to the place, after the unction and   [95
fricace;—for the *vertigine* in the head, putting but a drop into your
nostrils, likewise behind the ears, a most sovereign and approved
remedy; the *mal caduco,* cramps, convulsions, paralyses, epilepsies,
tremor cordia, retired nerves, ill vapors of the spleen, stoppings of the
liver, the stone, the strangury, *hernia ventosa, iliaca passio;*   [100
stops a *dysenteria* immediately; easeth the torsion of the small guts;
and cures *melancholia hypochondriaca,* being taken and applied according to my printed receipt. [*Pointing to his bill and his glass*] For
this is the physician, this the medicine; this counsels, this cures;
this gives direction, this works the effect; and, in sum, both   [105
together may be termed an abstract of the theoric and practic
in the Aesculapian art. 'Twill cost you eight crowns.—And, Zan
Fritada, pray thee sing a verse, extempore, in honor of it.

---

76. *magazines:* storage places. 77. *moscadelli:* muscatel wine. 78. *cocted:*
boiled. 96. *fricace:* rubbing; *vertigine:* dizziness. 98. *mal caduco:* epilepsy.
99. *tremor cordia:* heart trouble; *retired:* shrunken. 100. *stone:* kidney
stone; *strangury:* strangulated urination. 100. *hernia ventosa:* "windy"
hernia, with gas on the stomach. 100. *Iliaca passio:* colic. 101. *torsion:*
griping. *melancholia hypochondria:* acute depression.

POL. How do you like him, sir?
PER.   Most strangely, I!
POL. Is not his language rare?
PER.   But alchemy,   110
I never heard the like, or Broughton's books.
NANO. [*Sings*]

> Had old Hippocrates, or Galen,
> That to their books put med'cines all in,
> But known this secret, they had never   115
> (Of which they will be guilty ever)
> Been murderers of so much paper,
> Or wasted many a hurtless taper;
> No Indian drug had e'er been famed,
> Tobacco, sassafras, not named;   120
> Ne yet of guacum one small stick, sir,
> Nor Raymund Lully's great elixir.
> Ne had been known the Danish Gonswart,
> Or Paracelsus, with his long-sword.

PER. All this, yet, will not do; eight crowns is high.   125
VOLP. No more.—Gentlemen, if I had but time to discourse to you
the miraculous effects of this my oil, surnamed *oglio del Scoto*, with
the countless catalogue of those I have cured of th' aforesaid, and
many more diseases; the patents and privileges of all the princes
and commonwealths of Christendom; or but the depositions   [130
of those that appeared on my part, before the signiory of the
Sanitâ and most learned College of Physicians; where I was author-
ized, upon notice taken of the admirable virtues of my medicaments,
and mine own excellency in matter of rare and unknown secrets, not
only to disperse them publicly in this famous city, but in all   [135
the territories that happily joy under the government of the most
pious and magnificent states of Italy. But may some other gallant
fellow say, "Oh, there be divers that make profession to have as good,
and as experimented receipts as yours." Indeed, very many have
assayed, like apes, in imitation of that which is really and   [140
essentially in me, to make of this oil; bestowed great cost in furnaces,

---

110. *But:* except for. 111. *Broughton:* an eccentric Puritan preacher. 113.
Hippocrates, Galen: pioneer Greek physicians. 118. *hurtless:* innocent. 121.
Ne: nor. *Guacum:* resin of the guaiac tree used to treat gout. 122. *Lully:*
thirteenth-century occulist and alchemist. 123. *Gonswort:* another alchemist, not identified. 124. *Paracelsus:* sixteenth-century Swiss-German alchemist who was reputed to have a familiar spirit living in his sword. 131.
signiory . . . Sanitâ: Venetian medical licensing board.

stills, alembics, continual fires, and preparation of the ingredients
(as indeed there goes to it six hundred several simples, besides some
quantity of human fat, for the conglutination, which we buy of the
anatomists); but when these practitioners come to the last   [145
devotion—blow, blow, puff, puff, and all flies in *fumo*. Ha, ha, ha!
Poor wretches! I rather pity their folly and indiscretion, than their
loss of time and money; for those may be recovered by industry; but
to be a fool born, is a disease incurable. For myself, I always from
my youth have endeavored to get the rarest secrets, and book   [150
them, either in exchange or for money; I spared nor cost nor labor
where anything was worthy to be learned. And, gentlemen, honorable gentlemen, I will undertake, by virtue of chemical art, out of the
honorable hat that covers your head, to extract the four elements;
that is to say, the fire, air, water, and earth, and return you   [155
your felt without burn or stain. For, whilst others have been at
the *balloo* I have been at my book; and am now past the craggy
paths of study, and come to the flow'ry plains of honor and reputation.

POL. I do assure you, sir, that is his aim.   160
VOLP. But, to our price.
PER.   And that withal, Sir Pol.
VOLP. You all know, honorable gentlemen, I never valued this
ampulla, or vial, at less than eight crowns; but for this time, I am
content to be deprived of it for six; six crowns is the price, and less
in courtesy I know you cannot offer me; take it or leave it,   [165
howsoever, both it and I am at your service. I ask you not as the
value of the thing, for then I should demand of you a thousand
crowns; so the Cardinals Montalto, Fernese, the great Duke of
Tuscany, my gossip, with divers other princes, have given me; but
I despise money. Only to show my affection to you, honor-   [170
able gentlemen, and your illustrious state here, I have neglected
the messages of these princes, mine own offices, framed my journey
hither, only to present you with the fruits of my travels.—Tune
your voices once more to the touch of your instruments, and give
the honorable assembly some delightful recreation.   175

PER. What monstrous and most painful circumstance
Is here, to get some three or four gazets,
Some threepence i' the whole! for that 'twill come to.

---

146. *fumo:* smoke. 157. *balloo:* ball game. 161. *that withal:* that too (i.e.,
money) is his aim. 168. *Montalto . . . Tuscany:* actual persons of the six-
teenth century. 169. *gossip:* intimate friend. 177. *gazets:* small coins.

NANO. [*Sings*]

> You that would last long, list to my song;   180
> Make no more coil, but buy of this oil.
> Would you be ever fair, and young?
> Stout of teeth and strong of tongue?
> Tart of palate? Quick of ear?
> Sharp of sight? of nostril clear?   185
> Moist of hand? and light of foot?
> Or (I will come nearer to 't)
> Would you live free from all diseases?
> Do the act your mistress pleases,
> Yet fright all áchĕs from your bones?   190
> Here's a med'cine for the nones.

VOLP. Well, I am in a humor, at this time, to make a present of the small quantity my coffer contains; to the rich in courtesy, and to the poor for God's sake. Wherefore now mark: I asked you six crowns; and six crowns, at other times, you have paid   [195 me; you shall not give me six crowns, nor five, nor four, nor three, nor two, nor one; nor half a ducat; no, nor a *muccinigo*. Sixpence it will cost you, or six hundred pound—expect no lower price, for, by the banner of my front, I will not bate a bagatine,—that I will have, only, a pledge of your loves, to carry something from   [200 amongst you, to show I am not contemned by you. Therefore, now, toss your handkerchiefs, cheerfully, cheerfully; and be advertised, that the first heroic spirit that deigns to grace me with a handkerchief, I will give it a little remembrance of something beside, shall please it better than if I had presented it with a double pistolet.   [205

PER. Will you be that heroic spark, Sir Pol?

[CELIA, *at the window, throws down her handkerchief.*
O, see! the window has prevented you.

VOLP. Lady, I kiss your bounty; and, for this timely grace you have done your poor Scoto of Mantua, I will return you, over   [210 and above my oil, a secret of that high and inestimable nature, shall make you for ever enamored on that minute wherein your eye first descended on so mean, yet not altogether to be despis'd, an object. Here is a powder concealed in this paper, of which, if I should speak to the worth, nine thousand volumes were but as one page,   [215 that page as a line, that line as a word; so short is this pilgrimage of

---

181. *coil:* fuss. 184. *Tart:* sensitive. 191. *nones:* purpose. 197. *muccinigo:* small coin. 199. *bagatine:* trifling coin. 205. *double pistolet:* gold coin. 208. *prevented:* anticipated.

man, which some call life, to the expressing of it. Would I reflect on
the price? Why, the whole world is but as an empire, that empire
as a province, that province as a bank, that bank as a private purse,
to the purchase of it. I will only tell you: it is the powder   [220
that made Venus a goddess, given her by Apollo, that kept her perpetually young, cleared her wrinkles, firmed her gums, filled her skin,
colored her hair; from her derived to Helen, and at the sack of
Troy unfortunately lost; till now, in this our age, it was as happily
recovered, by a studious antiquary, out of some ruins of Asia,   [225
who sent a moiety of it to the court of France (but much sophisticated), wherewith the ladies there now color their hair. The rest,
at this present, remains with me, extracted to a quintessence; so that,
wherever it but touches, in youth it perpetually preserves, in age
restores the complexion; seats your teeth, did they dance like   [230
virginal jacks, firm as a wall; makes them white as ivory, that were
black as—

SCENE III

[*Enter* CORVINO.]

COR. Spite o' the devil, and my shame! Come down here;
Come down!—No house but mine to make your scene?
Signior Flaminio, will you down, sir? down?
What, is my wife your Franciscina, sir?
No windows on the whole piazza, here,   5
To make your properties, but mine? but mine?
                         [*He beats away the mountebank, etc.*
Heart! ere tomorrow I shall be new christened,
And called the *Pantalone di Bisognosi;*
About the town.
PER.   What should this mean, Sir Pol?
POL. Some trick of state, believe it; I will home.   10
PER. It may be some design on you.
POL.   I know not.
I'll stand upon my guard.
PER.   It is your best, sir.
POL. This three weeks, all my advices, all my letters,
They have been intercepted.
PER.   Indeed, sir?

231. *virginal jacks:* musical keys.
    sc. III: 3. *Flaminio:* Italian actor. 4. *Franciscina:* flirtatious servant girl,
stock stage character. 8. *Pantalone di Bisognosi:* fool of the beggars,
another theatrical type, frequently an old cuckold.

Best have a care.
POL.   Nay, so I will.
PER. [*Aside*]   This knight,   15
I may not lose him, for my mirth, till night.   [*Exeunt.*

SCENE IV. *A room in Volpone's house.*

[*Enter* VOLPONE *and* MOSCA.]

VOLP. O, I am wounded.
MOS.   Where, sir?
VOLP.   Not without;
Those blows were nothing; I could bear them ever.
But angry Cupid, bolting from her eyes,
Hath shot himself into me like a flame;
Where now he flings about his burning heat,   5
As in a furnace some ambitous fire
Whose vent is stopped. The fight is all within me.
I cannot live, except thou help me, Mosca;
My liver melts, and I, without the hope
Of some soft air from her refreshing breath,   10
Am but a heap of cinders.
MOS.   'Las, good sir,
Would you had never seen her.
VOLP.   Nay, would thou
Hadst never told me of her.
MOS.   Sir, 'tis true;
I do confess I was unfortunate,
And you unhappy; but I am bound in conscience,   15
No less than duty, to effect my best
To your release of torment, and I will, sir.
VOLP. Dear Mosca, shall I hope?
MOS.   Sir, more than dear,
I will not bid you to despair of aught
Within a human compass.
VOLP.   O, there spoke   20
My better angel. Mosca, take my keys,
Gold, plate, and jewels, all 's at thy devotion;
Employ them how thou wilt—nay, coin me too—
So thou in this but crown my longings, Mosca!
MOS. Use but your patience.
VOLP.   So I have.
MOS.   I doubt not   25
To bring success to your desires.

VOLP.   Nay, then,
I not repent me of my late disguise.
  MOS. If you can horn him, sir, you need not.
    VOLP.   True.
Besides, I never meant him for my heir.
Is not the color o' my beard and eyebrows   30
To make me known?
  MOS.   No jot.
    VOLP.   I did it well.
  MOS. So well, would I could follow you in mine,
With half the happiness; and yet I would
Escape your epilogue.
    VOLP.   But were they gulled
With a belief that I was Scoto?
  MOS.   Sir,   35
Scoto himself could hardly have distinguished!
I have not time to flatter you now; we'll part,
And as I prosper, so applaud my art.   [*Exeunt.*

SCENE V. *A room in Corvino's house.*

[*Enter* CORVINO, *with his sword in his hand, dragging in* CELIA.]

  CORV. Death of mine honor, with the city's fool!
A juggling, tooth-drawing, prating mountebank!
And at a public window! where, whilst he,
With his strained action, and his dole of faces,
To his drug-lecture draws your itching ears,   5
A crew of old, unmarried, noted lechers,
Stood leering up like satyrs; and you smile
Most graciously! and fan your favors forth,
To give your hot spectators satisfaction!
What, was your mountebank their call? their whistle?   10
Or were you enamored on his copper rings,
His saffron jewel, with the toad-stone in 't,
Or his embroidered suit, with the cope-stitch,
Made of a hearse cloth, or his old tilt-feather,
Or his starched beard? Well! you shall have him, yes.   15
He shall come home, and minister unto you

---

sc. IV: 28. *horn:* two-time. 34. *epilogue:* i.e., the blows.
    sc. V: 4. *dole of faces:* theatrical expressions. 12. *toad-stone:* stone-like object reputed to be formed in the head of a toad and to have therapeutic properties. 14. *tilt-feather:* helmet plume.

The fricace for the mother. Or, let me see,
I think you'd rather mount! Would you not mount?
Why, if you'll mount, you may; yes, truly, you may.
And so you may be seen, down to th' foot.   20
Get you a cittern, Lady Vanity,
And be a dealer with the virtuous man;
Make one. I'll but protest myself a cuckold,
And save your dowry. I am a Dutchman, I!
For if you thought me an Italian,   25
You would be damned ere you did this, you whore.
Thou 'dst tremble to imagine that the murder
Of father, mother, brother, all thy race,
Should follow, as the subject of my justice!
    CEL. Good sir, have patience!
    CORV.   What couldst thou propose   30
Less to thyself, than in this heat of wrath,
And stung with my dishonor, I should strike
This steel into thee, with as many stabs
As thou wert gazed upon with goatish eyes?
    CEL. Alas, sir, be appeased! I could not think   35
My being at the window should more now
Move your impatience than at other times.
    CORV. No? not to seek and entertain a parley
With a known knave? before a multitude?
You were an actor with your handkerchief!   40
Which he most sweetly kissed in the receipt,
And might, no doubt, return it with a letter
And 'point the place where you might meet; your sister's,
Your mother's, or your aunt's might serve the turn.
    CEL. Why, dear sir, when do I make these excuses,   45
Or ever stir abroad, but to the church?
And that so seldom—
    CORV.   Well, it shall be less;
And thy restraint before was liberty,
To what I now decree; and therefore mark me.
First, I will have this bawdy light damned up;   50
And till 't be done, some two or three yards off
I'll chalk a line; o'er which if thou but chance

---

17. *fricace . . . mother:* massage for hysteria (with a sexual undermeaning, as also in "mount," and "Make one"). 18. *mount:* go on the stage. 21. *cittern:* guitar. 22. *dealer:* whore. 24. *Dutchman:* thrifty. 30. *propose:* expect. 50. *light:* window.

To set thy desp'rate foot, more hell, more horror,
More wild remorseless rage shall seize on thee
Than on a conjuror that had heedless left   55
His circle's safety ere his devil was laid.
Then here's a lock which I will hang upon thee,
And, now I think on 't, I will keep thee backwards;
Thy lodging shall be backwards, thy walks backwards,
Thy prospect—all be backwards, and no pleasure,   60
That thou shalt know but backwards. Nay, since you force
My honest nature, know it is your own
Being too open, makes me use you thus.
Since you will not contain your subtle nostrils
In a sweet room, but they must snuff the air   65
Of rank and sweaty passengers—[*Knock within*] one knocks.
Away, and be not seen, pain of thy life;
Nor look toward the window; if thou dost—
Nay, stay, hear this—let me not prosper, whore,
But I will make thee an anatomy,   70
Dissect thee mine own self, and read a lecture
Upon thee to the city, and in public.
Away!—   [*Exit* CELIA.

[*Enter* SERVITORE.]

Who's there?
    SER.   'Tis Signior Mosca, sir.

SCENE VI

[CORVINO *and* SERVITORE *remain.*]

CORV. Let him come in. [*Exit* SERVITORE.]—His master's dead!
    There's yet
Some good to help the bad.—[*Enter* MOSCA.] My Mosca, welcome;
I guess your news.
    MOS.   I fear you cannot, sir.
    CORV. Is 't not his death?
    MOS.   Rather the contrary.
    CORV. Not his recovery?
    MOS.   Yes, sir.
    CORV.   I am cursed;   5
I am bewitched; my crosses meet to vex me.
How? how? how? how?

55-6. *conjuror . . . laid:* a safety-measure in invoking the devil was to draw
a magic circle. 57. *lock:* chastity belt. 66. *passengers:* passers-by. 70. *anat*
omy: cadaver.

MOS.   Why, sir, with Scoto's oil!
Corbaccio and Voltore brought of it,
Whilst I was busy in an inner room—
   CORV. Death! that damned mountebank! but for the law,   10
Now, I could kill the rascal. 'T cannot be
His oil should have that virtue. Ha' not I
Known him a common rogue, come fiddling in
To th' *osteria,* with a tumbling whore,
And, when he has done all his forced tricks, been glad   15
Of a poor spoonful of dead wine, with flies in 't?
It cannot be. All his ingredients
Are a sheep's gall, a roasted bitch's marrow,
Some few sod earwigs, pounded caterpillars,
A little capon's grease, and fasting spittle: 20
I know 'em to a dram.
   MOS.   I know not, sir;
But some on 't, there, they poured into his ears,
Some in his nostrils, and recovered him;
Applying but the fricace.
   CORV.   Pox o' that fricace.
   MOS. And, since, to seem the more officious   25
And flatt'ring of his health, there, they have had,
At extreme fees, the college of physicians
Consulting on him, how they might restore him;
Where one would have a cataplasm of spices,
Another a flayed ape clapped to his breast,   30
A third would ha' it a dog, a fourth an oil,
With wildcats' skins. At last, they all resolved
That, to preserve him, was no other means
But some young woman must be straight sought out,
Lusty, and full of juice, to sleep by him;   35
And to this service most unhappily,
And most unwillingly, am I now employed,
Which here I thought to pre-acquaint you with,
For your advice, since it concerns you most;
Because I would not do that thing might cross   40
Your ends, on whom I have my whole dependence, sir.
Yet, if I do not they may delate
My slackness to my patron, work me out
Of his opinion; and there all your hopes,

---

sc. VI: 14. *osteria:* inn; *tumbling whore:* female acrobat. 19. *sod earwigs:*
boiled beetles. 25. *officious:* dutiful. 29. *cataplasm:* poultice. 42. *delate:* report.

Ventures, or whatsoever, are all frustrate.   45
I do but tell you, sir. Besides, they are all
Now striving who shall first present him. Therefore—
I could entreat you, briefly, conclude somewhat:
Prevent 'em if you can.
  CORV.   Death to my hopes!
This is my villainous fortune! Best to hire   50
Some common courtesan!
  MOS.   Ay, I thought on that, sir;
But they are all so subtle, full of art—
And age again doting and flexible,
So as—I cannot tell—we may, perchance,
Light on a quean may cheat us all.
  CORV.   'Tis true.   55
  MOS. No, no; it must be one that has no tricks, sir,
Some simple thing, a creature made unto it;
Some wench you may command. Ha' you no kinswoman?
Gods so—Think, think, think, think, think, think, think, sir.
One o' the doctors offered there his daughter.   60
  CORV. How!
  MOS. Yes, Signior Lupo, the physician.
  CORV. His daughter!
  MOS.   And a virgin, sir. Why alas,
He knows the state of 's body, what it is:
That naught can warm his blood, sir, but a fever,
Nor any incantation raise his spirit;   65
A long forgetfulness hath seized that part.
Besides, sir, who shall know it? Someone or two—
  CORV. I pray thee give me leave.—[*Stepping aside*] If any man
But I had had this luck—The thing in 't self,
I know, is nothing.—Wherefore should not I   70
As well command my blood and my affections
As this dull doctor? In this point of honor,
The cases are all one of wife and daughter.
  MOS. [*Aside*] I hear him coming.
  CORV. [*Aside*] She shall do 't; 'tis done.   75
'Slight! if this doctor, who is not engaged,
Unless 't be for his counsel, which is nothing,
Offer his daughter, what should I, that am
So deeply in? I will prevent him. Wretch!

---

49. *Prevent:* get ahead of. 53. *age again:* "old" Volpone also. 57. *made unto:* coached for. 74. *coming:* coming round. 76. *engaged:* involved.

Covetous wretch!—Mosca, I have determined.
  MOS. How, sir?
  CORV.   We'll make all sure. The party you wot of   80
Shall be mine own wife, Mosca.
  MOS.   Sir, the thing,
But that I would not seem to counsel you,
I should have motioned to you, at the first;
And make your count, you have cut all their throats.
Why! 'tis directly taking a possession!   85
And in his next fit, we may let him go.
'Tis but to pull the pillow from his head,
And he is throttled; it had been done before
But for your scrupulous doubts.
  CORV.   Ay, a plague on 't;
My conscience fools my wit! Well, I'll be brief,   90
And so be thou, lest they should be before us.
Go home; prepare him; tell him with what zeal
And willingness I do it. Swear it was
On the first hearing, as thou mayst do, truly,
Mine own free motion.
  MOS.   Sir, I warrant you,   95
I'll so possess him with it, that the rest
Of his starved clients shall be banished all;
And only you received. But come not, sir,
Until I send, for I have something else
To ripen for your good—you must not know 'f.   100
  CORV. But do not you forget to send, now.
  MOS.   Fear not.   [*Exit.*

SCENE VII

[CORVINO *remains.*]

  CORV. Where are you, wife? My Celia! Wife!

[*Enter* CELIA.]

                          —What, blubbering?
Come, dry those tears. I think thou thought'st me in earnest;
Ha? By this light I talked so but to try thee.
Methinks, the lightness of the occasion
Should ha' confirmed thee. Come, I am not jealous.   5

---

83. *motioned:* proposed.
  SC. VII: 5. *confirmed:* reassured.

CEL. No?

CORV.   Faith I am not, I, nor never was;
It is a poor, unprofitable humor.
Do not I know, if women have a will,
They'll do 'gainst all the watches o' the world,
And that the fiercest spies are tamed with gold?   10
Tut, I am confident in thee, thou shalt see 't;
And see I'll give thee cause, too, to believe it.
Come, kiss me.—Go, and make thee ready straight,
In all thy best attire, thy choicest jewels,
Put 'em all on, and, with 'em, thy best looks: 15
We are invited to a solemn feast,
At old Volpone's, where it shall appear
How far I am free from jealousy or fear.   [Exeunt.

Act III

SCENE I. *A street.*

[*Enter* MOSCA.]

MOS. I fear I shall begin to grow in love
With my dear self and my most prosp'rous parts;
They do so spring and burgeon. I can feel
A whimsy i' my blood—I know not how—
Success hath made me wanton. I could skip   5
Out of my skin now, like a subtle snake,
I am so limber. Oh! your parasite
Is a most precious thing, dropped from above,
Not bred 'mongst clods and clodpolls, here on earth
I muse the mystery was not made a science,   10
It is so liberally professed! Almost
All the wise world is little else, in nature,
But parasites or sub-parasites. And yet
I mean not those that have your bare town-art,
To know who's fit to feed 'em; have no house,   15
No family, no care, and therefore mold
Tales for men's ears, to bait that sense; or get
Kitchen-invention, and some stale receipts

ACT III, SC. I: 10. *mystery:* profession.   11. *liberally:* widely.   17. *bait:* feed.

To please the belly, and the groin; nor those,
With their court dog-tricks, that can fawn and fleer,　　2(
Make their revénue out of legs and faces,
Echo my lord, and lick away a mote:
But your fine, elegant rascal, that can rise
And stoop, almost together, like an arrow;
Shoot through the air as nimbly as a star;　　25
Turn short as doth a swallow; and be here,
And there, and here, and yonder, all at once;
Present to any humor, all occasion;
And change a visor swifter than a thought!
This is the creature had the art born with him;　　30
Toils not to learn it, but doth practise it
Out of most excellent nature; and such sparks
Are the true parasites, others but their zanies.

SCENE II

[*Enter* BONARIO.]

MOS. Who's this? Bonario, old Corbaccio's son?
The person I was bound to seek. Fair sir,
You are happ'ly met.
BON.　　　　　　That cannot be by thee.
MOS. Why, sir?
BON.　　　　　Nay, 'pray thee know thy way, and leave me.
I would be loth to interchange discourse　　5
With such a mate as thou art.
MOS.　　　　　　　Courteous sir,
Scorn not my poverty.
BON.　　　　　Not I, by heaven;
But thou shalt give me leave to hate thy baseness.
MOS. Baseness!
BON.　　　　Ay; answer me, is not thy sloth
Sufficient argument? thy flattery?　　10
Thy means of feeding?
MOS.　　　　　Heaven be good to me.
These imputations are too common, sir,
And eas'ly stuck on virtue, when she's poor.
You are unequal to me, and howe'er

21. *legs:* bows. 22. *lick . . . mote:* i.e., removing an invisible spot from
the lord's coat. 29. *visor:* expression, put on like a mask.
　SC. II: *14. unequal:* unjust.

Your sentence may be righteous, yet you are not,   15
That, ere you know me, thus proceed in censure.
St. Mark bear witness 'gainst you, 'tis inhuman.   [*Weeps.*
   BON. [*Aside*] What! does he weep? the sign is soft and good!
I do repent me that I was so harsh.
   MOS. 'Tis true, that, swayed by strong necessity,   20
I am enforced to eat my careful bread
With too much obsequy; 'tis true, beside,
That I am fain to spin mine own poor raiment
Out of my mere observance, being not born
To a free fortune; but that I have done   25
Base offices, in rending friends asunder,
Dividing families, betraying counsels,
Whispering false lies, or mining men with praises,
Trained their credulity with perjuries,
Corrupted chastity, or am in love   30
With mine own tender ease, but would not rather
Prove the most rugged and laborious course,
That might redeem my present estimation,
Let me here perish, in all hope of goodness.
   BON. [*Aside*] This cannot be a personated passion!—   35
I was to blame, so to mistake thy nature;
'Pray thee forgive me; and speak out thy bus'ness.
   MOS. Sir, it concerns you; and though I may seem
At first to make a main offence in manners,
And in my gratitude unto my master,   40
Yet for the pure love which I bear all right,
And hatred of the wrong, I must reveal it.
This very hour your father is in purpose
To disinherit you—
   BON.   How!
   MOS.   And thrust you forth,
As a mere stranger to his blood; 'tis true, sir.   45
The work no way engageth me, but as
I claim an interest in the general state
Of goodness and true virtue, which I hear
T' abound in you; and for which mere respect,
Without a second aim, sir, I have done it.   50
   BON. This tale hath lost thee much of the late trust
Thou hadst with me; it is impossible.

---

22. *obsequy:* obsequiousness. 24. *observance:* service. 28. *mining:* undermining. 29. *Trained:* led on.

I know not how to lend it any thought
My father should be so unnatural.
   MOS. It is a confidence that well becomes   55
Your piety; and formed, no doubt, it is
From your own simple innocence; which makes
Your wrong more monstrous and abhorred. But, sir,
I now will tell you more. This very minute,
It is, or will be doing; and if you   60
Shall be but pleased to go with me, I'll bring you,
I dare not say where you shall see, but where
Your ear shall be a witness of the deed;
Hear yourself written bastard, and professed
The common issue of the earth.
   BON.   I'm mazed!   65
   MOS. Sir, if I do it not, draw your just sword,
And score your vengeance on my front and face;
Mark me your villain. You have too much wrong,
And I do suffer for you, sir. My heart   69
Weeps blood in anguish—
   BON.   Lead. I follow thee.   [*Exeunt.*

SCENE III. *A room in Volpone's house.*

[*Enter* VOLPONE, NANO, ANDROGYNO, *and* CASTRONE.]

   VOLP. Mosca stays long, methinks.—Bring forth your sports,
And help to make the wretched time more sweet.
   NAN. Dwarf, fool, and eunuch, well met here we be.
A question it were now, whether of us three,
Being all the known delicates of a rich man,   5
In pleasing him, claim the precedency can?
   CAS. I claim for myself.
   AND.   And so doth the fool.
   NAN. 'Tis foolish indeed; let me set you both to school.
First for your dwarf, he's little and witty,
And everything, as it is little, is pretty;   10
Else why do men say to a creature of my shape,
So soon as they see him, "It's a pretty little ape"?
And why a pretty ape, but for pleasing imitation
Of greater men's action, in a ridiculous fashion?

   SC. III: 4. *whether:* which.

Beside, this feat body of mine doth not crave   15
Half the meat, drink, and cloth, one of your bulks will have.
Admit your fool's face be the mother of laughter,
Yet, for his brain, it must always come after;
And though that do feed him, it's a pitiful case,
His body is beholding to such a bad face.   20

                                                     [*One knocks.*

    VOLP. Who's there? My couch; away! Look, Nano, see.—
                      [*Exeunt* ANDROGYNO *and* CASTRONE.
Give me my caps first—go, inquire. [*Exit* NANO.] Now, Cupid
Send it be Mosca, and with fair return.

                  [*Re-enter* NANO.]

    NAN. It is the beauteous Madam—
    VOLP.   Would-be—is it?
    NAN. The same.
    VOLP.   Now torment on me! Squire her in;   25
For she will enter, or dwell here for ever.
Nay, quickly. [*Exit* NANO; VOLPONE *retires to his couch.*]—That my
    fit were past! I fear
A second hell too, that my loathing this
Will quite expel my appetite to the other.
Would she were taking now her tedious leave.   30
Lord, how it threats me what I am to suffer!

                    SCENE IV

      [*Enter* NANO *and* LADY POLITIC WOULD-BE.]

    LADY. I thank you, good sir. Pray you signify
Unto your patron I am here.—This band
Shows not my neck enough.—I trouble you, sir;
Let me request you bid one of my women
Come hither to me. [*Exit* NANO.]—In good faith, I am dressed   5
Most favorably today; it is no matter;
'Tis well enough.

        [*Re-enter* NANO *with a* WAITING WOMAN.]

              Look, see, these petulant things!
How they have done this!
    VOLP. [*Aside*]   I do feel the fever

---

15. *feat:* dainty.

Ent'ring in at mine ears; oh, for a charm
To fright it hence.
    LADY.   Come nearer. Is this curl   10
In his right place? or this? Why is this higher
Than all the rest? You ha' not washed your eyes yet?
Or do they not stand even i' your head?
Where's your fellow? call her.   [*Exit* WOMAN.
    NAN. [*Aside*]   Now, St. Mark
Deliver us! anon she'll beat her women,   15
Because her nose is red.

          [*Re-enter* WOMAN *with another.*]

    LADY.   I pray you view
This tire, forsooth. Are all things apt, or no?
    WOM. One hair a little here sticks out, forsooth.
    LADY. Does 't so, forsooth! and where was your dear sight,
When it did so, forsooth? What now! bird-eyed?   20
And you, too? 'Pray you, both approach and mend it.
Now, by that light I muse you're not ashamed!
I, that have preached these things so oft unto you,
Read you the principles, argued all the grounds,
Disputed every fitness, every grace,   25
Called you to counsel of so frequent dressings—
    NAN. [*Aside*] More carefully than of your fame or honor.
    LADY. Made you acquainted what an ample dowry
The knowledge of these things would be unto you,
Able alone to get you noble husbands   30
At your return; and you thus to neglect it!
Besides, you seeing what a curious nation
Th' Italians are, what will they say of me?
"The English lady cannot dress herself."
Here's a fine imputation to our country!   35
Well, go your ways, and stay i' the next room.
This fucus was too coarse too; it's no matter.—
Good sir, you'll give 'em entertainement?
          [*Exeunt* NANO *and* WAITING WOMEN.
    VOLP. [*Aside*] The storm comes toward me.
    LADY. [*Going to the couch*]   How does my Volpone?
    VOLP. Troubled with noise; I cannot sleep. I dreamt   40
That a strange Fury ent'red now my house,

SC. IV: 17. *tire:* headdress. 20. *bird-eyed:* startled and jumpy (the maid
ducks a blow). 32. *curious:* fastidious. 37. *fucus:* rouge.

And, with the dreadful tempest of her breath,
Did cleave my roof asunder.
    LADY.   Believe me, and I
Had the most fearful dream, could I remember 't—
    VOLP. [*Aside*] Out on my fate! I ha' given her the occasion   45
How to torment me: she will tell me hers.
    LADY. Methought the golden mediocrity,
Polite, and delicate—
    VOLP.   O, if you do love me,
No more; I sweat, and suffer, at the mention
Of any dream. Feel how I tremble yet.   50
    LADY. Alas, good soul! the passion of the heart.
Seed-pearl were good now, boiled with syrup of apples,
Tincture of gold, and coral, citron-pills,
Your elecampane root, myrobalans—
    VOLP. Ay me, I have ta'en a grasshopper by the wing!   55
    LADY. Burnt silk and amber. You have muscadel
Good i' the house—
    VOLP.   You will not drink, and part?
    LADY. No, fear not that. I doubt we shall not get
Some English saffron—half a dram would serve;
Your sixteen cloves, a little musk, dried mints,   60
Bugloss, and barley meal—
    VOLP. [*Aside*]   She's in again;
Before I feigned diseases—now I have one.
    LADY. And these applied with a right scarlet cloth—
    VOLP. [*Aside*] Another flood of words! a very torrent!
    LADY. Shall I, sir, make you a poultice?
    VOLP.   No, no, no.   65
I am very well; you need prescribe no more.
    LADY. I have a little studied physic; but now
I'm all for music, save i' the forenoons,
An hour or two for painting. I would have
A lady, indeed, t' have all letters and arts,   70
Be able to discourse, to write, to paint;
But principal, as Plato holds, your music
(And so does wise Pythagoras, I take it)

---

47. *golden mediocrity:* Her dream, inappropriate for her, was apparently of
Aristotle's golden mean personified. 51. *passion:* heartburn. 54. *myroba-*
lans: dried fruit containing tannin, and regarded as a cure for melancholy
like the preceding items. 55. *grasshopper:* cicada, and therefore noisy. 61.
Bugloss: small plant, the ox tongue, a heart stimulant. 63. *right:* genuine.

Is your true rapture, when there is concent
In face, in voice, and clothes, and is, indeed,   75
Our sex's chiefest ornament.
    VOLP.   The poet
As old in time as Plato, and as knowing,
Says that your highest female grace is silence.
    LADY. Which o' your poets? Petrarch, or Tasso, or Dante?
Guarini? Ariosto? Aretine?   80
Cieco di Hadria? I have read them all.
    VOLP. [*Aside*] Is everything a cause to my destruction?
    LADY. I think I ha' two or three of 'em about me.
    VOLP. [*Aside*] The sun, the sea, will sooner both stand still
Than her eternal tongue! Nothing can 'scape it.   85
    LADY. Here's *Pastor Fido*—
    VOLP. [*Aside*]   Profess obstinate silence;
That's now my safest.
    LADY.   All our English writers,
I mean such as are happy in th' Italian,
Will deign to steal out of this author, mainly;
Almost as much as from Montagnié: 90
He has so modern and facile a vein,
Fitting the time, and catching the court-ear.
Your Petrarch is more passionate, yet he,
In days of sonneting, trusted 'em with much.
Dante is hard, and few can understand him.   95
But for a desperate wit, there's Aretine!
Only, his pictures are a little obscene—
You mark me not!
    VOLP.   Alas, my mind's perturbed.
    LADY. Why, in such cases, we must cure ourselves,
Make use of our philosophy—
    VOLP.   Oh, ay me!   100
    LADY. And as we find our passions do rebel,
Encounter 'em with reason, or divert 'em,
By giving scope unto some other humor
Of lesser danger; as, in politic bodies,

---

74. *concent:* harmony. 76. *poet:* Sophocles, *Ajax,* 293. 79-81. *poets:* Lady W.
suggests Italian Renaissance poets as the poet as old as Plato. Cieco (the
blind one) was Luigi Groto (1541-85), a prolific poet and playwright. 86.
Pastor Fido: The Faithful Shepherd, a pastoral drama by Guarini. 90. *Mon-*
tagnié: Lady Would-be's English-French pronunciation. 94. *trusted:* provided. 97. *obscene:* love sonnets by Pietro Aretino on illustrations by Giulio
Romano, 1523.

There's nothing more doth overwhelm the judgment,　　　105
And clouds the understanding, than too much
Settling and fixing, and, as 'twere, subsiding
Upon one object. For the incorporating
Of these same outward things into that part
Which we call mental, leaves some certain faeces　　　110
That stop the organs, and, as Plato says,
Assassinates our knowledge.

VOLP. [*Aside*]　　　　　　Now, the spirit
Of patience help me.

LADY.　　　　　　　Come, in faith, I must
Visit you more, a'days, and make you well—
Laugh and be lusty.

VOLP. [*Aside*]　　　My good angel save me!　　　115

LADY. There was but one sole man in all the world
With whom I e'er could sympathise; and he
Would lie you, often, three, four hours together
To hear me speak; and be sometime so rapt,
As he would answer me quite from the purpose,　　　120
Like you, and you are like him, just. I'll discourse,
An 't be but only, sir, to bring you asleep,
How we did spend our time and loves together,
For some six years.

VOLP.　　　　　　Oh, oh, oh, oh, oh, oh!

LADY. For we were coaetanei, and brought up—　　　125

VOLP. [*Aside*] Some power, some fate, some fortune rescue me!

SCENE V

[*Enter* MOSCA.]

MOS. God save you, madam.

LADY.　　　　　　Good sir.

VOLP.　　　　　　　　Mosca! welcome—
[*Aside*] Welcome to my redemption.

MOS. [*Aside*]　　　　　Why, sir?

VOLP. [*Aside*]　　　　　　　Oh,
Rid me of this my torture, quickly, there;
My madam with the everlasting voice.
The bells, in time of pestilence, ne'er made　　　5
Like noise, or were in that perpetual motion—
The cockpit comes not near it. All my house,

---

111. *Plato:* characteristically inaccurate. 125. *coaetanei:* of the same age.

But now, steamed like a bath with her thick breath,
A lawyer could not have been heard; nor scarce
Another woman, such a hail of words   10
She has let fall. For hell's sake, rid her hence.
  MOS. Has she presented?
  VOLP.   Oh, I do not care:
I'll take her absence upon any price,
With any loss.
  MOS.   Madam—
  LADY.   I ha' brought your patron
A toy, a cap here, of mine own work—
  MOS.   'Tis well.   15
I had forgot to tell you I saw your knight
Where you'd little think it—
  LADY.   Where?
  MOS.   Marry,
Where yet, if you make haste, you may apprehend him,
Rowing upon the water in a gondole,
With the most cunning courtesan of Venice.   20
  LADY. Is 't true?
  MOS.   Pursue 'em, and believe your eyes;
Leave me to make your gift. [*Exit* LADY.]—I knew 'twould take;
For, lightly, they that use themselves most licence,
Are still most jealous.
  VOLP.   Mosca, hearty thanks
For thy quick fiction, and delivery of me.   25
Now to my hopes, what say'st thou?

                    [*Re-enter* LADY.]

  LADY.   But do you hear, sir?—
  VOLP. [*Aside*] Again! I fear a paroxysm.
  LADY.   Which way
Rowed they together?
  MOS.   Toward the Rialto.
  LADY. I pray you lend me your dwarf.
  MOS.   I pray you take him.
                                              [*Exit* LADY.
Your hopes, sir, are like happy blossoms, fair,   30
And promise timely fruit, if you will stay
But the maturing. Keep you at your couch;
Corbaccio will arrive straight, with the will;

SC. V: 12. *presented:* given you a present. 23. *lightly:* generally.

When he is gone, I'll tell you more.   [*Exit.*

    VOLP.   My blood,

My spirits are returned; I am alive;   35

And, like your wanton gamester at primero,

Whose thought had whisper'd to him, not go less,

Methinks I lie, and draw—for an encounter.

SCENE VI

[*Enter* MOSCA *and* BONARIO.]

    MOS. Sir, here concealed [*Opening a door*] you may hear all. But,
    pray you,

Have patience, sir; [*One knocks.*] the same 's your father knocks.

I am compelled to leave you.   [*Exit*

    BON.   Do so.—Yet

Cannot my thought imagine this a truth. [*Goes in.*]

SCENE VII

[*Enter* MOSCA, CORVINO, *and* CELIA.]

    MOS. Death on me! You are come too soon. What meant you?

Did not I say I would send?

    CORV.   Yes, but I feared

You might forget it, and then they prevent us.

    MOS. Prevent!—[*Aside*] Did e'er man haste so for his horns?

A courtier would not ply it so for a place.—   5

Well, now there is no helping it, stay here;

I'll presently return.   [*Exit.*

    CORV.   Where are you, Celia?

You know not wherefore I have brought you hither?

    CEL. Not well, except you told me.

    CORV.   Now I will.

Hark hither.   [*They retire to one side.*

[*Re-enter* MOSCA.]

    MOS. [*To* BONARIO] Sir, your father hath sent word   10

It will be half an hour ere he come;

And therefore, if you please to walk the while

---

36. *primero:* a card game. 37. *go:* bet. 38. *draw, encounter:* terms in primero, used punningly as Volpone draws the curtain.

    SC. VII: 9. *except . . . me:* unless you tell me.

Into that gallery—at the upper end,
There are some books to entertain the time;
And I'll take care no man shall come unto you, sir.　　　15
  BON. Yes, I will stay there.—[*Aside*] I do doubt this fellow. [*Exit.*
  MOS. [*Looking after him*] There; he is far enough; he can hear
    nothing.
And for his father, I can keep him off.
  CORV. [*Advancing with* CELIA] Nay, now, there is no starting back,
    and therefore,
Resolve upon it; I have so decreed.　　　20
It must be done. Nor would I move 't afore,
Because I would avoid all shifts and tricks,
That might deny me.
  CEL.　　　　　　　Sir, let me beseech you,
Affect not these strange trials; if you doubt
My chastity, why, lock me up for ever;　　　25
Make me the heir of darkness. Let me live
Where I may please your fears, if not your trust.
  CORV. Believe it, I have no such humor, I.
All that I speak I mean; yet I am not mad;
Not horn-mad, see you? Go to, show yourself　　　30
Obedient, and a wife.
  CEL.　　　　　　O heaven!
  CORV.　　　　　　　　I say it,
Do so.
  CEL. Was this the train?
  CORV.　　　　　　　　I have told you reasons;
What the physicians have set down; how much
It may concern me; what my engagements are;
My means, and the necessity of those means　　　35
For my recovery. Wherefore, if you be
Loyal, and mine, be won; respect my venture.
  CEL. Before your honor?
  CORV.　　　　　　　Honor! tut, a breath.
There's no such thing in nature; a mere term
Invented to awe fools. What is my gold　　　40
The worse for touching, clothes for being looked on?
Why, this 's no more. An old decrepit wretch,
That has no sense, no sinew; takes his meat
With others' fingers; only knows to gape

---

21. *move 't:* suggest it. 30. *horn-mad:* madly jealous. 32. *train:* plot.

When you do scald his gums; a voice, a shadow;   45
And what can this man hurt you?
   CEL. [*Aside*]   Lord! what spirit
Is this hath ent'red him?
   CORV.   And for your fame,
That's such a jig; as if I would go tell it,
Cry it on the Piazza! Who shall know it
But he that cannot speak it, and this fellow,   50
Whose lips are i' my pocket? Save yourself—
If you'll proclaim 't, you may,—I know no other
Should come to know it.
   CEL.   Are heaven and saints then nothing?
Will they be blind or stupid?
   CORV.   How?
   CEL.   Good sir,
Be jealous still, emulate them; and think   55
What hate they burn with toward every sin.
   CORV. I grant you; if I thought it were a sin
I would not urge you. Should I offer this
To some young Frenchman, or hot Tuscan blood
That had read Aretine, conned all his prints,   60
Knew every quirk within lust's labyrinth,
And were professed critic in lechery;
And I would look upon him, and applaud him;
This were a sin: but here, 'tis contrary,
A pious work, mere charity, for physic,   65
And honest polity, to assure mine own.
   CEL. O heaven! canst thou suffer such a change?
   VOLP. [*Aside*] Thou art mine honor, Mosca, and my pride,
My joy, my tickling, my delight! Go bring 'em.
   MOS. Please you draw near, sir.
   CORV.   Come on, what—   70
You will not be rebellious? By that light—
   MOS. Sir, Signior Corvino, here, is come to see you.
   VOLP. Oh.
   MOS.   And hearing of the consultation had,
So lately, for your health, is come to offer,
Or rather, sir, to prostitute—
   BORV.   Thanks, sweet Mosca.   75
   MOS. Freely, unasked, or unentreated—

---

48. *jig:* joke.

CORV.   Well.
MOS. As the true fervent instance of his love,
His own most fair and proper wife, the beauty
Only of price in Venice—
  CORV.   'Tis well urged.
MOS. To be your comfortress, and to preserve you.   80
  VOLP. Alas, I am past, already! 'Pray you, thank him
For his good care and promptness; but for that,
'Tis a vain labor e'en to fight 'gainst heaven;
Applying fire to a stone—uh, uh, uh, uh!—
Making a dead leaf grow again. I take   85
His wishes gently, though; and you may tell him
What I have done for him; marry, my state is hopeless!
Will him to pray for me; and t' use his fortune
With reverence when he comes to 't.
  MOS.   Do you hear, sir?
Go to him with your wife.
  CORV.   Heart of my father!   90
Wilt thou persist thus? Come, I pray thee, come.
Thou seest 'tis nothing, Celia. By this hand,
I shall grow violent. Come, do 't, I say.
  CEL. Sir, kill me, rather. I will take down poison,
Eat burning coals, do anything—
  CORV.   Be damned!   95
Heart, I will drag thee hence home by the hair;
Cry thee a strumpet through the streets; rip up
Thy mouth unto thine ears; and slit thy nose,
Like a raw rochet—Do not tempt me, come;
Yield; I am loth—Death! I will buy some slave   100
Whom I will kill, and bind thee to him alive,
And at my window hang you forth, devising
Some monstrous crime, which I, in capital letters,
Will eat into thy flesh with aqua fortis,
And burning cor'sives, on this stubborn breast.   105
Now, by the blood thou hast incensed, I'll do it!
  CEL. Sir, what you please, you may; I am your martyr.
  CORV. Be not thus obstinate; I ha' not deserved it.
Think who it is entreats you. 'Pray thee, sweet;
Good faith, thou shalt have jewels, gowns, attires,   110

78. *proper:* very own. 79. *only of price:* most precious. 99. *rochet:* a red, large-headed fish. 104. *aqua fortis:* nitric acid. 105. *cor'sives:* corrosives.

What thou wilt think, and ask. Do but go kiss him.
Or touch him but. For my sake. At my suit.
This once. No? not? I shall remember this.
Will you disgrace me thus? Do you thirst my undoing?
  MOS. Nay, gentle lady, be advised.
  CORV.   No, no.   115
She has watched her time. God's precious, this is scurvy,
'Tis very scurvy; and you are—
  MOS.   Nay, good sir.
  CORV. An errant locust—by heaven, a locust!—Whore,
Crocodile, that hast thy tears prepared,
Expecting how thou'lt bid 'em flow.
  MOS.   Nay, 'pray you, sir!   120
She will consider.
  CEL.   Would my life would serve
To satisfy—
  CORV.   'Sdeath! if she would but speak to him,
And save my reputation, 'twere somewhat;
But spitefully to affect my utter ruin!
  MOS. [Aside to CORVINO] Ay, now you have put your fortune in her
      hands.   125
Why, i' faith, it is her modesty, I must quit her.
If you were absent, she would be more coming;
I know it, and dare undertake for her.
What woman can before her husband? 'Pray you,
Let us depart and leave her here.
  CORV.   Sweet Celia,   130
Thou mayst redeem all yet; I'll say no more.
If not, esteem yourself as lost.—Nay, stay there.
                                      [Exit with MOSCA.
  CEL. O God, and his good angels! whither, whither,
Is shame fled human breasts? that with such ease,
Men dare put off your honors, and their own?   135
Is that which ever was a cause of life
Now plac'd beneath the basest circumstance,
And modesty an exile made, for money?
  VOLP. Ay, in Corvino, and such earth-fed minds,
                                      [He leaps off from his couch.
That never tasted the true heav'n of love.   140

---

118. *errant:* out-and-out. 126. *quit:* defend. 127. *coming:* flexible. 128. *undertake:* vouch. 136. *cause of life:* the honor of marriage which has always
been defended at the cost of life.

Assure thee, Celia, he that would sell thee,
Only for hope of gain, and that uncertain,
He would have sold his part of Paradise
For ready money, had he met a copeman.
Why art thou mazed to see me thus revived?   145
Rather applaud thy beauty's miracle;
'Tis thy great work, that hath, not now alone,
But sundry times, raised me, in several shapes,
And, but this morning, like a mountebank,
To see thee at thy window; ay, before   150
I would have left my practice for thy love,
In varying figures I would have contended
With the blue Proteus, or the hornèd flood.
Now art thou welcome.
    CEL.   Sir!
    VOLP.   Nay, fly me not,
Nor let thy false imagination   155
That I was bedrid, make thee think I am so—
Thou shalt not find it. I am now as fresh,
As hot, as high, and in as jovial plight
As when, in that so celebrated scene,
At recitation of our comedy,   160
For entertainment of the great Valois,
I acted young Antinoüs, and attracted
The eyes and ears of all the ladies present,
T' admire each graceful gesture, note, and footing.   *[Sings.*

                Come, my Celia, let us prove,   165
                While we can, the sports of love.
                Time will not be ours for ever,
                He, at length, our good will sever.
                Spend not then his gifts in vain.
                Suns that set may rise again;   170
                But if once we lose this light,
                'Tis with us perpetual night.
                Why should we defer our joys?
                Fame and rumor are but toys.

---

144. *copeman:* buyer. 151. *practice:* plotting. 153. *Proteus:* sea-god who could take many shapes. *horned flood:* the shape-changing river-god Achelous whom Heracles had to wrestle for the hand of Deianira, and in the process broke off one of his horns, which is fabled to have become the horn of plenty. 161. *Valois:* Henry III of France at Venice in 1574. 162. *Antinoüs:* handsome boy beloved by the Roman emperor Hadrian. 165. *prove:* try.

Cannot we delude the eyes   175
Of a few poor household spies?
Or his easier ears beguile,
Thus removèd by our wile?
'Tis no sin love's fruits to steal,
But the sweet thefts to reveal;   180
To be taken, to be seen,
These have crimes accounted been.

CEL. Some serene blast me, or dire lightning strike
This my offending face.
VOLP.   Why droops my Celia?
Thou hast, in place of a base husband, found   185
A worthy lover; use thy fortune well,
With secrecy and pleasure. See, behold,
What thou art queen of; not in expectation,
As I feed others, but possessed and crowned.
See, here, a rope of pearl; and each more orient 190
Than that the brave Egyptian queen caroused.
Dissolve and drink 'em. See, a carbuncle,
May put out both the eyes of our St. Mark;
A diamond would have bought Lollia Paulina,
When she came in like starlight, hid with jewels 195
That were the spoils of provinces; take these,
And wear and lose 'em; yet remains an earring
To purchase them again, and this whole state.
A gem but worth a private patrimony
Is nothing; we will eat such at a meal.   200
The heads of parrots, tongues of nightingales,
The brains of peacocks and of ostriches,
Shall be our food; and, could we get the phoenix,
Though nature lost her kind, she were our dish.
CEL. Good sir, these things might move a mind affected 205
With such delights; but I, whose innocence
Is all I can think wealthy, or worth th' enjoying,
And which, once lost, I have naught to lose beyond it,
Cannot be taken with these sensual baits.
If you have conscience—
VOLP.   'Tis the beggar's virtue; 210

---

183. *serene:* poisonous evening fog. 191. *queen:* Cleopatra. 192. *carbuncle:*
ruby. 193. *May . . . out:* outshining. 194. *Lollia Paulina:* wife of the emperor Caligula. 204. *kind:* unique species

If thou hast wisdom, hear me, Celia.
Thy baths shall be the juice of July-flowers,
Spirit of roses and of violets,
The milk of unicorns, and panthers' breath
Gathered in bags and mixed with Cretan wines.   215
Our drink shall be preparèd gold and amber,
Which we will take until my roof whirl round
With the vertigo; and my dwarf shall dance,
My eunuch sing, my fool make up the antic,
Whilst we, in changèd shapes, act Ovid's tales: 220
Thou like Europa now, and I like Jove;
Then I like Mars, and thou like Erycine;
So of the rest, till we have quite run through
And wearied all the fables of the gods.
Then will I have thee in more modern forms,   225
Attirèd like some sprightly dame of France,
Brave Tuscan lady, or proud Spanish beauty;
Sometimes unto the Persian sophy's wife,
Or the Grand Signior's mistress; and, for change,
To one of our most artful courtesans,   230
Or some quick Negro, or cold Russian;
And I will meet thee in as many shapes,
Where we may so transfuse our wand'ring souls
Out at our lips, and score up sums of pleasures,

> That the curious shall not know   235
> How to tell them as they flow;
> And the envious, when they find
> What their number is, be pined.

CEL. If you have ears that will be pierced—or eyes
That can be opened—a heart, may be touched—   240
Or any part that yet sounds man about you—
If you have touch of holy saints, or heaven,
Do me the grace to let me 'scape. If not,
Be bountiful and kill me. You do know
I am a creature hither ill betrayed   245
By one whose shame I would forget it were;
If you will deign me neither of these graces,
Yet feed your wrath, sir, rather than your lust,

---

212. *July-flowers:* gilly flowers, clove-scented. 213. *spirit:* essence. 220.
tales: i.e., his *Metamorphoses.* 222. *Erycine:* Venus. 228. *sophy's:* Shah's.
236. *tell:* count.

(It is a vice comes nearer manliness)
And punish that unhappy crime of nature,   250
Which you miscall my beauty; flay my face,
Or poison it with ointments for seducing
Your blood to this rebellion. Rub these hands
With what may cause an eating leprosy,
E'en to my bones and marrow, anything   255
That may disfavor me, save in my honor.
And I will kneel to you, pray for you, pay down
A thousand hourly vows, sir, for your health;
Report, and think you virtuous—
    VOLP.   Think me cold,
Frozen, and impotent, and so report me!   260
That I had Nestor's hernia, thou wouldst think.
I do degenerate, and abuse my nation,
To play with opportunity thus long;
I should have done the act, and then have parleyed.
Yield, or I'll force thee.
    CEL.   O! just God!
    VOLP.   In vain—   265
    BON. [*Leaps out from where* MOSCA *had placed him*] Forbear, foul
ravisher, libidinous swine;
Free the forced lady, or thou di'st, impostor.
But that I am loth to snatch thy punishment
Out of the hand of justice, thou shouldst yet
Be made the timely sacrifice of vengeance,   270
Before this altar and this dross, thy idol.—
Lady, let's quit the place; it is the den
Of villainy; fear naught: you have a guard;
And he ere long shall meet his just reward.
                [*Exeunt* BONARIO *and* CELIA.
    VOLP. Fall on me, roof, and bury me in ruin;   275
Become my grace, that wert my shelter. Oh!
I am unmasked, unspirited, undone,
Betrayed to beggary, to infamy—

---

261. *Nestor's hernia:* impotence of age.

SCENE VIII

[*Enter* MOSCA.]

MOS. Where shall I run, most wretched shame of men,
To beat out my unlucky brains?
VOLP.   Here, here.
What! dost thou bleed?
MOS.   O, that his well-driven sword
Had been so courteous to have cleft me down
Unto the navel, ere I lived to see   5
My life, my hopes, my spirits, my patron, all
Thus desperately engaged, by my error.
    VOLP. Woe on thy fortune.
MOS.   And my follies, sir.
    VOLP. Th' hast made me miserable.
MOS.   And myself, sir.
Who would have thought he would have hearkened so?   10
    VOLP. What shall we do?
MOS.   I know not; if my heart
Could expiate the mischance, I'd pluck it out.
Will you be pleased to hang me, or cut my throat?
And I'll requite you, sir. Let's die like Romans,
Since we have lived like Grecians.   [*They knock without.*
    VOLP.   Hark! who's there?   15
I hear some footing; officers, the saffi,
Come to apprehend us! I do feel the brand
Hissing already at my forehead; now
Mine ears are boring.
MOS.   To your couch, sir, you;
Make that place good, however.   [VOLPONE *lies down as before.*
    —[*Aside*] Guilty men   20
Suspect what they deserve still.—Signior Corbaccio!

SCENE IX

[*Enter* CORBACCIO.]

CORB. Why, how now, Mosca?
MOS.   O, undone, amazed, sir.
Your son, I know not by what accident,

SC. VIII: 14. *Romans:* by suicide. 15. *Grecians:* luxuriously. 16. *saffi:*
bailiffs. 19. *boring:* being bored. 21. *still:* always.

Acquainted with your purpose to my patron,
Touching your will and making him your heir,
Ent'red our house with violence, his sword drawn,   5
Sought for you, called you wretch, unnatural,
Vowed he would kill you.
    CORB.   Me?
    MOS.   Yes, and my patron.
    CORB. This act shall disinherit him indeed.
Here is the will.
    MOS.   'Tis well, sir.
    CORB.   Right and well:
Be you as careful now for me.

               [*Enter* VOLTORE *behind.*]

    MOS.   My life, sir,   10
Is not more tendered; I am only yours.
    CORB. How does he? Will he die shortly, thinkest thou?
    MOS.   I fear
He'll outlast May.
    CORB.   Today?
    MOS.   No, last out May, sir.
    CORB. Couldst thou not gi' him a dram?
    MOS.   Oh, by no means, sir.
    CORB. Nay, I'll not bid you.
    VOLT. [*Coming forward*] This is a knave, I see.   15
    MOS. [*Aside*] How! Signior Voltore! did he hear me?
    VOLT.   Parasite!
    MOS. Who's that?—Oh, sir, most timely welcome—
    VOLT.   Scarce,
To the discovery of your tricks, I fear.
You are his, only? and mine also, are you not?
    MOS. Who? I, sir!
    VOLT.   You, sir. What device is this   20
About a will?
    MOS.   A plot for you, sir.
    VOLT.   Come,
Put not your foists upon me; I shall scent 'em.
    MOS. Did you not hear it?
    VOLT.   Yes, I hear Corbaccio

---

sc. IX: 11. *tendered:* care for. 17-18. *Scarce . . . tricks:* i.e., my discovery of your tricks will scarcely be welcome. 22. *foists:* (1) fraudulent deceptions, (2) silent breaking of wind.

Hath made your patron there his heir.
    MOS.   'Tis true,
By my device, drawn to it by my plot,   25
With hope—
    VOLT.   Your patron should reciprocate?
And you have promised?
    MOS.   For your good I did, sir.
Nay, more, I told his son, brought, hid him here,
Where he might hear his father pass the deed;
Being persuaded to it by this thought, sir,   30
That the unnaturalness, first, of the act,
And then his father's oft disclaiming in him
(Which I did mean t' help on), would sure enrage him
To do some violence upon his parent,
On which the law should take sufficient hold,   35
And you be stated in a double hope.
Truth be my comfort, and my conscience,
My only aim was to dig you a fortune
Out of these two rotten sepulchres—
    VOLT. I cry thee mercy, Mosca.
    MOS.   Worth your patience,   40
And your great merit, sir. And see the change!
    VOLT. Why, what success?
    MOS.   Most hapless! You must help, sir.
Whilst we expected th' old raven, in comes
Corvino's wife, sent hither by her husband—
    VOLT. What, with a present?
    MOS.   No, sir, on visitation   45
(I'll tell you how anon); and, staying long,
The youth he grows impatient, rushes forth,
Seizeth the lady, wounds me, makes her swear
(Or he would murder her—that was his vow)
T' affirm my patron to have done her rape;   50
Which how unlike it is, you see! and hence,
With that pretext he's gone, t' accuse his father,
Defame my patron, defeat you—
    VOLT.   Where's her husband?
Let him be sent for straight.
    MOS.   Sir, I'll go fetch him.
    VOLT. Bring him to the Scrutineo.

---

36. *stated:* estated.   43. *raven:* Corbaccio.   55. *Scrutineo:* Senate House.

MOS.   Sir, I will.   55
VOLT. This must be stopped.
MOS.   Oh, you do nobly, sir.
Alas, 'twas labored all, sir, for your good;
Nor was there want of counsel in the plot.
But Fortune can, at any time, o'erthrow
The projects of a hundred learned clerks, sir.   60
CORB. [*Listening*] What's that?
VOLT.   Wilt please you, sir, to go along?
                    [*Exit* CORBACCIO, *followed by* VOLTORE.
MOS. Patron, go in, and pray for our success.
VOLP. Need makes devotion; heaven your labor bless!   [*Exeunt.*

Act IV

SCENE I. *A street.*

[*Enter* SIR POLITIC WOULD-BE *and* PEREGRINE.]

POL. I told you, sir, it was a plot; you see
What observation is. You mentioned me
For some instructions; I will tell you, sir,
(Since we are met here in this height of Venice)
Some few particulars I have set down,   5
Only for this meridian, fit to be known
Of your crude traveller; and they are these.
I will not touch, sir, at your phrase, or clothes,
For they are old.
PER.   Sir, I have better.
POL.   Pardon,
I meant, as they are themes.
PER.   Oh, sir, proceed;   10
I'll slander you no more of wit, good sir.
POL. First, for your garb, it must be grave and serious,
Very reserved and locked; not tell a secret
On any terms, not to your father; scarce
A fable, but with caution; make sure choice   15
Both of your company and discourse; beware

---

60. *clerks:* scholars.

ACT IV, sc. i: 2. *mentioned:* called on. 11. *I'll . . . wit:* I'll never accuse
you of lacking wit. 12. *garb:* conduct.

You never speak a truth—
PER.   How!
POL.   Not to strangers.
For those be they you must converse with most;
Others I would not know, sir, but at distance
So as I still might be a saver in 'em—   20
You shall have tricks else passed upon you, hourly.
And then, for your religion, profess none,
But wonder at the diversity of all;
And, for your part, protest, were there no other
But simply the laws o' th' land, you could content you. 25
Nic. Machiavel and Monsieur Bodin, both
Were of this mind. Then must you learn the use
And handling of your silver fork at meals,
The metal of your glass (these are main matters
With your Italian); and to know the hour   30
When you must eat your melons and your figs.
 PER. Is that a point of state too?
POL.   Here, it is;
For your Venetian, if he see a man
Preposterous in the least, he has him straight;
He has; he strips him. I'll acquaint you, sir, 35
I now have lived here, 'tis some fourteen months.
Within the first week of my landing here,
All took me for a citizen of Venice,
I knew the forms so well—
 PER. [Aside]   And nothing else.
 POL. I had read Contarene, took me a house, 40
Dealt with my Jews to furnish it with movables—
Well, if I could but find one man, one man,
To mine own heart, whom I durst trust, I would—
 PER. What? what, sir?
POL.   Make him rich; make him a fortune:
He should not think again. I would command it. 45
 PER. As how?
POL.   With certain projects that I have,
Which I may not discover.

---

20. *might . . . 'em:* play it safe; *saver* (a gambling term) applies to one who escapes loss, though without gain. 26. *Bodin:* Jean Bodin, sixteenth-century French political phlosopher, whose advanced views were much discussed at the time. 34. *Preposterous:* doing things in inverted order. *has:* sets. *strips:* exposes. 40. *Contarene:* Cardinal Contarini, author of *Commonwealth and Government of Venice,* which appeared in London in 1599.

PER. [*Aside*]   If I had
But one to wager with, I would lay odds now,
He tells me instantly.

POL.   One is (and that
I care not greatly who knows) to serve the state   50
Of Venice with red herrings for three years,
And at a certain rate, from Rotterdam,
Where I have correspondence. There's a letter,
Sent me from one o' th' states, and to that purpose;
He cannot write his name, but that's his mark.   55

PER. He is a chandler?

POL.   No, a cheesemonger.
There are some other too with whom I treat
About the same negotiation;
And I will undertake it; for 'tis thus:
I'll do 't with ease; I have cast it all. Your hoy   60
Carries but three men in her, and a boy;
And she shall make me three returns a year:
So if there come but one of three, I save;
If two, I can defalk. But this is now,
If my main project fail.

PER.   Then you have others?   65

POL. I should be loth to draw the subtle air
Of such a place without my thousand aims.
I'll not dissemble, sir: where'er I come,
I love to be considerative; and 'tis true,
I have at my free hours thought upon   70
Some certain goods unto the state of Venice
Which I do call my cautions; and, sir, which
I mean, in hope of pension, to propound
To the Great Council, then unto the Forty,
So to the Ten. My means are made already—   75

PER. By whom?

POL.   Sir, one that though his place b' obscure,
Yet he can sway, and they will hear him. He's
A *commandadore*.

PER.   What, a common serjeant?

---

54. *states:* Low Countries. 56. *chandler:* candle merchant (suggested by a grease mark on the paper). 60. *cast:* calculated; *hoy:* small ship. 64. *defalk:* make a reduction. 72. *cautions:* precautions. 74-5. *Great . . . Ten:* governing bodies of the Venetian Republic.

POL. Sir, such as they are, put it in their mouths,
What they should say, sometimes; as well as greater.   80
I think I have my notes to show you—   [*Searching his pockets.*
   PER.   Good sir.
   POL. But you shall swear unto me, on your gentry,
Not to anticipate—
   PER.   I, sir?
   POL.   Nor reveal
A circumstance—my paper is not with me.
   PER. O, but you can remember, sir.
   POL.   My first is   85
Concerning tinder boxes. You must know,
No family is here without its box.
Now, sir, it being so portable a thing,
Put case that you or I were ill affected
Unto the state, sir; with it in our pockets,   90
Might not I go into the Arsenal,
Or you come out again, and none the wiser?
   PER. Except yourself, sir.
   POL.   Go to, then. I therefore
Advertise to the state, how fit it were
That none but such as were known patriots,   95
Sound lovers of their country, should be suffered
T' enjoy them in their houses; and even those
Sealed at some office, and at such a bigness
As might not lurk in pockets.
   PER.   Admirable!
   POL. My next is, how t' inquire, and be resolved   100
By present demonstration, whether a ship,
Newly arrived from Syria, or from
Any suspected part of all the Levant,
Be guilty of the plague; and where they use
To lie out forty, fifty days, sometimes,   105
About the Lazaretto, for their trial,
I'll save that charge and loss unto the merchant,
And in an hour clear the doubt.
   PER.   Indeed, sir?
   POL. Or—I will lose my labor.
   PER.   'My faith, that's much.
   POL. Nay, sir, conceive me. 'Twill cost me in onions,   110
Some thirty livres—

79-80. *such . . . greater:* i.e., one sometimes has to speak and work
through inferior agents, but they may do as well as greater ones. 89. *Put
case:* assume. 106. *Lazaretto:* quarantine.

PER.   Which is one pound sterling.
POL. Beside my waterworks. For this I do, sir:
First, I bring in your ship 'twixt two brick walls—
But those the state shall venture. On the one
I strain me a fair tarpaulin, and in that   115
I stick my onions, cut in halves; the other
Is full of loopholes, out at which I thrust
The noses of my bellows; and those bellows
I keep, with waterworks, in perpetual motion
(Which is the easiest matter of a hundred).   120
Now, sir, your onion, which doth naturally
Attract th' infection, and your bellows blowing
The air upon him, will show, instantly,
By his changed color, if there be contagion;
Or else remain as fair as at the first.   125
Now 'tis known, 'tis nothing.
PER.   You are right, sir.
POL. I would I had my note.
PER.   'Faith, so would I;
But you ha' done well for once, sir.
POL.   Were I false,
Or would be made so, I could show you reasons
How I could sell this state now to the Turk,   130
Spite of their galleys, or their—   [Examining his papers.
PER.   Pray you, Sir Pol.
POL. I have 'em not about me.
PER.   That I feared.
They are there, sir?
POL.   No, this is my diary,
Wherein I note my actions of the day.
PER. Pray you let's see, sir.—What is here? "Notandum,   135
A rat had gnawn my spur-leathers; notwithstanding,
I put on new, and did go forth; but first
I threw three beans over the threshold. Item,
I went and bought two toothpicks, whereof one
I burst immediately, in a discourse   140
With a Dutch merchant, 'bout ragion' del stato.
From him I went and paid a muccinigo
For piecing my silk stockings; by the way
I cheapened sprats; and at St. Mark's I urined."—
'Faith these are politic notes!

---

141. *ragion' del stato:* politics. 144. *cheapened:* priced.

POL. Sir, I do slip 145
No action of my life, thus, but I quote it.
PER. Believe me, it is wise!
POL. Nay, sir, read forth.

SCENE II

[*Enter, at a distance,* LADY POLITIC WOULD-BE, NANO, *and the two*
WAITING WOMEN.]

LADY. Where should this loose knight be, trow? Sure he's housed.
NAN. Why, then he's fast.
LADY. Ay, he plays both with me.
I pray you stay. This heat will do more harm
To my complexion than his heart is worth.
(I do not care to hinder, but to take him.) 5
How it comes off! [*Rubs her cheeks.*
WOM. My master's yonder.
LADY. Where?
WOM. With a young gentleman.
LADY. That same's the party!
In man's apparel.—Pray you, sir, jog my knight.
I will be tender to his reputation,
However he demerit.
POL. My lady!
PER. Where? 10
POL. 'Tis she indeed, sir; you shall know her. She is,
Were she not mine, a lady of that merit,
For fashion and behavior, and for beauty,
I durst compare—
PER. It seems you are not jealous,
That dare commend her.
POL. Nay, and for discourse— 15
PER. Being your wife, she cannot miss that.
POL. Madam,
Here is a gentleman, 'pray you use him fairly;
He seems a youth, but he is—

SC. II: 2. *fast:* safe. *both:* fast and loose. 18-21. *He seems . . . apprehend me:* i.e., Sir Pol introduces Peregrine as a young man but, he starts to add, one who knows the world by having entered it "soon." Lady Would-be, believing Peregrine to be a woman in disguise, agrees that he is indeed not a young man, and then she changes Pol's "soon" to "early," meaning,

LADY.   None?
POL.   Yes, one
Has put his face as soon into the world—
    LADY. You mean, as early? But today?
POL.   How's this!   20
    LADY. Why, in this habit, sir; you apprehend me.
Well, Master Would-be, this doth not become you;
I had thought the odor, sir, of your good name
Had been more precious to you; that you would not
Have done this dire massácre on your honor;   25
One of your gravity, and rank besides!
But knights, I see, care little for the oath
They make to ladies—chiefly their own ladies.
    POL. Now, by my spurs, the symbol of my knighthood—
    PER. [Aside] Lord, how his brain is humbled for an oath.   30
    POL. I reach you not.
    LADY.   Right, sir: your polity
May bear it through thus.—[To PEREGRINE] Sir, a word with you.
I would be loth to contest publicly
With any gentlewoman, or to seem
Froward, or violent, as the courtier says;   35
It comes too near rusticity in a lady,
Which I would shun by all means; and however
I may deserve from Master Would-be, yet
'T have one fair gentlewoman thus be made
Th' unkind instrument to wrong another,   40
And one she knows not, ay, and to perséver,
In my poor judgment, is not warranted
From being a solecism in our sex,
If not in manners.
    PER.   How is this!
    POL.   Sweet madam,
Come nearer to your aim.
    LADY.   Marry, and will, sir.   45
Since you provoke me with your impudence,

_____

as she explains, that Peregrine appeared just today in the habit (clothing)
of a man. "You apprehend (understand) me now?" 30. *humbled . . .
ath:* brought low, to his heels. 31. *reach:* understand. 35. *courtier:* as
    Baldassare Castiglione's *The Courtier* (*Il Cortegiano,* 1528), a famous
`iscussion of courtly behavior, translated into English by Sir Thomas
Hoby in 1561. 43. *From . . . sex:* because it would be a breach of etiquette
toward the female sex.

And laughter of your light land-siren here,
Your Sporus, your hermaphrodite—
   PER.   What's here?
Poetic fury and historic storms!
   POL. The gentleman, believe it, is of worth   50
And of our nation.
   LADY.   Ay, your Whitefriars nation?
Come, I blush for you, Master Would-be, I;
And am ashamed you should ha' no more forehead
Than thus to be the patron, or St. George,
To a lewd harlot, a base fricatrice,   55
A female devil, in a male outside.
   POL.   Nay,
An you be such a one! I must bid adieu
To your delights. The case appears too liquid.   [*Exit.*
   LADY. Ay, you may carry 't clear, with your state-face!—
But for your carnival concupiscence,   60
Who here is fled for liberty of conscience,
From furious persecution of the marshal,
Her will I disc'ple.
   PER.   This is fine, i' faith!
And do you use this often? Is this part
Of your wit's exercise, 'gainst you have occasion?   65
Madam—
   LADY. Go to, sir.
   PER.   Do you hear me, lady?
Why, if your knight have set you to beg shirts,
Or to invite me home, you might have done it
A nearer way by far.
   LADY.   This cannot work you
Out of my snare.
   PER.   Why, am I in it, then?   70
Indeed your husband told me you were fair,
And so you are; only your nose inclines,

---

48. *Sporus:* Nero's eunuch. 51. *Whitefriars:* a section of London where
criminals and perverts were safe from the law. 53. *forehead:* sense of
shame. 55. *fricatrice:* prostitute. 57. *An:* if. 58. *liquid:* clear. 59. *state-
face:* solemnity. 60-61. *carnival . . . conscience:* licentious and lecherous
desires which have come to Venice to have free play (with a satiric glance
at the Puritans' reason for liberty of conscience). 63. *disc'ple:* discipline.
65. *'gainst . . . occasion:* i.e., to keep it in trim till you have use for it.
67-8. *beg . . . home:* act as a beggar or street-walker.

That side that's next the sun, to the queen-apple.
  LADY. This cannot be endured by any patience.

SCENE III

[*Enter* MOSCA.]

  MOS. What's the matter, madam?
  LADY.   If the Senate
Right not my quest in this, I will protest 'em
To all the world no aristocracy.
  MOS. What is the injury, lady?
  LADY.   Why, the callet
You told me of, here I have ta'en disguised.   5
  MOS. Who? this? what means your Ladyship? The creature
I mentioned to you is apprehended now,
Before the Senate; you shall see her—
  LADY.   Where?
  MOS. I'll bring you to her. This young gentleman,
I saw him land this morning at the port.   10
  LADY. Is 't possible? How has my judgment wandered!
Sir, I must, blushing, say to you, I have erred;
And plead your pardon.
  PER.   What! more changes yet?
  LADY. I hope you've not the malice to remember
A gentlewoman's passion. If you stay   15
In Venice here, please you to use me, sir—
  MOS. Will you go, madam?
  LADY.   'Pray you, sir, use me; in faith,
The more you see me the more I shall conceive
You have forgot our quarrel.

[*Exeunt* LADY WOULD-BE, MOSCA, NANO, *and* WAITING WOMEN.

  PER.   This is rare!
Sir Politic Would-be? No, Sir Politic Bawd!   20
To bring me thus acquainted with his wife!
Well, wise Sir Pol, since you have practised thus
Upon my freshmanship, I'll try your salthead,
What proof it is against a counterplot.   [*Exit.*

---

73. *queen-apple:* which is red on the sunward side.
  SC. III: 4. *callet:* prostitute. 22. *practised:* plotted. 23. *salthead:* experience (with a derogatory comparison to a fishhead seasoned in brine).

SCENE IV. *The Senate House*

[*Enter* VOLTORE, CORBACCIO, CORVINO, *and* MOSCA.]

VOLT. Well, now you know the carriage of the business,
Your constancy is all that is required
Unto the safety of it.   [*He stands aside.*
    MOS.   Is the lie
Safely conveyed amongst us? Is that sure?
Knows every man his burden?
    CORV.   Yes.
    MOS.   Then shrink not.   5
    CORV. But knows the advocate the truth?
    MOS.   Oh, sir,
By no means; I devised a formal tale,
That salved your reputation. But be valiant, sir.
    CORV. I fear no one but him, that this his pleading
Should make him stand for a co-heir—
    MOS.   Co-halter!   10
Hang him; we will but use his tongue, his noise,
As we do croaker's here.
    CORV.   Ay, what shall he do?
    MOS. When we ha' done, you mean?
    CORV.   Yes.
    MOS.   Why, we'll think;
Sell him for mummia: he's half dust already.—
[*To* VOLTORE] Do you not smile, to see this buffalo,   15
How he doth sport it with his head?—[*Aside*] I should,
If all were well and past.—[*To* CORBACCIO] Sir, only you
Are he that shall enjoy the crop of all,
And these not know for whom they toil.
    CORB.   Ay, peace.
    MOS. [*To* CORVINO] But you shall eat it.—[*Aside*] Much!—[*Then
        to* VOLTORE *again*] Worshipful sir,   20
Mercury sit upon your thund'ring tongue,
Or the French Hercules, and make your language
As conquering as his club, to beat along,
As with a tempest, flat, our adversaries;
But much more yours, sir.

SC. IV: 4. *conveyed:* arranged. 12. *croaker's:* Corbaccio's. 14. *mummia:*
drug made from mummies. 15. *buffalo:* cuckold. 21. *Mercury:* god of eloquence. 22. *French Hercules:* surnamed Ogmius, pictured, to symbolize
his eloquence, with chains from his tongue to the ears of his audience.

VOLT.   Here they come; ha' done.   25
MOS. I have another witness, if you need, sir,
I can produce.
VOLT.   Who is it?
MOS.   Sir, I have her.

SCENE V

[*Enter four* AVOCATORI, BONARIO, CELIA, NOTARIO, COMMANDADORI,
SAFFI, *and other* OFFICERS OF JUSTICE.]

1 AVOC. The like of this the Senate never heard of.
2 AVOC. 'Twill come most strange to them when we report it.
4 AVOC. The gentlewoman has been ever held
Of unreprovèd name.
3 AVOC.   So, the young man.
4 AVOC. The more unnatural part that of his father.   5
2 AVOC. More of the husband.
1 AVOC.   I not know to give
His act a name, it is so monstrous!
4 AVOC. But the impostor, he is a thing created
T' exceed example!
1 AVOC.   And all after-times!
2 AVOC. I never heard a true voluptuary   10
Described but him.
3 AVOC.   Appear yet those were cited?
NOT. All but the old magnifico, Volpone.
1 AVOC. Why is not he here?
MOS.   Please your fatherhoods.
Here is his advocate. Himself's so weak,
So feeble—
4 AVOC. What are you?
BON.   His parasite,   15
His knave, his pander. I beseech the court
He may be forced to come, that your grave eyes
May bear strong witness of his strange impostures.
VOLT. Upon my faith and credit with your virtues,
He is not able to endure the air.   20
2 AVOC. Bring him, however.
3 AVOC.   We will see him.
4 AVOC.   Fetch him.

---

sc. v. *Avocatori:* legal officers of the state. *Saffi:* bailiffs.

VOLT. Your fatherhoods' fit pleasures be obeyed;

[*Exeunt* OFFICERS.

But sure, the sight will rather move your pities
Than indignation. May it please the court,
In the meantime, he may be heard in me. 25
I know this place most void of prejudice,
And therefore crave it, since we have no reason
To fear our truth should hurt our cause.
   3 AVOC.   Speak free.
   VOLT. Then know, most honored fathers, I must now
Discover to your strangely abusèd ears, 30
The most prodigious and most frontless piece
Of solid impudence and treachery
That ever vicious nature yet brought forth
To shame the state of Venice. This lewd woman,
That wants no artificial looks or tears 35
To help the visor she has now put on,
Hath long been known a close adulteress
To that lascivious youth there; not suspected,
I say, but known, and taken in the act
With him; and by this man, the easy husband, 40
Pardoned; whose timeless bounty makes him now
Stand here, the most unhappy, innocent person
That ever man's own goodness made accused.
For these, not knowing how to owe a gift
Of that dear grace, but with their shame, being placed 45
So above all powers of their gratitude,
Began to hate the benefit, and, in place
Of thanks, devise t' extirp the memory
Of such an act. Wherein I pray your fatherhoods
To observe the malice, yea, the rage of creatures 50
Discovered in their evils; and what heart
Such take, ev'n from their crimes. But that anon
Will more appear. This gentleman, the father,
Hearing of this foul fact, with many others,
Which daily struck at his too tender ears, 55
And grieved in nothing more than that he could not
Preserve himself a parent (his son's ills
Growing to that strange flood), at last decreed
To disinherit him.

---

31. *frontless:* shameless. 37. *close:* secret. 41. *timeless bounty:* untimely mercy. 44. *owe:* value. 54. *fact:* crime.

1 AVOC.   These be strange turns!
2 AVOC. The young man's fame was ever fair and honest.   60
VOLT. So much more full of danger is his vice,
That can beguile so, under shade of virtue.
But, as I said, my honored sires, his father
Having this settled purpose, by what means
To him betrayed, we know not, and this day   65
Appointed for the deed; that parricide
I cannot style him better, by confederacy
Preparing this his paramour to be there,
Ent'red Volpone's house (who was the man,
Your fatherhoods must understand, designed   70
For the inheritance), there sought his father:—
But with what purpose sought he him, my lords?
I tremble to pronounce it, that a son
Unto a father, and to such a father,
Should have so foul, felonious intent—   75
It was to murder him; when, being prevented
By his more happy absence, what then did he?
Not check his wicked thoughts; no, now new deeds
(Mischief doth ever end where it begins)—
An act of horror, fathers! He dragged forth   80
The aged gentleman that had there lain bedrid
Three years and more, out off his innocent couch,
Naked upon the floor; there left him; wounded
His servant in the face; and with this strumpet,
The stale to his forged practice, who was glad   85
To be so active,—I shall here desire
Your fatherhoods to note but my collections,
As most remarkable,—thought at once to stop
His father's ends, discredit his free choice
In the old gentleman, redeem themselves,   90
By laying infamy upon this man,
To whom, with blushing, they should owe their lives.
    1 AVOC. What proofs have you of this?
    BON.   Most honored fathers,
I humbly crave there be no credit given
To this man's mercenary tongue.
    2 AVOC.   Forbear.   95
    BON. His soul moves in his fee.
    3 AVOC.   O, sir.

85. *stale . . . practice:* front to his fabricated plot. 87. *collections:* evidence.

BON.   This fellow,
For six sols more would plead against his Maker.
    1 AVOC. You do forget yourself.
    VOLT.   Nay, nay, grave fathers,
Let him have scope! Can any man imagine
That he will spare his accuser, that would not   100
Have spared his parent?
    1 AVOC.   Well, produce your proofs.
    CEL. I would I could forget I were a creature.
    VOLT. Signior Corbaccio.
    4 AVOC.   What is he?
    VOLT.   The father.
    2 AVOC. Has he had an oath?
    NOT.   Yes.
    CORB   What must I do now?
    NOT. Your testimony's craved.
    CORB.   Speak to the knave?   105
I'll ha' my mouth first stopped with earth; my heart
Abhors his knowledge: I disclaim in him.
    1 AVOC. But for what cause?
    CORB.   The mere portent of nature.
He is an utter stranger to my loins.
    BON. Have they made you to this!
    CORB.   I will not hear thee,   110
Monster of men, swine, goat, wolf, parricide;
Speak not, thou viper.
    BON.   Sir, I will sit down,
And rather wish my innocence should suffer
Than I resist the authority of a father.
    VOLT. Signior Corvino.
    2 AVOC.   This is strange!
    1 AVOC.   Who's this?   115
    NOT. The husband.
    4 AVOC.   Is he sworn?
    NOT.   He is.
    3 AVOC.   Speak then.
    CORV. This woman, please your fatherhoods, is a whore,
Of most hot exercise, more than a partridge,
Upon record—
    1 AVOC.   No more.

_____

97. *sols:* small coin. 102. *a creature:* alive. 107. *disclaim in:* disown. 110.
made: coached.

CORV.   Neighs like a jennet.

NOT. Preserve the honor of the court.

CORV.   I shall,   120
And modesty of your most reverend ears.
And yet I hope that I may say these eyes
Have seen her glued unto that piece of cedar,
That fine well-timber'd gallant; and that here
The letters may be read, thorough the horn,   125
That make the story perfect.

 MOS. [*Aside to* CORVINO] Excellent, sir!

 CORV. [*Aside to* MOSCA] There is no shame in this now, is there?

 MOS. [*Aside to* CORVINO]   None.

 CORV. Or if I said, I hoped that she were onward
To her damnation, if there be a hell
Greater than whore and woman, a good Catholic   130
May make the doubt.

 3 AVOC.   His grief hath made him frantic.

 1 AVOC. Remove him hence.

 2 AVOC.   Look to the woman.   [*She swoons.*

 CORV.   Rare!
Prettily feigned! again!

 4 AVOC.   Stand from about her.

 1 AVOC. Give her the air.

 3 AVOC. [*To* MOSCA]   What can you say?

 MOS.   My wound,
May 't please your wisdoms, speaks for me, received   135
In aid of my good patron, when he missed
His sought-for father, when that well-taught dame
Had her cue giv'n her to cry out, "A rape!"

 BON. O most laid impudence! Fathers—

 3 AVOC.   Sir, be silent;
You had your hearing free, so must they theirs.   140

 2 AVOC. I do begin to doubt th' imposture here.

 4 AVOC. This woman has too many moods.

 VOLT.   Grave fathers,
She is a creature of a most professed
And prostituted lewdness.

 CORV.   Most impetuous!

---

124. *here:* (touching his head and making the letter V, the sign of the cuckold). 125. *horn:* of a hornbook (primer) and a cuckold. 129-31. *damnation . . . doubt:* i.e., Wasn't it all right for me to wish her damned, since an orthodox Catholic may doubt that there is any greater hell than being a whore? 139. *laid:* contrived.

Unsatisfied, grave fathers!
VOLT.   May her feignings   145
Not take your wisdoms. But this day she baited
A stranger, a grave knight, with her loose eyes
And more lascivious kisses. This man saw 'em
Together on the water, in a gondola.
MOS. Here is the lady herself, that saw 'em too,   150
Without; who then had in the open streets
Pursued them, but for saving her knight's honor.
1 AVOC. Produce that lady.
2 AVOC.   Let her come.   [*Exit* MOSCA.
4 AVOC.   These things,
They strike with wonder!
3 AVOC.   I am turned a stone!

SCENE VI

[*Re-enter* MOSCA *with* LADY WOULD-BE.]

MOS. Be resolute, madam.
LADY.   Ay, this same is she.—
Out, thou chameleon harlot! now thine eyes
Vie tears with the hyena. Darest thou look
Upon my wronged face?—I cry your pardons.
I fear I have forgettingly transgressed   5
Against the dignity of the court—
2 AVOC.   No, madam.
LADY. And been exorbitant—
2 AVOC.   You have not, lady.
4 AVOC. These proofs are strong.
LADY.   Surely, I had no purpose
To scandalize your honors, or my sex's.
3 AVOC. We do believe it.
LADY.   Surely you may believe it.   10
2 AVOC. Madam, we do.
LADY.   Indeed you may; my breeding
Is not so coarse—
4 AVOC.   We know it.
LADY.   To offend
With pertinacy—
3 AVOC.   Lady—
LADY.   Such a presence;
No, surely.

I AVOC. We will think it.

LADY.   You may think it.

I AVOC. Let her o'ercome.—What witnesses have you,   15
To make good your report?

BON.   Our consciences.

CEL. And heaven, that never fails the innocent.

I AVOC. These are no testimonies.

BON.   Not in your courts,
Where multitude and clamor overcomes.

I AVOC. Nay, then you do wax insolent.

[VOLPONE *is brought in, as impotent.*]

VOLT.   Here, here,   20
The testimony comes that will convince,
And put to utter dumbness their bold tongues.
See here, grave fathers, here's the ravisher,
The rider on men's wives, the great impostor,
The grand voluptuary! Do you not think   25
These limbs should affect venery? or these eyes
Covet a concubine? Pray you mark these hands.
Are they not fit to stroke a lady's breasts?
Perhaps he doth dissemble!

BON.   So he does.

VOLT. Would you ha' him tortur'd?

BON.   I would have him proved.   30

VOLT. Best try him then with goads, or burning irons;
Put him to the strappado; I have heard
The rack hath cured the gout; faith, give it him,
And help him of a malady; be courteous.
I'll undertake, before these honored fathers,   35
He shall have yet as many left diseases,
As she has known adulterers, or thou strumpets.
O, my most equal hearers, if these deeds,
Acts of this bold and most exorbitant strain,
May pass with sufferance, what one citizen   40
But owes the forfeit of his life, yea, fame,
To him that dares traduce him? Which of you
Are safe, my honored fathers? I would ask,
With leave of your grave fatherhoods, if their plot
Have any face or color like to truth?   45
Or if, unto the dullest nostril here,

___

SC. VI: 32. *strappado:* torture that dislocated the shoulders. 38. *equal:*
just.

It smell not rank, and most abhorred slander?
I crave your care of this good gentleman,
Whose life is much endangered by their fable;
And as for them, I will conclude with this: 50
That vicious persons, when they are hot, and fleshed
In impious acts, their constancy abounds:
Damned deeds are done with greatest confidence.
   1 AVOC. Take 'em to custody, and sever them.
   2 AVOC. 'Tis pity two such prodigies should live.   55
   1 AVOC. Let the old gentleman be returned with care.
                       [*Exeunt* OFFICERS *with* VOLPONE.
I am sorry our credulity wronged him.
   4 AVOC. These are two creatures!
   3 AVOC.   I have an earthquake in me!
   2 AVOC. Their shame, even in their cradles, fled their faces.
   4 AVOC. You have done a worthy service to the state, sir,   60
In their discovery.
   1 AVOC.   You shall hear, ere night,
What punishment the court decrees upon 'em.
[*Exeunt* AVOCATORI, NOTARIO, *and* OFFICERS *with* BONARIO *and* CELIA.
   VOLT. We thank your fatherhoods.—How like you it?
   MOS.   Rare.
I'd ha' your tongue, sir, tipped with gold for this;
I'd ha' you be the heir to the whole city;   65
The earth I'd have want men ere you want living:
They are bound to erect your statue in St. Mark's.—
Signior Corvino, I would have you go
And show yourself that you have conquered.
   CORV.   Yes.
   MOS. It was much better that you should profess   70
Yourself a cuckold thus, than that the other
Should have been proved.
   CORV.   Nay, I consider'd that;
Now it is her fault.
   MOS.   Then, it had been yours.
   CORV. True.—[*Aside to* MOSCA] I do doubt this advocate still.
   MOS. [*Aside*]   I' faith,
You need not; I dare ease you of that care.   75
   CORV. [*Aside*] I trust thee, Mosca.
   MOS. [*Aside*]   As your own soul, sir.
                              [*Exit* CORVINO.

---

54. *severe:* i.e., put them in separate cells (a legal term).

CORB.   Mosca!
MOS. Now for your business, sir.
CORB.   How? ha' you business?
MOS. Yes, yours, sir.
CORB.   O, none else?
MOS.   None else, not I.
CORB. Be careful then.
MOS.   Rest you with both your eyes, sir.
CORB. Dispatch it.
MOS.   Instantly.
CORB.   And look that all,   80
Whatever, be put in, jewels, plate, monies,
Household stuff, bedding, curtains.
MOS.   Curtain-rings, sir;
Only, the advocate's fee must be deducted.
CORB. I'll pay him now; you'll be too prodigal.
MOS. Sir, I must tender it.
CORB.   Two *cecchines* is well.   85
MOS. No, six, sir.
CORB.   'Tis too much.
MOS.   He talked a great while;
You must consider that, sir.
CORB.   Well, there's three—
MOS. I'll give it him.
CORB.   Do so, and there's for thee.   [*Exit.*
MOS. [*Aside*] Bountiful bones! What horrid strange offence
Did he commit 'gainst nature, in his youth,   90
Worthy this age?—[*Aside to* VOLTORE] You see, sir, how I work
Unto your ends; take you no notice.
VOLT.   No,
I'll leave you.
MOS. [*Aside*] All is yours, the devil and all,
Good advocate.—Madam, I'll bring you home.
LADY. No, I'll go see your patron.   95
MOS.   That you shall not;
I'll tell you why. My purpose is to urge
My patron to reform his will, and for
The zeal you have shown today, whereas before
You were but third or fourth, you shall be now
Put in the first; which would appear as begged   100
If you were present. Therefore—

---

79. *Rest . . . eyes:* leave it to me. 97. *reform:* revise.

LADY.   You shall sway me.

[*Exeunt.*

Act V

SCENE I. *A room in Volpone's house.*

[*Enter* VOLPONE.]

VOLP. Well, I am here, and all this brunt is past.
I ne'er was in dislike with my disguise
Till this fled moment: here 'twas good, in private;
But in your public,—*cave,* whilst I breathe.
'Fore God my left leg 'gan to have the cramp.   5
And I apprehended straight some power had struck me
With a dead palsy. Well, I must be merry,
And shake it off. A many of these fears
Would put me into some villainous disease,
Should they come thick upon me. I'll prevent 'em.   10
Give me a bowl of lusty wine, to fright
This humor from my heart.—[*He drinks.*] Hum, hum, hum!—
'Tis almost gone already; I shall conquer.
Any device now of rare ingenious knavery,
That would possess me with a violent laughter,   15
Would make me up again!—[*Drinks again.*] So, so, so, so!—
This heat is life; 'tis blood by this time.—Mosca!

SCENE II

[*Enter* MOSCA.]

MOS. How now, sir? Does the day look clear again?
Are we recovered, and wrought out of error,
Into our way, to see our path before us?
Is our trade free once more?
        VOLP.   Exquisite Mosca!
MOS. Was it not carried learnedly?
        VOLP.   And stoutly: 5
Good wits are greatest in extremities.
        MOS. It were folly beyond thought to trust

ACT V, SC. I: 4. *cave:* beware.

Any grand act unto a cowardly spirit.
You are not taken with it enough, methinks.
   VOLP. Oh, more than if I had enjoyed the wench;   10
The pleasure of all womankind's not like it.
   MOS. Why, now you speak, sir. We must here be fixed;
Here we must rest; this is our masterpiece;
We cannot think to go beyond this.
   VOLP.   True,
Thou hast played thy prize, my precious Mosca.
   MOS.   Nay, sir,   15
To gull the court—
   VOLP.   And quite divert the torrent
Upon the innocent.
   MOS.   Yes, and to make
So rare a music out of discords—
   VOLP.   Right.
That yet to me's the strangest! how th' hast borne it!
That these, being so divided 'mongst themselves,   20
Should not scent somewhat, or in me or thee,
Or doubt their own side.
   MOS.   True, they will not see 't.
Too much light blinds 'em, I think. Each of 'em
Is so possessed and stuffed with his own hopes
That anything unto the contrary,   25
Never so true, or never so apparent,
Never so palpable, they will resist it—
   VOLP. Like a temptation of the Devil.
   MOS.   Right, sir.
Merchants may talk of trade, and your great signiors
Of land that yields well; but if Italy   30
Have any glebe more fruitful than these fellows,
I am deceived. Did not your advocate rare?
   VOLP. Oh—"My most honored fathers, my grave fathers,
Under correction of your fatherhoods,
What face of truth is here? If these strange deeds   35
May pass, most honored fathers"—I had much ado
To forbear laughing.
   MOS.   'T seemed to me you sweat, sir.
   VOLP. In troth, I did a little.
   MOS.   But confess, sir,
Were you not daunted?

SC. II: 32. *rare:* rarely.

VOLP.   In good faith, I was
A little in a mist, but not dejected;   40
Never, but still myself.
    MOS.   I think it, sir.
Now, so truth help me, I must needs say this, sir,
And out of conscience for your advocate,
He has taken pains, in faith, sir, and deserved,
In my poor judgment, I speak it under favor,   45
Not to contrary you, sir, very richly—
Well—to be cozened.
    VOLP.   Troth, and I think so too,
By that I heard him in the latter end.
    MOS. O, but before, sir: had you heard him first
Draw it to certain heads, then aggravate,   50
Then use his vehement figures—I looked still
When he would shift a shirt; and doing this
Out of pure love, no hope of gain—
    VOLP.   'Tis right.
I cannot answer him, Mosca, as I would,
Not yet; but for thy sake, at thy entreaty,   55
I will begin, ev'n now—to vex 'em all,
This very instant.
    MOS.   Good sir.
    VOLP.   Call the dwarf
And eunuch forth.
    MOS.   Castrone, Nano!

              [*Enter* CASTRONE *and* NANO.]

    NANO.   Here.
    VOLP. Shall we have a jig now?
    MOS.   What you please, sir.
    VOLP.   Go,
Straight give out about the streets, you two,   60
That I am dead; do it with constancy,
Sadly, do you hear? Impute it to the grief
Of this late slander.   [*Exeunt* CASTRONE *and* NANO.
    MOS.   What do you mean, sir?
    VOLP.   Oh,
I shall have instantly my Vulture, Crow,

---

47. *cozened:* tricked. 50. *aggravate:* emphasize. 51. *figures:* of speech. *still:* constantly. 52. *shift:* change his shirt (sweaty because of his oratorical exertions). 62. *Sadly:* seriously.

Raven, come flying hither, on the news,   65
To peck for carrion, my she-wolf, and all,
Greedy, and full of expectation—
 MOS. And then to have it ravished from their mouths?
 VOLP. 'Tis true. I will ha' thee put on a gown,
And take upon thee, as thou wert mine heir;   70
Show 'em a will. Open that chest, and reach
Forth one of those that has the blanks. I'll straight
Put in thy name.
 MOS.   It will be rare, sir.
 VOLP.   Ay,
When they e'en gape, and find themselves deluded—
 MOS. Yes.
 VOLP. And thou use them scurvily. Dispatch;   75
Get on thy gown.
 MOS.   But what, sir, if they ask
After the body?
 VOLP. Say, it was corrupted.
 MOS. I'll say it stunk, sir; and was fain t' have it
Coffined up instantly, and sent away.
 VOLP. Anything; what thou wilt.—Hold, here's my will.   80
Get thee a cap, a count-book, pen and ink,
Papers afore thee; sit as thou wert taking
An inventory of parcels. I'll get up
Behind the curtain, on a stool, and hearken;
Sometime peep over, see how they do look,   85
With what degrees their blood doth leave their faces!
O, 'twill afford me a rare meal of laughter.
 MOS. Your advocate will turn stark dull upon it.
 VOLP. It will take off his oratory's edge.
 MOS. But your clarissimo, old roundback, he   90
Will crump you like a hog-louse, with the touch.
 VOLP. And what Corvino?
 MOS.   O, sir, look for him,
Tomorrow morning, with a rope and a dagger,
To visit all the streets; he must run mad.
My lady too, that came into the court,   95
To bear false witness for your worship—
 VOLP.   Yes.

---

90. *clarissimo*: Corbaccio. 91. *crump you*: curl up; *hog-louse*: the wood-louse (hog-shaped because of its fat, oval body).

And kissed me 'fore the fathers, when my face
Flowed all with oils—
   MOS.   And sweat, sir. Why, your gold
Is such another med'cine, it dries up
All those offensive savors. It transforms   100
The most deformed, and restores 'em lovely,
As 'twere the strange poetical girdle. Jove
Could not invent t' himself a shroud more subtle
To pass Acrisius' guards. It is the thing
Makes all the world her grace, her youth, her beauty.   105
   VOLP. I think she loves me.
   MOS.   Who? the lady, sir?
She's jealous of you.
   VOLP.   Dost thou say so?   [*Knocking within*
   MOS.   Hark.
There's some already.
   VOLP.   Look.
   MOS.   It is the Vulture;
He has the quickest scent.
   VOLP.   I'll to my place,
Thou to thy posture.   [*Goes behind the curtain.*
   MOS.   I am set.
   VOLP.   But, Mosca,   110
Play the artificer now: torture 'em rarely.

SCENE III

[*Enter* VOLTORE.]

   VOLT. How now, my Mosca?
   MOS. [*Writing*]   Turkey carpets, nine—
   VOLT. Taking an inventory! that is well.
   MOS. Two suits of bedding, tissue—
   VOLT.   Where's the will?
Let me read that the while.

[*Enter* SERVANTS *with* CORBACCIO *in a chair.*]

   CORB.   So, set me down,
And get you home.   [*Exeunt* SERVANTS.
   VOLT.   Is he come now, to trouble us?   5

102. *girdle:* of Venus. 104. *Acrisius:* father of Danae, to whom amorous
Jove descended as a shower of gold. 105. *Makes:* gives to.

MOS. Of cloth of gold, two more—
CORB.   Is it done, Mosca?
MOS. Of several velvets, eight—
VOLT.   I like his care.
CORB. Dost thou not hear?

[*Enter* CORVINO.]

CORV.   Ha! is the hour come, Mosca?
VOLP. [*Aside*] Ay, now they muster.

[*Peeps from behind a traverse.*

CORV.   What does the advocate here?
Or this Corbaccio?
CORB.   What do these here?

[*Enter* LADY WOULD-BE.]

LADY.   Mosca!   10
Is his thread spun?
MOS.   Eight chests of linen—
VOLP. [*Aside*]   Oh,
My fine Dame Would-be, too!
CORV.   Mosca, the will,
That I may show it these, and rid 'em hence.
MOS. Six chests of diaper, four of damask—there. [*Gives the will,*
CORB. Is that the will?
MOS. [*Writing*]   Down-beds, and bolsters—
VOLP. [*Aside*]   Rare!   15
Be busy still. Now they begin to flutter;
They never think of me. Look, see, see, see!
How their swift eyes run over the long deed,
Unto the name, and to the legacies,
What is bequeathed them there—
MOS.   Ten suits of hangings—   20
VOLP. [*Aside*] Ay, in their garters, Mosca. Now their hopes
Are at the gasp.
VOLT.   Mosca the heir!
CORB.   What's that?
VOLP. [*Aside*] My advocate is dumb; look to my merchant—
He has heard of some strange storm; a ship is lost—
He faints. My lady will swoon. Old glazen-eyes,   25

───────────

SC. III: 7. *several:* individual pieces of. 14. *diaper:* kind of damask. 21.
garters: i.e., suicide by hanging in their own garters.

He hath not reached his despair yet.
    CORB.   All these
Are out of hope; I am, sure, the man.   *[Takes the will.*
    CORV.   But, Mosca—
    MOS. Two cabinets—
    CORV.   Is this in earnest?
    MOS.   One
Of ebony—
    CORV.   Or do you but delude me?
    MOS. The other, mother-of-pearl—I am very busy.   30
Good faith, it is a fortune thrown upon me—
Item, one salt of agate—not my seeking.
    LADY. Do you hear, sir?
    MOS.   A perfumed box—'pray you forbear;
You see I am troubled—made of an onyx—
    LADY.   How!
    MOS. Tomorrow or next day, I shall be at leisure   35
To talk with you all.
    CORV.   Is this my large hope's issue?
    LADY. Sir, I must have a fairer answer.
    MOS.   Madam!
Marry, and shall: 'pray you, fairly quit my house.
Nay, raise no tempest with your looks; but hark you,
Remember what your ladyship offered me   40
To put you in an heir; go to; think on it.
And what you said e'en your best madams did
For maintenance, and why not you? Enough.
Go home, and use the poor Sir Pol, your knight, well,
For fear I tell some riddles; go, be melancholic.   45
                        [Exit LADY WOULD-BE.
    VOLP. *[Aside]* Oh, my fine devil!
    CORV.   Mosca, pray you a word.
    MOS. Lord! will not you take your dispatch hence yet?
Methinks, of all, you should have been th' example.
Why should you stay here? with what thought, what promise?
Hear you; do not you know, I know you an ass,   50
And that you would most fain have been a wittol
If fortune would have let you? that you are
A declared cuckold, on good terms? This pearl,
You'll say, was yours? right; this diamond?

---

32. *salt:* saltcellar. 45. *melancholic:* have the blues in a fashionably
genteel way. 51. *wittol:* willing cuckold.

I'll not deny 't, but thank you. Much here else?   55
It may be so. Why, think that these good works
May help to hide your bad. I'll not betray you;
Although you be but extraordinary,
And have it only in title, it sufficeth: 59
Go home; be melancholic too, or mad.   [*Exit* CORVINO.
  VOLP. [*Aside*] Rare Mosca! how his villainy becomes him!
  VOLT. [*Aside*] Certain he doth delude all these for me.
  CORB. Mosca the heir?
  VOLP. [*Aside*]   O, his four eyes have found it!
  CORB. I am cozened, cheated, by a parasite-slave;
Harlot, th' hast gulled me.
  MOS.   Yes, sir. Stop your mouth,   65
Or I shall draw the only tooth is left.
Are not you he, that filthy covetous wretch,
With the three legs, that here, in hope of prey,
Have, any time this three year, snuffed about,
With your most grov'ling nose, and would have hired   70
Me to the pois'ning of my patron, sir?
Are not you he that have today in court
Professed the disinheriting of your son?
Perjured yourself? Go home, and die, and stink;
If you but croak a syllable, all comes out: 75
Away, and call your porters! [*Exit* CORBACCIO.] Go, go, stink.
  VOLP. [*Aside*] Excellent varlet!
  VOLT.   Now, my faithful Mosca,
I find thy constancy—
  MOS.   Sir!
  VOLT.   Sincere.
  MOS. [*Writing*]   A table
Of porphyry—I mar'l you'll be thus troublesome.
  VOLT. Nay, leave off now, they are gone.
  MOS.   Why, who are you?   80
What! who did send for you? Oh, cry you mercy,
Reverend sir! Good faith, I am grieved for you,
That any chance of mine should thus defeat
Your (I must needs say) most deserving travails;
But I protest, sir, it was cast upon me,   85
And I could almost wish to be without it,
But that the will o' th' dead must be observed.

---

58. *but extraordinary:* only an unusual, nominal cuckold. 63. *four eyes:*
glasses. 79. *mar'l:* marvel.

Marry, my joy is that you need it not;
You have a gift, sir, (thank your education)
Will never let you want, while there are men,   90
And malice, to breed causes. Would I had
But half the like, for all my fortune, sir.
If I have any suits, as I do hope,
Things being so easy and direct, I shall not,
I will make bold with your obstreperous aid;   95
Conceive me—for your fee, sir. In meantime,
You that have so much law, I know ha' the conscience
Not to be covetous of what is mine.
Good sir, I thank you for my plate; 'twill help
To set up a young man. Good faith, you look   100
As you were costive; best go home and purge, sir.
                                             [*Exit* VOLTORE.
   VOLP. [*Coming from behind the curtain*] Bid him eat lettuce well.
   My witty mischief,
Let me embrace thee. O that I could now
Transform thee to a Venus!—Mosca, go,
Straight take my habit of clarissimo,   105
And walk the streets; be seen, torment 'em more;
We must pursue, as well as plot. Who would
Have lost this feast?
   MOS.   I doubt it will lose them.
   VOLP. O, my recovery shall recover all.
That I could now but think on some disguise   110
To meet 'em in, and ask 'em questions.
How I would vex 'em still at every turn!
   MOS. Sir, I can fit you.
   VOLP.   Canst thou?
   MOS.   Yes, I know
One o' the commandadori, sir; so like you,
Him will I straight make drunk, and bring you his habit.   115
   VOLP. A rare disguise, and answering thy brain!
O, I will be a sharp disease unto 'em.
   MOS. Sir, you must look for curses—

---

91. *causes:* lawsuits. 95. *obstreperous:* leather-lunged. 96. *Conceive . . .
fee:* i.e., having tricked Voltore out of a fortune, Mosca further insults
him by saying that if he should ever need a lawyer he would certainly
hire him, and "conceive me" (understand me) at your usual fee. 101.
costive: constipated. 102. *eat lettuce well:* i.e., take a sleeping pill; wild
lettuce was thought to contain opium and therefore to induce sleep. 105.
habit of clarissimo: grandee's suit.

VOLP.   Till they burst;
The Fox fares ever best when he is cursed.   [*Exeunt.*

SCENE IV. *A hall in Sir Politic's house.*

[*Enter* PEREGRINE *disguised and three* MERCATORI.]

PER. Am I enough disguised?
1 MER.   I warrant you.
PER. All my ambition is to fright him only.
2 MER. If you could ship him away, 'twere excellent.
3 MER. To Zant, or to Aleppo!
PER.   Yes, and ha' his
Adventures put i' th' Book of Voyages,   5
And his gulled story regist'red for truth!
Well, gentlemen, when I am in awhile,
And that you think us warm in our discourse,
Know your approaches.
1 MER.   Trust it to our care.

                              [*Exeunt* MERCATORI.

[*Enter* WAITING WOMAN.]

PER. Save you, fair lady! Is Sir Pol within?   10
WOM. I do not know, sir.
PER.   'Pray you say unto him
Here is a merchant, upon earnest business,
Desires to speak with him.
WOM.   I will see, sir.   [*Exit.*
PER.   'Pray you.
I see the family is all female here.

[*Re-enter* WAITING WOMAN.]

WOM. He says, sir, he has weighty affairs of state,   15
That now require him whole; some other time
You may possess him.
PER.   'Pray you say again,
If those require him whole, these will exact him,
Whereof I bring him tidings. [*Exit* WOMAN.] What might be
His grave affair of state now! How to make   20
Bolognian sausages here in Venice, sparing

sc. IV: 4. *Zant:* a Greek island. 5. *Book of Voyages:* Hakluyt's *Principall Navigations, Voiages, and Discoveries of the English Nation,* which had just appeared in a second edition.

One o' th' ingredients?

[*Re-enter* WAITING WOMAN.]

WOM.   Sir, he says he knows
By your word "tidings," that you are no statesman,
And therefore wills you stay.
PER.   Sweet, 'pray you return him
I have not read so many proclamations,   25
And studied them for words, as he has done—
But—here he deigns to come.   [*Exit* WOMAN.

[*Enter* SIR POLITIC.]

POL.   Sir, I must crave
Your courteous pardon. There hath chanced today
Unkind disaster 'twixt my lady and me;
And I was penning my apology,   30
To give her satisfaction, as you came now.
PER. Sir, I am grieved I bring you worse disaster.
The gentleman you met at th' port today,
That told you he was newly arrived—
POL.   Ay, was
A fugitive punk?
PER.   No, sir, a spy set on you;   35
And he has made relation to the Senate,
That you professed to him to have a plot
To sell the state of Venice to the Turk.
POL. O me!
PER.   For which warrants are signed by this time,
To apprehend you, and to search your study   40
For papers—
POL.   Alas, sir, I have none, but notes
Drawn out of play-books—
PER.   All the better, sir.
POL. And some essays. What shall I do?
PER.   Sir, best
Convey yourself into a sugar-chest;
Or, if you could lie round, a frail were rare;   45
And I could send you aboard.
POL.   Sir, I but talked so,

---

23. *"tidings"*: a plain word for "intelligence." 35. *punk*: whore. 41-2. *notes . . . play-books*: fine phrases from plays. 45. *frail were rare*: basket would be perfect.

For discourse sake merely.   [*They knock without.*

    PER.   Hark! they are there.

    POL. I am a wretch, a wretch!

    PER.   What will you do, sir?

Have you ne'er a currant-butt to leap into?

They'll put you to the rack; you must be sudden.   50

    POL. Sir, I have an engine—

    3 MER. [*Within*]   Sir Politic Would-be!

    2 MER. [*Within*] Where is he?

    POL.   That I've thought upon, before time.

    PER. What is it?

    POL.   I shall ne'er endure the torture.—

Marry, it is, sir, of a tortoise shell,

Fitted for these extremities; 'pray you, sir, help me.   55

Here I have a place, sir, to put back my legs,

Please you to lay it on, sir, [*Lies down while* PEREGRINE *places the
    shell upon him.*] with this cap,

And my black gloves. I'll lie, sir, like a tortoise,

Till they are gone.

    PER.   And call you this an engine?

    POL. Mine own device.—Good sir, bid my wife's women   60

To burn my papers.   [*Exit* PEREGRINE.

[*The three* MERCATORI *rush in.*]

    1 MER.   Where's he hid?

    3 MER.   We must,

And will, sure, find him.

    2 MER.   Which is his study?

[*Re-enter* PEREGRINE.]

    1 MER.   What

Are you, sir?

    PER.   I am a merchant, that came here

To look upon this tortoise.

    3 MER.   How?

    1 MER.   St. Mark!

What beast is this?

    PER.   It is a fish.

    2 MER.   Come out here!   65

    PER. Nay, you may strike him, sir, and tread upon him;

He'll bear a cart.

---

49. *currant-butt:* wine cask. 51. *engine:* contraption.

1 MER.   What, to run over him?
PER.   Yes, sir.
3 MER. Let's jump upon him.
2 MER.   Can he not go?
PER.   He creeps, sir.
1 MER. Let's see him creep.
PER.   No, good sir, you will hurt him.
2 MER. Heart, I'll see him creep, or prick his guts.   70
3 MER. Come out here.
PER.   Pray you, sir!—[*Aside to* SIR POLITIC] Creep a little.
1 MER.   Forth.
2 MER. Yet further.
PER.   Good sir!—[*Aside*] Creep!
2 MER.   We'll see his legs.
          [*They pull off the shell and discover him.*
3 MER. Gods so, he has garters!
1 MER.   Ay, and gloves!
2 MER.   Is this
Your fearful tortoise?
     PER. [*Discovering himself*] Now, Sir Pol, we are even;
For your next project I shall be prepared;   75
I am sorry for the funeral of your notes, sir.
     1 MER. 'Twere a rare motion to be seen in Fleet Street.
     2 MER. Ay, i' the term.
     1 MER.   Or Smithfield, in the fair.
     3 MER. Methinks 'tis but a melancholic sight!
     PER. Farewell, most politic tortoise.
                    [*Exeunt* PEREGRINE *and* MERCATORI.

          [*Re-enter* WAITING WOMAN.]

     POL.   Where's my lady?   80
Knows she of this?
     WOM.   I know not, sir.
     POL.   Inquire.—
Oh, I shall be the fable of all feasts,
The freight of the gazetti, ship-boys' tale;
And, which is worst, even talk for ordinaries.
     WOM. My lady's come most melancholic home,   85
And says, sir, she will straight to sea, for physic.
     POL. And I, to shun this place and clime for ever,

---

77. *motion*: sight. 78. *term*: during the season, when courts are in session.
83. *freight . . . gazetti*: theme of the newspapers. 84. *ordinaries*: taverns.

Creeping with house on back, and think it well
To shrink my poor head in my politic shell.   [*Exeunt.*

SCENE V. *A room in Volpone's house.*

[*Enter* VOLPONE *and* MOSCA, *the first in the habit of a commandadore,
the other of a clarissimo.*]

VOLP. Am I then like him?
MOS.   O, sir, you are he;
No man can sever you.
VOLP.   Good.
MOS.   But what am I?
VOLP. 'Fore heav'n, a brave clarissimo; thou becom'st it!
Pity thou wert not born one.
MOS.   If I hold
My made one, 'twill be well.
VOLP.   I'll go and see   5
What news first at the court.   [*Exit.*
MOS.   Do so.—My Fox
Is out on his hole, and ere he shall re-enter,
I'll make him languish in his borrowed case,
Except he come to composition with me.—
Androgyno, Castrone, Nano!

[*Enter* ANDROGYNO, CASTRONE, *and* NANO.]

ALL.   Here.   10
MOS. Go, recreate yourselves abroad; go, sport.—
                                    [*Exeunt all but* MOSCA.
So, now I have the keys, and am possessed.
Since he will needs be dead afore his time,
I'll bury him, or gain by him. I am his heir,
And so will keep me, till he share, at least.   15
To cozen him of all, were but a cheat
Well placed; no man would construe it a sin;
Let his sport pay for 't. This is called the Fox-trap.   [*Exit.*

————————

sc. v: 2. *sever:* tell you apart. 8. *case:* skin. 9. *composition:* terms.

SCENE VI. *A street.*

[*Enter* CORBACCIO *and* CORVINO.]

CORB. They say the court is set.
CORV.   We must maintain
Our first tale good, for both our reputations.
  CORB. Why, mine's no tale; my son would there have killed me.
  CORV. That's true; I had forgot;—[*Aside*] mine is, I am sure.—
But for your will, sir.
  CORB.   Ay, I'll come upon him   5
For that hereafter, now his patron's dead.

[*Enter* VOLPONE *disguised.*]

  VOLP. Signior Corvino! and Corbaccio! sir,
Much joy unto you.
  CORV.   Of what?
  VOLP.   The sudden good
Dropped down upon you—
  CORB.   Where?
  VOLP.   And none knows how—
From old Volpone, sir.
  CORB.   Out, errant knave!   10
  VOLP. Let not your too much wealth, sir, make you furious.
  CORB. Away, thou varlet.
  VOLP.   Why, sir?
  CORB.   Dost thou mock me?
  VOLP. You mock the world, sir; did you not change wills?
  CORB. Out, harlot.
  VOLP.   O! belike you are the man,
Signior Corvino? Faith, you carry it well;   15
You grow not mad withal; I love your spirit.
You are not overleavened with your fortune.
You should ha' some would swell now like a wine-fat,
With such an autumn.—Did he gi' you all, sir?
  CORV. Avoid, you rascal.
  VOLP.   Troth, your wife has shown   20
Herself a very woman; but you are well,
You need not care, you have a good estate,
To bear it out, sir, better by this chance—
Except Corbaccio have a share.

SC. VI: 17. *overleavened:* puffed up. 18. *fat:* vat. 19. *autumn:* harvest.
20. *Avoid:* get out.

CORB.   Hence, varlet.
VOLP. You will not be acknown, sir; why, 'tis wise.   25
Thus do all gamesters, at all games, dissemble:
No man will seem to win.   [*Exeunt* CORVINO *and* CORBACCIO.
   Here comes my vulture,
Heaving his beak up i' the air, and snuffing.

SCENE VII

[*Enter* VOLTORE.]

VOLT. Outstripped thus, by a parasite! a slave!
Would run on errands, and make legs for crumbs!
Well, what I'll do—
   VOLP.   The court stays for your worship.
I e'en rejoice, sir, at your worship's happiness,
And that it fell into so learned hands,   5
That understand the fingering—
   VOLT.   What do you mean?
   VOLP. I mean to be a suitor to your worship,
For the small tenement, out of reparations,
That at the end of your long row of houses,
By the Piscaria; it was, in Volpone's time,   10
Your predecessor, ere he grew diseased,
A handsome, pretty, customed bawdyhouse
As any was in Venice, none dispraised;
But fell with him: his body and that house
Decayed together.
   VOLT.   Come, sir, leave your prating.   15
   VOLP. Why, if your worship give me but your hand
That I may ha' the refusal, I have done.
'Tis a mere toy to you, sir, candle-rents;
As your learned worship knows—
   VOLT.   What do I know?
   VOLP. Marry, no end of your wealth, sir; God decrease it!   20
   VOLT. Mistaking knave! what, mockest thou my misfortune?
                                          [*Exit.*
   VOLP. His blessing on your heart, sir; would 'twere more!—
Now to my first again, at the next corner.   [*Exit.*

---

25. *be acknown:* admit it.

  SC. VII: 2. *make legs:* scrape and bow. 8. *reparations:* repair. 10. *Piscaria:*
fishmarket. 12. *customed:* popular. 18. *candle-rents:* small revenue from
run-down low-income property.

SCENE VIII. *Another corner of the street.*

[*Enter* CORBACCIO *and* CORVINO, MOSCA *passant.*]

CORB. See, in our habit! see the impudent varlet!
CORV. That I could shoot mine eyes at him, like gun-stones.

[*Enter* VOLPONE.]

VOLP. But is this true, sir, of the parasite?
CORB. Again, t' afflict us? monster!
VOLP.   In good faith, sir,
I am heartily grieved, a beard of your grave length   5
Should be so overreached. I never brooked
That parasite's hair; methought his nose should cozen:
There still was somewhat in his look, did promise
The bane of a clarissimo.
        CORB.   Knave—
        VOLP.   Methinks
Yet you, that are so traded i' the world,   10
A witty merchant, the fine bird, Corvino,
That have such moral emblems on your name,
Should not have sung your shame, and dropped your cheese,
To let the Fox laugh at your emptiness.
        CORV. Sirrah, you think the privilege of the place,   15
And your red saucy cap, that seems to me
Nailed to your jolt-head with those two *cecchines,*
Can warrant your abuses; come you hither;
You shall perceive, sir, I dare beat you; approach.
        VOLP. No haste, sir, I do not know your valor well,   20
Since you durst publish what you are, sir.
        CORV.   Tarry,
I'd speak with you.
        VOLP.   Sir, sir, another time—
        CORV. Nay, now.
        VOLP.   O God, sir! I were a wise man,
Would stand the fury of a distracted cuckold.

[MOSCA *walks by them.*

        CORB. What, come again!
        VOLP.   Upon 'em, Mosca; save me.   25

---

sc. viii: Stage direction. *passant:* passing by. 1. *habit:* dress. 6. *brooked:* could endure. 12. *moral . . . name:* instructive fables about the crow. 13. *sung:* like the crow, cf. Act I, Sc. II, 96. 16-17. *red . . . cecchines:* i.e., Volpone is disguised as an officer of the law with a red cap on his jolt (block) head with two gilt buttons.

CORB. The air's infected where he breathes.
CORV.   Let's fly him.
                    [*Exeunt* CORVINO *and* CORBACCIO.
VOLP. Excellent basilisk! turn upon the Vulture.

SCENE IX

[*Enter* VOLTORE.]

VOLT. Well, flesh-fly, it is summer with you now;
Your winter will come on.
    MOS.   Good advocate,
'Pray thee not rail, nor threaten out of place thus;
Thou 'lt make a solecism, as Madam says.
Get you a biggin more; your brain breaks loose.   5
                                                         [*Exit.*

    VOLT. Well sir.
    VOLP.   Would you ha' me beat the insolent slave?
Throw dirt upon his first good clothes?
    VOLT.   This same
Is doubtless some familiar!
    VOLP.   Sir, the court,
In troth, stays for you. I am mad, a mule
That never read Justinian should get up   10
And ride an advocate. Had you no quick
To avoid gullage, sir, by such a creature?
I hope you do but jest; he has not done 't;
This 's but confederacy to blind the rest.
You are the heir?
    VOLT.   A strange, officious,   15
Troublesome knave! Thou dost torment me.
    VOLP.   I know—
It cannot be, sir, that you should be cozened;
'Tis not within the wit of man to do it;
You are so wise, so prudent; and 'tis fit
That wealth and wisdom still should go together.   20
                                                         [*Exeunt.*

---

27. *basilisk:* mythical beast that killed with a look.
    SC. IX: I. *flesh fly:* born from carrion (as Mosca has been). 5. *biggin
more:* larger lawyer's cap. 8. *familiar:* attendant demon. 10. *never . . .
Justinian:* knows no legal tricks. 12. *gullage:* being tricked.

SCENE X. *The Senate House.*

[*Enter four* AVOCATORI, NOTARIO, BONARIO, CELIA, CORBACCIO, CORVINO,
COMMANDADORI, SAFFI, *etc.*]

1 AVOC. Are all the parties here?
NOT.   All but the advocate.
2 AVOC. And here he comes.

[*Enter* VOLTORE *and* VOLPONE.]

1 AVOC.   Then bring 'em forth to sentence.
VOLT. O, my most honored fathers, let your mercy
Once win upon your justice, to forgive—
I am distracted—
   VOLP. [*Aside*]   What will he do now?
VOLT.   Oh,   5
I know not which t' address myself to first;
Whether your fatherhoods, or these innocents—
   CORV. [*Aside*] Will he betray himself?
VOLT.   Whom equally
I have abused, out of most covetous ends—
   CORV. The man is mad!
   CORB.   What's that?
   CORV.   He is possessed.   10
   VOLT. For which, now struck in conscience, here I prostrate
Myself at your offended feet, for pardon.
   1, 2 AVOC. Arise.
   CEL.   O heav'n, how just thou art!
VOLP.   I am caught
I' mine own noose—
   CORV. [*To* CORBACCIO] Be constant, sir; naught now
Can help but impudence.
   1 AVOC.   Speak forward.
   COM.   Silence!   15
   VOLT. It is not passion in me, reverend fathers,
But only conscience, conscience, my good sires,
That makes me now tell truth. That parasite,
That knave, hath been the instrument of all.
   1 AVOC. Where is that knave? Fetch him.
VOLP.   I go.   [*Exit.*
   CORV.   Grave fathers, 20
This man's distracted; he confessed it now:
For, hoping to be old Volpone's heir,
Who now is dead—

3 AVOC.   How?
2 AVOC.   Is Volpone dead?
CORV. Dead since, grave fathers.
BON.   O sure vengeance!
1 AVOC.   Stay;
Then he was no deceiver?
VOLT.   Oh, no, none.   25
This parasite, grave fathers—
CORV.   He does speak
Out of mere envy, 'cause the servant's made
The thing he gaped for. Please your fatherhoods,
This is the truth, though I'll not justify
The other, but he may be somedeal faulty.   30
    VOLT. Ay, to your hopes, as well as mine, Corvino;
But I'll use modesty. Pleaseth your wisdoms
To view these certain notes, and but confer them;
As I hope favor, they shall speak clear truth.
    CORV. The Devil has ent'red him!
BON.   Or bides in you.   35
    4 AVOC. We have done ill, by a public officer
To send for him, if he be heir.
    2 AVOC.   For whom?
    4 AVOC. Him that they call the parasite.
    3 AVOC.   'Tis true,
He is a man of great estate, now left.
    4 AVOC. Go you, and learn his name, and say the court   40
Entreats his presence here, but to the clearing
Of some few doubts.   [_Exit_ NOTARIO.
    2 AVOC.   This same's a labyrinth!
    1 AVOC. Stand you unto your first report?
CORV.   My state,
My life, my fame—
BON.   Where is 't?
CORV.   Are at the stake.
    1 AVOC. Is yours so too?
CORB.   The advocate's a knave,   45
And has a forkèd tongue—
    2 AVOC.   Speak to the point.
    CORB. So is the parasite too.
    1 AVOC.   This is confusion.

SC. X: 24. _since:_ since the trial. 32. _modesty:_ moderation. 33. _confer:_
compare.

VOLT. I do beseech your fatherhoods, read but those—

[Giving them papers.

CORV. And credit nothing the false spirit hath writ:
It cannot be but he's possessed, grave fathers.   50

[The scene closes.

SCENE XI. *A street.*

[Enter VOLPONE.]

VOLP. To make a snare for mine own neck, and run
My head into it, wilfully! with laughter!
When I had newly 'scaped, was free and clear!
Out of mere wantonness! Oh, the dull devil
Was in this brain of mine when I devised it,   5
And Mosca gave it second; he must now
Help to sear up this vein, or we bleed dead.

[Enter NANO, ANDROGYNO, *and* CASTRONE.]

How now! Who let you loose? Whither go you now?
What, to buy gingerbread, or to drown kitlings?
NAN. Sir, Master Mosca called us out of doors,   10
And bid us all go play, and took the keys.
AND. Yes.
VOLP.   Did Master Mosca take the keys? Why, so!
I'm farther in. These are my fine conceits!
I must be merry, with a mischief to me!
What a vile wretch was I, that could not bear   15
My fortune soberly? I must ha' my crochets,
And my conundrums!—Well, go you, and seek him;
His meaning may be truer than my fear.
Bid him he straight come to me to the court;
Thither will I, and, if 't be possible,   20
Unscrew my advocate, upon new hopes.
When I provoked him, then I lost myself.   *[Exeunt.*

SC. XI: 13. *conceits:* ideas. 16. *crochets:* eccentric whims.

SCENE XII. *The Senate House.*

[AVOCATORI, *etc., are discovered, as before.*]

1 AVOC. These things can ne'er be reconciled. He here
                              [*Shows the papers.*]
Professeth that the gentleman was wronged,
And that the gentlewoman was brought thither,
Forced by her husband, and there left.
    VOLT.   Most true.
    CEL. How ready is heav'n to those that pray!
    1 AVOC.   But that   5
Volpone would have ravished her, he holds
Utterly false, knowing his impotence.
    CORV. Grave fathers, he is possessed; again, I say,
Possessed; nay, if there be possession,
And obsession, he has both.
    3 AVOC.   Here comes our officer.   10

[*Enter* VOLPONE.]

    VOLP. The parasite will straight be here, grave fathers.
    4 AVOC. You might invent some other name, Sir Varlet.
    3 AVOC. Did not the notary meet him?
    VOLP.   Not that I know.
    4 AVOC. His coming will clear all.
    2 AVOC.   Yet it is misty.
    VOLT. May 't please your fatherhoods—
    VOLP. [*Whispers to the* ADVOCATE]   Sir, the parasite   15
Willed me to tell you that his master lives;
That you are still the man; your hopes the same;
And this was only a jest—
    VOLT.   How?
    VOLP.   Sir, to try
If you were firm, and how you stood affected.
    VOLT. Art sure he lives?
    VOLP.   Do I live, sir?
    VOLT.   O me!   20
I was too violent.
    VOLP.   Sir, you may redeem it.
They said you were possessed; fall down, and seem so:
I'll help to make it good. [VOLTORE *falls.*] God bless the man!—

SC. XII: 9-10. *possession . . . obsession:* attack by the devil from within
and without.

[*Aside to* VOLTORE] Stop your wind hard, and swell.—See, see, see, see!
He vomits crooked pins! His eyes are set,   25
Like a dead hare's hung in a poulters' shop!
His mouth's running away! Do you see, signior?
Now it is in his belly.

CORV.   Ay, the devil!

VOLP. Now in his throat.

CORV.   Ay, I perceive it plain.

VOLP. 'Twill out, 'twill out! stand clear. See where it flies!   30
In shape of a blue toad, with a bat's wings!
Do not you see it, sir?

CORB.   What? I think I do.

CORV. 'Tis too manifest.

VOLP.   Look! he comes t' himself!

VOLT. Where am I?

VOLP.   Take good heart, the worst is past, sir.
You're dispossessed.

1 AVOC.   What accident is this?   35

2 AVOC. Sudden and full of wonder!

3 AVOC.   If he were
Possessed, as it appears, all this is nothing.

CORV. He has been often subject to these fits.

1 AVOC. Show him that writing:—do you know it, sir?

VOLP. [*Aside to* VOLTORE] Deny it, sir, forswear it; know it not.   40

VOLT. Yes, I do know it well: it is my hand;
But all that it contains is false.

BON.   O practice!

2 AVOC. What maze is this!

1 AVOC.   Is he not guilty then,
Whom you there name the parasite?

VOLT.   Grave fathers,
No more than his good patron, old Volpone.   45

4 AVOC. Why, he is dead.

VOLT.   O no, my honored fathers.
He lives—

1 AVOC. How! lives?

VOLT.   Lives.

2 AVOC.   This is subtler yet!

3 AVOC. You said he was dead!

VOLT.   Never.

---

sc. XII: 25-8. *He . . . belly:* symptoms of being possessed by the devil.
35. *dispossessed:* i.e., of the devil. 42. *practice:* trickery.

3 AVOC.   You said so!
CORV.   I heard so.
4 AVOC. Here comes the gentleman; make him way.

[*Enter* MOSCA.]

3 AVOC.   A stool.
4 AVOC. [*Aside*] A proper man! and, were Volpone dead,   50
A fit match for my daughter.
3 AVOC.   Give him way.
VOLP. [*Aside to* MOSCA] Mosca, I was a'most lost: the advocate
Had betrayed all; but now it is recovered;
All's on the hinge again—say I am living.
MOS. What busy knave is this?—Most reverend fathers,   55
I sooner had attended your grave pleasures,
But that my order for the funeral
Of my dear patron did require me—
VOLP. [*Aside*]   Mosca!
MOS. Whom I intend to bury like a gentleman.
VOLP. [*Aside*] Ay, quick, and cozen me of all.
2 AVOC.   Still stranger!   60
More intricate!
1 AVOC.   And come about again!
4 AVOC. [*Aside*] It is a match; my daughter is bestowed.
MOS. [*Aside to* VOLPONE] Will you gi' me half?
VOLP. [*Aside*]   First I'll be hanged.
MOS. [*Aside*]   I know
Your voice is good; cry not so loud.
1 AVOC.   Demand
The advocate.—Sir, did not you affirm   65
Volpone was alive?
VOLP.   Yes, and he is;
This gent'man told me so.—[*Aside to* MOSCA] Thou shalt have half.
MOS. Whose drunkard is this same? Speak, some that know him;
I never saw his face.—[*Aside to* VOLPONE] I cannot now
Afford it you so cheap.
VOLP. [*Aside*]   No?
1 AVOC.   What say you?   70
VOLT. The officer told me.
VOLP.   I did, grave fathers,
And will maintain he lives, with mine own life,
And that this creature [*Pointing to* MOSCA] told me.—[*Aside*]

---

50. *proper:* handsome. 60. *quick:* alive.

I was born
With all good stars my enemies.
    MOS.   Most grave fathers,
If such an insolence as this must pass
Upon me, I am silent; 'twas not this   75
For which you sent, I hope.
    2 AVOC.   Take him away.
    VOLP. Mosca!
    3 AVOC.   Let him be whipped.
    VOLP. [*Aside to* MOSCA] Wilt thou betray me? Cozen me?
    3 AVOC.   And taught to bear himself
Toward a person of his rank.
    4 AVOC.   Away.   80
    MOS. I humbly thank your fatherhoods.
    VOLP.   Soft, soft;—[*Aside*] Whipped!
And lose all that I have! If I confess,
It cannot be much more.
    4 AVOC.   Sir, are you married?
    VOLP. They'll be allied anon; I must be resolute;
The Fox shall here uncase.   [*He puts off his disguise.*
    MOS. [*Aside*]   Patron!
    VOLP.   Nay, now   85
My ruins shall not come alone; your match
I'll hinder sure; my substance shall not glue you,
Nor screw you into a family.
    MOS. [*Aside*]   Why, patron!
    VOLP. I am Volpone, and this [*Pointing to* MOSCA] is my knave;
This [*To* VOLTORE], his own knave; this [*To* CORBACCIO], avarice's
    fool;   90
This [*To* CORVINO], a chimaera of wittol, fool, and knave:
And, reverend fathers, since we all can hope
Naught but a sentence, let's not now despair it.
You hear me brief.
    CORV.   May it please your fatherhoods—
    COM.   Silence.
    1 AVOC. The knot is now undone, by miracle!   95
    2 AVOC. Nothing can be more clear.
    3 AVOC.   Or can more prove
These innocent.
    1 AVOC.   Give 'em their liberty.
    BON. Heaven could not long let such gross crimes be hid.
    2 AVOC. If this be held the highway to get riches,
May I be poor.

3 AVOC. This 's not the gain, but torment.   100
1 AVOC. These possess wealth, as sick men possess fevers,
Which trulier may be said to possess them.
2 AVOC. Disrobe that parasite.
CORV. and MOS.   Most honored fathers—
1 AVOC. Can you plead aught to stay the course of justice?
If you can, speak.
CORV. and VOLT. We beg favor.
CEL.   And mercy.   105
1 AVOC. You hurt your innocence, suing for the guilty.
Stand forth; and, first, the parasite. You appear
T' have been the chiefest minister, if not plotter,
In all these lewd impostures, and now, lastly,
Have with your impudence abused the court,   110
And habit of a gentleman of Venice,
Being a fellow of no birth or blood;
For which our sentence is, first, thou be whipped:
Then live perpetual prisoner in our galleys.
VOLP. I thank you for him.
MOS.   Bane to thy wolfish nature!   115
1 AVOC. Deliver him to the saffi.—Thou, Volpone,
By blood and rank a gentleman, canst not fall
Under like censure; but our judgment on thee
Is that thy substance all be straight confiscate
To the hospital of the Incurabili.   120
And since the most was gotten by imposture,
By feigning lame, gout, palsy, and such diseases,
Thou art to lie in prison, cramped with irons,
Till thou be'st sick and lame indeed.—Remove him.
VOLP. This is called mortifying of a Fox.   125
1 AVOC. Thou, Voltore, to take away the scandal
Thou hast given all worthy men of thy profession,
Art banished from their fellowship, and our state.—
Corbaccio!—Bring him near.—We here possess
Thy son of all thy state, and confine thee   130
To the monastery of San' Spirito;
Where, since thou knewest not how to live well here,
Thou shalt be learned to die well.
CORB.   Ha! what said he?
COM. You shall know anon, sir.

---

115. *Bane to:* may evil come to. 125. *mortifying:* (1) slowly killing (2) tenderizing for cooking.

1 AVOC.   Thou, Corvino, shalt
Be straight embarked from thine own house, and rowed   135
Round about Venice, through the Grand Canal,
Wearing a cap, with fair long ass's ears,
Instead of horns; and so to mount, a paper
Pinned on thy breast, to the Berlina.
    CORV.   Yes,
And have mine eyes beat out with stinking fish,   140
Bruised fruit, and rotten eggs—'tis well. I am glad
I shall not see my shame yet.
    1 AVOC.   And to expiate
Thy wrongs done to thy wife, thou art to send her
Home to her father, with her dowry trebled;
And these are all your judgments.
    ALL.   Honored fathers—   145
    1 AVOC. Which may not be revoked. Now you begin,
When crimes are done and past, and to be punished,
To think what your crimes are.—Away with them!
Let all that see these vices thus rewarded,
Take heart, and love to study 'em. Mischiefs feed   150
Like beasts, till they be fat, and then they bleed.   [Exeunt.

VOLPONE

The seasoning of a play is the applause.
Now, though the Fox be punished by the laws,
He yet doth hope, there is no suff'ring due,
For any fact which he hath done 'gainst you;   155
If there be, censure him; here he doubtful stands.
If not, fare jovially, and clap your hands.   [Exit.

---

139. Berlina: pillory. 155. fact: crime.

The Duchess of Malfi

The Duchess of Malfi

DRAMATIS PERSONAE

FERDINAND, *Duke of Calabria*

CARDINAL, *his brother*

ANTONIO BOLOGNA, *steward of the household to the Duchess*

DELIO, *his friend*

DANIEL DE BOSOLA, *gentleman of the horse to the Duchess*

CASTRUCHIO

MARQUIS OF PESCARA

COUNT MALATESTE

RODERIGO

SILVIO

GRISOLAN

DOCTOR

THE SEVERAL MADMEN

DUCHESS OF MALFI

CARIOLA, *her woman*

JULIA, *Castruchio's wife, and the Cardinal's mistress.*

OLD LADY

LADIES, CHILDREN, PILGRIMS, EXE-CUTIONERS, OFFICERS, *and* AT-TENDANTS, *etc.*

SCENE—*The Duchess's palace, Amalfi; Cardinal's palace, Rome; Loretto and neighboring country; Milan.*

Act I

SCENE I. *The Duchess's Palace, Amalfi.*

[ANTONIO *and* DELIO.]

DELIO. You are welcome to your country, dear Antonio;
You have been long in France, and you return
A very formal Frenchman in your habit.
How do you like the French court?

ANT.   I admire it.
In seeking to reduce both state and people   5
To a fixed order, their judicious king

ACT I, SC. I: 3. *habit:* dress.

Begins at home; quits first his royal palace
Of flattering sycophants, of dissolute
And infamous persons,—which he sweetly terms
His Master's masterpiece, the work of heaven;   10
Considering duly that a prince's court
Is like a common fountain, whence should flow
Pure silver drops in general, but if 't chance
Some cursed example poison 't near the head,
Death and diseases through the whole land spread.   15
And what is 't makes this blessèd government
But a most provident council, who dare freely
Inform him the corruption of the times?
Though some o' th' court hold it presumption
To instruct princes what they ought to do,   20
It is a noble duty to inform them
What they ought to foresee.—Here comes Bosola,
The only court-gall; yet I observe his railing
Is not for simple love of piety:
Indeed, he rails at those things which he wants;   25
Would be as lecherous, covetous, or proud,
Bloody, or envious, as any man,
If he had means to be so.—Here's the cardinal.

[*Enter* CARDINAL *and* BOSOLA.]

BOS. I do haunt you still.

CARD. So.   30

BOS. I have done you better service than to be slighted thus. Miserable age, where only the reward of doing well is the doing of it!

CARD. You enforce your merit too much.

BOS. I fell into the galleys in your service; where, for two years
together, I wore two towels instead of a shirt, with a knot on   [35
the shoulder, after the fashion of a Roman mantle. Slighted thus! I
will thrive some way. Blackbirds fatten best in hard weather; why
not I in these dog-days?

CARD. Would you could become honest!

BOS. With all your divinity do but direct me the way to it.   [40
I have known many travel far for it, and yet return as arrant knaves
as they went forth, because they carried themselves always along with
them. [*Exit* CARDINAL.] Are you gone? Some fellows, they say, are
possessed with the devil, but this great fellow were able to possess the
greatest devil, and make him worse.   45

---

13. *in general:* invariably. 23. *gall:* bitter critic. 34. *galleys:* slave-ships.

ANT. He hath denied thee some suit?

BOS. He and his brother are like plum-trees that grow crooked over standing-pools; they are rich and o'erladen with fruit. but none but crows, pies, and caterpillars feed on them. Could I be one of their flattering panders, I would hang on their ears like a horseleech,   [50 till I were full, and then drop off. I pray, leave me. Who would rely upon these miserable dependances, in expectation to be advanced tomorrow? What creature ever fed worse than hoping Tantalus? Nor ever died any man more fearfully than he that hoped for a pardon. There are rewards for hawks and dogs when they have done   [55 us service; but for a soldier that hazards his limbs in a battle, nothing but a kind of geometry is his last supportation.

DELIO. Geometry?

BOS. Ay, to hang in a fair pair of slings, take his latter swing in the world upon an honourable pair of crutches, from hospital to   [60 hospital. Fare ye well, sir: and yet do not you scorn us; for places in the court are but like beds in the hospital, where this man's head lies at that man's foot, and so lower and lower.   [*Exit.*

DEL. I knew this fellow seven years in the galleys
For a notorious murder; and 't was thought   65
The cardinal suborned it: he was released
By the French general, Gaston de Foix,
When he recovered Naples.

ANT.   'Tis great pity
He should be thus neglected: I have heard
He 's very valiant. This foul melancholy   70
Will poison all his goodness; for, I'll tell you,
If too immoderate sleep be truly said
To be an inward rust unto the soul,
It then doth follow want of action
Breeds all black malcontents; and their close rearing,   75
Like moths in cloth, do hurt for want of wearing.

SCENE II. *The same.*

[ANTONIO, DELIO.]

DELIO. The presence 'gins to fill; you promised me
To make me the partaker of the natures

---

48. *standing:* stagnant and scum-covered. 49. *pies:* magpies. 57. *geometry . . . supportation:* only support a pair of crutches, looking like arms of a compass, with which he measures the ground. 67. *Gaston de Foix:* young French leader who fell while taking Ravenna, not Naples, from the Spanish in 1512.

Of some of your great courtiers.

ANT.   The lord cardinal's
And other strangers' that are now in court?
I shall.—Here comes the great Calabrian duke.   5

[*Enter* FERDINAND *and* ATTENDANTS.]

FERD. Who took the ring oft'nest?

SIL. Antonio Bologna, my lord.

FERD. Our sister duchess' great master of her household? Give him
the jewel.—When shall we leave this sportive action, and fall to action indeed?   10

CAST. Methinks, my lord, you should not desire to go to war in
person.

FERD. Now for some gravity.—Why, my lord?

CAST. It is fitting a soldier arise to be a prince, but not necessary a
prince descend to be a captain.   15

FERD. No?

CAST. No, my lord; he were far better do it by a deputy.

FERD. Why should he not as well sleep or eat by a deputy? This
might take idle, offensive, and base office from him, whereas the other
deprives him of honour.   20

CAST. Believe my experience: that realm is never long in quiet where
the ruler is a soldier.

FERD. Thou told'st me thy wife could not endure fighting.

CAST. True, my lord.

FERD. And of a jest she broke of a captain she met full of   [25
wounds: I have forgot it.

CAST. She told him, my lord, he was a pitiful fellow, to lie, like the
children of Ismael, all in tents.

FERD. Why, there's a wit were able to undo all the chirurgeons o'
the city; for although gallants should quarrel, and had drawn   [30
their weapons, and were ready to go to it, yet her persuasions would
make them put up.

CAST. That she would, my lord.—How do you like my Spainish
jennet?

ROD. He is all fire.   35

FERD. I am of Pliny's opinion: I think he was begot by the wind; he

_____

SC. II: 6. *ring:* a suspended ring which knights rode at and tried to carry
off on their lances. 28. *tents:* with a play on the meaning, rolls of bandage.
29. *chirurgeons:* surgeons. 34. *jennet:* light horse. 36. *Pliny's opinion:* Pliny
(23-79), a Roman writer, recorded in his widely read *Natural History* the
old belief that mares could be impregnated by the west wind and give birth
to fleet foals who lived only three years.

runs as if he were ballassed with quicksilver.

SIL. True, my lord, he reels from the tilt often.

ROD., GRIS. Ha, ha, ha!

FERD. Why do you laugh? Methinks you that are courtiers   [40
should be my touch-wood, take fire when I give fire; that is, laugh
when I laugh, were the subject never so witty.

CAST. True, my lord: I myself have heard a very good jest, and have
scorned to seem to have so silly a wit as to understand it.

FERD. But I can laugh at your fool, my lord.   45

CAST. He cannot speak, you know, but he makes faces; my lady cannot abide him.

FERD. No?

CAST. Nor endure to be in merry company; for she says too much
laughing, and too much company, fills her too full of the
wrinkle.   51

FERD. I would, then, have a mathematical instrument made for her
face, that she might not laugh out of compass.—I shall shortly visit
you at Milan, Lord Silvio.

SIL. Your grace shall arrive most welcome.   55

FERD. You are a good horseman, Antonio: you have excellent riders
in France. What do you think of good horsemanship?

ANT. Nobly, my lord: as out of the Grecian horse issued many
famous princes, so out of brave horsemanship arise the first sparks of
growing resolution, that raise the mind to noble action.   60

FERD. You have bespoke it worthily.

SIL. Your brother, the lord cardinal, and sister duchess.

[*Enter* CARDINAL, *with* DUCHESS, *and* CARIOLA.]

CARD. Are the galleys come about?

GRIS.   They are, my lord.

FERD. Here's the Lord Silvio is come to take his leave.

DELIO. Now, sir, your promise: what's that cardinal?   65
I mean his temper. They say he's a brave fellow,
Will play his five thousand crowns at tennis, dance,
Court ladies, and one that hath fought single combats.

ANT. Some such flashes superficially hang on him for form; but
observe his inward character: he is a melancholy churchman.   [70
The spring in his face is nothing but the engendering of toads; where
he is jealous of any man, he lays worse plots for them than ever was
imposed on Hercules, for he strews in his way flatterers, panders,
intelligencers, atheists, and a thousand such political monsters. He

---

38. *reels from the tilt:* refuses or turns aside in jousting.

should have been Pope; but instead of coming to it by the   [75
primitive decency of the church, he did bestow bribes so largely and
so impudently as if he would have carried it away without heaven's
knowledge. Some good he hath done——

    DELIO. You have given too much of him. What's his brother?

    ANT. The duke there? A most perverse and turbulent nature.   80
What appears in him mirth is merely outside;
If he laugh heartily, it is to laugh
All honesty out of fashion.

    DELIO.   Twins?

    ANT.   In quality.
He speaks with others' tongues, and hears men's suits
With others' ears; will seem to sleep o' th' bench   85
Only to entrap offenders in their answers;
Dooms men to death by information;
Rewards by hearsay.

    DELIO.   Then the law to him
Is like a foul, black cobweb to a spider,—
He makes it his dwelling and a prison   90
To entangle those shall feed him.

    ANT.   Most true:
He never pays debts unless they be shrewd turns,
And those he will confess that he doth owe.
Last, for his brother there, the cardinal,
They that do flatter him most say oracles   95
Hang at his lips; and verily I believe them,
For the devil speaks in them.
But for their sister, the right noble duchess,
You never fixed your eye on three fair medals
Cast in one figure, of so different temper.   100
For her discourse, it is so full of rapture,
You only will begin then to be sorry
When she doth end her speech, and wish, in wonder,
She held it less vain-glory to talk much,
Than your penance to hear her. Whilst she speaks,   105
She throws upon a man so sweet a look
That it were able raise one to a galliard
That lay in a dead palsy, and to dote
On that sweet countenance; but in that look
There speaketh so divine a continence   110

---

87. *information:* evidence from spies. 92. *shrewd:* ill. 107. *galliard:* gay
dance.

As cuts off all lascivious and vain hope.
Her days are practised in such noble virtue,
That sure her nights, nay, more, her very sleeps,
Are more in heaven than other ladies' shrifts.
Let all sweet ladies break their flattering glasses,   115
And dress themselves in her.
    DELIO.   Fie, Antonio,
You play the wire-drawer with her commendations.
    ANT. I'll case the picture up: only thus much;
All her particular worth grows to this sum,—
She stains the time past, lights the time to come.   120
    CARI. You must attend my lady in the gallery,
Some half an hour hence.
    ANT. I shall.   [*Exeunt* ANTONIO *and* DELIO.
    FERD. Sister, I have a suit to you.
    DUCH.   To me, sir?
    FERD. A gentleman here, Daniel de Bosola,   125
One that was in the galleys——
    DUCH.   Yes, I know him.
    FERD. A worthy fellow he's: pray, let me entreat for
The provisorship of your horse.
    DUCH.   Your knowledge of him
Commends him and prefers him.
    FERD.   Call him hither. [*Exit* ATTENDANTS.
We are now upon parting. Good Lord Silvio,   130
Do us commend to all our noble friends
At the leaguer.
    SIL.   Sir, I shall.
    DUCH.   You are for Milan?
    SIL. I am.
    DUCH. Bring the caroches.—We'll bring you down
To the haven.   135

        [*Exeunt* DUCHESS, SILVIO, CASTRUCHIO, RODERIGO,
              GRISOLAN, CARIOLA, JULIA, *and* ATTENDANTS.

    CARD. Be sure you entertain that Bosola
For your intelligence. I would not be seen in 't;
And therefore many times I have slighted him,
When he did court our furtherance, as this morning.

---

114. *shrifts:* confessions. 117. *wire-drawer:* exaggerator. 120. *stains:* deprives
of luster, surpasses. 128. *provisorship:* job of supervising. 132. *leaguer:*
camp. 134. *caroches:* coaches. 136. *entertain:* employ. 137. *intelligence:*
secret service.

FERD. Antonio, the great master of her household,   140
Had been far fitter.
     CARD.   You are deceived in him.
His nature is too honest for such business.—
He comes: I'll leave you.   [*Exit.*

[*Re-enter* BOSOLA.]

BOS.   I was lured to you.
     FERD. My brother here, the cardinal, could never
Abide you.
     BOS.   Never since he was in my debt.   145
     FERD. May be some oblique character in your face
Made him suspect you.
     BOS.   Doth he study physiognomy?
There's no more credit to be given to th' face
Than to a sick man's urine, which some call
The physician's whore, because she cozens him.   150
He did suspect me wrongfully.
     FERD.   For that
You must give great men leave to take their times.
Distrust doth cause us seldom be deceived.
You see, the oft shaking of the cedar-tree
Fastens it more at root.
     BOS.   Yet take heed;   155
For to suspect a friend unworthily
Instructs him the next way to suspect you,
And prompts him to deceive you.
     FERD.   There's gold.
     BOS.   So:
What follows?—(*Aside.*) Never rained such showers as these
Without thunderbolts i' th' tail of them.—Whose throat must I cut?
     FERD. Your inclination to shed blood rides post   161
Before my occasion to use you. I give you that
To live i' th' court here, and observe the duchess;
To note all the particulars of her haviour,
What suitors do solicit her for marriage,
And whom she best affects. She's a young widow: 166
I would not have her marry again.
     BOS.   No, sir?
     FERD. Do not you ask the reason; but be satisfied.
I say I would not.

143. *lured:* a metaphor from hawking; a lure was a bunch of feathers on
a frame waved in the air to recall the hawk from flight.

BOS.　　　　　　It seems you would create me
One of your familiars.

FERD.　　　　　　Familiar! What's that?　　　170

BOS. Why, a very quaint invisible devil in flesh,—
An intelligencer.

FERD.　　　Such a kind of thriving thing
I would wish thee; and ere long thou mayst arrive
At a higher place by 't.

BOS.　　　　　Take your devils,
Which hell calls angels! These cursed gifts would make　175
You a corrupter, me an impudent traitor;
And should I take these, they'd take me to hell.

FERD. Sir, I'll take nothing from you that I have given.
There is a place that I procured for you
This morning, the provisorship o' th' horse.　　　180
Have you heard on 't?

BOS.　　　　　No.

FERD.　　　　　　　'Tis yours: is 't not worth thanks?

BOS. I would have you curse yourself now, that your bounty
(Which makes men truly noble) e'er should make me
A villain. O, that to avoid ingratitude
For the good deed you have done me, I must do　185
All the ill man can invent! Thus the devil
Candies all sins o'er: and what heaven terms vile,
That names he complimental.

FERD.　　　　　　Be yourself;
Keep your old garb of melancholy; 't will express
You envy those that stand above your reach,　　　190
Yet strive not to come near 'em. This will gain
Access to private lodgings, where yourself
May, like a politic dormouse——

BOS.　　　　　　As I have seen some
Feed in a lord's dish, half asleep, not seeming
To listen to any talk; and yet these rogues　　　195
Have cut his throat in a dream. What's my place?
The provisorship o' th' horse? Say, then, my corruption
Grew out of horse-dung: I am your creature.

FERD.　　　　　　　　Away!　　　[Exit.

BOS. Let good men, for good deeds, covet good fame,

---

170. *familiars:* a sinister word, like intelligencers (informers), applied both to evil spirits and to agents of the Inquisition. 171. *quaint:* cunning. 175. *angels:* coins. 188. *complimental:* commendable accomplishment.

Since place and riches oft are bribes of shame.   200
Sometimes the devil doth preach.   [*Exit* BOSOLA.

SCENE III.

[*Enter* FERDINAND, DUCHESS, CARDINAL, *and* CARIOLA.]

CARD. We are to part from you; and your own discretion
Must now be your director.
   FERD.   You are a widow:
You know already what man is; and therefore
Let not youth, high promotion, eloquence——
   CARD. No,   5
Nor anything without the addition, honour,
Sway your high blood.
   FERD.   Marry! They are most luxurious
Will wed twice.
   CARD.   O, fie!
   FERD.   Their livers are more spotted
Than Laban's sheep.
   DUCH.   Diamonds are of most value,
They say, that have passed through most jewellers' hands.   10
   FERD. Whores by that rule are precious.
   DUCH.   Will you hear me?
I'll never marry.
   CARD.   So most widows say;
But commonly that motion lasts no longer
Than the turning of an hour-glass: the funeral sermon
And it end both together.
   FERD.   Now hear me: 15
You live in a rank pasture, here, i' th' court;
There is a kind of honey-dew that's deadly;
'Twill poison your fame; look to 't. Be not cunning;
For they whose faces do belie their hearts
Are witches ere they arrive at twenty years,   20
Ay, and give the devil suck.
   DUCH. This is terrible good counsel.
   FERD. Hypocrisy is woven of a fine small thread,
Subtler than Vulcan's engine: yet, believe 't,

SC. III: 7. *luxurious:* lustful. 9. *Laban's sheep:* Genesis XXX, 31-42—Laban, Jacob's father-in-law, received all the streaked and spotted sheep. 24. *Vulcan's engine:* the invisible net in which he caught his wife (Venus) with Mars.

Your darkest actions, nay, your privat'st thoughts,   25
Will come to light.
    CARD.   You may flatter yourself,
And take your own choice; privately be married
Under the eaves of night——
    FERD.   Think 't the best voyage
That e'er you made; like the irregular crab,
Which, though 't goes backward, thinks that it goes right   30
Because it goes its own way: but observe,
Such weddings may more properly be said
To be executed than celebrated.
    CARD.   The marriage night
Is the entrance into some prison.
    FERD.   And those joys,
Those lustful pleasures, are like heavy sleeps   35
Which do fore-run man's mischief.
    CARD.   Fare you well.
Wisdom begins at the end: remember it.   [*Exit.*
    DUCH. I think this speech between you both was studied,
It came so roundly off.
    FERD.   You are my sister;
This was my father's poniard, do you see?   40
I'd be loath to see 't look rusty, 'cause 't was his.
I would have you to give o'er these chargeable revels:
A vizor and a mask are whispering-rooms
That were never built for goodness. Fare ye well—
And women like that part which, like the lamprey,   45
Hath never a bone in 't.
    DUCH.   Fie, sir!
    FERD.   Nay,
I mean the tongue: variety of courtship.
What cannot a neat knave with a smooth tale
Make a woman believe? Farewell, lusty widow.   [*Exit.*
    DUCH. Shall this move me? If all my royal kindred   50
Lay in my way unto this marriage,
I'd make them my low footsteps. And even now,
Even in this hate, as men in some great battles,
By apprehending danger, have achieved
Almost impossible actions (I have heard soldiers say so),   55
So I through frights and threatenings will assay
This dangerous venture. Let old wives report

---

42. *chargeable:* expensive.

I winked and chose a husband.—Cariola,
To thy known secrecy I have given up
More than my life,—my fame.
CARI.   **Both shall be safe;**   60
For I'll conceal this secret from the world
As warily as those that trade in poison
Keep poison from their children.
DUCH.   Thy protestation
Is ingenious and hearty; I believe it.
Is Antonio come?
CARI.   He attends you.
DUCH.   Good dear soul,   65
Leave me; but place thyself behind the arras,
Where thou may'st overhear us. Wish me good speed;
For I am going into a wilderness,
Where I shall find nor path nor friendly clue
To be my guide.   [CARIOLA *goes behind the arras.*

[*Enter* ANTONIO.]

              I sent for you: sit down;   70
Take pen and ink, and write. Are you ready?
ANT.   Yes.
DUCH. What did I say?
ANT. That I should write somewhat.
DUCH.   O, I remember.
After these triumphs and this large expense
It's fit, like thrifty husbands, we inquire   75
What's laid up for tomorrow.
ANT. So please your beauteous excellence.
DUCH.   Beauteous!
Indeed, I thank you. I look young for your sake;
You have ta'en my cares upon you.
ANT.   I'll fetch your grace
The particulars of your revenue and expense.   80
DUCH. O, you are
An upright treasurer, but you mistook;
For when I said I meant to make inquiry
What's laid up for to-morrow, I did mean
What's laid up yonder for me.
ANT.   Where?
DUCH.   In heaven.   85

---

58. *winked:* closed my eyes. 64. *ingenious.* frank. 74. *triumphs:* festivities.

I am making my will (as 't is fit princes should,
In perfect memory), and, I pray, sir, tell me,
Were not one better make it smiling, thus,
Than in deep groans and terrible ghastly looks,
As if the gifts we parted with procured   90
That violent distraction?
    ANT.   O, much better.
    DUCH. If I had a husband now, this care were quit:
But I intend to make you overseer.
What good deed shall we first remember? Say.
    ANT. Begin with that first good deed began i' th' world.   95
After man's creation, the sacrament of marriage.
I'd have you first provide for a good husband:
Give him all.
    DUCH.   All!
    ANT.   Yes, your excellent self.
    DUCH. In a winding-sheet?
    ANT.   In a couple.
    DUCH. Saint Winfrid, that were a strange will!   100
    ANT. 'Twere stranger if there were no will in you
To marry again.
    DUCH.   What do you think of marriage?
    ANT. I take 't, as those that deny purgatory:
It locally contains or heaven or hell;
There's no third place in 't.
    DUCH.   How do you affect it?   105
    ANT. My banishment, feeding my melancholy,
Would often reason thus:—
    DUCH.   Pray, let's hear it.
    ANT. Say a man never marry, nor have children,
What takes that from him? Only the bare name
Of being a father, or the weak delight   110
To see the little wanton ride a-cock-horse
Upon a painted stick, or hear him chatter
Like a taught starling.
    DUCH.   Fie, fie, what's all this?
One of your eyes is blood-shot; use my ring to 't.
They say 't is very sovereign. 'Twas my wedding-ring,   115
And I did vow never to part with it
But to my second husband.
    ANT. You have parted with it now.
    DUCH. Yes, to help your eye-sight.
    ANT. You have made me stark blind.

DUCH.   How?
ANT. There is a saucy and ambitious devil
Is dancing in this circle.
    DUCH.   Remove him.
    ANT.   How?
    DUCH. There needs small conjuration, when your finger
May do it: thus. Is it fit?
                  [*She puts the ring upon his finger; he kneels.*
    ANT.   What said you?
    DUCH.   Sir,
This goodly roof of yours is too low built;   125
I cannot stand upright in 't nor discourse,
Without I raise it higher. Raise yourself;
Or, if you please my hand to help you: so!   [*Raises him.*
    ANT. Ambition, madam, is a great man's madness,
That is not kept in chains and close-pent rooms,   130
But in fair lightsome lodgings, and is girt
With the wild noise of prattling visitants,
Which makes it lunatic beyond all cure.
Conceive not I am so stupid but I aim
Whereto your favours tend: but he's a fool   135
That, being a-cold, would thrust his hands i' th' fire
To warm them.
    DUCH.   So, now the ground's broke,
You may discover what a wealthy mine
I make you lord of.
    ANT.   O my unworthiness!
    DUCH. You were ill to sell yourself: 140
This darkening of your worth is not like that
Which tradesmen use i' th' city; their false lights
Are to rid bad wares off: and I must tell you,
If you will know where breathes a complete man
(I speak it without flattery), turn your eyes,   145
And progress through yourself.
    ANT. Were there nor heaven nor hell,
I should be honest: I have long served virtue,
And never ta'en wages of her.
    DUCH.   Now she pays it.
The misery of us that are born great!   150
We are forced to woo, because none dare woo us;
And as a tyrant doubles with his words
And fearfully equivocates, so we
Are forced to express our violent passions

In riddles and in dreams, and leave the path   155
Of simple virtue, which was never made
To seem the thing it is not. Go, go brag
You have left me heartless; mine is in your bosom:
I hope 't will multiply love there. You do tremble:
Make not your heart so dead a piece of flesh,   160
To fear more than to love me. Sir, be confident:
What is 't distracts you? This is flesh and blood, sir;
'Tis not the figure cut in alabaster
Kneels at my husband's tomb. Awake, awake, man!
I do here put off all vain ceremony,   165
And only do appear to you a young widow
That claims you for her husband, and, like a widow,
I use but half a blush in 't.
    ANT.   Truth speak for me:
I will remain the constant sanctuary
Of your good name.
    DUCH.   I thank you, gentle love: 170
And 'cause you shall not come to me in debt,
(Being now my steward) here upon your lips
I sign your *Quietus est.* This you should have begged now.
I have seen children oft eat sweetmeats thus,
As fearful to devour them too soon.   175
    ANT. But for your brothers?
    DUCH.   Do not think of them:
All discord without this circumference
Is only to be pitied, and not feared:
Yet, should they know it, time will easily
Scatter the tempest.
    ANT.   These words should be mine,   180
And all the parts you have spoke, if some part of it
Would not have savoured flattery.
    DUCH.   Kneel.
                [CARIOLA *comes from behind the arras.*
    ANT.   Ha!
    DUCH. Be not amazed: this woman's of my counsel.
I have heard lawyers say, a contract in a chamber
Per verba [de] presenti is absolute marriage.   185
                [*She and* ANTONIO *kneel.*

---

173. *Quietus est:* acquittance of debt. 185. *Per . . . presenti:* In the present tense; according to canon law a marriage contract was valid if it was an immediate agreement rather than a future plan.

Bless, heaven, this sacred Gordian, which let violence
Never untwine.

ANT. And may our sweet affections, like the spheres,
Be still in motion!

DUCH.   Quickening, and make
The like soft music!   190

ANT. That we may imitate the loving palms,
Best emblem of a peaceful marriage,
That never bore fruit, divided!

DUCH. What can the church force more?

ANT. That fortune may not know an accident,   195
Either of joy or sorrow, to divide
Our fixèd wishes!

DUCH.   How can the church build faster?
We now are man and wife, and 'tis the church
That must but echo this.—Maid, stand apart:
I now am blind.

ANT.   What's your conceit in this?   200
DUCH. I would have you lead your fortune by the hand
Unto your marriage-bed:
(You speak in me this, for we now are one).
We'll only lie and talk together, and plot
T' appease my humorous kindred; and if you please,   205
Like the old tale in *Alexander and Lodowick,*
Lay a naked sword between us, keep us chaste.
O, let me shroud my blushes in your bosom,
Since 'tis the treasury of all my secrets!
                              [*Exeunt* DUCHESS *and* ANTONIO.

CARI. Whether the spirit of greatness or of woman   210
Reign most in her, I know not; but it shows
A fearful madness. I owe her much of pity.   [*Exit.*

Act II

SCENE I. *The Palace, Amalfi.*

[*Enter* BOSOLA *and* CASTRUCHIO.]

BOS. You say you would fain be taken for an eminent courtier?
CAST. 'Tis the very main of my ambition.

---

186. *Gordian:* knot. 205. *humorous:* unreasonable. 206. *Alexander and Lodowick:* a ballad version of a story, appearing in many forms, in which two friends impersonate each other, so that one has to place a sword between himself and the other's wife.
ACT II, SC. I: 2. *main:* target.

BOS. Let me see: you have a reasonable good face for 't already, and
your night-cap expresses your ears sufficient largely. I would have you
learn to twirl the strings of your band with a good grace, and   [5
in a set speech, at th' end of every sentence, to hum three or four
times, or blow your nose till it smart again, to recover your memory.
When you come to be a president in criminal causes, if you smile upon
a prisoner, hang him; but if you frown upon him and threaten him,
let him be sure to scape the gallows.   10

CAST. I would be a very merry president.

BOS. Do not sup o' nights; 'twill beget you an admirable wit.

CAST. Rather it would make me have a good stomach to quarrel;
for they say, your roaring boys eat meat seldom, and that makes them
so valiant. But how shall I know whether the people take me   [15
for an eminent fellow?

BOS. I will teach a trick to know it: give out you lie a-dying, and if
you hear the common people curse you, be sure you are taken for one
of the prime night-caps.

[Enter an OLD LADY.*]*

You come from painting now.   20

OLD LADY. From what?

BOS. Why, from your scurvy face-physic. To behold thee not
painted inclines somewhat near a miracle. These in thy face here were
deep ruts and foul sloughs the last progress. There was a lady in
France that, having had the small-pox, flayed the skin off her   [25
face to make it more level; and whereas before she looked like a nut-
meg-grater, after she resembled an abortive hedgehog.

OLD LADY. Do you call this painting?

BOS. No, no, but I call it careening of an old morphewed lady, to
make her disembogue again: there's rough-cast phrase to your plastic.

OLD LADY. It seems you are well acquainted with my closet.   [31

BOS. One would suspect it for a shop of witchcraft, to find in it the
fat of serpents, spawn of snakes, Jews' spittle, and their young children's ordure: and all these for the face. I would sooner eat a dead
pigeon taken from the soles of the feet of one sick of the   [35

---

4. *night-cap . . . ears:* lawyer's coif, a white silk skull cap, shows your
ass-like ears. 5. *band:* a collar with a pair of strips or bands hanging
down in front was a conventional part of a lawyer's dress. 14. *roaring
boys:* bullies. 24. *sloughs:* bogs and dead flesh. 29. *careening:* turning
a ship on its side for scraping; *morphewed:* scaly-skinned. 30. *disembogue:*
put out to sea; *rough-cast:* coarse plaster; *plastic:* beautifying. 35. *pigeon:*
fowls were applied to the feet of the patient to draw poisons from his
head.

plague, than kiss one of you fasting. Here are two of you, whose sin
of your youth is the very patrimony of the physician; makes him re-
new his foot-cloth with the spring, and change his high-priced courte-
san with the fall of the leaf. I do wonder you do not loathe yourselves.
Observe my meditation now: 40
What thing is in this outward form of man
To be beloved? We account it ominous,
If nature do produce a colt, or lamb,
A fawn, or goat, in any limb resembling
A man, and fly from 't as a prodigy.   45
Man stands amazed to see his deformity
In any other creature but himself.
But in our own flesh though we bear diseases
Which have their true names only ta'en from beasts,—
As the most ulcerous wolf and swinish measle,—   50
Though we are eaten up of lice and worms,
And though continually we bear about us
A rotten and dead body, we delight
To hide it in rich tissue: all our fear,
Nay, all our terror, is, lest our physician   55
Should put us in the ground to be made sweet.—
Your wife's gone to Rome: you two couple, and get you to the wells
at Lucca to recover your aches. I have other work on foot.

                      [Exeunt CASTRUCHIO *and* OLD LADY.

I observe our duchess
Is sick a-days, she pukes, her stomach seethes,   60
The fins of her eye-lids look most teeming blue,
She wanes i' th' cheek, and waxes fat i' th' flank,
And, contrary to our Italian fashion,
Wears a loose-bodied gown: there's somewhat in 't.
I have a trick may chance discover it,   65
A pretty one: I have bought some apricocks,
The first our spring yields.

        [Enter ANTONIO *and* DELIO, *talking together apart.]*

DELIO.   And so long since married?
You amaze me.

---

36. *fasting:* when you are fasting and your breath is therefore strongest.
38. *foot-cloth:* trappings of his horse or mule—a sign of the successful physician. 50. *wolf:* a lupus or tubercular sore; *swinish measle:* the older meaning of "measle" was leprosy, which was popularly thought to be like a skin
disease of swine, actually caused by tape-worm. 61. *fins . . . blue:* rims
. . . blue like those of a teeming (pregnant) woman.

ANT.　　　　Let me seal your lips for ever:
For, did I think that anything but th' air
Could carry these words from you, I should wish　　　70
You had no breath at all.—Now, sir, in your contemplation?
You are studying to become a great wise fellow.

BOS. O, sir, the opinion of wisdom is a foul tetter that runs all over
a man's body: if simplicity direct us to have no evil, it directs us to
a happy being; for the subtlest folly proceeds from the subtlest　　[75
wisdom. Let me be simply honest.

ANT. I do understand your inside.

BOS.　　　　　　　　　　　　Do you so?

ANT. Because you would not seem to appear to th' world
Puffed up with your preferment, you continue
This out-of-fashion melancholy: leave it, leave it.　　　80

BOS. Give me leave to be honest in any phrase, in any compliment
whatsoever. Shall I confess myself to you? I look no higher than
I can reach: they are the gods that must ride on winged horses. A
lawyer's mule of a slow pace will both suit my disposition and business; for, mark me, when a man's mind rides faster than his　　[85
horse can gallop, they quickly both tire.

ANT. You would look up to heaven, but I think
The devil, that rules i' th' air, stands in your light.

BOS. O, sir, you are lord of the ascendant, chief man with the duchess: a duke was your cousin-german removed. Say you were　　[90
lineally descended from King Pepin, or he himself, what of this?
Search the heads of the greatest rivers in the world, you shall find
them but bubbles of water. Some would think the souls of princes
were brought forth by some more weighty cause than those of meaner
persons: they are deceived, there's the same hand to them; the　　[95
like passions sway them; the same reason that makes a vicar go to law
for a tithe-pig, and undo his neighbours, makes them spoil a whole
province, and batter down goodly cities with the cannon.

[*Enter* DUCHESS *and* LADIES.]

DUCH. Your arm, Antonio: do I not grow fat?
I am exceeding short-winded.—Bosola,　　　100
I would have you, sir, provide for me a litter;
Such a one as the Duchess of Florence rode in.

---

73. *tetter:* eczema. 89. *ascendant:* in astrology the heavens are divided
into twelve houses or sections; the ascendant or first is the house of life
or childbirth. 91. *King Pepin:* ruler of the Franks, 751-768; this passage
is based on Montaigne.

BOS. The duchess used one when she was great with child.

DUCH. I think she did.—Come hither, mend my ruff:
Here, when? thou art such a tedious lady; and   105
Thy breath smells of lemon-peels: would thou hadst done!
Shall I sound under thy fingers? I am
So troubled with the mother!

    BOS. (*aside*).   I fear, too much.

DUCH. I have heard you say that the French courtiers
Wear their hats on 'fore the king.   110

    ANT. I have seen it.

    DUCH.   In the presence?

    ANT.   Yes.

DUCH. Why should not we bring up that fashion?
'Tis ceremony more than duty that consists
In the removing of a piece of felt.
Be you the example to the rest o' th' court;   115
Put on your hat first.

    ANT.   You must pardon me:
I have seen, in colder countries than in France,
Nobles stand bare to th' prince; and the distinction
Methought showed reverently.

    BOS. I have a present for your grace.

    DUCH.   For me, sir?   120

    BOS. Apricocks, madam.

    DUCH.   O, sir, where are they?
I have heard of none to-year.

    BOS. (*aside*).   Good; her colour rises.

DUCH. Indeed, I thank you: they are wondrous fair ones.
What an unskilful fellow is our gardener!
We shall have none this month.   125

    BOS. Will not your grace pare them?

    DUCH. No: they taste of musk, methinks; indeed they do.

    BOS. I know not: yet I wish your grace had pared 'em.

    DUCH. Why?

    BOS. I forgot to tell you, the knave gardener,   130
(Only to raise his profit by them the sooner)
Did ripen them in horse-dung.

    DUCH.   O, you jest.—
You shall judge: pray, taste one.

    ANT.   Indeed, madam,
I do not love the fruit.

---

104. *mend:* arrange. 107. *sound:* swoon. 108. *mother:* nervousness and feeling of suffocation in the throat (with a pun). 127. *musk:* highly thought of in fruit.

DUCH.   Sir, you are loath
To rob us of our dainties. 'Tis a delicate fruit;   135
They say they are restorative.
BOS.   'Tis a pretty art,
This grafting.
DUCH.   'Tis so; a bettering of nature.
BOS. To make a pippin grow upon a crab,
A damson on a black-thorn.—(*Aside*.) How greedily she eats them!
A whirlwind strike off these bawd-farthingales!   140
For, but for that and the loose-bodied gown,
I should have discovered apparently
The young springal cutting a caper in her belly.
DUCH. I thank you, Bosola: they were right good ones,
If they do not make me sick.
ANT.   How now, madam!   145
DUCH. This green fruit and my stomach are not friends:
How they swell me!
BOS. (*aside*). Nay, you are too much swelled already.
DUCH. O, I am in an extreme cold sweat!
BOS.   I am very sorry.   [*Exit.*
DUCH. Lights to my chamber!—O good Antonio,   150
I fear I am undone!
DELIO.   Lights there, lights!   [*Exit* DUCHESS *with* LADIES.
ANT. O my most trusty Delio, we are lost!
I fear she's fallen in labour; and there's left
No time for her remove.
DELIO.   Have you prepared
Those ladies to attend her; and procured   155
That politic safe conveyance for the midwife
Your duchess plotted?
ANT.   I have.
DELIO. Make use, then, of this forced occasion.
Give out that Bosola hath poisoned her
With these apricocks; that will give some colour   160
For her keeping close.
ANT.   Fie, fie, the physicians
Will then flock to her.
DELIO. For that you may pretend
She'll use some prepared antidote of her own,
Lest the physicians should re-poison her.   165
ANT. I am lost in amazement: I know not what to think on 't.
                                        [*Exeunt.*

---

142. *apparently:* clearly. 143. *springal:* stripling.

SCENE II. *A gallery in the same.*

[BOSOLA *(and a little later)* OLD LADY.]

BOS. So, so, there's no question but her techiness and most vulturous
eating of the apricocks are apparent signs of breeding.—Now?

OLD LADY. I am in haste, sir.

BOS. There was a young waiting-woman had a monstrous desire
to see the glass-house——   5

OLD LADY. Nay, pray, let me go.

BOS. And it was only to know what strange instrument it was
should swell up a glass to the fashion of a woman's belly.

OLD LADY. I will hear no more of the glass-house. You are still abus-
ing women!   10

BOS. Who? I? No; only (by the way now and then) mention your
frailties. The orange-tree bears ripe and green fruit and blossoms all
together; and some of you give entertainment for pure love, but more
for more precious reward. The lusty spring smells well; but drooping
autumn tastes well. If we have the same golden showers that   [15
rained in the time of Jupiter the thunderer, you have the same Danaës
still, to hold up their laps to receive them. Didst thou never study the
mathematics?

OLD LADY. What's that, sir?

BOS. Why, to know the trick how to make a many lines   [20
meet in one centre. Go, go, give your foster-daughters good counsel:
tell them, that the devil takes delight to hang at a woman's girdle,
like a false rusty watch, that she cannot discern how the time passes.
                                                                [*Exit* OLD LADY.

[*Enter* ANTONIO, RODERIGO, *and* GRISOLAN.]

ANT. Shut up the court-gates.

ROD.   Why, sir? What's the danger?

ANT. Shut up the posterns presently, and call   25
All the officers o' th' court.

GRIS.   I shall instantly.   [*Exit.*

ANT. Who keeps the key o' th' park-gate?

ROD.   Forobosco.

ANT. Let him bring 't presently.

SC. II: 2. *breeding:* pregnancy. 5. *glass-house:* a glass factory near the
Blackfriars Theater, where this play was presented, was one of the sights
of London. 15. *golden showers:* Jupiter in the form of a golden shower
made love to Danae; she thus became the symbol of mercenary love.

[Re-enter GRISOLAN *with* SERVANTS.]

I SERV. O, gentlemen o' th' court, the foulest treason!

BOS. (*aside*). If that these apricocks should be poisoned now,   30
Without my knowledge!

   I SERV. There was taken even now a Switzer in the duchess' bed-
     chamber——

   2 SERV. A Switzer!

   I SERV. With a pistol in his great codpiece.

BOS. Ha, ha, ha!   35

   I SERV. The codpiece was the case for 't.

   2 SERV. There was a cunning traitor. Who would have searched his
codpiece?

   I SERV. True; if he had kept out of the ladies' chambers. And all
the moulds of his buttons were leaden bullets.   40

   2 SERV. O wicked cannibal! A fire-lock in 's codpiece!

   I SERV. 'Twas a French plot, upon my life.

   2 SERV. To see what the devil can do!

ANT. All the officers here?

SERVANTS. We are.   45

ANT. Gentlemen,
We have lost much plate, you know; and but this evening
Jewels, to the value of four thousand ducats,
Are missing in the duchess' cabinet.
Are the gates shut?

SERV.   Yes.

ANT.   'Tis the duchess' pleasure   50
Each officer be locked into his chamber
Till the sun-rising; and to send the keys
Of all their chests and of their outward doors
Into her bed-chamber. She is very sick.

ROD. At her pleasure.   55

ANT. She entreats you take 't not ill: the innocent
Shall be the more approved by it.

   BOS. Gentleman o' th' wood-yard, where's your Switzer now?

   I SERV. By this hand, 'twas credibly reported by one o' th' black
guard.   *[Exeunt all except* ANTONIO *and* DELIO.

DELIO. How fares it with the duchess?

ANT.   She's exposed   61
Unto the worst of torture, pain and fear.

   DELIO. Speak to her all happy comfort.

---

34. *codpiece:* a cloth pouch enclosing the male genitals. 59-60. *black guard:*
kitchen servants.

ANT. How I do play the fool with mine own danger!
You are this night, dear friend, to post to Rome: 65
My life lies in your service.
    DELIO.   Do not doubt me.
    ANT. O, 'tis far from me: and yet fear presents me
Somewhat that looks like danger.
    DELIO.   Believe it,
'Tis but the shadow of your fear, no more.
How superstitiously we mind our evils!   70
The throwing down salt, or crossing of a hare,
Bleeding at nose, the stumbling of a horse,
Or singing of a cricket, are of power
To daunt whole man in us. Sir, fare you well:
I wish you all the joys of a blessed father;   75
And (for my faith) lay this unto your breast:
Old friends, like old swords, still are trusted best.   [*Exit.*

[Enter CARIOLA.]

CARI. Sir, you are the happy father of a son:
Your wife commends him to you.
    ANT.   Blessed comfort!—
For heaven' sake, tend her well: I'll presently   80
Go set a figure for 's nativity.   [*Exeunt.*

SCENE III. *The same.*

[BOSOLA (*with a dark lantern*).]

BOS. Sure I did hear a woman shriek: list, ha!
And the sound came, if I received it right,
From the duchess' lodgings. There's some stratagem
In the confining all our courtiers
To their several wards: I must have part of it;   5
My intelligence will freeze else. List, again!
It may be 't was the melancholy bird,
Best friend of silence and of solitariness,
The owl, that screamed so.—Ha! Antonio!

[Enter ANTONIO *with a candle, his sword drawn.*]

ANT. I heard some noise.—Who's there? What are thou? Speak.
BOS. Antonio? put not your face nor body   11
To such a forced expression of fear:

---

81. *set a figure:* cast a horoscope.
    SC. III: 5. *have part:* get to the bottom.

I am Bosola, your friend.
 ANT.   Bosola?—
(*Aside.*) This mole does undermine me.—Heard you not
A noise even now?
 BOS.   From whence?
 ANT.   From the duchess' lodging. 15
 BOS. Not I: did you?
 ANT.   I did, or else I dreamed.
 BOS. Let's walk towards it.
 ANT.   No: it may be 'twas
But the rising of the wind.
 BOS.   Very likely.
Methinks 'tis very cold, and yet you sweat:
You look wildly.
 ANT.   I have been setting a figure 20
For the duchess' jewels.
 BOS.   Ah, and how falls your question?
Do you find it radical?
 ANT.   What's that to you?
'Tis rather to be questioned what design,
When all men were commanded to their lodgings,
Makes you a night-walker.
 BOS.   In sooth, I'll tell you: 25
Now all the court's asleep, I thought the devil
Had least to do here. I came to say my prayers;
And if it do offend you I do so,
You are a fine courtier.
 ANT. (*aside*). This fellow will undo me!— 30
You gave the duchess apricocks to-day:
Pray heaven they were not poisoned!
 BOS. Poisoned! a Spanish fig
For the imputation!
 ANT.   Traitors are ever confident
Till they are discovered. There were jewels stol'n too: 35
In my conceit, none are to be suspected
More than yourself.
 BOS.   You are a false steward.
 ANT. Saucy slave, I'll pull thee up by the roots.
 BOS. May be the ruin will crush you to pieces.
 ANT. You are an impudent snake indeed, sir: 40
Are you scarce warm, and do you show your sting?

---

22. *radical:* fit for astrological solution.

You libel well, sir?

BOS.   No, sir: copy it out,
And I will set my hand to 't.

ANT. (*aside*).   My nose bleeds.
One that were superstitious would count
This ominous, when it merely comes by chance.   45
Two letters, that are wrought here for my name,
Are drowned in blood!
Mere accident.—For you, sir, I'll take order.
I' th' morn you shall be safe.—(*Aside*.) 'Tis that must colour
Her lying-in.—Sir, this door you pass not: 50
I do not hold it fit that you come near
The duchess' lodgings, till you have quit yourself.—
(*Aside*.) The great are like the base; nay, they are the same,
When they seek shameful ways to avoid shame.   [*Exit.*

BOS. Antonio hereabout did drop a paper:—   55
Some of your help, false friend.—O, here it is.
What's here? a child's nativity calculated!   [*Reads.*
'*The duchess was delivered of a son, 'tween the hours twelve and
one in the night, Anno Dom.* 1504.'—that's this year—'*decimo nono
Decembris,*'—that's this night—'*taken according to the me-*   [60
ridian of Malfi,'—that's our duchess: happy discovery!—'*The lord
of the first house being combust in the ascendant signifies short life;
and Mars being in a human sign, joined to the tail of the Dragon,
in the eight house, doth threaten a violent death. Cætera non
scrutantur.*'   65
Why now 'tis most apparent; this precise fellow
Is the duchess' bawd:—I have it to my wish!
This is a parcel of intelligency
Our courtiers were cased up for. It needs must follow
That I must be committed on pretence   70
Of poisoning her; which I'll endure, and laugh at.
If one could find the father now! but that
Time will discover. Old Castruchio
I' th' morning posts to Rome: by him I'll send
A letter that shall make her brothers' galls   75
O'erflow their livers. This was a thrifty way!
Though Lust do mask in ne'er so strange disguise,
She's oft found witty, but is never wise.   [*Exit.*

---

42. *libel:* bring formal charges in writing. 56. *false friend:* the dark-lantern.
65-6. *Caetera non scrutantur:* the other signs are not examined. 66. *precise:*
puritanical.

SCENE IV. *Rome: the* CARDINAL'S *palace.*

[CARDINAL *and* JULIA.]

CARD. Sit: thou art my best of wishes. Prithee, tell me
What trick didst thou invent to come to Rome
Without thy husband?
JULIA.   Why, my lord, I told him
I came to visit an old anchorite
Here for devotion.
    CARD.   Thou art a witty false one,—   5
I mean, to him.
    JULIA.   You have prevailed with me
Beyond my strongest thoughts; I would not now
Find you inconstant.
    CARD.   Do not put thyself
To such a voluntary torture, which proceeds
Out of your own guilt.
    JULIA.   How, my lord!
    CARD.   You fear   10
My constancy, because you have approved
Those giddy and wild turnings in yourself.
    JULIA. Did you e'er find them?
    CARD.   Sooth, generally for women,
A man might strive to make glass malleable,
Ere he should make them fixèd.
    JULIA.   So, my lord.   15
    CARD. We had need go borrow that fantastic glass
Invented by Galileo, the Florentine,
To view another spacious world i' th' moon,
And look to find a constant woman there.
    JULIA. This is very well, my lord.
    CARD.   Why do you weep?   20
Are tears your justification? The self-same tears
Will fall into your husband's bosom, lady,
With a loud protestation that you love him
Above the world. Come, I'll love you wisely,
That's jealously; since I am very certain   25
You cannot make me cuckold.

---

sc. IV: 11. *approved:* experienced. 16. *fantastic glass:* Galileo's telescope,
actually invented in 1609.

JULIA.   I'll go home
To my husband.
    CARD.   You may thank me, lady.
I have taken you off your melancholy perch,
Bore you upon my fist, and showed you game,
And let you fly at it.—I pray thee, kiss me.—   30
When thou wast with thy husband, thou wast watched
Like a tame elephant:—still you are to thank me:—
Thou hadst only kisses from him and high feeding;
But what delight was that? 'T was just like one
That hath a little fingering on the lute,   35
Yet cannot tune it:—still you are to thank me.
    JULIA. You told me of a piteous wound i' th' heart,
And a sick liver, when you wooed me first,
And spake like one in physic.
    CARD.   Who's that?—

[Enter SERVANT.*]*

Rest firm! for my affection to thee,   40
Lightning moves slow to 't.
    SERV.   Madam, a gentleman
That's comes post from Malfi, desires to see you.
    CARD. Let him enter: I'll withdraw.   *[Exit.*
    SERV.   He says
Your husband, old Castruchio, is come to Rome,   44
Most pitifully tired with riding post.   *[Exit.*

[Enter DELIO.*]*

JULIA. (*aside*). Signior Delio! 't is one of my old suitors.
DELIO. I was bold to come and see you.
    JULIA.   Sir, you are welcome.
DELIO. Do you lie here?
    JULIA.   Sure, your own experience
Will satisfy you no: our Roman prelates
Do not keep lodging for ladies.
    DELIO.   Very well: 50
I have brought you no commendations from your husband,
For I know none by him.
    JULIA.   I hear he's come to Rome.
DELIO. I never knew man and beast, of a horse and a knight,

31-2. *watched . . . elephant:* hawks and elephants were tamed by being
kept awake all night. 36. *tune:* play. 39. *in physic:* under physician's care.

So weary of each other. If he had had a good back,
He would have undertook to have borne his horse,   55
His breech was so pitifully sore.
   JULIA.   Your laughter
Is my pity.
   DELIO. Lady, I know not whether
You want money, but I have brought you some.
   JULIA. From my husband?
   DELIO.   No, from mine own allowance.   60
   JULIA. I must hear the condition, ere I be bound to take it.
   DELIO. Look on 't, 't is gold; hath it not a fine colour?
   JULIA. I have a bird more beautiful.
   DELIO.   Try the sound on 't.
   JULIA. A lute-string far exceeds it.
It hath no smell, like cassia or civet;   65
Nor is it physical, though some fond doctors
Persuade us seethe 't in cullises. I'll tell you,
This is a creature bred by——

                 [*Re-enter* SERVANT.]

   SERV.   Your husband's come,
Hath delivered a letter to the Duke of Calabria   69
That, to my thinking, hath put him out of his wits.   [*Exit.*
   JULIA. Sir, you hear:
Pray, let me know your business and your suit
As briefly as can be.
   DELIO. With good speed: I would wish you
(At such time as you are non-resident   75
With your husband) my mistress.
   JULIA. Sir, I'll go ask my husband if I shall,
And straight return your answer.   [*Exit.*
   DELIO.   Very fine!
Is this her wit, or honesty, that speaks thus?
I heard one say the duke was highly moved   80
With a letter sent from Malfi. I do fear
Antonio is betrayed. How fearfully
Shows his ambition now! Unfortunate fortune!
They pass through whirl-pools, and deep woes do shun,
Who the event weigh ere the action's done.   85
                     [*Exit.*

---

65. *cassia:* cinnamon; *civet:* perfume. 66. *physical:* medicinal; *fond:* foolish
67. *cullises:* broths.

SCENE V. *The same.*

[CARDINAL *and* FERDINAND *with a letter.*]

FERD. I have this night digged up a mandrake.
    CARD.   Say you?
FERD. And I am grown mad with 't.
    CARD.   What's the prodigy?
    FERD. Read there,—a sister damned: she's loose i' th' hilts;
Grown a notorious strumpet.
    CARD.   Speak lower.
    FERD.   Lower!
Rogues do not whisper 't now, but seek to publish 't   5
(As servants do the bounty of their lords)
Aloud; and with a covetous searching eye,
To mark who note them. O, confusion seize her!
She hath had most cunning bawds to serve her turn,
And more secure conveyances for lust   10
Than towns of garrison for service.
    CARD.   Is 't possible?
Can this be certain?
    FERD.   Rhubarb! O, for rhubarb
To purge this choler! Here's the cursèd day
To prompt my memory; and here 't shall stick
Till of her bleeding heart I make a sponge   15
To wipe it out.
    CARD.   Why do you make yourself
So wild a tempest?
    FERD.   Would I could be one,
That I might toss her palace 'bout her ears,
Root up her goodly forests, blast her meads,
And lay her general territory as waste   20
As she hath done her honours.
    CARD.   Shall our blood,
The royal blood of Aragon and Castile,
Be thus attainted?
    FERD.   Apply desperate physic:
We must not now use balsamum, but fire,
The smarting cupping-glass, for that's the mean   25

SC. V: I. *mandrake:* poisonous root, with forked human shape. 24. *balsamum:* salve. 25. *cupping-glass:* for drawing blood.

To purge infected blood, such blood as hers.
There is a kind of pity in mine eye,—
I'll give it to my handkerchief; and now 'tis here.
I'll bequeath this to her bastard.
    CARD.   What to do?
    FERD. Why, to make soft lint for his mother's wounds,   30
When I have hewed her to pieces.
    CARD.   Cursed creature!
Unequal nature, to place women's hearts
So far upon the left side!
    FERD.   Foolish men,
That e'er will trust their honour in a bark
Made of so slight weak bulrush as is woman,   35
Apt every minute to sink it!
    CARD. Thus ignorance, when it hath purchased honour,
It cannot wield it.
    FERD.   Methinks I see her laughing,—
Excellent hyena! Talk to me somewhat, quickly,
Or my imagination will carry me   40
To see her in the shameful act of sin.
    CARD. With whom?
    FERD.   Happily with some strong-thighed bargeman
Or one o' th' wood-yard that can quoit the sledge
Or toss the bar, or else some lovely squire
That carries coals up to her privy lodgings.   45
    CARD. You fly beyond your reason.
    FERD.   Go to, mistress!
'Tis not your whore's milk that shall quench my wild-fire,
But your whore's blood.
    CARD. How idly shows this rage, which carries you,
As men conveyed by witches through the air,   50
On violent whirlwinds! This intemperate noise
Fitly resembles deaf men's shrill discourse,
Who talk aloud, thinking all other men
To have their imperfection.
    FERD.   Have not you
My palsy?
    CARD. Yes, yet I can be angry   55
Without this rupture. There is not in nature
A thing that makes man so deformed, so beastly,
As doth intemperate anger. Chide yourself.

---

32. *Unequal:* unjust. 33. *left:* "sinister." 43. *quoit the sledge:* throw the
hammer.

You have divers men who never yet expressed
Their strong desire of rest but by unrest,　　　　　　　60
By vexing of themselves. Come, put yourself
In tune.
　　FERD. So I will only study to seem
The thing I am not. I could kill her now,
In you, or in myself; for I do think
It is some sin in us heaven doth revenge　　　　　　65
By her.
　　CARD. Are you stark mad?
　　FERD.　　　　　　　　　I would have their bodies
Burnt in a coal-pit with the ventage stopped,
That their cursed smoke might not ascend to heaven;
Or dip the sheets they lie in in pitch or sulphur,　　　70
Wrap them in 't, and then light them like a match;
Or else to boil their bastard to a cullis,
And give 't his lecherous father to renew
The sin of his back.
　　CARD.　　　　　I'll leave you.
　　FERD.　　　　　　　　　Nay, I have done.
I am confident, had I been damned in hell,　　　　　75
And should have heard of this, it would have put me
Into a cold sweat. In, in; I'll go sleep.
Till I know who leaps my sister, I'll not stir:
That known, I'll find scorpions to string my whips,　79
And fix her in a general eclipse.　　　　　　　　[*Exeunt.*

Act III

SCENE I. *Amalfi: the* DUCHESS's *palace.*

[ANTONIO *and* DELIO.]

　　ANT. Our noble friend, my most belovèd Delio!
O, you have been a stranger long at court.
Came you along with the Lord Ferdinand?
　　DELIO. I did, sir: and how fares your noble duchess?
　　ANT. Right fortunately well: she's an excellent　　　5
Feeder of pedigrees; since you last saw her,
She hath had two children more, a son and daughter.
　　DELIO. Methinks 't was yesterday. Let me but wink,
And not behold your face, which to mine eye
Is somewhat leaner, verily I should dream　　　　　10

It were within this half hour.

ANT. You have not been in law, friend Delio,
Nor in prison, nor a suitor at the court,
Nor begged the reversion of some great man's place,
Nor troubled with an old wife, which doth make   15
Your time so insensibly hasten.

DELIO.   Pray, sir, tell me,
Hath not this news arrived yet to the ear
Of the lord cardinal?

ANT.   I fear it hath:
The Lord Ferdinand, that's newly come to court,
Doth bear himself right dangerously.

DELIO.   Pray, why?   20

ANT. He is so quiet that he seems to sleep
The tempest out, as dormice do in winter.
Those houses that are haunted are most still,
Till the devil be up.

DELIO.   What say the common people?

ANT. The common rabble do directly say   25
She is a strumpet.

DELIO.   And your graver heads
Which would be politic, what censure they?

ANT. They do observe I grow to infinite purchase,
The left-hand way; and all suppose the duchess
Would amend it, if she could; for, say they,   30
Great princes, though they grudge their officers
Should have such large and unconfinèd means
To get wealth under them, will not complain,
Lest thereby they should make them odious
Unto the people. For other obligation,   35
Of love or marriage between her and me,
They never dream of.

DELIO.   The Lord Ferdinand
Is going to bed.

[*Enter* DUCHESS, FERDINAND, *and* ATTENDANTS.]

FERD.   I'll instantly to bed,
For I am weary.—I am to bespeak
A husband for you.

DUCH.   For me, sir! Pray, who is 't?   40

FERD. The great Count Malateste.

ACT III, SC. I: 28. *purchase:* fortune.

DUCH.   Fie upon him!
A count! He's a mere stick of sugar-candy;
You may look quite thorough him. When I choose
A husband, I will marry for your honour.
   FERD. You shall do well in 't.—How is 't, worthy Antonio?   45
   DUCH. But, sir, I am to have private conference with you
About a scandalous report is spread
Touching mine honour.
   FERD.   Let me be ever deaf to 't:
One of Pasquil's paper-bullets, court-calumny,
A pestilent air, which princes' palaces   50
Are seldom purged of. Yet, say that it were true,
I pour it in your bosom, my fixed love
Would strongly excuse, extenuate, nay, deny
Faults, were they apparent in you. Go, be safe
In your own innocency.
   DUCH. (*aside*).   O blessed comfort!   55
This deadly air is purged.
              [*Exeunt* DUCHESS, ANTONIO, DELIO, *and* ATTENDANTS.
   FERD.   Her guilt treads on
Hot-burning coulters.

              [*Enter* BOSOLA.]

        Now, Bosola,
How thrives our intelligence?
   BOS.   Sir, uncertainly:
'Tis rumoured she hath had three bastards, but
By whom we may go read i' th' stars.
   FERD.   Why, some   60
Hold opinion all things are written there.
   BOS. Yes, if we could find spectacles to read them.
I do suspect there hath been some sorcery
Used on the duchess.
   FERD.   Sorcery! to what purpose?
   BOS. To make her dote on some desertless fellow   65
She shames to acknowledge.
   FERD.   Can your faith give way
To think there's power in potions or in charms,
To make us love whether we will or no?

---

49. *Pasquil's paper-bullets:* The name of Pasquillo, a sharp-tongued Roman
of the fourteenth century, was given to a mutilated statue excavated in
Rome in 1501 on which were hung lampoons and satiric verses. 57. *coulters:*
iron blade in front of the plow-share.

bos. Most certainly.

ferd. Away! these are mere gulleries, horrid things,   70
Invented by some cheating mountebanks
To abuse us. Do you think that herbs or charms
Can force the will? Some trials have been made
In this foolish practice, but the ingredients
Were lenitive poisons, such as are of force   75
To make the patient mad; and straight the witch
Swears by equivocation they are in love.
The witchcraft lies in her rank blood. This night
I will force confession from her. You told me
You had got, within these two days, a false key   80
Into her bed-chamber.

bos.   I have.

ferd.   As I would wish.

bos. What do you intend to do?

ferd.   Can you guess?

bos.   No.

ferd.   Do not ask, then:
He that can compass me, and know my drifts,
May say he hath put a girdle 'bout the world,
And sounded all her quick-sands.

bos.   I do not   85
Think so.

ferd.   What do you think, then, pray?

bos.   That you
Are your own chronicle too much, and grossly
Flatter yourself.

ferd.   Give me thy hand; I thank thee:
I never gave pension but to flatterers,
Till I entertainèd thee. Farewell.   90
That friend a great man's ruin strongly checks,
Who rails into his belief all his defects.   [*Exeunt.*

SCENE II. *The* duchess's *bed-chamber.*

[DUCHESS, ANTONIO, CARIOLA.]

duch. Bring me the casket hither, and the glass.—
You get no lodging here tonight, my lord.

ant. Indeed, I must persuade one.

duch.   Very good:

---

75 *lenitive:* softening, hypnotic.

I hope in time 't will grow into a custom,
That noblemen shall come with cap and knee   5
To purchase a night's lodging of their wives.
   ANT. I must lie here.
   DUCH.   Must! You are a lord of mis-rule.
   ANT. Indeed, my rule is only in the night.
   DUCH. To what use will you put me?
   ANT.   We'll sleep together.
   DUCH. Alas, what pleasure can two lovers find in sleep?   10
   CARI. My lord, I lie with her often, and I know
She'll much disquiet you.
   ANT.   See, you are complained of.
   CARI. For she's the sprawling'st bedfellow.
   ANT. I shall like her the better for that.
   CARI. Sir, shall I ask you a question?   15
   ANT. I pray thee, Cariola.
   CARI. Wherefore still when you lie with my lady
Do you rise so early?
   ANT.   Labouring men
Count the clock oft'nest, Cariola,
Are glad when their task's ended.
   DUCH.   I'll stop your mouth. [*Kisses him.*
   ANT. Nay, that's but one; Venus had two soft doves   21
To draw her chariot: I must have another.— [*She kisses him again.*
When wilt thou marry, Cariola?
   CARI.   Never, my lord.
   ANT. O, fie upon this single life! forgo it.
We read how Daphne, for her peevish slight,   25
Became a fruitless bay-tree; Syrinx turned
To the pale empty reed; Anaxarete
Was frozen into marble: whereas those
Which married, or proved kind unto their friends,
Were by a gracious influence trans-shaped   30
Into the olive, pomegranate, mulberry,
Became flowers, precious stones, or eminent stars.
   CARI. This is a vain poetry: but I pray you, tell me,
If there were proposed me wisdom, riches, and beauty,
In three several young men, which should I choose?   35

SC. II: 25. *peevish slight:* obstinate refusal of Apollo. 26. *Syrinx:* she
repulsed Pan and was turned into a reed from which he made his pipe. 27.
Anaxarete: she was turned into stone by Venus because she rejected Iphis,
who hanged himself in despair at her door.

ANT. 'Tis a hard question. This was Paris' case,
And he was blind in 't, and there was great cause;
For how was 't possible he could judge right,
Having three amorous goddesses in view,
And they stark naked? 'Twas a motion   40
Were able to benight the apprehension
Of the severest counsellor of Europe.
Now I look on both your faces so well formed,
It puts me in mind of a question I would ask.
  CARI. What is 't?
  ANT.   I do wonder why hard-favoured ladies,   45
For the most part, keep worse-favoured waiting-women
To attend them, and cannot endure fair ones.
  DUCH. O, that's soon answered.
Did you ever in your life know an ill painter
Desire to have his dwelling next door to the shop   50
Of an excellent picture-maker? 'Twould disgrace
His face-making, and undo him. I prithee,
When were we so merry? My hair tangles.
  ANT. Pray thee, Cariola, let's steal forth the room,
And let her talk to herself. I have divers times   55
Served her the like, when she hath chafed extremely.
I love to see her angry. Softly, Cariola.
                 [*Exeunt* ANTONIO *and* CARIOLA.
  DUCH. Doth not the colour of my hair 'gin to change?
When I wax gray, I shall have all the court
Powder their hair with arras, to be like me.   60
You have cause to love me; I entered you into my heart

        [*Enter* FERDINAND *unseen.*]

Before you would vouchsafe to call for the keys.
We shall one day have my brothers take you napping.
Methinks his presence, being now in court,
Should make you keep your own bed; but you'll say   65
Love mixed with fear is sweetest. I'll assure you,
You shall get no more children till my brothers
Consent to be your gossips. Have you lost your tongue?
'Tis welcome:
For know, whether I am doomed to live or die,   70
I can do both like a prince.

———————

40. *motion:* show or spectacle. 60. *arras:* white powdered iris root. 68.
gossips: god-parents to your children.

FERD.   Die, then, quickly.

> [FERDINAND *gives her a poniard.*

Virtue, where art thou hid? What hideous thing
Is it that doth eclipse thee?
   DUCH.   Pray, sir, hear me.
   FERD. Or is it true thou art but a bare name,
And no essential thing?
   DUCH.   Sir——
   FERD.   Do not speak.   75
   DUCH. No, sir:
I will plant my soul in mine ears, to hear you.
   FERD. O most imperfect light of human reason,
That mak'st us so unhappy to foresee
What we can least prevent! Pursue thy wishes,   80
And glory in them: there's in shame no comfort
But to be past all bounds and sense of shame.
   DUCH. I pray, sir, hear me: I am married.
   FERD.   So!
   DUCH. Happily, not to your liking: but for that,
Alas, your shears do come untimely now   85
To clip the bird's wings that's already flown!
Will you see my husband?
   FERD.   Yes, if I could change
Eyes with a basilisk.
   DUCH.   Sure, you came hither
By his confederacy.
   FERD.   The howling of a wolf
Is music to thee, screech-owl: prithee, peace.—   90
Whate'er thou art that hast enjoyed my sister,
For I am sure thou hear'st me, for thine own sake
Let me not know thee. I came hither prepared
To work thy discovery; yet am now persuaded
It would beget such violent effects   95
As would damn us both. I would not for ten millions
I had beheld thee: therefore use all means
I never may have knowledge of thy name.
Enjoy thy lust still, and a wretched life,
On that condition.—And for thee, vile woman,   100
If thou do wish thy lecher may grow old
In thy embracements, I would have thee build
Such a room for him as our anchorites

---

88. *basilisk:* fabulous monster with a serpent's body and a cock's head,
whose look was fatal. 103. *anchorites:* hermits.

To holier use inhabit. Let not the sun
Shine on him till he's dead; let dogs and monkeys   105
Only converse with him, and such dumb things
To whom nature denies use to sound his name;
Do not keep a paraquito, lest she learn it.
If thou do love him, cut out thine own tongue,
Lest it bewray him.
    DUCH.   Why might not I marry?   110
I have not gone about in this to create
Any new world or custom.
    FERD.   Thou art undone;
And thou hast ta'en that massy sheet of lead
That hid thy husband's bones, and folded it
About my heart.
    DUCH.   Mine bleeds for 't.
    FERD.   Thine! thy heart!   115
What should I name 't, unless a hollow bullet
Filled with unquenchable wild-fire?
    DUCH.   You are in this
Too strict; and were you not my princely brother,
I would say, too wilful: my reputation
Is safe.
    FERD. Dost thou know what reputation is?   120
I'll tell thee,—to small purpose, since th' instruction
Comes now too late.
Upon a time Reputation, Love, and Death
Would travel o'er the world; and it was concluded
That they should part, and take three several ways.   125
Death told them, they should find him in great battles,
Or cities plagued with plagues; Love gives them counsel
To inquire for him 'mongst unambitious shepherds,
Where dowries were not talked of, and sometimes
'Mongst quiet kindred that had nothing left   130
By their dead parents. 'Stay,' quoth Reputation,
'Do not forsake me; for it is my nature,
If once I part from any man I meet,
I am never found again.' And so for you:
You have shook hands with Reputation,   135
And made him invisible. So, fare you well:
I will never see you more.
    DUCH.   Why should only I,

---

108. *paraquito:* parrot.

Of all the other princes of the world,
Be cased up, like a holy relic? I have youth
And a little beauty.

    FERD.   So you have some virgins   140
That are witches. I will never see thee more.   [*Exit.*

        [*Enter* ANTONIO, *with a pistol, and* CARIOLA.]

    DUCH. You saw this apparition?
    ANT.   Yes: we are
Betrayed. How came he hither? I should turn
This to thee, for that.
    CARI.   Pray, sir, do; and when
That you have cleft my heart, you shall read there   145
Mine innocence.
    DUCH.   That gallery gave him entrance.
  ANT. I would this terrible thing would come again,
That, standing on my guard, I might relate
My warrantable love.—   [*She shows the poniard.*
              Ha! what means this?
    DUCH. He left this with me.
    ANT.   And it seems did wish   150
You would use it on yourself?
    DUCH.   His action seemed
To intend so much.
    ANT.   This hath a handle to 't,
As well as a point: turn it towards him, and
So fasten the keen edge in his rank gall.   [*Knocking within.*
How now! who knocks? More earthquakes?
    DUCH.   I stand   155
As if a mine beneath my feet were ready
To be blown up.
    CARI.   'Tis Bosola.
    DUCH.   Away!
O misery! methinks unjust actions
Should wear these masks and curtains, and not we.
You must instantly part hence: I have fashioned it already.   160
            [*Exit* ANTONIO.

           [*Enter* BOSOLA.]

    BOS. The duke your brother is ta'en up in a whirlwind;
Hath took horse, and 's rid post to Rome.
    DUCH.   So late?
    BOS. He told me, as he mounted into th' saddle,

You were undone.

DUCH.   Indeed, I am very near it.

BOS. What's the matter?   165

DUCH. Antonio, the master of our household,
Hath dealt so falsely with me in 's accounts.
My brother stood engaged with me for money
Ta'en up of certain Neapolitan Jews,
And Antonio lets the bonds be forfeit.   170

BOS. Strange!—(*Aside.*) This is cunning.

DUCH.   And hereupon
My brother's bills at Naples are protested
Against.—Call up our officers.

BOS.   I shall.   [*Exit.*

[*Re-enter* ANTONIO.]

DUCH. The place that you must fly to is Ancona:
Hire a house there. I'll send after you   175
My treasure and my jewels. Our weak safety
Runs upon enginous wheels: short syllables
Must stand for periods. I must now accuse you
Of such a feignèd crime as Tasso calls
Magnanima menzogna, a noble lie,   180
'Cause it must shield our honours.—Hark! they are coming.

[*Re-enter* BOSOLA *and* OFFICERS.]

ANT. Will your grace hear me?

DUCH. I have got well by you; you have yielded me
A million of loss: I am like to inherit
The people's curses for your stewardship.   185
You had the trick in audit-time to be sick,
Till I had signed your quietus; and that cured you
Without help of a doctor.—Gentlemen,
I would have this man be an example to you all;
So shall you hold my favour; I pray, let him;   190
For h'as done that, alas, you would not think of,
And (because I intend to be rid of him)
I mean not to publish.—Use your fortune elsewhere.

ANT. I am strongly armed to brook my overthrow,
As commonly men bear with a hard year.   195
I will not blame the cause on 't; but do think

---

169. *ta'en up:* borrowed. 177. *enginous:* rapid and intricate. 178. *periods:*
sentences. 190. *let:* dismiss.

The necessity of my malevolent star
Procures this, not her humour. O, the inconstant
And rotten ground of service! You may see,
'Tis e'en like him, that in a winter night,   200
Takes a long slumber o'er a dying fire,
As loath to part from 't; yet parts thence as cold
As when he first sat down.
   DUCH.   We do confiscate,
Towards the satisfying of your accounts,
All that you have.
   ANT.   I am all yours; and 'tis very fit   205
All mine should be so.
   DUCH.   So, sir, you have your pass.
   ANT. You may see, gentlemen, what 'tis to serve
A prince with body and soul.   [*Exit.*
   BOS. Here's an example for extortion: what moisture is drawn out
of the sea, when foul weather comes, pours down, and runs into the
sea again.   211
   DUCH. I would know what are your opinions
Of this Antonio.
   2 OFF. He could not abide to see a pig's head gaping: I thought
your grace would find him a Jew.   215
   3 OFF. I would you had been his officer, for your own sake.
   4 OFF. You would have had more money.
   1 OFF. He stopped his ears with black wool, and to those came to
him for money said he was thick of hearing.
   2 OFF. Some said he was an hermaphrodite, for he could not abide
a woman.   221
   4 OFF. How scurvy proud he would look when the treasury was full!
Well, let him go.
   1 OFF. Yes, and the chippings of the buttery fly after him, to scour
his gold chain.   225
   DUCH. Leave us.——   [*Exeunt* OFFICERS.
What do you think of these?
   BOS. That these are rogues that in 's prosperity,
But to have waited on his fortune, could have wish'd
His dirty stirrup riveted through their noses,   230
And followed after 's mule, like a bear in a ring;
Would have prostituted their daughters to his lust;
Made their first-born intelligencers; thought none happy
But such as were born under his blest planet.

———————

224. *chippings:* bread crumbs.

And wore his livery: and do these lice drop off now?　　　235
Well, never look to have the like again:
He hath left a sort of flattering rogues behind him;
Their doom must follow. Princes pay flatterers
In their own money: flatterers dissemble their vices,
And they dissemble their lies; that's justice.　　　240
Alas, poor gentleman!
　　DUCH. Poor! he hath amply filled his coffers.
　　BOS. Sure, he was too honest. Pluto, the god of riches,
When he's sent by Jupiter to any man,
He goes limping, to signify that wealth　　　245
That comes on God's name comes slowly; but when he's sent
On the devil's errand, he rides post and comes in by scuttles.
Let me show you what a most unvalued jewel
You have in a wanton humour thrown away,
To bless the man shall find him. He was an excellent　　　250
Courtier and most faithful; a soldier that thought it
As beastly to know his own value too little
As devilish to acknowledge it too much.
Both his virtue and form deserved a far better fortune:
His discourse rather delighted to judge itself than show itself:　　　255
His breast was filled with all perfection,
And yet it seemed a private whispering-room,
It made so little noise of 't.
　　DUCH. But he was basely descended.
　　BOS. Will you make yourself a mercenary herald,　　　260
Rather to examine men's pedigrees than virtues?
You shall want him:
For know, an honest statesman to a prince
Is like a cedar planted by a spring;
The spring bathes the tree's root, the grateful tree　　　265
Rewards it with his shadow: you have not done so.
I would sooner swim to the Bermoothes on
Two politicians' rotten bladders, tied
Together with an intelligencer's heart-string,
Than depend on so changeable a prince's favour.　　　270
Fare thee well, Antonio! Since the malice of the world
Would needs down with thee, it cannot be said yet
That any ill happened unto thee, considering thy fall
Was accompanied with virtue.
　　DUCH. O, you render me excellent music!

---

237. *sort:* crew. 248. *unvalued:* invaluable. 262. *want:* miss 267. *Bermoothes:* Bermudas.

BOS.   Say you?   275
 DUCH. This good one that you speak of is my husband.
 BOS. Do I not dream? Can this ambitious age
Have so much goodness in 't as to prefer
A man merely for worth, without these shadows
Of wealth and painted honours? Possible?   280
 DUCH. I have had three children by him.
 BOS.   Fortunate lady!
For you have made your private nuptial bed
The humble and fair seminary of peace,
No question but: many an unbeneficed scholar
Shall pray for you for this deed, and rejoice   285
That some preferment in the world can yet
Arise from merit. The virgins of your land
That have no dowries shall hope your example
Will raise them to rich husbands. Should you want
Soldiers, 'twould make the very Turks and Moors   290
Turn Christians, and serve you for this act.
Last, the neglected poets of your time,
In honour of this trophy of a man,
Raised by that curious engine, your white hand,
Shall thank you in your grave for 't, and make that   295
More reverend than all the cabinets
Of living princes. For Antonio,
His fame shall likewise flow from many a pen,
When heralds shall want coats to sell to men.
 DUCH. As I taste comfort in this friendly speech,   300
So would I find concealment.
 BOS. O, the secret of my prince,
Which I will wear on th' inside of my heart!
 DUCH. You shall take charge of all my coin and jewels,
And follow him; for he retires himself   305
To Ancona.
 BOS.   So.
 DUCH.   Whither, within few days,
I mean to follow thee.
 BOS.   Let me think:
I would wish your grace to feign a pilgrimage
To our Lady of Loretto, scarce seven leagues
From fair Ancona; so may you depart   310
Your country with more honour, and your flight

---

283. *seminary:* seed-bed. 293. *trophy:* monument. 299. *coats:* of arms.

Will seem a princely progress, retaining
Your usual train about you.
    DUCH.   Sir, your direction
Shall lead me by the hand.
    CARI.   In my opinion,
She were better progress to the baths at Lucca,   315
Or go visit the Spa
In Germany; for, if you will believe me,
I do not like this jesting with religion,
This feignèd pilgrimage.
    DUCH. Thou art a superstitious fool!   320
Prepare us instantly for our departure.
Past sorrows, let us moderately lament them,
For those to come, seek wisely to prevent them.
               [*Exit* DUCHESS *with* CARIOLA.
    BOS. A politician is the devil's quilted anvil;
He fashions all sins on him, and the blows
Are never heard: he may work in a lady's chamber   325
(As here for proof). What rests but I reveal
All to my lord? O, this base quality
Of intelligencer! Why, every quality i' th' world
Prefers but gain or commendation:
Now, for this act I am certain to be raised,   330
And men that paint weeds to the life are praised.   [*Exit.*

SCENE III. *Rome: the* CARDINAL's *palace.*

[CARDINAL, FERDINAND, MALATESTE, PESCARA, SILVIO, DELIO.]

    CARD. Must we turn soldier, then?
    MAL.   The emperor,
Hearing your worth that way (ere you attained
This reverend garment), joins you in commission
With the right fortunate soldier, the Marquis of Pescara,
And the famous Lannoy.
    CARD.   He that had the honour   5
Of taking the French king prisoner?
    MAL.   The same.
Here's a plot drawn for a new fortification
At Naples.

---

327. *quality:* profession. 329. *Prefers:* offers.
    SC. III: 1. *emperor:* Charles V. 4-5. *Pescara . . . Lannoy:* Charles' commanders in his victory over Francis I at Pavia in 1525.

FERD.   This great Count Malateste, I perceive,
Hath got employment?
DELIO.   No employment, my lord;
A marginal note in the muster-book that he is   10
A voluntary lord.
FERD.   He's no soldier?
DELIO. He has worn gun-powder in 's hollow tooth for the tooth-
  ache.
SIL. He comes to the leaguer with a full intent
To eat fresh beef and garlic, means to stay
Till the scent be gone, and straight return to court.   15
DELIO. He hath read all the late service
As the City Chronicle relates it;
And keeps two pewterers going, only to express
Battles in model.
SIL.   Then he'll fight by the book.
DELIO. By the almanac, I think,   20
To choose good days and shun the critical.
That's his mistress' scarf.
SIL.   Yes, he protests
He would do much for that taffeta.
DELIO. I think he would run away from a battle,
To save it from taking prisoner.
SIL.   He is horribly afraid   25
Gun-powder will spoil the perfume on 't.
DELIO. I saw a Dutchman break his pate once
For calling him a pot-gun; he made his head
Have a bore in 't like a musket.
SIL. I would he had made a touch-hole to 't.   30
He is indeed a guarded sumpter-cloth,
Only for the remove of the court.

[*Enter* BOSOLA.]

PES. Bosola arrived! What should be the business?
Some falling-out amongst the cardinals.
These factions amongst great men, they are like   35
Foxes: when their heads are divided,
They carry fire in their tails, and all the country

16. *service:* military operations. 25. *taking:* being taken. 28. *pot-gun:* pop-
gun, braggart. 31. *guarded sumpter-cloth:* ornamented saddle blanket. 32.
remove: progress from place to place. 36. *Foxes:* like Samson's jackals
which he tied together by the tails ("heads are divided") to fire the
Philistines' corn.

About them goes to wrack for 't.

SIL.   What's that Bosola?

DELIO. I knew him in Padua,—a fantastical scholar, like such who
study to know how many knots was in Hercules' club, of   [40
what colour Achilles' beard was, or whether Hector were not
troubled with the tooth-ache. He hath studied himself half blear-
eyed to know the true symmetry of Cæsar's nose by a shoeing-horn;
and this he did to gain the name of a speculative man.

PES. Mark Prince Ferdinand: 45
A very salamander lives in 's eye,
To mock the eager violence of fire.

SIL. That cardinal hath made more bad faces with his oppression
than ever Michael Angelo made good ones. He lifts up 's nose, like
a foul porpoise before a storm.   50

PES. The Lord Ferdinand laughs.

DELIO.   Like a deadly cannon
That lightens ere it smokes.

PES. These are your true pangs of death,
The pangs of life, that struggle with great statesmen.

DELIO. In such a deformèd silence witches whisper their charms.

CARD. Doth she make religion her ridinghood   56
To keep her from the sun and tempest?

FERD. That, that damns her. Methinks her fault and beauty,
Blended together, show like leprosy,
The whiter the fouler. I make it a question   57
Whether her beggarly brats were ever christened.

CARD. I will instantly solicit the state of Ancona
To have them banished.

FERD.   You are for Loretto?
I shall not be at your ceremony, fare you well.—
Write to the Duke of Malfi, my young nephew,   65
She had by her first husband, and acquaint him
With 's mother's honesty.

BOS.   I will.

FERD.   Antonio!
A slave that only smelled of ink and counters,
And never in 's life looked like a gentleman,
But in the audit-time.—Go, go presently,   70
Draw me out an hundreth and fifty of our horse,
And meet me at the fort-bridge.   [*Exeunt.*

---

48. *oppression:* emotionalism.

SCENE IV.

[*Two* PILGRIMS *to the Shrine of our Lady of Loretto.*]

1 PIL. I have not seen a goodlier shrine than this;
Yet I have visited many.
2 PIL.   The Cardinal of Aragon
Is this day to resign his cardinal's hat;
His sister duchess likewise is arrived
To pay her vow of pilgrimage. I expect   5
A noble ceremony.
    1 PIL.   No question.—They come.
            [*Here the ceremony of the* CARDINAL's *instalment in
            the habit of a soldier: performed in delivering up his
            cross, hat, robes and ring at the shrine, and investing
            him with sword, helmet, shield, and spurs. Then* AN-
            TONIO, *the* DUCHESS *and their children, having presented
            themselves at the shrine, are (by a form of banishment
            in dumb show expressed towards them by the* CARDINAL
            *and the state of Ancona) banished. During all which
            ceremony, this ditty is sung, to very solemn music, by
            divers churchmen; and then exeunt all except the two*
            PILGRIMS.]
Arms and honours deck thy story,
To thy fame's eternal glory!   *The Author dis-*
Adverse fortune ever fly thee;   *claims this ditty*
No disastrous fate come nigh thee!   *to be his*   [10
I alone will sing thy praises,
Whom to honour virtue raises,
And thy study, that divine is,
Bent to martial discipline is.
Lay aside all those robes lie by thee;   15
Crown thy arts with arms, they'll beautify thee.
O worthy of worthiest name, adorned in this manner,
Lead bravely thy forces on under war's warlike banner!
O, mayst thou prove fortunate in all martial courses!
Guide thou still by skill in arts and forces!   20
Victory attend thee nigh, whilst fame sings loud thy powers;
Triumphant conquest crown thy head, and blessings pour down
        showers!
    1 PIL. Here's a strange turn of state! who would have thought
So great a lady would have matched herself
Unto so mean a person? Yet the cardinal   25

Bears himself much too cruel.

2 PIL   They are banished.

1 PIL. But I would ask what power hath this state
Of Ancona to determine of a free prince?

2 PIL. They are a free state, sir, and her brother showed
How that the Pope, fore-hearing of her looseness,   30
Hath seized into th' protection of the church
The dukedom which she held as dowager.

1 PIL. But by what justice?

2 PIL   Sure, I think by none,
Only her brother's instigation.

1 PIL. What was it with such violence he took   35
Off from her finger?

2 PIL.   'Twas her wedding-ring;
Which he vowed shortly he would sacrifice
To his revenge.

1 PIL.   Alas, Antonio!
If that a man be thrust into a well,
No matter who sets hand to 't, his own weight   40
Will bring him sooner to th' bottom. Come, let's hence.
Fortune makes this conclusion general:
All things do help th' unhappy man to fall.   [*Exeunt.*

SCENE V. *A road near Loretto.*

[ANTONIO, DUCHESS, CHILDREN, CARIOLA, SERVANTS.]

DUCH. Banished Ancona!

ANT.   Yes, you see what power
Lightens in great men's breath.

DUCH.   Is all our train
Shrunk to this poor remainder?

ANT.   These poor men,
Which have got little in your service, vow
To take your fortune: but your wiser buntings,   5
Now they are fledged, are gone.

DUCH.   They have done wisely.
This puts me in mind of death: physicians thus,
With their hands full of money, use to give o'er
Their patients.

ANT.   Right the fashion of the world:
From decayed fortunes every flatterer shrinks;   10

sc. v: 5. *buntings:* small birds that follow the summer.

Men cease to build where the foundation sinks.

DUCH. I had a very strange dream tonight.

ANT.   What was 't?

DUCH. Methought I wore my coronet of state,
And on a sudden all the diamonds
Were changed to pearls.

ANT.   My interpretation   15
Is, you'll weep shortly; for to me the pearls
Do signify your tears.

DUCH.   The birds, that live i' th' field
On the wild benefit of nature, live
Happier than we: for they may choose their mates,
And carol their sweet pleasures to the spring.   20

[*Enter* BOSOLA *with a letter.*]

BOS. You are happily o'erta'en.

DUCH.   From my brother?

BOS. Yes, from the Lord Ferdinand, your brother,
All love and safety.

DUCH.   Thou dost blanch mischief,
Would'st make it white. See, see, like to calm weather
At sea before a tempest, false hearts speak fair   25
To those they intend most mischief.   [*Reads.
                                                            A Letter.*

"Send Antonio to me; I want his head in a business."
A politic equivocation!
He doth not want your counsel, but your head;
That is, he cannot sleep till you be dead.   30
And here's another pitfall that's strewed o'er
With roses; mark it, 'tis a cunning one: [*Reads.*
"I stand engaged for your husband for several debts at Naples: let
not that trouble him; I had rather have his heart than his money."—
And I believe so too.

BOS.   What do you believe?   35

DUCH. That he so much distrusts my husband's love,
He will by no means believe his heart is with him
Until he see it. The devil is not cunning enough
To circumvent us in riddles.

BOS. Will you reject that noble and free league   40
Of amity and love which I present you?

DUCH. Their league is like that of some politic kings,

---

12. *tonight:* last night.

Only to make themselves of strength and power
To be our after-ruin: tell them so.
   BOS. And what from you?
   ANT.   Thus tell him: I will not come.   45
   BOS. And what of this?
   ANT.   My brothers have dispersed
Bloodhounds abroad; which till I hear are muzzled,
No truce, though hatched with ne'er such politic skill,
Is safe, that hangs upon our enemies' will.
I'll not come at them.
   BOS.   This proclaims your breeding.   50
Every small thing draws a base mind to fear
As the adamant draws iron. Fare you well, sir;
You shall shortly hear from 's.   [*Exit.*
   DUCH.   I suspect some ambush;
Therefore by all my love I do conjure you
To take your eldest son, and fly towards Milan,   55
Let us not venture all this poor remainder
In one unlucky bottom.
   ANT.   You counsel safely.
Best of my life, farewell. Since we must part,
Heaven hath a hand in 't; but no otherwise
Than as some curious artist takes in sunder   60
A clock or watch, when it is out of frame,
To bring 't in better order.
   DUCH. I know not which is best,
To see you dead, or part with you. Farewell, boy:
Thou art happy that thou hast not understanding   65
To know thy misery; for all our wit
And reading brings us to a truer sense
Of sorrow.—In the eternal church, sir,
I do hope we shall not part thus.
   ANT.   O, be of comfort!
Make patience a noble fortitude,   70
And think not how unkindly we are used:
Man, like to cassia, is proved best, being bruised.
   DUCH. Must I, like to a slave-born Russian,
Account it praise to suffer tyranny?
And yet, O heaven, thy heavy hand is in 't!   75
I have seen my little boy oft scourge his top,
And compared myself to 't: naught made me e'er

76. *scourge:* whip or spin with a string.

Go right but heaven's scourge-stick.

ANT.   Do not weep:
Heaven fashioned us of nothing; and we strive
To bring ourselves to nothing.—Farewell, Cariola,   80
And thy sweet armful.—If I do never see thee more,
Be a good mother to your little ones,
And save them from the tiger: fare you well.

DUCH. Let me look upon you once more, for that speech
Came from a dying father. Your kiss is colder   85
Than that I have seen an holy anchorite
Give to a dead man's skull.

ANT. My heart is turned to a heavy lump of lead,
With which I sound my danger: fare you well. [*Exit with his son.*
DUCH. My laurel is all witherèd.   90
CARI. Look, madam, what a troop of armèd men
Make toward us!

[*Enter* BOSOLA *vizarded, with a Guard.*]

DUCH.   O, they are very welcome:
When Fortune's wheel is over-charged with princes,
The weight makes it move swift: I would have my ruin
Be sudden.—I am your adventure, am I not?   95
BOS. You are: you must see your husband no more.
DUCH. What devil art thou that counterfeits heaven's thunder?
BOS. Is that terrible? I would have you tell me whether
Is that note worse that frights the silly birds
Out of the corn, or that which doth allure them   100
To the nets? You have hearkened to the last too much.
DUCH. O misery! like to a rusty o'ercharged cannon,
Shall I never fly in pieces? Come, to what prison?
BOS. To none.
DUCH.   Whither, then?
BOS.   To your palace.
DUCH.   I have heard
That Charon's boat serves to convey all o'er   105
The dismal lake, but brings none back again.
BOS. Your brothers mean you safety and pity.
DUCH.   Pity!
With such a pity men preserve alive
Pheasants and quails, when they are not fat enough
To be eaten.

---

95. *adventure:* quarry.

BOS.   These are your children?
DUCH.   Yes.
BOS.   Can they prattle?   110
DUCH. No:
But I intend, since they were born accursed,
Curses shall be their first language.
    BOS.   Fie, madam!
Forget this base, low fellow.
    DUCH.   Were I a man,
I'd beat that counterfeit face into thy other.   115
    BOS. One of no birth.
    DUCH.   Say that he was born mean,
Man is most happy when 's own actions
Be arguments and examples of his virtue.
    BOS. A barren, beggarly virtue.
    DUCH. I prithee, who is greatest? Can you tell?   120
Sad tales befit my woe: I'll tell you one.
A salmon, as she swam unto the sea,
Met with a dog-fish, who encounters her
With this rough language: 'Why art thou so bold
To mix thyself with our high state of floods,   125
Being no eminent courtier, but one
That for the calmest and fresh time o' th' year
Dost live in shallow rivers, rank'st thyself
With silly smelts and shrimps? And darest thou
Pass by our dog-ship without reverence?'   130
'O,' quoth the salmon, 'sister, be at peace:
Thank Jupiter we both have passed the net!
Our value never can be truly known,
Till in the fisher's basket we be shown:
I' th' market then my price may be the higher,   135
Even when I am nearest to the cook and fire.'
So to great men the moral may be stretchèd;
Men oft are valued high, when th' are most wretched.—
But come, whither you please. I am armed 'gainst misery;
Bent to all sways of the oppressor's will.   140
There's no deep valley but near some great hill.   [*Exeunt.*

Act IV

[FERDINAND, BOSOLA.]

FERD. How doth our sister duchess bear herself
In her imprisonment?
    BOS.   Nobly: I'll describe her.
She's sad as one long used to 't, and she seems
Rather to welcome the end of misery
Than shun it; a behaviour so noble   5
As gives a majesty to adversity.
You may discern the shape of loveliness
More perfect in her tears than in her smiles:
She will muse four hours together; and her silence,
Methinks, expresseth more than if she spake.   10
    FERD. Her melancholy seems to be fortified
With a strange disdain.
    BOS.   'Tis so; and this restraint,
(Like English mastiffs that grow fierce with tying)
Makes her too passionately apprehend
Those pleasures she's kept from.
    FERD.   Curse upon her!   15
I will no longer study in the book
Of another's heart. Inform her what I told you.   [*Exit.*

[*Enter* DUCHESS *and* ATTENDANTS.]

BOS. All comfort to your grace!
    DUCH.   I will have none.
Pray thee, why dost thou wrap thy poisoned pills
In gold and sugar?   20
    BOS. Your elder brother, the Lord Ferdinand,
Is come to visit you, and sends you word,
'Cause once he rashly made a solemn vow
Never to see you more, he comes i' th' night;
And prays you gently neither torch nor taper   25
Shine in your chamber. He will kiss your hand,
And reconcile himself; but for his vow
He dares not see you.
    DUCH.   At his pleasure.—
Take hence the lights.—He's come.   [*Exeunt* ATTENDANTS *with lights.*

[Enter FERDINAND.]

FERD.   Where are you?
DUCH.   Here, sir.
FERD. This darkness suits you well.
DUCH.   I would ask you pardon.   30
FERD. You have it;
For I account it the honourablest revenge,
Where I may kill, to pardon.—Where are your cubs?
   DUCH. Whom?
   FERD.   Call them your children;
For though our national law distinguish bastards   35
From true legitimate issue, compassionate nature
Makes them all equal.
   DUCH.   Do you visit me for this?
You violate a sacrament o' th' church
Shall make you howl in hell for 't.
   FERD.   It had been well,
Could you have lived thus always; for, indeed,   40
You were too much i' th' light.—But no more;
I come to seal my peace with you. Here's a hand
                         [*Gives her a dead man's hand.*
To which you have vowed much love; the ring upon 't
You gave.
   DUCH.   I affectionately kiss it.
   FERD. Pray, do, and bury the print of it in your heart.   45
I will leave this ring with you for a love-token;
And the hand as sure as the ring: and do not doubt
But you shall have the heart too. When you need a friend,
Send it to him that owed it; you shall see
Whether he can aid you.
   DUCH.   You are very cold: 50
I fear you are not well after your travel.—
Ha! lights!——O, horrible!
   FERD.   Let her have lights enough.   [*Exit.*
   DUCH. What witchcraft doth he practise, that he hath left
A dead man's hand here?
           [*Here is discovered, behind a traverse, the artificial
           figures of* ANTONIO *and his children, appearing as if
           they were dead.*]
   BOS. Look you, here's the piece from which 't was ta'en.   55
He doth present you this sad spectacle,
That, now you know directly they are dead,
Hereafter you may wisely cease to grieve

For that which cannot be recoverèd.

    DUCH. There is not between heaven and earth one wish   60
I stay for after this. It wastes me more
Than were 't my picture, fashioned out of wax,
Stuck with a magical needle, and then buried
In some foul dung-hill; and yond's an excellent property
For a tyrant, which I would account mercy.

    BOS.   What's that?   65
    DUCH. If they would bind me to that liveless trunk,
And let me freeze to death.

    BOS.   Come, you must live.
    DUCH. That's the greatest torture souls feel in hell:
In hell that they must live, and cannot die.
Portia, I'll new-kindle thy coals again,   70
And revive the rare and almost dead example
Of a loving wife.

    BOS.   O, fie! despair? Remember
You are a Christian.

    DUCH.   The church enjoins fasting:
I'll starve myself to death.

    BOS.   Leave this vain sorrow.
Things being at the worst begin to mend: the bee   75
When he hath shot his sting into your hand,
May then play with your eye-lid.

    DUCH.   Good comfortable fellow,
Persuade a wretch that's broke upon the wheel
To have all his bones new set; entreat him live
To be executed again. Who must despatch me?   80
I account this world a tedious theatre,
For I do play a part in 't 'gainst my will.

    BOS. Come, be of comfort; I will save your life.
    DUCH. Indeed, I have not leisure to tend so small a business.
    BOS. Now, by my life, I pity you.
    DUCH.   Thou art a fool, then,   85
To waste thy pity on a thing so wretched
As cannot pity itself. I am full of daggers.
Puff, let me blow these vipers from me.

[Enter SERVANT.]

    ACT IV, SC. I: 64. *dung-hill:* whose heat would melt the waxen image;
property: appropriate act. 70. *Portia:* died by holding burning candles in
her mouth after her husband Brutus' death at Philippi.

What are you?
    SERV.   One that wishes you long life.
    DUCH. I would thou wert hanged for the horrible curse   90
Thou hast given me: I shall shortly grow one
Of the miracles of pity. I'll go pray!—   [*Exit* SERVANT.
No, I'll go curse.
    BOS.   O, fie!
    DUCH.   I could curse the stars—
    BOS.   O, fearful!
    DUCH. And those three smiling seasons of the year
Into a Russian winter; nay, the world   95
To its first chaos.
    BOS.   Look you, the stars shine still.
    DUCH. O, but you must
Remember, my curse hath a great way to go.—
Plagues, that make lanes through largest families,
Consume them!—
    BOS.   Fie, lady!
    DUCH.   Let them, like tyrants,   100
Never be remembered but for the ill they have done;
Let all the zealous prayers of mortified
Churchmen forget them!—
    BOS.   O, uncharitable!
    DUCH. Let heaven a little while cease crowning martyrs,
To punish them!—   105
Go, howl them this, and say, I long to bleed:
It is some mercy when men kill with speed.   [*Exit.*

                    [*Re-enter* FERDINAND.]

    FERD. Excellent, as I would wish; she's plagued in art.
These presentations are but framed in wax
By the curious master in that quality,   110
Vincentio Lauriola, and she takes them
For true substantial bodies.
    BOS.   Why do you do this?
    FERD. To bring her to despair.
    BOS.   Faith, end here,
And go no farther in your cruelty.
Send her a penitential garment to put on   115
Next to her delicate skin, and furnish her
With beads and prayer-books.
    FERD.   Damn her! that body of hers,
While that my blood ran pure in 't, was more worth

Than that which thou wouldst comfort, called a soul.
I will send her masques of common courtesans,   120
Have her meat served up by bawds and ruffians,
And, 'cause she'll needs be mad, I am resolved
To remove forth the common hospital
All the mad-folk, and place them near her lodging;
There let them practise together, sing and dance,   125
And act their gambols to the full o' th' moon:
If she can sleep the better for it, let her.
Your work is almost ended.

BOS.   Must I see her again?
FERD. Yes.
BOS.   Never.
FERD.   You must.
BOS.   Never in mine own shape;
That's forfeited by my intelligence   130
And this last cruel lie: when you send me next,
The business shall be comfort.
FERD.   Very likely!
Thy pity is nothing of kin to thee. Antonio
Lurks about Milan: thou shalt shortly thither,
To feed a fire as great as my revenge,   135
Which never will slack till it hath spent his fuel:
Intemperate agues make physicians cruel.   [*Exeunt.*

SCENE II.

[DUCHESS, CARIOLA.]

DUCH. What hideous noise was that?
CARI.   'Tis the wild consort
Of madmen, lady, which your tyrant brother
Hath placed about your lodging. This tyranny,
I think, was never practised till this hour.
DUCH. Indeed, I thank him. Nothing but noise and folly   5
Can keep me in my right wits; whereas reason
And silence make me stark mad. Sit down;
Discourse to me some dismal tragedy.
CARI. O, 'twill increase your melancholy!
DUCH.   Thou art deceived:
To hear of greater grief would lessen mine.   10
This is a prison?

_____
130. *intelligence:* acting as spy.

CARI.   Yes, but you shall live
To shake this durance off.
    DUCH.   Thou art a fool:
The robin-red-breast and the nightingale
Never live long in cages.
    CARI.   Pray, dry your eyes.
What think you of, madam?
    DUCH.   Of nothing;   15
When I muse thus, I sleep.
    CARI. Like a madman, with your eyes open?
    DUCH. Dost thou think we shall know one another
In th' other world?
    CARI.   Yes, out of question.
    DUCH. O, that it were possible we might   20
But hold some two days' conference with the dead!
From them I should learn somewhat, I am sure,
I never shall know here. I'll tell thee a miracle:
I am not mad yet, to my cause of sorrow:
Th' heaven o'er my head seems made of molten brass,   25
The earth of flaming sulphur, yet I am not mad.
I am acquainted with sad misery
As the tanned galley-slave is with his oar;
Necessity makes me suffer constantly,
And custom makes it easy. Who do I look like now?   30
    CARI. Like to your picture in the gallery,
A deal of life in show, but none in practice;
Or rather like some reverend monument
Whose ruins are even pitied.
    DUCH.   Very proper;
And Fortune seems only to have her eye-sight   35
To behold my tragedy.—How now!
What noise is that?

[Enter SERVANT.]

    SERV.   I am come to tell you,
Your brother hath intended you some sport.
A great physician, when the Pope was sick
Of a deep melancholy, presented him   40
With several sorts of madmen, which wild object
(Being full of change and sport) forced him to laugh,
And so th' imposthume broke: the self-same cure
The duke intends on you.

    SC. II: 43. *imposthume:* ulcer.

DUCH.   Let them come in.

SERV. There's a mad laywer; and a secular priest;   45
A doctor that hath forfeited his wits
By jealousy; an astrologian
That in his works said such a day o' th' month
Should be the day of doom, and, failing of 't,
Ran mad; an English tailor, crazed i' th' brain   50
With the study of new fashions; a gentleman-usher
Quite beside himself with care to keep in mind
The number of his lady's salutations,
Or 'How do you,' she employed him in each morning;
A farmer, too, an excellent knave in grain,   55
Mad 'cause he was hindered transportation:
And let one broker that's mad loose to these,
You'd think the devil were among them.

DUCH. Sit, Cariola.—Let them loose when you please,
For I am chained to endure all your tyranny.   60

[*Enter* MADMEN.]

Here by a MADMAN *this song is sung to a dismal kind of music.*

> O, let us howl some heavy note,
>   Some deadly dogged howl,
> Sounding as from the threatening throat
>   Of beasts and fatal fowl!
> As ravens, screech-owls, bulls, and bears,   65
>   We'll bell, and bawl our parts,
> Till irksome noise have cloy'd your ears
>   And corrosived your hearts.
> At last, when as our choir wants breath,
>   Our bodies being blest,   70
> We'll sing, like swans, to welcome death,
>   And die in love and rest.

1 MADMAN. Doom's-day not come yet! I'll draw it nearer by a perspective, or make a glass that shall set all the world on fire upon an
instant. I cannot sleep; my pillow is stuffed with a litter of   [75
porcupines.

2 MADMAN. Hell is a mere glass-house, where the devils are continually blowing up women's souls on hollow irons, and the fire never
goes out.

3 MADMAN. I will lie with every woman in my parish the   [80

---

55. *in grain:* in the grain trade and ingrained. 73-4. *perspective:* telescope.

tenth night. I will tithe them over like hay-cocks.

4 MADMAN. Shall my 'pothecary out-go me, because I am a cuckold?
I have found out his roguery: he makes alum of his wife's urine, and
sells it to Puritans that have sore throats with over-straining.

1 MADMAN. I have skill in heraldry.   85

2 MADMAN. Hast?

1 MADMAN. You do give for your crest a woodcock's head with the
brains picked out on 't; you are a very ancient gentleman.

3 MADMAN. Greek is turned Turk: we are only to be saved by the
Helvetian translation.   90

1 MADMAN. Come on, sir, I will lay the law to you.

2 MADMAN. O, rather lay a corrosive: the law will eat to the bone.

3 MADMAN. He that drinks but to satisfy nature is damned.

4 MADMAN. If I had my glass here, I would show a sight should
make all the women here call me mad doctor.   95

1 MADMAN. What's he? A rope-maker?

2 MADMAN. No, no, no; a snuffling knave that while he shows the
tombs, will have his hand in a wench's placket.

3 MADMAN. Woe to the caroche that brought home my wife from
the masque at three o'clock in the morning! It had a large   [100
feather-bed in it.

4 MADMAN. I have pared the devil's nails forty times, roasted them
in raven's eggs, and cured agues with them.

3 MADMAN. Get me three hundred milch-bats, to make possets to
procure sleep.   105

4 MADMAN. All the college may throw their caps at me: I have made
a soap-boiler costive; it was my masterpiece.

[*Here the dance, consisting of Eight Madmen, with music answerable
thereunto; after which,* BOSOLA (*like an old man*) *enters.*]

DUCH. Is he mad too?

SERV.   Pray, question him. I'll leave you.

                              [*Exeunt* SERVANT *and* MADMEN.

BOS. I am come to make thy tomb.

DUCH.   Ha! my tomb!

Thou speak'st as if I lay upon my death-bed,   110
Gasping for breath. Dost thou perceive me sick?

---

84. *straining:* preaching. 87. *woodcock:* proverbially stupid bird. 89-90.
Greek . . . translation: the Greek text of the Bible has been turned to
Turkish (infidel) uses, so we can be saved only by the Genevan translation,
which was made in 1560 by Puritan exiles from England. 96. *rope-maker:*
hangman's assistant. 107. *costive:* constipated; a masterpiece since soap is
used for suppositories.

BOS. Yes, and the more dangerously, since thy sickness is insensible.

DUCH. Thou art not mad, sure: dost know me?

BOS.   Yes.

DUCH.   Who am I?

BOS. Thou art a box of worm-seed, at best but a salvatory of green
mummy. What's this flesh? A little crudded milk, fantasti-   [115
cal puff-paste. Our bodies are weaker than those paper-prisons boys
use to keep flies in; more contemptible, since ours is to preserve earth-
worms. Didst thou ever see a lark in a cage? Such is the soul in the
body: this world is like her little turf of grass, and the heaven o'er our
heads, like her looking-glass, only gives us a miserable knowl-   [120
edge of the small compass of our prison.

DUCH. Am not I thy duchess?

BOS. Thou art some great woman, sure, for riot begins to sit on thy
forehead (clad in gray hairs) twenty years sooner than on a merry
milk-maid's. Thou sleep'st worse than if a mouse should be   [125
forced to take up her lodging in a cat's ear: a little infant that breeds
its teeth, should it lie with thee, would cry out, as if thou wert the
more unquiet bedfellow.

DUCH. I am Duchess of Malfi still.

BOS. That makes thy sleeps so broken: 130
Glories, like glow-worms, afar off shine bright,
But, looked to near, have neither heat nor light.

DUCH. Thou art very plain.

BOS. My trade is to flatter the dead, not the living; I am a tomb-
maker.   135

DUCH. And thou com'st to make my tomb?

BOS. Yes.

DUCH. Let me be a little merry:—of what stuff wilt thou make it?

BOS. Nay, resolve me first of what fashion?

DUCH. Why, do we grow fantastical in our deathbed?   140
Do we affect fashion in the grave?

BOS. Most ambitiously. Princes' images on their tombs do not lie,
as they were wont, seeming to pray up to heaven; but with their hands
under their cheeks, as if they died of the tooth-ache. They are not
carved with their eyes fixed upon the stars; but, as their   [145
minds were wholly bent upon the world, the self-same way they seem
to turn their faces.

DUCH. Let me know fully therefore the effect

---

114. *salvatory:* ointment box; *green:* fresh. 115. *mummy:* a drug from
embalmed bodies; *crudded:* curded.

Of this thy dismal preparation,
This talk fit for a charnel.
BOS.　　　　　　　　Now I shall:— 150

[*Enter* EXECUTIONERS, *with a coffin, cords, and a bell.*]

Here is a present from your princely brothers;
And may it arrive welcome, for it brings
Last benefit, last sorrow.
DUCH.　　　　　　Let me see it:
I have so much obedience in my blood,
I wish it in their veins to do them good. 155
　BOS. This is your last presence-chamber.
　CARI. O my sweet lady!
DUCH.　　　　　　　Peace; it affrights not me.
　BOS. I am the common bellman
That usually is sent to condemned persons
The night before they suffer.
DUCH.　　　　　　Even now thou saidest 160
Thou wast a tomb-maker.
BOS.　　　　　　'Twas to bring you
By degrees to mortification. Listen.

> *Hark, now everything is still,*
> *The screech-owl and the whistler shrill*
> *Call upon our dame aloud,* 165
> *And bid her quickly don her shroud!*
> *Much you had of land and rent;*
> *Your length in clay's now competent:*
> *A long war disturbed your mind;*
> *Here your perfect peace is signed.* 170
> *Of what is 't fools make such vain keeping?*
> *Sin their conception, their birth weeping,*
> *Their life a general mist of error,*
> *Their death a hideous storm of terror.*
> *Strew your hair with powders sweet,* 175
> *Don clean linen, bathe your feet,*
> *And (the foul fiend more to check)*
> *A crucifix let bless your neck.*
> *'Tis now full tide 'tween night and day;*
> *End your groan, and come away.* 180

168. *competent:* adequate.

CARI. Hence, villains, tyrants, murderers! Alas!
What will you do with my lady?—Call for help!
   DUCH. To whom? To our next neighbours? They are mad-folks.
   BOS. Remove that noise.
   DUCH.   Farewell, Cariola.
In my last will I have not much to give: 185
A many hungry guests have fed upon me;
Thine will be a poor reversion.
   CARI.   I will die with her.
   DUCH. I pray thee, look thou giv'st my little boy
Some syrup for his cold, and let the girl
Say her prayers ere she sleep.
              [CARIOLA *is forced out by the* EXECUTIONERS.
              Now what you please!   190
What death?
   BOS.   Strangling: here are your executioners.
   DUCH. I forgive them:
The apoplexy, catarrh, or cough o' th' lungs,
Would do as much as they do.
   BOS. Doth not death fright you?
   DUCH.   Who would be afraid on 't,   195
Knowing to meet such excellent company
In th' other world?
   BOS. Yet, methinks,
The manner of your death should much afflict you:
This cord should terrify you.
   DUCH.   Not a whit: 200
What would it pleasure me to have my throat cut
With diamonds? or to be smothered
With cassia? or to be shot to death with pearls?
I know death hath ten thousand several doors
For men to take their exits; and 'tis found   205
They go on such strange geometrical hinges,
You may open them both ways: any way, for heaven-sake,
So I were out of your whispering. Tell my brothers
That I perceive death, now I am well awake,
Best gift is they can give or I can take.   210
I would fain put off my last woman's-fault:
I'd not be tedious to you.
   EXECUT.   We are ready.
   DUCH. Dispose my breath how please you; but my body

---

193. catarrh: cerebral hemorrhage.

Bestow upon my women, will you?
    EXECUT.   Yes.
    DUCH. Pull, and pull strongly, for your able strength   215
Must pull down heaven upon me:—
Yet stay; heaven-gates are not so highly arched
As princes' palaces; they that enter there
Must go upon their knees (*kneels*).—Come, violent death,
Serve for mandragora to make me sleep!—   220
Go tell my brothers, when I am laid out,
They then may feed in quiet.   [*They strangle her.*
    BOS. Where's the waiting-woman?
Fetch her: some other strangle the children.

[Enter CARIOLA.]

Look you, there sleeps your mistress.
    CARI.   O, you are damned   225
Perpetually for this! My turn is next;—
Is 't not so ordered?
    BOS.   Yes, and I am glad
You are so well prepared for 't.
    CARI.   You are deceived, sir,
I am not prepared for 't, I will not die;
i will first come to my answer, and know   230
How I have offended.
    BOS.   Come, despatch her.—
You kept her counsel; now you shall keep ours.
    CARI. I will not die, I must not; I am contracted
To a young gentleman.
    EXECUT.   Here's your wedding-ring.
    CARI. Let me but speak with the duke. I'll discover   235
Treason to his person.
    BOS.   Delays:—throttle her.
    EXECUT. She bites and scratches.
    CARI.   If you kill me now,
I am damned; I have not been at confession
This two years.
    BOS. (*To* EXECUTIONERS.) When!
    CARI.   I am quick with child.
    BOS.   Why, then,
Your credit's saved. (EXECUTIONERS *strangle* CARIOLA.)
              Bear her into th' next room;   240
Let this lie still.   [*Exeunt* EXECUTIONERS *with body of* CARIOLA.

[Enter FERDINAND.]

FERD.   Is she dead?

BOS.   She is what
You'd have her. But here begin your pity:
                            [*Shows the Children strangled.*]
Alas, how have these offended?

FERD.   The death
Of young wolves is never to be pitied.

    BOS. Fix your eye here.

FERD.   Constantly.

BOS.   Do you not weep?   245
Other sins only speak; murther shrieks out.
The element of water moistens the earth,
But blood flies upwards and bedews the heavens.

    FERD. Cover her face; mine eyes dazzle: she died young.

    BOS. I think not so; her infelicity   250
Seemed to have years too many.

    FERD. She and I were twins;
And should I die this instant, I had lived
Her time to a minute.

    BOS.   It seems she was born first:
You have bloodily approved the ancient truth,   255
That kindred commonly do worse agree
Than remote strangers.

    FERD.   Let me see her face
Again. Why didst not thou pity her? What
An excellent honest man mightst thou have been,
If thou hadst borne her to some sanctuary!   260
Or, bold in a good cause, opposed thyself,
With thy advancèd sword above thy head,
Between her innocence and my revenge!
I bade thee, when I was distracted of my wits,
Go kill my dearest friend, and thou hast done 't.   265
For let me but examine well the cause:
What was the meanness of her match to me?
Only I must confess I had a hope,
Had she continued widow, to have gained
An infinite mass of treasure by her death: 270
And that was the main cause,—her marriage,
That drew a stream of gall quite through my heart.
For thee (as we observe in tragedies
That a good actor many times is cursed
For playing a villain's part) I hate thee for 't.   275
And, for my sake, say, thou hast done much ill well.

BOS. Let me quicken your memory, for I perceive
You are falling into ingratitude: I challenge
The reward due to my service.

FERD.   I'll tell thee
What I'll give thee.

BOS.   Do.

FERD.   I'll give thee a pardon   280
For this murther.

BOS.   Ha!

FERD.   Yes, and 'tis
The largest bounty I can study to do thee.
By what authority didst thou execute
This bloody sentence?

BOS.   By yours.

FERD. Mine! Was I her judge?   285
Did any ceremonial form of law
Doom her to not-being? Did a complete jury
Deliver her conviction up i' th' court?
Where shalt thou find this judgment registered,
Unless in hell? See, like a bloody fool,   290
Thou'st forfeited thy life, and thou shalt die for 't.

BOS. The office of justice is perverted quite
When one thief hangs another. Who shall dare
To reveal this?

FERD.   O, I'll tell thee;
The wolf shall find her grave, and scrape it up,   295
Not to devour the corpse, but to discover
The horrid murther.

BOS.   You, not I, shall quake for 't.

FERD. Leave me.

BOS.   I will first receive my pension.

FERD. You are a villain.

BOS.   When your ingratitude
Is judge, I am so.

FERD.   O horror,   300
That not the fear of him which binds the devils
Can prescribe man obedience!—
Never look upon me more.

BOS.   Why, fare thee well.
Your brother and yourself are worthy men!
You have a pair of hearts are hollow graves,   305
Rotten, and rotting others; and your vengeance,
Like two chained bullets, still goes arm in arm.

You may be brothers; for treason, like the plague,
Doth take much in a blood. I stand like one
That long hath ta'en a sweet and golden dream: 310
I am angry with myself, now, that I wake.
    FERD. Get thee into some unknown part o' th' world,
That I may never see thee.
    BOS.   Let me know
Wherefore I should be thus neglected. Sir,
I served your tyranny, and rather strove   315
To satisfy yourself than all the world:
And though I loathed the evil, yet I loved
You that did counsel it; and rather sought
To appear a true servant than an honest man.
    FERD. I'll go hunt the badger by owl-light;   320
'Tis a deed of darkness.   [*Exit.*
    BOS. He's much distracted. Off, my painted honour!
While with vain hopes our faculties we tire,
We seem to sweat in ice and freeze in fire.
What would I do, were this to do again?   325
I would not change my peace of conscience
For all the wealth of Europe.—She stirs; here's life:—
Return, fair soul, from darkness, and lead mine
Out of this sensible hell!—she's warm, she breathes:—
Upon thy pale lips I will melt my heart,   330
To store them with fresh colour.—Who's there?
Some cordial drink!—Alas! I dare not call:
So pity would destroy pity.—Her eye opes,
And heaven in it seems to ope, that late was shut,
To take me up to mercy.   335
    DUCH. Antonio!
    BOS.   Yes, madam, he is living;
The dead bodies you saw were but feigned statues.
He's reconciled to your brothers; the Pope hath wrought
The atonement.
    DUCH.   Mercy!   [*She dies.*
    BOS. O, she's gone again! there the cords of life broke.   340
O sacred innocence, that sweetly sleeps
On turtles' feathers, whilst a guilty conscience
Is a black register wherein is writ
All our good deeds and bad, a perspective

---

309. *take . . . blood:* runs through a family. 329. *sensible:* felt by the
senses. 342. *turtles':* doves'. 344. *perspective:* glass.

That shows us hell! That we cannot be suffered   345
To do good when we have a mind to it!
This is manly sorrow!
These tears, I am very certain, never grew
In my mother's milk. My estate is sunk
Below the degree of fear: where were   350
These penitent fountains while she was living?
O, they were frozen up! Here is a sight
As direful to my soul as is the sword
Unto a wretch hath slain his father.
Come, I'll bear thee hence,   355
And execute thy last will; that's deliver
Thy body to the reverend dispose
Of some good women: that the cruel tyrant
Shall not deny me. Then I'll post to Milan,
Where somewhat I will speedily enact   360
Worth my dejection.   [*Exit with the body.*

Act V.

SCENE I. *Milan: A public place.*

[ANTONIO, DELIO.]

ANT. What think you of my hope of reconcilement
To the Aragonian brethren?
    DELIO.   I misdoubt it;
For though they have sent their letters of safe-conduct
For your repair to Milan, they appear
But nets to entrap you. The Marquis of Pescara,   5
Under whom you hold certain land in cheat,
Much 'gainst his noble nature hath been moved
To seize those lands; and some of his dependants
Are at this instant making it their suit
To be invested in your revenues.   10
I cannot think they mean well to your life
That do deprive you of your means of life,
Your living.
    ANT.   You are still an heretic
To any safety I can shape myself.
    DELIO. Here comes the marquis: I will make myself   15

ACT V, SC. I: 6. *in cheat:* subject to escheat or forfeiture.

Petitioner for some part of your land,
To know whether it is flying.

ANT.   I pray, do.   *[Withdraws*

[*Enter* PESCARA.]

DELIO. Sir, I have a suit to you.

PES.   To me?

DELIO.   An easy one:
There is the Citadel of Saint Bennet,
With some demesnes, of late in the possession   20
Of Antonio Bologna,—please you bestow them on me.

PES. You are my friend; but this is such a suit,
Nor fit for me to give, nor you to take.

DELIO. No, sir?

PES.   I will give you ample reason for 't
Soon in private. Here's the cardinal's mistress.   25

[*Enter* JULIA.]

JULIA. My lord, I am grown your poor petitioner,
And should be an ill beggar, had I not
A great man's letter here (the cardinal's)
To court you in my favour.   *[Gives a letter.*

PES.   He entreats for you
The Citadel of Saint Bennet, that belonged   30
To the banished Bologna.

JULIA.   Yes.

PES. I could not have thought of a friend I could rather
Pleasure with it: 'tis yours.

JULIA.   Sir, I thank you;
And he shall know how doubly I am engaged,
Both in your gift, and speediness of giving,   35
Which makes your grant the greater.   *[Exit.*

ANT. (*aside*).   How they fortify
Themselves with my ruin!

DELIO.   Sir, I am
Little bound to you.

PES.   Why?

DELIO. Because you denied this suit to me, and gave 't
To such a creature.

PES.   Do you know what it was?   40
It was Antonio's land: not forfeited
By course of law, but ravished from his throat
By the cardinal's entreaty. It were not fit
I should bestow so main a piece of wrong

Upon my friend: 'tis a gratification　　45
Only due to a strumpet, for it is injustice.
Shall I sprinkle the pure blood of innocents
To make those followers I call my friends
Look ruddier upon me? I am glad
This land, ta'en from the owner by such wrong,　　50
Returns again unto so foul an use
As salary for his lust. Learn, good Delio,
To ask noble things of me, and you shall find
I'll be a noble giver.

DELIO.　　　　You instruct me well.

ANT. (*aside*). Why, here's a man now would fright impudence　　55
From sauciest beggars.

PES.　　　　　Prince Ferdinand's come to Milan,
Sick, as they give out, of an apoplexy;
But some say 'tis a frenzy. I am going
To visit him.　　　　　　　　　　　　　　[*Exit.*

ANT.　　'Tis a noble old fellow.

DELIO. What course do you mean to take, Antonio?　　60

ANT. This night I mean to venture all my fortune,
Which is no more than a poor lingering life,
To the cardinal's worst of malice. I have got
Private access to his chamber; and intend
To visit him about the mid of night,　　65
As once his brother did our noble duchess.
It may be that the sudden apprehension
Of danger,—for I'll go in mine own shape,—
When he shall see it fraight with love and duty,
May draw the poison out of him, and work　　70
A friendly reconcilement. If it fail,
Yet it shall rid me of this infamous calling;
For better fall once than be ever falling.

DELIO. I'll second you in all danger; and, howe'er,
My life keeps rank with yours.　　75

ANT. You are still my loved and best friend.　　[*Exeunt.*

SCENE II.

[PESCARA, *a* DOCTOR.]

PES. Now, doctor, may I visit your patient?

DOC. If 't please your lordship; but he's instantly
To take the air here in the gallery
By my direction.

---

69. *fraight:* fraught.

PES.   Pray thee, what's his disease?

DOC. A very pestilent disease, my lord,   5
They call lycanthropia.

PES.   What's that?
I need a dictionary to 't.

DOC.   I'll tell you.
In those that are possessed with 't there o'erflows
Such melancholy humour they imagine
Themselves to be transformèd into wolves;   10
Steal forth to church-yards in the dead of night,
And dig dead bodies up: as two nights since
One met the duke 'bout midnight in a lane
Behind Saint Mark's church, with the leg of a man
Upon his shoulder; and he howled fearfully;   15
Said he was a wolf, only the difference
Was, a wolf's skin was hairy on the outside,
His on the inside; bade them take their swords,
Rip up his flesh, and try. Straight I was sent for,
And, having ministered to him, found his grace   20
Very well recovered.

PES. I am glad on 't.

DOC.   Yet not without some fear
Of a relapse. If he grow to his fit again,
I'll go a nearer way to work with him
Than ever Paracelsus dreamed of; if   25
They'll give me leave, I'll buffet his madness out of him.
Stand aside; he comes.

[*Enter* FERDINAND, CARDINAL, MALATESTE, *and* BOSOLA.]

FERD. Leave me.

MAL. Why doth your lordship love this solitariness?

FERD. Eagles commonly fly alone: they are crows, daws, and   [30
starlings that flock together. Look, what's that follows me?

MAL. Nothing, my lord.

FERD. Yes.

MAL. 'Tis your shadow.

FERD. Stay it; let it not haunt me.   35

MAL. Impossible, if you move, and the sun shine.

FERD. I will throttle it.   [*Throws himself down on his shadow.*

MAL. O, my lord, you are angry with nothing.

FERD. You are a fool: how is 't possible I should catch my shadow,
unless I fall upon 't? When I go to hell, I mean to carry a   [40
bribe; for, look you, good gifts evermore make way for the worst
persons.

PES. Rise, good my lord.

FERD. I am studying the art of patience.

PES. 'Tis a noble virtue.   45

FERD. To drive six snails before me from this town to Moscow; neither use goad nor whip to them, but let them take their own time; —the patientest man i' th' world match me for an experiment! And I'll crawl after like a sheep-biter.   49

CARD. Force him up.   [*They raise him.*

FERD. Use me well, you were best. What I have done, I have done: I'll confess nothing.

DOC. Now let me come to him.—Are you mad, my lord? Are you out of your princely wits?

FERD.   What's he?

PES.   Your doctor.

FERD. Let me have his beard sawed off, and his eyebrows filed more civil.   56

DOC. I must do mad tricks with him, for that's the only way on 't.— I have brought your grace a salamander's skin to keep you from sunburning.

FERD. I have cruel sore eyes.   60

DOC. The white of a cockatrix's egg is present remedy.

FERD. Let it be a new-laid one, you were best. Hide me from him: physicians are like kings,— They brook no contradiction.

DOC. Now he begins to fear me: now let me alone with him   [65
                          [*Puts off his four cloaks, one after another.*

CARD. How now! put off your gown?

DOC. Let me have some forty urinals filled with rose-water: he and I'll go pelt one another with them.—Now he begins to fear me.—Can you fetch a frisk, sir?—Let him go, let him go, upon my peril. I find by his eye he stands in awe of me: I'll make him as tame as a   [70
dormouse.

FERD. Can you fetch your frisks, sir!—I will stamp him into a cullis, flay off his skin to cover one of the anatomies this rogue hath set i' th' cold yonder in Barber-Chirurgeon's-hall.—Hence, hence! You are all of you like beasts for sacrifice. (*Throws the* DOCTOR *down and*   [75
beats him.) There's nothing left of you but tongue and belly, flattery and lechery.   [*Exit.*

PES. Doctor, he did not fear you thoroughly.

SC. II: 49. *sheep-biter:* stealthy sheep-stealing dog. 69. *fetch a frisk:* cut a caper. 73. *anatomies:* skeletons. 74. *Barber . . . hall:* The Barber Surgeons were granted the bodies of four felons annually.

DOC. True; I was somewhat too forward.

BOS. Mercy upon me, what a fatal judgment   80
Hath fallen upon this Ferdinand!

PES.   Knows your grace
What accident hath brought unto the prince
This strange distraction?

CARD. (*aside*). I must feign somewhat.—Thus they say it grew.
You have heard it rumored, for these many years,   85
None of our family dies but there is seen
The shape of an old woman, which is given
By tradition to us to have been murthered
By her nephews for her riches. Such a figure
One night, as the prince sat up late at 's book,   90
Appeared to him; when crying out for help,
The gentlemen of chamber found his grace
All on a cold sweat, altered much in face
And language: since which apparition,
He hath grown worse and worse, and I much fear   95
He cannot live.

BOS.   Sir, I would speak with you.

PES. We'll leave your grace,
Wishing to the sick prince, our noble lord,
All health of mind and body.

CARD.   You are most welcome.

[*Exeunt* PESCARA, MALATESTE, *and* DOCTOR.
Are you come? so.—(*Aside.*) This fellow must not know   100
By any means I had intelligence
In our duchess' death; for, though I counselled it,
The full of all th' engagement seemed to grow
From Ferdinand.—Now, sir, how fares our sister?
I do not think but sorrow makes her look   105
Like to an oft-dyed garment: she shall now
Taste comfort from me. Why do you look so wildly?
O, the fortune of your master here, the prince,
Dejects you; but be you of happy comfort:
If you'll do one thing for me I'll entreat,   110
Though he had a cold tomb-stone o'er his bones,
I'd make you what you would be.

BOS.   Anything!
Give it me in a breath, and let me fly to 't.
They that think long small expedition win,

---

114. *expedition:* speed.

For musing much o' th' end cannot begin.   115

[*Enter* JULIA.]

JULIA. Sir, will you come in to supper?

CARD.   I am busy; leave me.

JULIA (*aside*). What an excellent shape hath that fellow! [*Exit.*

CARD. 'Tis thus. Antonio lurks here in Milan:
Inquire him out, and kill him. While he lives,
Our sister cannot marry; and I have thought   120
Of an excellent match for her. Do this, and style me
Thy advancement.

BOS. But by what means shall I find him out?

CARD. There is a gentleman called Delio
Here in the camp, that hath been long approved   125
His loyal friend. Set eye upon that fellow;
Follow him to mass; may be Antonio,
Although he do account religion
But a school-name, for fashion of the world
May accompany him; or else go inquire out   130
Delio's confessor, and see if you can bribe
Him to reveal it. There are a thousand ways
A man might find to trace him: as to know
What fellows haunt the Jews for taking up
Great sums of money, for sure he's in want;   135
Or else to go to th' picture-makers, and learn
Who bought her picture lately: some of these
Happily may take.

BOS.   Well, I'll not freeze i' th' business:
I would see that wretched thing, Antonio,   139
Above all sights i' th' world.

CARD.   Do, and be happy.   [*Exit.*

BOS. This fellow doth breed basilisks in 's eyes,
He's nothing else but murder; yet he seems
Not to have notice of the duchess' death.
'Tis his cunning: I must follow his example;
There cannot be a surer way to trace   145
Than that of an old fox.

[*Re-enter* JULIA, *with a pistol.*]

JULIA. So, sir, you are well met.

BOS.   How now!

JULIA. Nay, the doors are fast enough:
Now, sir, I will make you confess your treachery.

BOS. Treachery!

JULIA.   Yes, confess to me   150
Which of my women 'twas you hired to put
Love-powder into my drink?
  BOS. Love-powder!
JULIA.   Yes, when I was at Malfi.
Why should I fall in love with such a face else?
I have already suffered for thee so much pain,   155
The only remedy to do me good
Is to kill my longing.
  BOS.   Sure, your pistol holds
Nothing but perfumes or kissing-comfits.
Excellent lady!
You have a pretty way on 't to discover   160
Your longing. Come, come, I'll disarm you.
And arm you thus: yet this is wondrous strange.
  JULIA. Compare thy form and my eyes together,
You'll find my love no such great miracle.
Now you'll say   165
I am wanton. This nice modesty in ladies
Is but a troublesome familiar
That haunts them.
  BOS. Know you me: I am a blunt soldier.
JULIA.   The better:
Sure, there wants fire where there are no lively sparks   170
Of roughness.
  BOS.   And I want compliment.
JULIA.   Why, ignorance
In courtship cannot make you do amiss,
If you have a heart to do well.
  BOS.   You are very fair.
JULIA. Nay, if you lay beauty to my charge,
I must plead unguilty.
  BOS.   Your bright eyes   175
Carry a quiver of darts in them, sharper
Than sun-beams.
  JULIA.   You will mar me with commendation,
Put yourself to the charge of courting me,
Whereas now I woo you.
  BOS. (aside). I have it, I will work upon this creature.--   180
Let us grow most amorously familiar.
If the great cardinal now should see me thus,

---

158. kissing-comfits: candies to sweeten the breath.

Would he not count me a villain?

JULIA. No; he might count me a wanton,
Not lay a scruple of offence on you;   185
For if I see and steal a diamond,
The fault is not i' th' stone, but in me the thief
That purloins it. I am sudden with you.
We that are great women of pleasure use to cut off
These uncertain wishes and unquiet longings,   190
And in an instant join the sweet delight
And the pretty excuse together. Had you been i' th' street,
Under my chamber-window, even there
I should have courted you.

BOS. O, you are an excellent lady!   195

JULIA. Bid me do somewhat for you presently
To express I love you.

BOS.   I will; and if you love me,
Fail not to effect it.
The cardinal is grown wondrous melancholy:
Demand the cause, let him not put you off   200
With feigned excuse; discover the main ground on 't.

JULIA. Why would you know this?

BOS.   I have depended on him,
And I hear that he is fallen in some disgrace
With the emperor: if he be, like the mice
That forsake falling houses, I would shift   205
To other dependance.

JULIA.   You shall not need
Follow the wars: I'll be your maintenance.

BOS. And I your loyal servant: but I cannot
Leave my calling.

JULIA.   Not leave an ungrateful
General for the love of a sweet lady!   21C
You are like some cannot sleep in feather-beds,
But must have blocks for their pillows.

BOS.   Will you do this?

JULIA. Cunningly.

BOS. Tomorrow I'li expect th' intelligence.

JULIA. Tomorrow! Get you into my cabinet;   215
You shall have it with you. Do not delay me,
No more than I do you: I am like one
That is condemned; I have my pardon promised,
But I would see it sealed. Go, get you in:
You shall see me wind my tongue about his heart   220
Like a skein of silk.   [*Exit* BOSOLA.

[*Re-enter* CARDINAL.]

CARD.   Where are you?

[*Enter* SERVANTS.]

SERVANTS.   Here.
CARD. Let none, upon your lives, have conference
With the Prince Ferdinand, unless I know it.—
(*Aside.*) In this distraction he may reveal
The murther.   [*Exeunt* SERVANTS.
                Yond's my lingering consumption: 225
I am weary of her, and by any means
Would be quit of.
    JULIA.   How now, my lord! what ails you?
    CARD. Nothing.
    JULIA.   O, you are much altered:
Come, I must be your secretary, and remove
This lead from off your bosom: what's the matter?   230
    CARD. I may not tell you.
    JULIA. Are you so far in love with sorrow
You cannot part with part of it? Or think you
I cannot love your grace when you are sad
As well as merry? Or do you suspect   235
I, that have been a secret to your heart
These many winters, cannot be the same
Unto your tongue?
    CARD.   Satisfy thy longing.—
The only way to make thee keep my counsel
Is, not to tell thee.
    JULIA.   Tell your echo this,   240
Or flatterers, that like echoes still report
What they hear, though most imperfect, and not me;
For if that you be true unto yourself,
I'll know.
    CARD.   Will you rack me?
    JULIA.   No, judgment shall
Draw it from you: it is an equal fault,   245
To tell one's secrets unto all or none.
    CARD. The first argues folly.
    JULIA. But the last tyranny.
    CARD. Very well: why, imagine I have committed

---

229. *secretary:* confidante.

Some secret deed which I desire the world   250
May never hear of.
    JULIA.   Therefore may not I know it?
You have concealed for me as great a sin
As adultery. Sir, never was occasion
For perfect trial of my constancy
Till now; sir, I beseech you——
    CARD.   You'll repent it.   255
    JULIA. Never.
    CARD. It hurries thee to ruin: I'll not tell thee.
Be well advised, and think what danger 'tis
To receive a prince's secrets. They that do,
Had need have their breasts hooped with adamant   260
To contain them. I pray thee, yet be satisfied;
Examine thine own frailty; 'tis more easy
To tie knots than unloose them. 'Tis a secret
That, like a lingering poison, may chance lie
Spread in thy veins, and kill thee seven year hence.   265
    JULIA. Now you dally with me.
    CARD.   No more; thou shalt know it.
By my appointment, the great Duchess of Malfi
And two of her young children, four nights since,
Were strangled.
    JULIA.   O heaven! sir, what have you done!
    CARD. How now? How settles this? Think you your bosom   270
Will be a grave dark and obscure enough
For such a secret?
    JULIA.   You have undone yourself, sir.
    CARD. Why?
    JULIA.   It lies not in me to conceal it.
    CARD.   No?
Come, I will swear you to 't upon this book.   274
    JULIA. Most religiously.
    CARD.   Kiss it.   [*She kisses the book.*
Now you shall never utter it; thy curiosity
Hath undone thee: thou 'rt poisoned with that book.
Because I knew thou couldst not keep my counsel,
I have bound thee to 't by death.

[*Re-enter* BOSOLA.]

    BOS. For pity sake, hold!
    CARD.   Ha, Bosola!
    JULIA.   I forgive you   280

This equal piece of justice you have done,
For I betrayed your counsel to that fellow.
He overheard it: that was the cause I said
It lay not in me to conceal it.

BOS. O foolish woman,   285
Couldst not thou have poisoned him?

JULIA.   'Tis weakness
Too much to think what should have been done. I go,
I know not whither.   [*Dies.*

CARD.   Wherefore com'st thou hither?

BOS. That I might find a great man like yourself,
Not out of his wits, as the Lord Ferdinand,   290
To remember my service.

CARD. I'll have thee hewed in pieces.

BOS. Make not yourself such a promise of that life
Which is not yours to dispose of.

CARD.   Who placed thee here?

BOS. Her lust, as she intended.

CARD.   Very well: 295
Now you know me for your fellow-murderer.

BOS. And wherefore should you lay fair marble colours
Upon your rotten purposes to me?
Unless you imitate some that do plot great treasons,
And when they have done, go hide themselves i' th' graves   300
Of those were actors in 't?

CARD.   No more; there is
A fortune attends thee.

BOS. Shall I go sue to Fortune any longer?
'Tis the fool's pilgrimage.

CARD. I have honours in store for thee.   305

BOS. There are a many ways that conduct to seeming
Honour, and some of them very dirty ones.

CARD. Throw to the devil
Thy melancholy. The fire burns well;
What need we keep a-stirring of 't, and make   310
A greater smother? Thou wilt kill Antonio?

BOS. Yes.

CARD.   Take up that body.

BOS.   I think I shall
Shortly grow the common bier for church-yards.

CARD. I will allow thee some dozen of attendants

---

297. *marble colours:* paint applied to wood to make it look like marble.

To aid thee in the murther.   315

   BOS. O, by no means. Physicians that apply horse-leeches to any
rank swelling use to cut off their tails, that the blood may run
through them the faster: let me have no train when I go to shed
blood, less it make me have a greater when I ride to the gallows.

   CARD. Come to me after midnight, to help to remove   320
That body to her own lodging. I'll give out
She died o' the plague; 't will breed the less inquiry
After her death.

   BOS. Where's Castruchio her husband?

   CARD. He's rode to Naples, to take possession   325
Of Antonio's citadel.

   BOS. Believe me, you have done a very happy turn.

   CARD. Fail not to come. There is the master-key
Of our lodgings; and by that you may conceive
What trust I plant in you.   [*Exit.*

   BOS.   You shall find me ready.   330
O poor Antonio, though nothing be so needful
To thy estate as pity, yet I find
Nothing so dangerous! I must look to my footing.
In such slippery ice-pavements men had need
To be frost-nailed well: they may break their necks else.   335
The precedent's here afore me. How this man
Bears up in blood! seems fearless! Why, 'tis well:
Security some men call the suburbs of hell,
Only a dead wall between. Well, good Antonio,
I'll seek thee out; and all my care shall be   340
To put thee into safety from the reach
Of these most cruel biters that have got
Some of thy blood already. It may be,
I'll join with thee in a most just revenge.
The weakest arm is strong enough that strikes   345
With the sword of justice. Still methinks the duchess
Haunts me: there, there!—'Tis nothing but my melancholy.
O Penitence, let me truly taste thy cup,
That throws men down only to raise them up!   [*Exit.*

SCENE III.

[ANTONIO, DELIO, ECHO (*from the* DUCHESS'S *grave*).]

   DELIO. Yond's the cardinal's window. This fortification
Grew from the ruins of an ancient abbey;

---

335. *frost-nailed:* hobnailed.

And to yond side o' th' river lies a wall,
Piece of a cloister, which in my opinion
Gives the best echo that you ever heard,   5
So hollow and so dismal, and withal
So plain in the distinction of our words,
That many have supposed it is a spirit
That answers.
    ANT.   I do love these ancient ruins.
We never tread upon them but we set   10
Our foot upon some reverend history;
And, questionless, here in this open court,
Which now lies naked to the injuries
Of stormy weather, some men lie interred
Loved the church so well, and gave so largely to 't,   15
They thought it should have canopied their bones
Till dooms-day. But all things have their end;
Churches and cities, which have diseases like to men,
Must have like death that we have.
    ECHO.   *Like death that we have.*
    DELIO. Now the echo hath caught you.   20
    ANT. It groaned, methought, and gave
A very deadly accent.
    ECHO.   *Deadly accent.*
    DELIO. I told you 't was a pretty one. You may make it
A huntsman, or a falconer, a musician,
Or a thing of sorrow.
    ECHO.   *A thing of sorrow.*   25
    ANT. Ay, sure, that suits it best.
    ECHO.   *That suits it best.*
    ANT. 'Tis very like my wife's voice.
    ECHO.   *Ay, wife's voice.*
    DELIO. Come, let's us walk farther from 't.
I would not have you go to th' cardinal's tonight:
Do not.   30
    ECHO. *Do not.*
    DELIO. Wisdom doth not more moderate wasting sorrow
Than time. Take time for 't; be mindful of thy safety.
    ECHO. *Be mindful of thy safety.*
    ANT. Necessity compels me.   35
Make scrutiny throughout the passages
Of your own life, you'll find it impossible
To fly your fate.
    ECHO.   *O, fly your fate!*

DELIO. Hark! the dead stones seem to have pity on you,
And give you good counsel.   40
    ANT. Echo, I will not talk with thee,
For thou art a dead thing.
    ECHO.   *Thou art a dead thing.*
    ANT. My duchess is asleep now,
And her little ones, I hope sweetly. O heaven,
Shall I never see her more?
    ECHO.   *Never see her more.*   45
    ANT. I marked not one repetition of the echo
But that; and on the sudden a clear light
Presented me a face folded in sorrow.
    DELIO. Your fancy merely.
    ANT.   Come, I'll be out of this ague.
For to live thus is not indeed to live: 50
It is a mockery and abuse of life.
I will not henceforth save myself by halves;
Lose all, or nothing.
    DELIO.   Your own virtue save you!
I'll fetch your eldest son, and second you.
It may be that the sight of his own blood,   55
Spread in so sweet a figure, may beget
The more compassion. However, fare you well.
Though in our miseries Fortune have a part,
Yet in our noble sufferings she hath none.   59
Contempt of pain, that we may call our own.   [*Exeunt.*

SCENE IV.

[CARDINAL, PESCARA, MALATESTE, RODERIGO, GRISOLAN.]

CARD. You shall not watch tonight by the sick prince;
His grace is very well recovered.
    MAL. Good my lord, suffer us.
    CARD.   O, by no means;
The noise, and change of object in his eye,
Doth more distract him. I pray, all to bed;   5
And though you hear him in his violent fit,
Do not rise, I entreat you.
    PES. So, sir; we shall not.
    CARD.   Nay, I must have you promise
Upon your honours, for I was enjoined to 't
By himself; and he seemed to urge it sensibly.   10

---

sc. IV: 10. *sensibly:* with feeling.

PES. Let our honours bind this trifle!
CARD. Nor any of your followers.
MAL. Neither.
CARD. It may be, to make trial of your promise,
When he's asleep, myself will rise and feign   15
Some of his mad tricks, and cry out for help,
And feign myself in danger.
    MAL. If your throat were cutting,
I'd not come at you, now I have protested against it.
CARD. Why, I thank you.
GRIS.   'Twas a foul storm tonight.   20
ROD. The Lord Ferdinand's chamber shook like an osier.
MAL. 'Twas nothing but pure kindness in the devil
To rock his own child.   [Exeunt all except the CARDINAL.
CARD. The reason why I would not suffer these
About my brother, is, because at midnight   25
I may with better privacy convey
Julia's body to her own lodging. O, my conscience!
I would pray now; but the devil takes away my heart
For having any confidence in prayer.
About this hour I appointed Bosola   30
To fetch the body. When he hath served my turn,
He dies.   [Exit.

[Enter BOSOLA.]

BOS. Ha! 'twas the cardinal's voice; I heard him name Bosola and
my death. Listen; I hear one's footing.

[Enter FERDINAND.]

FERD. Strangling is a very quiet death.   35
BOS. (aside). Nay, then, I see I must stand upor my guard.
FERD. What say to that? Whisper softly: do you agree to 't? So; it
must be done i' th' dark: the cardinal would not for a thousand
pounds the doctor should see it.   [Exit.
BOS. My death is plotted; here's the consequence of murther.   40
We value not desert nor Christian breath,
When we know black deeds must be cured with death.

[Enter ANTONIO and SERVANT.]

SERV. Here stay, sir, and be confident, I pray;
I'll fetch you a dark lantern.   [Exit.
ANT. Could I take him at his prayers,   45
There were hope of pardon.

BOS. Fall right, my sword!—   [*Stabs him.*
I'll not give thee so much leisure as to pray.
    ANT. O, I am gone! Thou hast ended a long suit
In a minute.
    BOS.   What art thou?
    ANT.   A most wretched thing,   50
That only have thy benefit in death,
To appear myself.

                [*Re-enter* SERVANT *with a lantern.*]

    SERV. Where are you, sir?
    ANT. Very near my home.—Bosola!
    SERV. O, misfortune!   55
    BOS. Smother thy pity, thou art dead else.—Antonio!
The man I would have saved 'bove mine own life!
We are merely the stars' tennis-balls, struck and bandied
Which way please them.—O good Antonio,
I'll whisper one thing in thy dying ear   60
Shall make thy heart break quickly! Thy fair duchess
And two sweet children——
    ANT.   Their very names
Kindle a little life in me.
    BOS.   Are murdered.
    ANT. Some men have wished to die
At the hearing of sad tidings; I am glad   65
That I shall do 't in sadness. I would not now
Wish my wounds balmed nor healed, for I have no use
To put my life to. In all our quest of greatness,
Like wanton boys whose pastime is their care,
We follow after bubbles blown in th' air.   70
Pleasure of life, what is 't? Only the good hours
Of an ague; merely a preparative to rest,
To endure vexation. I do not ask
The process of my death; only commend me
To Delio.   75
    BOS. Break, heart!
    ANT. And let my son fly the courts of princes.   [*Dies.*
    BOS. Thou seemest to have loved Antonio.
    SERV. I brought him hither,
To have reconciled him to the cardinal.   80
    BOS. I do not ask thee that.
Take him up, if thou tender thine own life,

66. *sadness:* fact (with a pun).

And bear him where the lady Julia
Was wont to lodge.—O, my fate moves swift!
I have this cardinal in the forge already;
Now I'll bring him to th' hammer. O direful misprision!   85
I will not imitate things glorious,
No more than base: I'll be mine own example.—
On, on, and look thou represent, for silence,
The thing thou bearest.   [*Exeunt.*

SCENE V.

[CARDINAL, *with a book.*]

CARD. I am puzzled in a question about hell;
He says, in hell there's one material fire,
And yet it shall not burn all men alike.
Lay him by. How tedious is a guilty conscience!
When I look into the fish-ponds in my garden,   5
Methinks I see a thing armed with a rake,
That seems to strike at me.

[*Enter* BOSOLA *and* SERVANT *bearing* ANTONIO's *body.*]

               Now, art thou come?
Thou look'st ghastly;
There sits in thy face some great determination,
Mixed with some fear.
    BOS.   Thus it lightens into action: 10
I am come to kill thee.
    CARD.   Ha!—Help! our guard!
    BOS. Thou art deceived: they are out of thy howling.
    CARD. Hold; and I will faithfully divide
Revenues with thee.
    BOS.   Thy prayers and proffers
Are both unseasonable.
    CARD.   Raise the watch!   15
We are betrayed!
    BOS.   I have confined your flight:
I'll suffer your retreat to Julia's chamber,
But no further.
    CARD.   Help! we are betrayed!

[*Enter, above,* PESCARA, MALATESTE, RODERIGO, *and* GRISOLAN.]

MAL. Listen.

---

85. *misprision:* mistake.

CARD. My dukedom for rescue!   20
ROD. Fie upon his counterfeiting!
MAL. Why, 'tis not the cardinal.
ROD. Yes, yes, 'tis he;
But I'll see him hanged ere I'll go down to him.
CARD. Here's a plot upon me; I am assaulted! I am lost,   25
Unless some rescue!
GRIS.   He doth this pretty well;
But it will not serve to laugh me out of mine honour.
CARD. The sword's at my throat!
ROD. You would not bawl so loud then.
MAL. Come, come, let's go to bed: he told us thus much aforehand.
PES. He wished you should not come at him; but, believe 't,   31
The accent of the voice sounds not in jest.
I'll down to him, howsoever, and with engines
Force ope the doors.   [*Exit above.*
ROD.   Let's follow him aloof,
And note how the cardinal will laugh at him.   35
          [*Exeunt, above,* MALATESTE, RODERIGO, *and* GRISOLAN.
BOS. There's for you first,
'Cause you shall not unbarricade the door
To let in rescue.   [*He kills the* SERVANT.
CARD.   What cause hast thou to pursue my life?
BOS.   Look there.
CARD. Antonio!
BOS.   Slain by my hand unwittingly.
Pray, and be sudden. When thou kill'd'st thy sister,   40
Thou took'st from Justice her most equal balance,
And left her naught but her sword.
CARD.   O, mercy!
BOS. Now it seems thy greatness was only outward;
For thou fall'st faster of thyself than calamity
Can drive thee. I'll not waste longer time; there   [*Stabs him.*
CARD. Thou hast hurt me.
BOS.   Again!
CARD.   Shall I die like a leveret,   46
Without any resistance?—Help, help, help!
I am slain!

[*Enter* FERDINAND.]

FERD.   Th' alarum! Give me a fresh horse!

___

sc. v: 46. *leveret:* young hare.

Rally the vaunt-guard, or the day is lost!
Yield, yield! I give you the honour of arms,   50
Shake my sword over you; will you yield?
    CARD. Help me; I am your brother!
    FERD.   The devil!
My brother fight upon the adverse party!
            [*He wounds the* CARDINAL, *and in the scuffle gives*
                    BOSOLA *his death-wound.*]
There flies your ransom.
    CARD. O justice!   55
I suffer now for what hath former been:
Sorrow is held the eldest child of sin.
    FERD. Now you're brave fellows. Cæsar's fortune was harder than
Pompey's: Cæsar died in the arms of prosperity, Pompey at the feet
of disgrace. You both died in the field. The pain's nothing;   [60
pain many times is taken away with the apprehension of greater, as
the tooth-ache with the sight of a barber that comes to pull it out.
There's philosophy for you.
    BOS. Now my revenge is perfect.—Sink, thou main cause
                                        [*He kills Ferdinand.*
Of my undoing!—The last part of my life   65
Hath done me best service.
    FERD. Give me some wet hay; I am broken-winded.
I do account this world but a dog-kennel:
I will vault credit and affect high pleasures
Beyond death.
    BOS.   He seems to come to himself,   70
Now he's so near the bottom.
    FERD. My sister, O my sister! there's the cause on 't.
Whether we fall by ambition, blood, or lust,
Like diamonds, we are cut with our own dust.   [*Dies.*
    CARD. Thou hast thy payment too.   75
    BOS. Yes, I hold my weary soul in my teeth;
'Tis ready to part from me. I do glory
That thou, which stood'st like a huge pyramid
Begun upon a large and ample base,
Shalt end in a little point, a kind of nothing.   80

        [*Enter, below,* PESCARA, MALATESTE, RODERIGO, *and* GRISOLAN.]

    PES. How now, my lord!
    MAL.   O sad disaster!

---

62. *barber:* surgeon. 69. *vault credit:* go beyond what is credible.

ROD.   How comes this?
BOS. Revenge for the Duchess of Malfi murdered
By th' Aragonian brethren; for Antonio
Slain by this hand; for lustful Julia
Poisoned by this man; and lastly for myself,   85
That was an actor in the main of all
Much 'gainst mine own good nature, yet i' th' end
Neglected.
    PES.   How now, my lord!
    CARD.   Look to my brother:
He gave us these large wounds, as we were struggling
Here i' th' rushes. And now, I pray, let me   90
Be laid by and never thought of.   [*Dies.*
    PES. How fatally, it seems, he did withstand
His own rescue!
    MAL.   Thou wretched thing of blood,
How came Antonio by his death?
    BOS. In a mist; I know not how.   95
Such a mistake as I have often seen
In a play. O, I am gone!
We are only like dead walls or vaulted graves,
That, ruined, yield no echo. Fare you well!
It may be pain, but no harm, to me to die   100
In so good a quarrel. O, this gloomy world!
In what a shadow, or deep pit of darkness,
Doth womanish and fearful mankind live!
Let worthy minds ne'er stagger in distrust
To suffer death or shame for what is just: 105
Mine is another voyage.   [*Dies.*
    PES. The noble Delio, as I came to th' palace,
Told me of Antonio's being here, and showed me
A pretty gentleman, his son and heir.

[*Enter* DELIO, *and* ANTONIO'S *son.*]

    MAL. O, sir, you come too late!
    DELIO.   I heard so, and   110
Was armed for 't, ere I came. Let us make noble use
Of this great ruin; and join all our force
To establish this young hopeful gentleman
In 's mother's right. These wretched eminent things
Leave no more fame behind 'em, than should one   115

---

90. *rushes:* used to cover the floors.

Fall in a frost, and leave his print in snow:
As soon as the sun shines, it ever melts,
Both form and matter. I have ever thought
Nature doth nothing so great for great men
As when she's pleased to make them lords of truth: 120
Integrity of life is fame's best friend,
Which nobly, beyond death, shall crown the end.   [*Exeunt.*

FINIS

Biographical and Bibliographical References

CHRISTOPHER MARLOWE

LIFE: Born 1564 in Canterbury, son of a shoemaker and parish clerk. He was educated at King's School, Canterbury, and Corpus Christi College, Cambridge, where he was graduated A.B. in 1583 and M.A. in 1587(?). Thereafter he was a successful London dramatist, attached to the Admiral's and Lord Strange's companies, and an occasional secret agent for the government. A warrant for his arrest was issued by the Privy Council on the charge of atheism in 1593, but the real reason may have been his activities as a secret agent. He was killed in May 1593, before coming to trial, by another government agent, Ingram Frizer, after a tavern quarrel.

LITERARY CAREER:

1587: *Tamburlaine*	*Massacre at Paris*
1588-1593: *Doctor Faustus*	*Hero and Leander*
The Jew of Malta	Translations of Ovid's
Edward II	*Amores* and Lucan's
	Pharsalia

BIOGRAPHY AND CRITICISM: Una Ellis-Fermor, *Christopher Marlowe* (1927), *The Frontiers of Drama* (1945); *The Tragical History of Doctor Faustus*, ed. F. S. Boas (1932); John Bakeless, *The Tragical History of Christopher Marlowe* (1942); R. B. Heilman, "The Tragedy of Knowledge: Marlowe's Treatment of Faustus," *Quart. Rev. of Lit.,* II (1946), 316-332; L. Kirschbaum, "Marlowe's Faustus: A Reconsideration," *RES,* XIX (1943), 225-241; J. C. Maxwell, "The Sin of Faustus," *The Wind and the Rain,* IV (1947), 49-52; *Doctor Faustus*, ed. by W. Greg (1950); H. Levin, *The Overreacher* (1952); R. Ornstein, "The Comic Synthesis in Dr. Faustus," *ELH,* XXII (1955), 165-72; F. P. Wilson, *Marlowe and the Early Shakespeare* (1953).

WILLIAM SHAKESPEARE

LIFE: Born 1564 (baptized 26 April) in Stratford-on-Avon (a thriving rural center of about 2,000) to John Shakespeare, a fancy tanner and town official, and his wife Mary Arden, whose well-to-do Roman Catholic family lived in a nearby village. William probably attended the Stratford grammar school, which was unusually well endowed, and where he would have studied the major Latin authors. On 26 November 1582 he married Anne Hathaway (1556-1623) of Stratford; their first child Susanna was baptized 26 May 1583, and twins Hamnet and Judith were baptized 2 February 1585. By 1592 Shakespeare was a successful London dramatist; and in 1594 he became a leading member, with the famous actors William Kempe and Richard Burbage, of the players known as the Chamberlain's Men. In 1596 he moved from his house near The Theatre to Southwark; and in the following year he bought and restored a large house called New Place in Stratford. The Theatre was torn down in 1598, and the larger Globe was built across the Thames by a syndicate of which Shakespeare was a member. They prospered, and were favored by both Elizabeth and James I, under the latter of whom they were known as the King's Men. When the enclosed Blackfriars' Theatre became vacant in 1609 it was taken over by the King's Men and operated profitably by them during the winter seasons. The Globe was accidentally burned down in 1613, and in the same year Shakespeare bought a house near the Blackfriars'. He revised his will in March 1616, and died on April 23, leaving £350 and a considerable amount of property. He was survived by his wife, two daughters, and one granddaughter.

LITERARY CAREER:

1588: *Sonnets* begun (?)
1589: *Comedy of Errors*
1590: *I Henry VI*
1591: *II* and *III Henry VI*
　　　Titus Andronicus
　　　Taming of the Shrew
1592: *Two Gentlemen of Verona*
1593: *Venus and Adonis*
　　　Richard III
1594: *Rape of Lucrece*
　　　Love's Labours Lost
　　　King John
1595: *Richard II*
　　　A Midsummer Night's Dream
　　　Romeo and Juliet
1596: *Merchant of Venice*
1597: *I Henry IV*
　　　Merry Wives of Windsor
1598: *II Henry IV*

　　　Much Ado About Nothing
1599: *Henry V*
　　　Julius Caesar
1600: *As You Like It*
　　　Twelfth Night
1601: *Hamlet*
　　　Troilus and Cressida
1602: *All's Well That Ends Well*
1604: *Measure for Measure*
　　　Othello
1605: *King Lear*
1606: *Macbeth*
1607: *Antony and Cleopatra*
　　　Timon of Athens
1608: *Coriolanus*
　　　Pericles
1609: *Sonnets* published
1610: *Cymbeline*
1611: *The Winter's Tale*
　　　The Tempest

BIOGRAPHY AND CRITICISM: E. K. Chambers, *William Shakespeare. A Study of Facts and Problems* (1930), *The Elizabethan Stage* (1923); *Shakespeare's England,* ed. Walter Raleigh (1916); Alfred Harbage, *Shakespeare's Audience* (1941); J. C. Adams, *The Globe Playhouse* (1942); *Shakespeare Criticism,* ed. by D. N. Smith (1916); *Shakespeare Criticism,* ed. by Anne Bradby (1936); *Shakespeare: Modern Essays In Criticism,* ed. by L. Dean (1957). On *King Lear:* A. C. Bradley, *Shakespearian Tragedy* (1905); G. W. Knight, *The Wheel of Fire* (1930); H.

G. Granville-Barker, *Prefaces to Shakespeare* (1947); S. L. Bethell, *Shakespeare and the Popular Dramatic Tradition* (1944); R. B. Heilman, *This Great Stage* (1948); M. Van Doren, *Shakespeare* (1939); J. F. Danby, *Shakespeare's Doctrine of Nature: A Study of King Lear* (1949); D. Stauffer, *Shakespeare's World of Images* (1949); H. C. Goddard, *The Meaning of Shakespeare* (1951); A. Sewell, *Character and Society in Shakespeare* (1951); R. M. Speaight, *Nature in Shakespeare's Tragedy* (1955); G. Bush, *Shakespeare and the Natural Condition* (1956); B. Stirling, *Unity in Shakespearean Tragedy* (1956); D. Traversi, *An Approach to Shakespeare,* 2nd rev. ed. (1956); H. S. Wilson, *On the Design of Shakespearian Tragedy* (1957); W. Rosen, *Shakespeare and the Craft of Tragedy* (1960).

BEN JONSON

LIFE: Born 1572, posthumous son of a clergyman and stepson of a master bricklayer of Westminster. Ben Jonson attended Westminster School (until about 1588), where he studied under the historian, William Camden, "to whom I owe / All that I am in arts, all that I know." Unable to afford a university education, Jonson was apprenticed to a bricklayer, served in the army in Flanders, married in 1594, and three years later had given up bricklaying and become an actor and then a playwright. His first notable play was a comedy, *Everyman in His Humour* (1598), in which Shakespeare acted. In the same year Jonson killed an actor in self-defense and while in prison was converted (to Catholicism) for twelve years. Under James I he wrote masques and entertainments for the court, and in 1612-13 he was abroad as tutor to the young Walter Raleigh. In 1616 he collected and published his best writings to 1612—plays, masques, epigrams, and poems. He was given an honorary degree by Oxford in 1619, and during his later years he enjoyed the respect and affection of leading writers and men of affairs, including Bacon, Shakespeare, Donne, Chapman, Herrick, Carew, and Sir Kenelm Digby, who published a second edition of his works in 1640-41 containing later plays, masques, poems, and essays. He suffered a stroke in 1628, died in 1637, and was buried in Westminster Abbey.

PRINCIPAL PLAYS:

1598: *Everyman in His Humour*	1610: *The Alchemist*
1599: *Everyman Out of His Humour*	1611: *Catiline*
	1614: *Bartholomew Fair*
1601: *Cynthia's Revels; The Poetaster*	1616: *The Devil Is an Ass*
	1626: *The Staple of News*
1603: *Sejanus*	1629: *The New Inn*
1606: *Volpone*	1632: *The Magnetic Lady*
1609: *Epicoene or The Silent Woman*	1633: *A Tale of a Tub*

MODERN EDITIONS, BIOGRAPHY, AND CRITICISM: *Ben Jonson* (works, with life, introductions, and notes), ed. by C. H. Herford & P. & E. Simpson, 11 vols. (1925-53); *Ben Jonson: Selected Works*, ed., with introduction, by Harry Levin (1938); *Volpone*, ed. by J. D. Rea (1919); M. Chute, *Ben Jonson of Westminster* (1953); L. C. Knights, *Drama and Society in the Age of Jonson* (1937); A. H. Sancton, *Rhetoric as a Dramatic Language in Ben Jonson* (1948); J. A. Barish, "The Double Plot in *Volpone*," *Modern Philology*, li (1953), 83-92; J. J. Enck, *Jonson and the Comic Truth* (1957); E. B. Partridge, *The Broken Compass: A Study of the Major Comedies of Ben Jonson* (1958).

JOHN WEBSTER

LIFE: Born around 1580 in London. Very little is known of his private life. In 1602 Henslowe, the London dramatic producer, paid Webster for collaborating on a play called *Caesar's Fall*. Practically the only information thereafter comes from his plays and a few occasional verses.

LITERARY CAREER: Webster wrote six or seven plays in collaboration with Dekker, Heywood, Massinger, Ford, and others; his most important original plays aside from *The Duchess of Malfi* (performed 1613-14?) are *The While Devil* (1612) and *The Devil's Law Case* (1623). He died some time before 1635.

EDITIONS AND CRITICISM: *Complete Works*, ed. F. L. Lucas (1927, 1937); *The Duchess of Malfi*, ed. by F. L. Lucas, rev. with additions (1958); Rupert Brooke, *John Webster and The Elizabethan Drama* (1917); M. C. Bradbrook, *Themes and Conventions of Elizabethan Tragedy* (1935); U. M. Ellis-Fermor, *The Jacobean Drama* (1936), *The Frontiers of Drama* (1945); M. E. Prior, *The Language of Tragedy* (1947); C. Leech, *John Webster* (1951); H. T. Price, "The Function of Imagery in Webster," *PMLA*, LXX (1955), 717-39; T. M. Bogard, *The Tragic Satire of John Webster* (1955); C. G. Thayer, "The Ambiguity of Bosola," *SP*, LIV (1957), 162-71; I. Ekeblad, "The 'Impure Art' of John Webster," *RES*, IX (1958), 253-67; McD. Emslie, "Motive in Malfi," *EIC*, IX (1959), 391-405.